QUILTS
in America

QUILTS
in America

PATSY AND MYRON ORLOFSKY

ABBEVILLE PRESS PUBLISHERS
NEW YORK   LONDON

AUTHOR'S NOTE:
I would like to thank my good friend Kate Dodge, who helped
me bring this project to fruition.

JACKET FRONT:
Phebe Warner Coverlet, c. 1803. See page 225.

JACKET BACK:
Sarah Furman Warner Coverlet, c. 1800. See page 225.

FRONTISPIECE:
Framed Center Variation Quilt, c. 1780. Pieced cotton and
block-printed fabrics, 88½ x 84 in. Noah Webster Foundation,
West Hartford, Connecticut. "1769" is stitched at the top and
bottom of the center square.

First paperback edition.
10 9 8 7 6 5 4 3 2 1

Plate 109 from *Historic Wallpapers,* by Nancy McClelland.
Copyright © 1924 by J. B. Lippincott Company.
Copyright © renewed 1952 by Nancy McClelland.
Reproduced by permission of J. B. Lippincott Company.

Paperback ISBN 0-7892-0857-1

The hardcover edition is cataloged as follows:
Library of Congress Cataloging-in-Publication Data

Orlofsky, Patsy.
Quilts in America / Patsy and Myron Orlofsky.
p. cm.
Originally published: New York : McGraw-Hill, 1974.
Includes bibliographical references and index.
ISBN 1-55859-334-9
1. Quilts—United States. I. Orlofsky, Myron. II. Title.
NK9112.074 1992
746.9'7'0973—dc20   92-315

For bulk and premium sales and for text adoption procedures, write
to Customer Service Manager, Abbeville Press, 137 Varick Street,
Suite 504, New York, NY 10013 or call 1-800-ARTBOOK.

Acknowledgments

Many people have shared generously of their time, knowledge, and enthusiasm in the production of this book. Of invaluable help were the research resources of numerous museums, historical societies, and other institutions. To the following we acknowledge our gratitude and thanks:

Elizabeth Ann Coleman, Department of Decorative Arts, Brooklyn Museum, Brooklyn, New York; Christa C. Mayer-Thurman, Curator, Department of Textiles, Art Institute of Chicago, Chicago, Illinois; Eleanor L. Nowlin, Shelburne Museum, Shelburne, Vermont; Maude E. Banta, Conservator, Historic Deerfield, Inc., Deerfield, Massachusetts; Linda Baumgarten, Associate Curator of Textiles, Valentine Museum, Richmond, Virginia; Mildred B. Lanier, Curator of Textiles, and Sandra C. Shaffer, Assistant Curator, Colonial Williamsburg, Williamsburg, Virginia; Jane C. Nylander, Curator, Ceramics and Textiles, and Etta Falkner, Librarian, Old Sturbridge Village, Sturbridge, Massachusetts; Imelda G. DeGraw, Curator of Textiles, Denver Art Museum, Denver, Colorado; C. R. Jones, Associate Curator, New York State Historical Association, Cooperstown, New York; Margaret Fikioris, Textile Conservator, and Karol A. Schmiegel, Assistant Registrar, The Henry Francis duPont Winterthur Museum, Winterthur, Delaware; Martin Leifer, New-York Historical Society, New York, New York; Doris M. Bowman, Needlework and Lace Specialist, Division of Textiles, Smithsonian Institution, Washington, D.C.; Sybil Daneman, Cooper-Hewitt Museum of Decorative Arts and Design, Smithsonian Institution, New York, New York; Lydia H. Davis, Registrar, Maryland Historical Society, Baltimore, Maryland; Gretchen Feldman and M. B. Munford, Assistant Curator of Decorative Arts, Baltimore Museum of Art, Baltimore, Maryland; Elise McGarvey, Curator of Costumes and Textiles, and Christine Jackson, Assistant, Philadelphia Museum of Art, Philadelphia, Pennsylvania; Betty C. Monkman, Registrar, Office of the Curator, White House, Washington, D.C.; William H. Watkins, Director, Mattatuck Museum, Waterbury, Connecticut; Yolanda Digaetano, Assistant Curator, Decorative Arts, Newark Museum, Newark, New Jersey; Lynn Bordes, American Wing, Metropolitan Museum of Art, New York, New York; Wesley R. Hurt, Director, University Museum, Indiana University, Bloomington, Indiana; Mrs. Gemmell Jainschigg, Darien Historical Society, Darien, Connecticut; Carol Steiro, Curator, Folk Art Collections, Museum of New Mexico, Santa Fe, New Mexico; J. Herbert Callister, Curator, Textiles and Costumes, Wadsworth Atheneum, Hartford, Connecticut; Gridley McKim Smith, Curator of Collections, Pamela D. Kingsbury, Assistant Curator of Prints and Drawings, Lea Rosson, Curatorial Assistant, University of Kansas Museum of Art, Lawrence, Kansas; D. Graeme Keith, Curator of Textiles, M. H. De Young Memorial Museum, San Francisco, California.

Abby Aldrich Rockefeller Folk Art Collection, Williamsburg, Virginia; Cincinnati Art Museum, Cincinnati, Ohio; American Museum in Britain, Claverton Manor, Bath, England; Museum of Fine Arts, Boston, Massachusetts; Connecticut Historical Society, Hartford, Connecticut; Charleston Museum, Charleston, South Carolina; Davenport Museum, Davenport, Iowa; Henry Ford Museum and Greenfield Village, Dearborn, Michigan; Gallier House, New Orleans, Louisiana; Honolulu Academy of Arts, Honolulu, Hawaii; Hennepin County Historical Society, Minneapolis, Minnesota; Illinois State Museum, Springfield, Illinois; Fall River Historical Society, Fall River, Massachusetts; Jefferson County Historical Society, Watertown, New York; Mount Vernon Ladies' Association of the Union, Mount Vernon, Virginia; Mint Museum of Art, Charlotte, North Carolina; Manchester Historic Association, Manchester, New Hampshire; National Gallery of Art, Washington, D.C.; National Tobacco-Textile Museum, Danville, Virginia; New Jersey Historical Society, Newark, New Jersey; Pennsylvania Historical and Museum Commission, Harrisburg, Pennsylvania; Queen Anne's County Historical Society, Centreville, Maryland; Royal Ontario Museum, Toronto, Canada; Suffolk County Whaling Museum of Sag

Harbor, Long Island, Sag Harbor, New York; Witte Memorial Museum, San Antonio, Texas; Woodlawn Plantation, Mount Vernon, Virginia; York Institute Museum, Saco, Maine; Kenmore, Fredericksburg, Virginia; Gunston Hall, Lorton, Virginia; Stratford Hall, Stratford, Virginia; Frank H. McClung Museum, University of Tennessee, Knoxville, Tennessee; Jefferson County Historical Society, Watertown, New York; Virginia Military Institute Museum, Lexington, Virginia; Victoria and Albert Museum, London, England; Star of the Republic Museum, Washington, Texas; Friends of the Hopkinton Village Library, Hopkinton, New Hampshire; Grand Rapids Public Museum, Grand Rapids, Michigan.

The following individuals loaned material from their collections or generously supplied information: Grace and Elliott Snyder; Frank Moran; Mr. and Mrs. George Anderson; Mary Borkowski; Frances M. Traynor; Prudence Fuchsmann; Joan Gilbert; Jonathan and Gail Holstein; Mrs. Chads O. Skinner; Governor and Mrs. Leverett Saltonstall; Stanley Polar; Joyce Gross; Mrs. Grace McConce Snyder; Mr. and Mrs. James O. Keene; Patsy Lee Leaders; Mrs. Fred Crebbin III: Julia Boyer Reinstein; Mrs. G. Gordon Gatchell; Susan Lewis Cockrell; Mrs. Pauline Pretzfelder Blumenfeld; Mrs. Louis E. Dallenbach; W. Clough Wallace; Mrs. Kim Brown McIlhenny; Mrs. Robert Keegan; Bill Pearson; Louise and Lloyd Francke; Betty Sterling; Barbara and Don Ladd; Mr. and Mrs. Alastair B. Martin; Miss Louise Judson Cooke; Mr. and Mrs. Ben Mildwoff; and Mr. and Mrs. Lenord Balish.

For technical assistance: Cathy Robinowitz; Kate Jennings; James M. Scott, Jr.; Marisha Hydeman; Edythe Stafford; Mary Herzog; Carolyn Vola; Barbara Kouba; Ann Bowman.

Very special thanks to our research librarian, Lois Keeler, Darien Library, Darien, Connecticut.

We also wish to acknowledge our gratitude to the following textile experts for their help: Mildred B. Lanier; Florence Montgomery; Margaret Fikioris; Cora Ginsburg.

We would like to express great appreciation to the following photographers: Roy L. Hale and Jim Enyeart, with special mention to Arthur Vitols of Helga Photo Studio.

The following made important recommendations regarding our manuscript: Kenneth Allebach, Beth Gutcheon, David Shapiro, and, most particularly, Ruth Cox Page. To all we are indebted.

Finally, we wish to thank our editor, Lou Ashworth, and Phyllis Levy and Bob Mitchell, without whom . . .

Contents

Cathedral Window Quilt (detail), 1991. Pieced cotton calicos, 72 x 108 in. Private collection.
Made by Shirley Frank Kulp.

Preface

For those who are fascinated by the study of America's quilt-making tradition, I am extremely pleased that this paperback edition of the 1974 book is being issued. As a collector, I am especially pleased that this edition, like the 1992 Abbeville Edition, has an additional picture that I am very happy to include—a quilt made by my mother. I own many quilts by diverse makers, and I have enjoyed them not only as works of art, but as evidence of regional and family history. Quilts have always had the aura of the heirloom about them, and it is quite satisfying to have a quilt that is part of my own family history. This new edition is also a tribute to my late husband and our shared interest in quilts. He would have greatly enjoyed knowing that our book lives on.

PATSY ORLOFSKY
2005

Introduction

Our interest in quilts began a number of years ago when we saw a collection at the home of a friend, Janet Ruttenberg. In those days, good quilts of all types were to be found for as little as 25 cents. The quilts were on shelves, hung on the walls, on beds. Many were worn and pale, sometimes almost tatters of material on which there was a faded pattern, others no more than huge fragments of beautiful old textiles. It was startling to see so many. These were not some exotic, rare, Peruvian or Coptic textiles, but simple, homemade American bedcovers. And they were as appealing as any textiles we had ever seen.

Soon after, we began to collect quilts of our own. As time went on we wanted to learn as much as possible about them: how they were made, something of their history, and, if possible, something about the women who created them. Though many quilts are signed and a number of quilt makers—such as Mary Totten, who created superb pieces during the early 1800s, and Bertha Stenge, who made quilts of great originality during the 1930s and 1940s—are remembered today, the vast majority are unknown, their names and personal histories forgotten.

We began to appreciate quilts for their historical importance, documenting the style and taste of different eras in the country's development. They provide rich examples of the textiles used in clothing and household furnishings, bringing alive the actual color, design, and types of materials during succeeding periods of our history.

More and more we became fascinated by the information surrounding textiles and the enormous complexity and range of skills required to make quilts. Quilt makers were not only expert needlewomen but had a great feeling for textiles, as they were often involved in every process of the fabrication of materials—from growing the flax or shearing the wool to the weaving and dyeing stage.

Enjoyable, also, is the knowledge that the quilt is an extremely personal object made of bits of clothing—petticoats and shirts and ties, party dresses and everyday dresses and furnishing materials that have seen wear. There is a look to the fabrics that only age and use can give them— rich patina in which the white turns ivory or beige; the blue a deep indigo, almost black. Colors that were once bright turn pale and fade, and little calicos, side by side with other prints, seem to become one. What appeared to be a single patch is actually made up of two or three pieces of infinitesimally small size. There are fabrics that are no longer made, tiny sprigged calicos and printed chintzes in subtle colors that, in themselves, evoke a whole era—old houses with porches, featherbeds, attics, sewing baskets, and thimbled fingers. Over a long period of time, quilts were an intimate part of the family life, used over and over again. We do not believe that quilts must be in pristine condition in order to be appreciated. Many quilts will be worn, the fabrics deteriorated, the colors faded, but we believe this to be the life of the quilt. A quilt was meant to be washed and it was made of materials that had been washed repeatedly. The sun, the use, the washing give a quilt its subtlety and patina.

We have traveled over the country and found interesting quilts wherever we went. We have talked to many people and it is startling to realize the degree of pleasure people feel about quilts. Everyone seems to have a quilt for which he or she has some special sentiment or memory or experience: helping at a quilting bee or sewing pieces together for a quilt top or owning a family heirloom quilt.

We believe we have uncovered many hitherto unknown quilts of particular beauty and interest, as well as historic quilts that have been previously identified but not illustrated.

Some of what is set forth, particularly in the chapter "Patterns and Pattern Names," is in the realm of folklore; but that is part of the record of quilts in America. The selection of photographs of the quilts has been based on the various methods of decoration for a quilt: appliquéing, piecing, stenciling, embroidering, and quilting. A great number are from public rather than private collections, in order to enable readers to see quilts at museums, restorations, and historical societies and familiarize themselves first hand. We have stressed everyday quilts of common goods as well as intricately designed counterpanes of rare imported materials. We have looked for the maverick design as well as the classic; and the historically important as well as the quilt of totally unknown provenance.

For a fuller understanding of the text, certain decisions have been made regarding definitions of textile techniques and terms.

The word *quilt* comes originally from the Latin word *culcita*, meaning a stuffed sack, mattress, or cushion; it comes into English from the French *cuilte*. The word has undergone various spelling changes since the thirteenth century; "cowltes," "qwhiltez," "quildes," and "twilts" have been mentioned in histories, inventories, plays, and poems. Today the word *quilt* means two cloths sewn together with something soft between or, to be more specific, two or more fabrics held together with stitches at frequent intervals to confine in place the several layers of cloth.

Some quilts do not really fit exactly into this definition. Many quilts are only two layers. The maker has chosen to leave out the interlining either to achieve a less weighty bedcover or to enable herself to do more delicate quilting. And then some quilts contain no quilting at all. The two layers may be joined together by tying or knotting or, as in the case of many "Log Cabin" quilts (a classic design category), they may be sewn together as they are being constructed. A simple definition that takes in all these contingencies is "textile sandwich."

There are two other words used frequently and interchangeably in literature on quilts: counterpane and coverlet. *Counterpane* simply means the spread used on top of the bed, the outer covering, and has the connotation of the "best spread." It is not necessarily a quilt. The word *coverlet* can be used interchangeably with counterpane to mean a bedcover or bedspread but it is also the name given to a whole family of heavy, patterned, woven blankets or spreads.

A simple description of *piecing* is joining two pieces of material together by a seam, and to *appliqué* is to sew a piece cut from one fabric onto a ground fabric. The term *patchwork* is used in our text as a general, nontechnical term referring to both techniques. We have also omitted the word *trapunto* in favor of *stuffing* because trapunto refers to a highly specialized type of Italian quilting seldom found on American quilts. Quilt sizes have been omitted where information was not available. In photographs that show details, we have chosen to omit the sizes, except in cases where overall quilt dimensions seemed pertinent.

Finally, we have elected to date quilts by quarter-century periods unless there is a realistic provenance or historic record or a specific date is indicated on the quilt. Because of the elusive nature of quilt dating, this offers more opportunity for accuracy.

What is set forth is the result of our investigations. More facts remain to be uncovered, new quilts to be found and studied, quilters to be named. The possibilities seem unending. We hope this book is a beginning.

QUILTS
in America

1
The History of Quilts in America

The ancient origins of quilting, appliqué, and piecing are somewhat obscure, but it is known that all three techniques were used on clothing and furnishings in diverse parts of the world at extremely early dates. Economy and warmth have been the major stimuli in the development of all three. Two layers of fabric quilted together were warmer and stronger than one, a weak fabric could be strengthened and decorated with a patch applied on top of it, and fabrics need not be discarded when remnants could be pieced together to make a new cloth. These techniques were natural answers to prehistoric decorative and clothing needs, and, as pointed out:

> *Such decoration may fairly have been used by most primitive civilizations as it has been by many peasant cultures and there is no need to marshall the rather scanty evidence in order to prove that all emanated from one or more original sources.*[1]

Although quilting undoubtedly dates back before written history, the earliest known example of a quilted garment is on a carved ivory figure of a Pharaoh of the Egyptian First Dynasty, c. 3400 B.C. The figure of the king, presently in the collection of the British Museum, strongly suggests a quilted mantle or robe covered with a diamond pattern characteristic of quilting. The effect is of a layer of soft quilted material. It appears to be wrapped closely around the figure as if it had been needed for warmth. This quilted type of robe echoes the suggestion that one of the earliest functions of quilting was for protective clothing, the padding acting as an insulator to keep the wearer either warm or cool.

An extremely early surviving example was believed to have been made between the first century B.C. and the second century A.D. It is a

---

1. "Notes on Applied Work and Patchwork," His Majesty's Stationery Office, London, 1949, page 5.

16 Quilts in America

quilted carpet or floor covering discovered in Mongolia in 1924, and "actually found on the floor of a tomb just as it might have been used in the tent or mountain stronghold of a great chieftain during life."[2] The piece is elaborately quilted in large scroll and spiral designs and has appliquéd forms of trees and animals along the border. This is not primitive stitchery but an example of fine artistic needlework. Again we see quilting as a practical response to the need for protection from the cold, as an article of furnishing, a floor covering, or mattress. Dirt floors were common in houses throughout history until the nineteenth century, and it may be that the quilt evolved from a form of mat. There are suggestions in seventeenth-century inventories and writings that quilts served as mats on beds. From an English inventory of 1683 there are references to "1 quilt bed" in the gatehouse, and "1 quilt bed and matt" in the drawing room.[3] John Locke, the seventeenth-century philosopher, wrote in his *Thoughts Concerning Education* of the correct type of bed for children:

> *Let his bed be hard, and rather quilts than feathers. Hard lodgings strengthen the parts, whereas being buried every night in feathers melts and dissolves the body.... Besides he that is used to hard lodgings at home will not miss his sleep (where he has most need of it) in his travels abroad for want of his soft bed, and his pillows laid in order.*

And Daniel Defoe in *Voyage Around the World* (1725) stated: "The way of lodging *upon* quilts, and in beds . . . I need not describe."

As we have already observed in the Egyptian quilted mantle, quilting was used in garments. During the eleventh, twelfth, and thirteenth centuries, quilting was used extensively as a protective device in defensive armor, two layers of strong linen or canvas being stuffed with padding and then sewn together. The garments of various types called the gambeson, the haketon, the pourpoint, and the habergon were worn as a form of coat, or under or over metal armor, or as head caps or hoods, the tightly quilted material acting to absorb the impact of weapons. Quilted armor was useless against gunshot and ceased to be used as guns became increasingly common. Although it is from the sixteenth century that we begin to find references to quilted garments for everyday clothing, presumably quilting was in everyday use prior to that time. An author

---

2. Mary Symonds (Mrs. Guy Antrobus) and Louisa Preece, *Needlework Through the Ages,* Hodder and Stoughton, London, 1928, page 82.
3. Mavis Fitzrandolph, *Traditional Quilting,* B. T. Batsford, London, 1954, page 156.

wrote in 1555: "The men's apparall is double and quilted."[4] Decorative quilting for clothing became popular in the seventeenth century and grew to rage proportions in the early eighteenth century. Men wore quilted jackets and waistcoats. One man wrote:

> *We goe brave in apparell that wee may be taken for better men that wee bee; we use much bombastings and quiltings to seem fitter formed, better shouldered, smaller waisted, fuller thyght than we are.*[5]

The garments were stuffed with as much as five or six pounds of bombast, rendering the wearer virtually unable to move. Women dressed in elaborately quilted petticoats; these became so stylish that they were responsible for a whole new fashion in women's dress: the skirt cut away in front to reveal the petticoat.

Throughout the centuries, quilting was also universally adapted to the use of household furnishings. Manor houses and cottages alike suffered from extreme cold, and quilting was an effective, inexpensive way to insulate the living quarters from the cold. Wall hangings, curtains, and bed furnishings were therefore quilted. By the end of the thirteenth century, the few references to quilts in dictionaries, inventories, and household accounts imply that the use of quilts as bedcoverings was common.

The earliest known surviving example of a bed quilt is a Sicilian quilt made toward the end of the fourteenth century (see plate 1). It is linen, quilted and outlined with brown and white linen thread, padded with wool. Stitched in blocks across the center of the quilt are narrative scenes from the legend of Tristan. The borders are exquisitely decorated with leaf branch and rose patterns, dispersed about pictorial episodes of the story of Tristan. Expertly executed, the quilt indicates a finely honed tradition of craftsmanship in quilting. One section of the quilt is in the Victoria and Albert Museum in London, and its other two sections live in Italy: one in the Bargello Museum in Florence, the other privately owned.

Records of world-traveling merchants in the early sixteenth century report quilts being made in India. Duarte Barbosa, a Portuguese in India, observed in 1516: "They also make here very beautiful quilts and testers of beds finely worked and painted and quilted articles of dress."[6] A later

---

4. Therle Hughes, *English Domestic Needlework, 1660–1860*, Macmillan Company, New York, 1961, page 139.
5. *Ibid.*, page 140.
6. Alice Baldwin Beer, *Trade Goods*, Smithsonian Institution Press, Washington, D.C., 1970, page 22.

Plate 1.
Sicilian Quilt, c. 1400. Linen quilted with brown and white linen thread, padded with wool, 122 x 106 in. Victoria and Albert Museum, London. This oldest known surviving bed quilt depicts scenes from the legend of Tristan.

report from Surat, India, in 1609 stated: "Quilts made both of white calicoes and all sorts of painted stuffs are to be had in abundance, and very reasonable."[7]

And the British Isles too had a long tradition of quilt making. Variations on the word *quilt* are found as early as the thirteenth century, and actual references to specific quilts are at least as early as the fifteenth century. Part of a cargo on a boat returning from Brittany to England in 1498–99 included "one quilt valued at 3s. 4d."[8] In the year 1540, it is recorded that Katherine Howard, fifth wife of Henry VIII, was presented with twenty-three quilts of sarsenet (silk), closely quilted.

7.   *Ibid.*, page 24.
8.   Fitzrandolph, *op. cit.*, page 153.

The early quilts were made of wool, linen, and cotton and some of taffeta and silk, elaborately quilted with floral arabesques, circles, intersecting lines, feather designs, running vines, and baskets of flowers. They were described as

a faire quilte of crymson sattin, vj breadths iij yards 3 quarters naile deepe [a naile measuring 2½ inches], all lozenged over with silver twiste, in the midst a cinquefoile within a garland of ragged staves, fringed rounde aboute with a small fringe of crymson silke, lyned through with white fustian [1584][9]

and "A China quilt stitched in chequer work with yellow silk the ground white" (1614).[10] Although white was the most popular color, there were quilts of green, crimson, and blue. Nor can there be any doubt as to the complexity of the quilting patterns. A schoolmaster reported in his journal in December 1750: "I finished the bed quilt after five days' close application. It gave satisfaction and I received 10 schillings, 6 d's for the drawing.[11]

By the middle of the eighteenth century quilts were made by professional workers. An article in the *London Tradesman*, 1747, states that quilted petticoats:

are made mostly by Women, and some Men, who are employed by the Shops and earn but little. They quilt like wise Quilt for Beds for the upholder. This they make more of than the Petticoats, but nothing very considerable, nothing to get rich by, unless they are able to purchase the materials and sell them finished to the Shops, which few of them do. They rarely take apprentices, and the Women they employ to help them, earn Three to Four Shillings a Week and their Diet.[12]

Appliqué work and pieced work, like quilting, have a long history. An early example of appliquéd work is found on the ceremonial canopy of the funeral tent of the Egyptian queen Esi-mem-kev, in about 980 B.C. It is in the Boulak Museum in Cairo. The canopy is made of gazelle hides dyed pink, primrose, bluish green, pale blue, and golden yellow. Patterns of scarabs, serpents, open blossom forms, and other Egyptian symbols are

---

9. "Notes on Quilting," *ibid.*
10. Hughes, *ibid.*
11. *Ibid.*, page 143.
12. *Ibid.*, page 143.

applied to the surface as an obvious form of decoration.

In Peru, pre-Columbian mummy bundles have been discovered with appliquéd copper masks and eyes. And·the Crusaders used appliqué techniques for sewing elaborate designs to banners and cloaks and heraldic devices.

During the fifteenth, sixteenth, and seventeenth centuries, appliqué gained increasing favor in Spain, Italy, England, and Northern Europe as a substitute for more costly embroidery on clothing, particularly imperial and ecclesiastical vestments, and household furnishings. Cut-out patterns of flowers and figures were widely used on curtains, wall hangings, canopies, bed hangings, and chair coverings.

Piecing may be the oldest technique of all. Animal skins pieced together probably predate all other types of covering. Actual chronicled data is scant, but striking pieced objects—a large votive hanging, banners, a small silk bag—were discovered in the caves of the Thousand Buddhas in the region of Serindia in India. The caves situated on the trade route between China and the West date during the period of the sixth to the ninth centuries. The votive hanging of rectangular pieces of silk and damask of different colors and designs is pieced together in the style of a "Hit and Miss" pattern of a quilt of today, while the bag is composed of triangular and square patches of silk. The technique used to sew the pieces together is identical to that used today. Saddle cloths and horse trappings made of small pieces of broadcloth sewn together in a patchwork style, the seams covered with needlework of various colors, were used by the Persians. And, of course, there is the biblical mention of Joseph's coat of many colors, which may well have been pieced. The first reference to appliqué or pieced work on a quilt occurs in a book of French poems or "lays" of the twelfth or thirteenth century called *La Lai del Désiré*. The reference is to a "bed prepared of which the quilt was of a check board pattern of two sorts of silk cloth, well made and rich." There is also a reference in Jonathan Swift's *Gulliver's Travels*, published in 1726, that Gulliver's clothes "looked like the patchwork made by the ladies in England, only that mine were all of a colour." The earliest known English pieced and appliquéd quilts are a set of coverlets at Levens Hall (see plate 2). Although there are no specific records and the quilts are not dated, family hearsay has it that they were made about 1708. Octagonal and cruciform patches containing fragments of Indian chintz in shades of red and blue have been applied to the tops while several patches are composed of smaller sections of chintz pieced together. The quilting in red thread is an all-over diamond pattern. There are also bed hangings of the same material. The Indian chintzes are said to have been imported during the last years of the seventeenth century. The quality of

Plate 2.
Levens Hall Quilt (detail),
c. 1700–1710. Levens Hall,
Cumberland, England. Appliquéd
and pieced quilt incorporating
fragments of 17th-century Indian
chintzes.

the needlework and design reflects enormous technical proficiency, which suggests that these were not the first quilts of the type.

Pieced and appliquéd work continued to be used in the making of quilts and, by the end of the eighteenth century, pieced quilts were common in English households. Quilting, appliqué, embroidery, and piecework were only a small part of the tradition of needlecraft in Europe. An encyclopedic book, *The Academy of Armoury*, published in 1688, listed literally scores of sewing techniques and stitches for the schoolmistress.

It is apparent that women were highly knowledgeable in the art of needlecraft. This is the tradition they brought with them to the new world. By the time of the American colonization, it can be assumed that quilts were in general use in Europe and a familiarity with them was common to the colonists.

QUILTS IN AMERICA

The first settlers of New England arrived in mid-November of 1620. They had traveled for days over a vast and desolate ocean toward an unknown wilderness. Governor William Bradford wrote of the landing of the Mayflower passengers:

> . . . they had now no freinds to wellcome them, nor inns to entertaine or refresh their weatherbeaten bodys, no houses or much less townes to repaire too, to seeke for succoure. . . . And for the season it was winter, and they that know the winters of that cuntrie know them to be sharp and violent, and subjecte to cruell and feirce stormes, deangerous to travill to known places, much more to serch an unknown coast.[13]

The 102 men, women, and children were ill prepared for the freezing cold of the New England weather. During the first winter half died of sickness, hunger, and lack of shelter. There was no relief except that which they could improvise. They were isolated from the rest of the world:

> For summer being done, all things stand upon them with a weatherbeaten face; and the whole countrie, full of woods and thickets, represented a wild and savage heiw. If they looked behind them, ther was the mighty ocean which they had passed, and was now as a maine barr and goulfe to separate them from all the civill parts of the world.[14]

In Europe were families and friends, great cities with cathedrals and vast libraries, doctors, skilled craftsmen and scientists, shops with goods from Asia, India, and all parts of Europe, the theater of Shakespeare, the art of Michelangelo. They were on a primitive continent separated by an overwhelming and frightening distance from all they knew.

The hardships faced by the first settlers of America were enormous. The dangerous Atlantic crossing, dependent upon the unpredictable winds, took seven to ten weeks on pathetically small ships. And when they arrived in the new world they were faced with hunger and disease, a harsh and unknown climate that varied dramatically from north to south, wars with Indians, and wars between the colonizing countries.

The settlers had to experience life in the new land—they had to learn about its seasons and its resources, when to plant, and what the

---

13. Daniel J. Boorstin, *The Americans: The Colonial Experience*, Vintage Books, Random House, New York, 1958, page vii.
14. *Ibid.*

harvest would produce. Houses had to be built, furniture made, the family clothed. Little accurate information was available to them about the conditions they would meet. The earlier explorations of DeSoto, Coronado, and others had produced a jumble of fantasy and fact about the new world. Stories of great wealth, of gold, of rich Indian empires, and of vast natural resources had created interest on the part of European princes, merchants, and traders in America. At the same time, restriction of religious liberties and bad economic and political conditions in Europe had created the right atmosphere for enormous numbers of people to undertake voluntarily the great colonization. Merchant companies could raise capital for ships and supplies. The crowns of Europe, anxious to share in the potential wealth, would readily give land grants. But only people could bring the skills necessary to develop the land. From England, France, and Holland, from Sweden and the Palatine, the colonists sailed, naive in their expectations, poorly prepared, knowing little or nothing of the new world. They brought with them only bare essentials—food, clothing, tools and furniture, a few personal items. The first minister at Salem, Reverend Francis Higginson, wrote in 1630:

> Before you come, be careful to be strongly instructed what things are fittest to bring with you for your more comfortable passage at sea, as also for your husbandry occasions when you come to the land. For when you are once parted with England you shall meete neither markets nor fayres to buy what you want. Therefore, be sure to furnish yourselves with things fitting to be had before you come: as meale for bread, malt for drinke, woolen and linnen cloath, and leather for shoes, and all manner of carpenters tools, and a great deale of iron and steele to make nails, and locks for houses, and furniture for ploughs and carts, and glasse for windows and many other things which were better for you to think of there than to want them here.[15]

The men and women who came to New England and Virginia, to Pennsylvania and Delaware and North Carolina, carried in their minds the memory of their homelands, the architecture, the forms of furniture, the style of dress, which they were to recreate in a fresh image in the new world. Each person had to adapt his or her skills and develop new ones if he was to survive. John Urmstone, a preacher in North Carolina, wrote in 1711:

> Men are generally of all trades, and women the like within their spheres. ... Men are generally carpenters, joiners, wheelwrights, coopers,

---

15. Francis Higginson, *New England's Plantation*, London, 1630.

butchers, tanners, shoemakers, tallow-chandlers, watermen and what not; women soap-makers, starch-makers, dyers, etc. He or she who cannot do all of these things . . . will have but a bad time of it.[16]

Although the colonists brought from Europe a heritage rich in needlework and quilting traditions, there are no records that the first settlers brought quilts with them. It is not until the end of the seventeenth century that we find references to quilts in America. "A quilt of calico, colored and flowered"[17] is listed in the inventory of the house of Captain George Corwin, who died in 1685 in Salem, Massachusetts. And among the inventory of the household furnishings of Captain John Kidd, the sea captain who later became the notorious pirate, and his wife, Sarah, when they began housekeeping in New York in 1692, is listed: "featherbeds, feather pillows, tablecloths, linen sheets, napkins, ten blankets and three 'quilts.' "[18]

Whether these quilts were made in the colonies is uncertain, but that quilts were made and used, as well as pelts and furs, for bedcoverings at an early date in the colonies can scarcely be doubted. Conditions in the new land were particularly conducive to the making and use of quilts, though it must be assumed that the quilts that were made during the first years of settlement were considerably more utilitarian than decorative.

Materials of all types were scarce in this relatively rudimentary economy. Imports were expensive and not readily obtainable. Months passed before goods ordered from England and the continent were received, and the mark-up on goods from Europe was customarily from 100 percent to 300 percent.

Inevitably, the colonists were forced to manufacture their own materials for clothing and household needs. Enormous quantities of linens were necessary for each family, and towels, napkins, sheets, pillow coverings, blankets, and coverlets of all types were made and stored and used. Every skill and effort was toward self-support.

Creating the raw materials, and from the raw materials the finished goods, was a long and difficult task.

---

16. John Urmstone, "Self-Reliance on the Frontier," *The Annals of America*, Vol. 1, *1493–1754, Discovery of a New World*, Encyclopaedia Britannica, Chicago, 1968, page 329.
17. Frances Little, *Early American Textiles*, Century Company, New York, 1931, page 223.
18. Marie D. Webster, *Quilts, Their Story and How to Make Them*, Doubleday, Page and Company, New York, 1915, page 70.

To turn flax into linen took sixteen months from planting to finished fabric: sowing, weeding, pulling up the ripened stalks, de-seeding, drying, retting (or rotting) them with a five day water treatment; cleaning still again, re-drying, and beating several times to remove the woody center; swingled (or scraped) to remove the coarse fibers, then carded with a heavy comb called a hetchel, and recarded several times to refine it into fibers fine enough for spinning into thread for weaving. Wound into skeins, the thread was bleached in ashes and water for a week, rinsed, washed, dried, and rewound onto weaving bobbins and shuttles. The final fabric itself had to be bleached for weeks in the sun before it was cut, sewed, or embroidered. Wool processing wasn't any easier, although it wasn't always necessary to raise the sheep themselves; fleece could sometimes be bought through trade. After shearing it was cleaned of burrs and twigs, washed, and dried, and then carded: the wool was rubbed with melted swine's grease, then pulled through the fine wire teeth of carding combs, sometimes dyed at that point, sometimes spun first, wound into skeins, and then dyed. [19]

After the textiles were made they were frequently dyed. As in other goods, there was a high import duty on dyes from Europe. Women had to develop a knowledge of the natural dyes that were available and how to use them. They had to know which leaves and which roots would yield color and what barks of trees and dried insects could be used. From the leaves of the indigo plant they derived blue dyes. The bark of the butternut and black walnut, hemlock, and maple trees yielded browns. Reds came from madder and pokeberries, yellow from yellowweed and smartweed. Lily of the valley leaves produced a greenish yellow. Yellow dyes could also be obtained from peach and pear tree leaves.

They were dependent upon the growing seasons to stock the natural materials that would be ground and powdered into dyes. Dyes were difficult to store and extracting the colors desired was a long process. Colonists also had to learn how to impart the colors to the cloth, what colors would remain "fast," and which would hold to linen, wool, or cotton. They also had to learn how to mix hues to expand the range of colors—red and yellow to produce orange, blue and yellow to create green.

Every scrap of fabric was scarce and precious, to be conserved and reused. Nothing was thrown away. Textiles were preserved and used as long as possible. Pioneer life was one of extreme hardship, and the lack of goods made fabrics so precious that this recycling of even the smallest

---

19. Museum of American Folk Art, "The Fabric of the State," 1972, unpaginated.

scraps was an abiding necessity. Not all of the scrap materials were from pieces of worn-out clothing; some were remnants from the fabrics used in making new garments and household furnishings.

It was not unusual for clothing to be worn twenty to thirty years, mended and patched and then cut down and restyled for use by another. A shirt or petticoat was used over and over again, sometimes refashioned into clothing for an infant, then as a fabric for a curtain, and then into the rag bag for a pieced quilt. There was a relentless resourcefulness, as when, due to the great cost of yarn, worn-out woolen clothing was often unwound and the threads used to make mittens or socks. A poem composed about 1630 describes the plight of the colonist in the clouting, or patching, of their garments:

> And now our garments begin to grow thin,
> And wool is much wanted to card and to spin.
> If we can get a garment to cover without,
> Our other in-garments are clout upon clout.
> Our clothes we brought with us are apt to be torn,
> They need to be clouted soon after they're worn,
> But clouting our garments they hinder us nothing;
> Clouts double are warmer than single whole clothing.[20]

Patching of clothing—and, of course, bed coverings—was a common and necessary technique. The idea of using saved scraps of materials in piecing was also natural to the Puritan and frontier mentality of thrift, utility, and economy. Quilters have used recycled materials for years.

Quilts, with their thick interlinings, were also an effective protection against the cold. The privation was acute in the paralyzingly cold weather of the north, "the dreary monotony of a New England winter, which leaves so large a blank, so melancholy a death-spot, in lives so brief that they ought to be all summertime."[21]

Samuel Sewall, a Boston businessman and judge, noted in his diary at the beginning of the eighteenth century: "An Extraordinary Cold Storm of Wind and Snow. Bread was frozen at Lords Table. . . . At six oclock my ink freezes so that I can hardly write by a good fire in my

---

20. From the "Forefathers' Song," collection of the Massachusetts Historical Society, in Martha Genung Stearns, *Homespun and Blue*, Charles Scribner's Sons, New York, 1963, page 8.
21. Alice Morse Earle, *Customs and Fashions in Old New England*, Charles E. Tuttle Company, Rutland, Vermont, 1973, page 129 (first edition published 1893 by Charles Scribner's Sons, New York).

Wives Chamber."[22] In later years Benjamin Franklin, referring to the cold, indicated it was so intense that it would give women head colds that "fell into their jaws and gums and have destroyed, early, many a fine set of teeth in these northern colonies."

The freezing cold in unheated or poorly heated bedrooms made effective insulation a life-and-death matter. Beds were shrouded with curtains and hangings, sometimes quilted, to keep out the dreaded chill and drafts. A fire alone was not sufficient for warmth, and the triple-layered quilt provided some measure of comfort from the cold. Under a quilt, a child could sleep warm.

In time, with the increase in imports and the development of manufacturing, more goods were available in the urban areas along the coast—Philadelphia, Boston, Charleston, New York. But many home crafts continued in rural areas with the migrations west throughout the nineteenth century.

The quilting tradition was to repeat itself as the boundaries of settlement moved in every direction over the country. The earliest types of appliqué and pieced quilts made in America developed out of necessity, probably as soon as the various bed coverings brought by the settlers were worn or no longer usable. There is no real evidence that elaborate decorative quilts were not made at the time or that quilt making was only a result of need, but the economic and physical conditions in the colonies was such that during the seventeenth century need almost certainly had to be the primary motivation in the making of quilts. Patches were appliquéd to an existing worn top, or pieces of saved scraps were used to replace a deteriorated section of a counterpane, or were sewn together to make a new top. The quilts were surely simple, constructed by patching or joining materials together in squares and triangles in whatever miscellaneous sizes and shapes the maker happened to have. As thread was costly and difficult to obtain and the quilter could afford neither the time nor materials to stitch the top elaborately, the quilted counterpane was also simply made. The American quilter traditionally used the more economical running stitch, rather than the backstitch common in European quilts.

We have no descriptions of seventeenth-century American quilts, and none seem to have survived. Consequently, the history of the earliest quilts must be an interpretive one. The problems of interpretation are especially numerous in American textile history—not only because of the lack of contemporary documentation, but also because of the greatly

---

22. *Ibid.*, page 128.

varying conditions that existed in the early years of colonization. The variety in the economic, social, cultural, and geographic conditions, as well as the differences imposed on each colony by its mother country, resulted in an enormous disparity of custom and style. What would be true of one group or area would not apply to another. Accordingly, it is virtually impossible to impose a chronology of styles onto quilts before 1700. Probably various types of quilts—pieced, appliquéd and quilted—developed simultaneously and were used throughout the colonies.

Certainly the quilt was not the only early bed covering. It doubtless vied with animal pelts and hand-woven wool blankets in popularity. However, pelts were difficult to clean and the hand-woven wool blankets were not easy to produce because of the tremendous amount of time that went into the carding, spinning, and weaving for the coverlet. A yard-wide piece of all-wool goods involved many months of work from the time the colonial housewife received the fleece. Quilts, however, provided a more creative outlet for the entire family and produced one of the few flamboyant elements of color and style in an otherwise utilitarian household.

To have a better idea of what the early quilts were like, one must examine the textiles used for clothing and house furnishings. As has been pointed out by Frances Little, the colonists were not "obliged to confine themselves to homespun materials. On the contrary, their contact with England assured them a constant supply of foreign fabrics."[23] American colonists received finished printed fabrics, clothing, and furnishings from England in return for their flax, wool, cotton, and so on. This was the basis of the British mercantile-colonial strategy. But, at the same time, home industry was encouraged to facilitate clothing the populace—and as a means of creating small outlets of manufacture that would not be in competition with large British concerns. This home industry flourished and became the main supplier of goods for many colonists and an important phenomenon in early quilt making. Although there may have been a constant flow of English textiles and textiles imported by England from the East and shipped to the colonies, their availability was limited. They were expensive and proximity to the ports of the eastern seaboard was crucial. Consequently, humble pioneers in remote areas had to depend largely on their home looms.

Materials and colors used in the making of quilts were basically a product of customs of dress. Of course, leftover bits of materials from household furnishings were also used, particularly in later periods, but we

23. Little, *op. cit.*, page 206.

will confine ourselves to dress. As it is today, not everybody dressed alike. There was a paradoxical variety even among the Puritans.

In the period from about 1620 to 1680, the dress of the New England colonist was simple. A Puritan colonist of the Massachusetts Bay Colony dressed in the typical fashion of the Puritans in England at the time. The austere style recommended for the men was a suit of black cloth; stockings of homespun dark gray or green wool fastened to the breeches with black ribbon; cuffs of white Holland linen; hat of black felt; and cloak of black cloth lined with fustian or drugget (coarse, plain-weave wool fabrics). The Puritan woman wore a gown of purple, gray, or brown plain cloth; petticoats of homespun; an apron of white Holland linen; white linen cuffs and large collar and white linen cap; woolen stockings; and a silk kerchief or a hood lined in silk. Distinction between rich and poor in Puritan dress related chiefly to the character of the linen found in the apron, collar, and cuffs. One could expect to see any of these materials in a New England pieced quilt of this period together with bits of worn-out flannel sheets, old coat and cloak linings, and home-dyed petticoats—in fact, home-woven remnants of all descriptions. As to colors used, one New England clothing legacy from 1670 listed puce, grain color, Kendall green, Lincoln green, Bristol red, Watchet blue, and Stammel red. Another earlier list included butternut, khaki, russet, tan, brown, tawny leather, grain red, scarlet, and a great range of brown tints. Thus, the quilt of the New England colonist was sturdy, homespun, warm, never gaudy, simple and rich in earth color, and plain rather than decorative.

In the southern colonies, a quilt made during the same period would have had very different characteristics. Early settlers in Virginia and the Carolinas were, in many cases, wealthy landed Englishmen who very quickly created large self-supporting estates and plantations. These planters with close ties to the mother country, with fortunes from tobacco, wished to achieve heights of elegance. The landed Virginian lady wore a gown of light velvet, opening over a brocaded petticoat. The neck ruff was of stiffened lace of very high workmanship. A farthingale supported the dress, which hung in heavy plaits to the ground. The gentleman planter wore a suit (doublet and padded breeches were the style at this time) of colored light velvet, silk stockings, and a felt hat adorned with embroidery and plumes. Even the workingman on the plantation was not poorly clothed. By 1650, linen of an excellent quality was being made on the plantation. The plantation owned looms on which materials were woven for the use of the family and indentured servants and slaves. The typical workingman's costume consisted of loose breeches and jerkin of canvas or frieze and hose of stout woolen cloths, and blue linen shifts. The woman wore a petticoat and waistcoat of strong wool (calimanco is listed in some accounts), two blue aprons, and two linen caps. The clothing of the slaves was typically "homespun cloths and homespun stuffs, crocus and Virginia cloth, and the women crowned their simple attire with gay turbans." The Indians that came to the plantations were described as wearing "gay dress of the wild woods."

Even at this early period (1620–80), in the southern colonies quilts were very likely constructed with finer stitchery and more elegant fabrics than those of their northern cousins. Though the plantation was largely self-sufficient, it regularly received the latest "fancy cloth" from England. A list of "fancy cloth" tells us very little, as the fabric names are foreign in meaning for the most part: "says and serges, druggets and darnicks, paduasoys and perpetuanas, tabbies and sarcenets, calimancoes and kidderminsters." One list, however, made in 1660, describes articles easily recognizable:

> *olive colored cambric petticoat*
> *flowered tabby petticoat*
> *velvet petticoat*
> *striped dimity petticoat*
> *printed calico gown lined with blue silk*
> *striped dimity jacket*
> *scarlet sleeves*
> *striped linen petticoat*
> *India silk petticoat*
> *calico petticoat*[24]

A clothing portrait of the settlers of the Dutch Colonies, New Amsterdam, Manhattan, and New Netherlands, again presents differences. Originally, they doubtlessly arrived in the dress of their mother country. The wife of the patroon wore fairly elegant clothing: her gown was of crimson silk, ruffs and cuffs of starched and wired lace, and a patterned woolen overgarment tied with silk ribbons. The patroon wore ample breeches of velvet, woolen hose, silk scarf, and white linen collars and cuffs.

From the simple Dutch housewife came the beginnings of a recognizable quilting heritage. Dutch housewives brought with them to New Amsterdam a strong tradition of quilted garments and petticoats.

---

24. Elisabeth McClellan, *History of American Costume*, Tudor Publishing Co., 1969, page 64 (originally *Historic Dress in America*, George W. Jacobs and Co., 1904).

Most interesting was their custom of wearing sewing pockets in which they carried scissors, pincushions, and all manner of functional household articles (see plate 127). These were large, were worn tied around the waist, and were fashioned out of patchwork. The Dutch housewife's costume was typically a petticoat of linsey-woolsey striped with a variety of brilliant dyes, covered by gowns described as uniformly gay, covered again by a long white apron of homespun linen, and topped by a waistcoat made of red and blue printed linen, with sleeves of red and yellow patterned cloth. Another distinguishing mark of the Dutch lady was a cap of quilted calico. Under the willing hands of the hardworking Dutch women, spinning and weaving became a routine part of the work of their homes. They created stores of household linens and bedding and petticoats, and were renowned for their comfortable habit of well-stocked linen closets. Surely a quilt, brightly colored and quilted by experienced hands, unique to the Dutch craftswoman, was born out of her very particular conditions. Such quilts were sturdy, coarse, and well made.

Though no quilts from the period remain, they can be visualized from the clothing and textiles of the period. The dress of most of the colonists of the seventeenth century was simple, fashioned primarily from goods spun, woven, dyed, and sewn in the household. The average pioneer of limited means, the dwellers of the isolated settlements and frontier farms, all the working people who depended on their own home production, undoubtedly found it more difficult to create a quilt with a variety of material, fancy stitchery, and elaborate designs than did their wealthy urban or plantation counterparts. Nonetheless, there were indeed people of property and affairs who would have had access to far more sophisticated fabrics—satins, velvets, brocades, and particularly the highly prized imported India calicoes and chintzes. Fashionable European women were wearing calicoes imported from India before 1650, and calico printing was undertaken in England as early as 1676. Along the seaboard there were rare materials brought by sailors and travelers returning from exotic voyages. Even during the earliest period, there must have been a variety of quilt types, though the cruder variety probably predominated.

The earliest surviving American pieced quilt known to the authors, the Saltonstall Quilt, is said to date from about 1704 (see plate 3). It is possibly the earliest pieced quilt still in existence, predating the English Levens Hall Quilt by four years. (As neither has a date written or sewn on it, the dating of each is based, of course, on circumstantial evidence.) The top of the Saltonstall Quilt is composed of hundreds of small pieces of silk, velvet, and brocade materials set together in a series of squares of two-patch and four-patch design. A winged angel has been appliquéd at

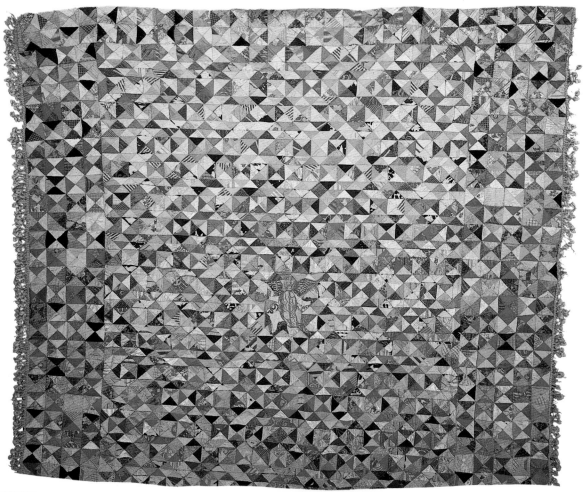

Plate 3 (ABOVE).
Saltonstall Quilt (detail), c. 1704. Pieced silk, brocade, and velvet, 75 x 82 in. Collection of Governor and Mrs. Leverett Saltonstall. This geometric framed center variation quilt, said to have been made by Sarah Sedgwick Leverett and her daughter Elizabeth Leverett, is believed to be the oldest known surviving pieced quilt.

Plate 4 (LEFT).
Coverlet with building, Connecticut, c. 1750. Pieced and appliquéd homespun wool, 65½ x 76 in. The Baltimore Museum of Art; Bequest of John H. Scarff, by exchange.

The History of Quilts in America 33

the center of the quilt, most likely at a later date, though we cannot be certain. There is no quilting or interlining.

The absence of an interlining is representative of early eighteenth-century English quilts, which were frequently constructed only of two layers of material stitched together without padding. There is an unusual handmade three-inch border of woolen ball fringe on three sides. The quilt is small, measuring two yards three inches by two yards ten inches. The quilt, believed to have been made by Sarah Sedgwick Leverett, wife of John Leverett, governor of the Massachusetts Bay Colony from 1673 to 1679, and her daughter Elizabeth represents an obvious attempt at design. The squares are not placed in a random fashion but are built up in an overall pattern that gives the effect of bowknots and windmills, and produces the added effect of vertical squares surrounding horizontal squares to create a geometric framed center.

The period of the quilt's construction has been confirmed ingeniously. A common technique used in piecing a quilt involved cutting the quilt pattern out of paper—newspapers, letters, scraps of whatever was available—over which the material was basted and then sewn together or to a set. The paper interlining was frequently left in the quilt to serve as an added layer of insulation against the cold. When the textile covering becomes worn, or is pushed back, the paper will show through. The Saltonstall Quilt reveals such an interlining of paper: bits of a Harvard College catalog of 1701. The quilt has remained in the Leverett-Saltonstall families since it was made, and it is presently owned by Governor and Mrs. Saltonstall of Massachusetts.

By the beginning of the eighteenth century, there are more frequent references to quilts in wills, journals, letters, household inventories, and advertisements. It is striking that the records are not descriptive of the patterns or types of quilt—pieced, appliquéd, or whole cloth. Everyday quilts may have been considered too commonplace for elaborate description.

Judge Samuel Sewall, delighted with his daughter's engagement, ordered house furnishings from England in 1720 as a wedding gift:

> *a true Looking Glass of Black Walnut Frame of the Newest Fashion if the Fashion be good, as good as can be bought for five or six pounds.*
>
> *A Duzen of good slack Walnut Chairs fine Cane with a Couch. Four pair of strong Iron Dogs with Brass heads about 5 or 6 shillings a pair.*
>
> *Curtains & Vallens for a Bed with Counterpane Head Cloth and Tester made of good yellow waterd worsted camlet with Triming well made and Bases if it be the Fashion. Send also of the Same Camlet & Triming*

as may be good enough to make Cushions for the Chamber Chairs.
A good fine large Chintz Quilt well made.[25]

References in wills and inventories of estates are sporadic. An "India Silk quilt"[26] was included in the inventory of the estate of Governor William Burnet of Boston in 1729, and "1 old quilt" was listed together with "1 Bedstead and curtains, 3 blankets"[27] in an inventory in Dorchester, Massachusetts, in 1732.

Peter Faneuil, the Boston merchant who made a fortune in the export of New England codfish and gave Faneuil Hall to the city of Boston, had a number of bedcovers and hangings, including quilts, itemized in the inventory of his estate in 1743: "1 Green Harrateen Bed, Bedstd . . . 2 Green Silk Quilts," "Yellow Mohair Bed . . . false Curtains," "1 workt Fustian Bed . . . 3/4 lined with Green Damask . . . blew Silk Quilt," "one Chints Field Mohogony Bedstd," "1 Blew Harateen Bed . . . Silk Quilt," and "a Red Harrateen Bed . . . & Silk Quilt."[28]

There was also a "Silk Quilt" in the estate of Reverend Benjamin Colman, Boston, 1747,[29] and an auction of household furnishings advertised in the *New England Journal* of March 20, 1727, offered: "three Feather Beds, two Bedsteads and Curtains . . . Ruggs, 'Quilts,' some pictures, together with Sundry other things."[30]

While we must assume the vast majority of bed covers during this period were homemade quilts, and other coverlets could be purchased in the colonies. John Housman, a Philadelphia upholsterer, advised his customers and creditors in a notice published June 14, 1722, in the *American Weekly Mercury*, that he was returning to England and had for sale: "Standing Beds, Feather-Beds, Quilts, Blankets, Stuffs for Curtains, Chairs, Looking-Glasses, Couches, &c. All Persons indebted to him are desired to come and make up their Accounts, and those who have any Demand on him may come and settle the same."[31]

"Bed-Camblets, Cotton Quilts and Deck Nails" from England were

25. Earle, *op. cit.*, page 118.
26. Abbott Lowell Cummings, *Bed Hangings*, Society for the Preservation of New England Antiquities, Boston, 1961, page 37.
27. Carleton L. Safford and Robert Bishop, *America's Quilts and Coverlets*, E. P. Dutton Co., Inc., New York, 1972, page 18.
28. Cummings, *op. cit.*, page 11.
29. *Ibid.*, page 37.
30. George Francis Dow, *The Arts & Crafts in New England, 1704–1775, Gleanings from Boston Newspapers*, Wayside Press, Topsfield, Mass., 1927, page 107.
31. Alfred Coxe Prime, *The Arts and Crafts in Philadelphia, Maryland, and South Carolina, 1721–1785*, Walpole Society, Topsfield, Mass., 1929, page 205.

Plate 5.
Framed Medallion Variation Quilt, Connecticut, c. 1775–1800. Pieced cotton and linen,
83 x 85 in. Smithsonian Institution, Washington, D.C. There are over 150 different printed dress
fabrics used in this quilt, which is one of the Copp Family Household textiles.

Plates 7 and 8.
Westover-Berkeley Coverlet (details).

Plate 6.
Westover-Berkeley Coverlet (detail), Virginia, c. 1775–1800. Appliquéd and embroidered
cotton, 93 ¾ x 105 ½ in. Valentine Museum, Richmond, Virginia.

advertised for sale in the *Boston News-Letter* of March 21, 1723,[32] while the June 22, 1727, issue offered "Quilts, Rugs and Wadings."[33] An advertisement in the *Boston Gazette* on September 12, 1757, listed for sale: "4 Blankets, 4 Coverlids, 4 Bed Quilts, and 4 Counterpins."[34]

Of course, quilting was used on clothing, particularly, as we have noted, among the Dutch of New Amsterdam. The women wore petticoats of many different colors and materials quilted in elaborate and fanciful designs. Legal notices in newspapers described runaway servants dressed in quilted garments. A 1728 notice in the *Boston News-Letter* reported:

> *Ran away, an Indian woman, indented servant, tall lusty, wore narrow striped Cherrederry gown, turned up with a little flowered red and white callico, stript homespun quilted petticoat, plain muslin apron, & a suit of plain pinners, & a red & white flowered know, pair green stone earings, white cotton stockings, leather heeled shoes.*[35]

There were also references to "Childrens quilted Peaks" (1737),[36] "Turkey Quilts fit for Lady's Skirts (1751),[37] and "a blue quilted Coat" (1757).[38]

Newspaper advertisements offered instruction in quilting and other needlework. A Mrs. Carroll placed a notice in the *New-York Mercury* on May 6, 1765, which read: "Mrs. Carroll proposes teaching young Ladies plain work, Samplars, French Quilting, knoting for Bed Quilts or Toilets, Dresden, flowering on Cat Gut, Shading with Silk or Worsted on Cambrick, Lawn, or Holland."[39]

The education of women in reading, writing, and arithmetic was considered of vastly less importance than instruction in household matters. At times in our history, too much abstract education for a girl was thought to be dangerous and even unhealthy. In 1645, John Winthrop, the aristocratic governor of the Massachusetts Bay Colony, wrote:

> *(April 13, 1645) Mr. Hopkins, the governor of Hartford upon Connecticut, came to Boston, and brought his wife with him, (a godly young woman, and of special parts,) who was fallen into a sad infirmity, the loss of her understanding and reason, which had been growing upon*

32. Dow, *op. cit.*, page 154.
33. *Ibid.*
34. *Ibid.*, page 166.
35. *Ibid.*, page 187.
36. *Ibid.*, page 274.
37. *Ibid.*, page 176.
38. *Ibid.*, page 201.
39. Rita Susswein Gottesman, *The Arts and Crafts in New York, 1726–1776*, New-York Historical Society, 1938, page 276.

her divers years, by occasion of her giving herself wholly to reading and writing, and had written many books. Her husband, being very loving and tender of her, was loath to grieve her; but he saw his error, when it was too late. For if she had attended her household affairs, and such things as belong to women, and not gone out of her way and calling to meddle in such things as are proper for men, whose minds are stronger, etc., she had kept her wits, and might have improved them usefully and honorably in the place God had set her. He brought her to Boston, and left her with her brother, one Mr. Yale, a merchant, to try what means might be had here for her. But no help could be had.[40]

The attitude toward education and the sins of idleness lasted into the eighteenth and nineteenth centuries. In a letter published in the *New-York Mercury* in October of 1758, a frustrated husband complained:

Needlework . . . My Wife's notion of education differs widely from mine. She is an irreconcileable enemy to Idleness, and considers every State of life as Idleness, in which the hands are not employed or some art acquired, by which she thinks money may be got or saved.

In pursuance of this principle, she calls up her Daughters at a certain hour, and appoints them a task of needle-work to be performed before breakfast. . . .

By this continual exercise of their diligence, she has obtained a very considerable number of laborious performances. We have twice as many fire-skreens and chimneys and three flourished quilts for every bed [authors' emphasis]. Half the rooms are adorned with a kind of futile pictures which imitate tapestry. But all their work is not set out to shew. She has boxes filled with knit garters and braided shoes. She has twenty coverns for side-saddles embroidered with silver flowers, and has curtains wrought with gold in various figures, which she resolves some time or other to hang up. . . .

About a month ago, Tent and Turkey-stitch seemed at a stand; my Wife knew not what New Work to introduce; I ventured to propose that the Girls should now learn to read and write and mentioned the necessity of a little arithmatick; but unhappily, my wife has discovered that linen wears out, and has brought the Girls three little wheels, that they may spin hukkaback for the servants' table.[41]

---

40. John Winthrop, "Journal," *American Literature Vol. 1, The 17th and 18th Centuries*, Carl Bode, Leon Howard, and Louis B. Wright, eds., Washington Square Press, New York, 1966, page 60.
41. Gottesman, *op. cit.*, page 276.

Plate 9.
Bowknots and Swags Quilt, early 19th century. Pieced, appliquéd, and embroidered cottons and linens, 93 x 89 in. Shelburne Museum, Shelburne, Vermont. The pillar prints (above and below the framed center) are typical of those block-printed in England between 1800 and 1805. The bowknot and swag motif is found throughout the 18th and into the first third of the 19th century on wallpapers and textiles. The floral motif centered in each swag is hand painted with flowers. The peacocks and flowers around the border are pieced cottons appliquéd with embroidery stitches.

Plate 10.
Framed Center Quilt, c. 1800–1825. Pieced cotton quilted in stuffed floral, feather, and grapevine motifs, 99 ½ x 98 in. Collection of the authors. The center panel (measuring 27 ¼ x 27 ¼ in.) was printed by John Hewson, who printed squares specifically for use as quilt centers in the late 18th and early 19th centuries. They are all variations of an urn surrounded by flowers, birds, and butterflies. Hewson's work resembles designs found in English furnishing and dress fabrics of the late 18th century.

Girls learned needlework at an astonishingly young age, almost as early as they learned to walk and talk. One woman described her childhood experiences as follows:

> *Before I was three years old, I was started at piecing a quilt. Patchwork, you know. My stint was at first only two blocks a day, but these were sewn together with the greatest care or they were unraveled and done over. Two blocks was called "a single," but when I got a little bigger I had to make two pairs of singles and sew the four blocks together, and I was pretty proud when I had finished them and achieved my first "wedding."*[42]

Girls were taught by their mothers, sisters, and grandmothers to thread needles, mend and repair worn quilts, and then, finally, to cut out patches and sew them together—four patches, nine patches, on to the more complex triangular and hexagonal patterns. Later, they mastered techniques of appliqué, applying pieces of calico and chintz to the quilt top and tying down the edges neatly with seemingly invisible stitches. Finally they learned to perform almost magical feats with needle and thread and created exquisite all-white quilts with thousands of infinitesimal stitches. There were patterns to learn and new designs to create: "Robbing Peter to Pay Paul," "Rose of Sharon," "Log Cabin," "Courthouse Steps," and hundreds of others. When a girl gained proficiency, she would embark on a series of quilts for her own hope chest, to be completed by the time she was engaged.

The well-to-do attended private classes where they learned various forms of needlework—plain work, dresden, point work, tent stitch, cross stitch, and how to make bone lace with pillows and bobbins. There was also papyrotamia (the art of paper cutouts), painting, and quilt piecing in a hundred different and difficult designs. Girls worked on samplers, which served the dual purpose of teaching types of stitches as well as the alphabet and numbers.

Boys, too, were taught all forms of sewing. In a society where manpower was critically short, everyone from the youngest to the oldest was expected to contribute toward the household needs. And, until the mid-eighteenth century, the average family simply could not afford to buy

---

42. Marion Nicholl Rawson, *When Antiques Were Young*, E. P. Dutton and Co., New York, 1931, page 129.

quantities of goods; everything possible had to be produced at home. As Governor Moore of New York was to say: "Every house swarmed with children, who are set to work as soon as they are able to Spin and Card."[43]

During the colonial period, as Daniel J. Boorstin pointed out in *The Americans: The Colonial Experience*: "Most crafts in America were still carried on as small family undertakings. Even at the end of the colonial period, a considerable proportion of the manufactures of the northern colonies still came from village craftsmen."[44]

In time, with the flowering of a philosophy of national self-determination, the development of a strong household manufacturing society was fundamental in securing economic independence from England.

Boys not only sewed but cut the materials to be pieced into a quilt. The lovely quilt shown in plate 137 was pieced by John W. Yeury in 1830 when he was a boy of seven. The fabrics are typical of the first quarter of the nineteenth century. That quilts are cherished as family heirlooms and handed down from generation to generation is attested to by the fact that this quilt is presently owned by Barbara B. Ladd, a great-great-granddaughter of John W. Yeury. Although quilt making is generally considered a woman's art, boys and men have made quilts to the present time. As young boys, Dwight D. Eisenhower and his brothers helped their mother piece the quilt shown in plate 15, while Calvin Coolidge cut the pieces for the Baby Blocks Quilt shown in plate 16 in 1882, when he was ten years old.

Needlework was an integral part of the school curriculum until the middle of the nineteenth century. Expert needleworkmanship was by no means a province restricted only to colonial society, or that of the women and girls who attended private schools, seminaries, or finishing colleges. It was part of the public school curriculum from the beginning. The Dame School, for example, was a combination nursery school, kindergarten, and first grade, run by a spinster or housewife who taught small children—boys as well as girls—their alphabet and instructed them in sewing and knitting. Fundamentals deemed necessary for the education of children were reading, the Bible, and sewing. The emphasis on sewing is seen in the curriculum of college preparatory academies. Atkinson Academy, founded in 1787 by Reverend Samuel Peabody of Atkinson,

---

43. Carl Bridenbaugh, *The Colonial Craftsman*, Phoenix Books, University of Chicago Press, Chicago, 1950, page 35.
44. Boorstin, *op. cit.*, page 23.

Plate 11.
Benjamin J. Harrison, *Annual Fair of the American Institute—at Niblo's Garden*, c. 1845. Watercolor, 20¼ x 27½ in. Museum of the City of New York; Gift of Mrs. J. Insley Blair. The fair was held to promote domestic and manufactured arts, including quilts of all types and patterns.

Plate 12.
Fannie Lou Spelce, *Quilting Bee*, 20th century. © Fannie Lou Spelce Associates. This painting depicts the women of Dyer, Arkansas, who gathered once each month to make quilts. The frame is of interest because it is hung from the ceiling on pulleys, making it possible to raise it out of the way when not in use.

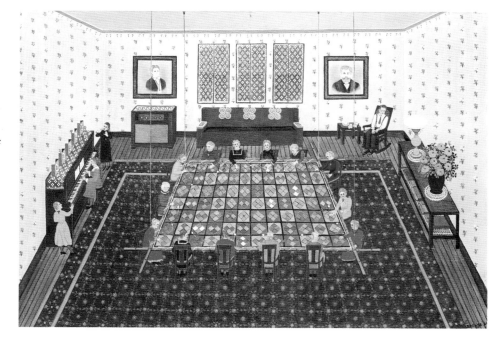

Plate 13.
Bertha Stenge, *Quilt Show*, Illinois, 1943. Pieced cotton, 78 x 93 in. Collection of Frances Stenge Traynor. This original design shows thirteen pieced quilts in miniature, each about 6 inches square and each a replica of a different well-known pattern. The border contains fifty-two pieced quilt patterns. This quilt won many prizes, including first prize in the Kentucky State Fair and first prize in the Florida State Fair of 1949.

Plate 14.
Bertha Stenge, *The Quilting Bee*, Illinois, c. 1948. Pieced and appliquéd cotton, 77 x 81 in. Collection of Frances Stenge Traynor. The center is an exact copy in appliqué of *The Quilting Party*, a painting by an unknown artist in Virginia, c. 1854. The pieced borders include original quilting designs.

Plate 15 (ABOVE LEFT).
Tumbling Blocks Quilt. Dwight D. Eisenhower Birthplace Museum, Denison, Texas. Dwight D. Eisenhower and his brothers helped their mother piece this quilt. Eisenhower noted that the striped materials came from shirts and the prints and checks from fabrics his mother used to make her dresses.

Plate 16 (ABOVE RIGHT).
Baby Blocks Quilt, President Coolidge Homestead, Plymouth Notch, Vermont. The quilt seen on the bed was pieced by Calvin Coolidge in 1882, when he was ten years old.

New Hampshire, taught painting, sewing, and embroidery as well as academic subjects.

Thomas Jefferson wrote to his daughter Martha in 1787 extolling the democratic virtues of an education in needlecraft. Patsy, as she was known, was at school in Paris during Jefferson's tenure as Minister to the Court of Louis XVI. She complained in a letter to her father of the difficulties in learning. Jefferson replied:

I do not like your saying that you are unable to read the ancient print of your Livy but with the aid of your master. We are always equal to what we undertake with resolution. A little degree of this will enable you to decipher your Livy. If you always lean on your master, you will never be able to proceed without him. It is a part of the American character to consider nothing as desperate; to surmount every difficulty by resolution and contrivance. In Europe there are shops for every want; its inhabitants, therefore have no idea that their wants can be supplied otherwise. Remote from all other aid, we are obliged to invent and to execute; to find means within ourselves, and not lean on others. Consider, therefore, the conquering your Livy as an exercise in the habit of surmounting difficulties; a habit which will be necessary to you in the country where you are to live, and without which you will be thought a very helpless animal, and less esteemed. Music, drawing, books, invention, and exercise, will be so many resources to you against ennui. But, there are others which, to this object, add that of utility. These are the needle and domestic economy. The latter you can

*not learn here, but the former you may. In the country life of America
there are many moments when a woman can have recourse to nothing
but her needle for employment. In a dull company, and in dull weather,
for instance, it is ill-manners to read, it is ill-manners to leave them; no
card-playing there among genteel people—that is abandoned to
blackguards. The needle is then a valuable resource. Besides without
knowing how to use it herself, how can the mistress of a family direct
the work of her servants?*[45]

Women applied their expertise, which in some instances was truly
professional, not only to the fashioning of lovely quilts, but to the sewing
of clothing and household furnishings on which they lavished exquisite
care and skill.

By the middle of the eighteenth century, the colonies had reached a
new level of stability and even affluence. The population had grown to
almost 1,500,000. Benjamin Franklin was moved in 1743 to advise his
fellow colonists: "The first Drudgery of Settling New Colonies, which
confines the Attention of People to mere Necessaries, is now pretty well
over; and there are many in every Province in Circumstances that set
them at Ease, and afford leisure to cultivate the finer Arts."[46]

Goods from all parts of the world were available in the coastal
ports, which in turn supplied the smaller centers of the New England,
Middle Atlantic, and southern colonies. Commerce between the
settlements flourished, made possible through extensive coastal trade and
a continually improving road system. Furniture, clothing, textiles, and
other goods from India, Russia, Austria, Sweden, France, Holland, and
England were to be found in almost every region of the colonies.

There was great variety from which to choose. A single
advertisement from the *Boston Gazette* of 1746 listed an astonishingly
wide assortment of goods for sale, including quilts:

*ENGLISH GOODS, a great Variety imported from London, in the
last Ships; and to be Sold by Albert Dennie, By Wholesale or Retail,
at his House on the Mill Bridge, upon the right Hand leading to
Charlestown-Ferry, all for ready Cash, viz. Allum, Balladine sewing Silk,*

45. Mildred J. Davis, *Early American Embroidery Designs*, Crown Publishers, New York,
    1969, page 25.
46. J. C. Furnas, *The Americans, A Social History 1587–1914*, Vol. 1, Capricorn Books,
    New York, 1971, page 190.

Plate 17.
Rising Sun or Star of Bethlehem, 1810. Pieced and appliquéd cotton, 94 x 94 in. Smithsonian Institution, Washington, D.C. Made by Mary (Betsy) Totten of Tottenville, Staten Island, New York. Vases, fruit, and birds, as well as hundreds of rosebuds and leaves, have been fashioned from calico. The roses and other flowers are soft-lustered chintz. Buds and the two chained-bud borders are worked in reverse appliqué. The initials "M.T." appear at the end of one of the vases. Other quilts by Mary Totten display the same magnificent sense of design and workmanship.

*raw Silk, colour'd and waxed Threads, Pins, Ozenbrigs, India Dimetys,
black Bombazeen and Alapene, silk Damask, Horse hair Buttons, Hair
Shapes, Wadding, Linnen and Cotton Checks, Velvet, and Everlasting
for Wast-coats, worsted Stuff plain and flower'd, worsted Damasks,
Ruffels, Fearnothing Great Coats, Kerseys, Druggets, Swanikins, Broad
Cloths, Serges, worsted & hair Plushes, Caps, Stockings, Cambricks,
Shalloons, Camblets, Garlets, yard wide Linnens, bed Ticks, cotton
Stockings, Chinces, Callicoes, Buttons and Mohair, Hats, Muslins, white
Callicoes, Ribbands, Necklaces, Fans, Scots Snuff, Pewter, Nails,
Buckles, Knives, Needles, Thimbles, short Cloaks, Taffieties, Persians,
Velvets, Hangers or Cutlasses, Looking Glasses, Wigg Cauls, Shirt
Buttons, Indigo, half Thick, bed Quilts [authors' emphasis], brass Wire,
Horse Whips, bed Baskets, Saws, and sundry Sorts of brazery Ware,
Paper for Room, Gloves, Sailors Cloths ready made, blue Callicoes.*[47]

For the quilt maker, the greater amount and variety of domestic and
imported fabrics available gave increased opportunities for expression.
Though thrift and economy were to remain an ever-present influence,
the quilt maker now had a choice of a wide assortment of colors and
fabrics, weaves of all types, and beautiful printed cottons and linens for
her quilts. No longer was the housewife confined, as in the leaner, earlier
days, to random scraps of leftover materials of random size and shapes.
Materials were used more extravagantly. The lush Indian chintz that was
the rage in Europe, printed with exotic birds and flowers and branches;
calicoes, the foreground red with lovely vine patterns of horse chestnut
blossoms and leaves; and blue- and yellow- and red-striped silks—all
these found their way into the quilt top. Linens, silks, cottons, and wools
used in clothing and house furnishings were used in quilts. The Framed
Medallion Quilt (plate 5) was made sometime about 1795. It is one of a
number of household textiles including sheets, dressing table covers,
pillow covers, table linens, toweling, and counterpanes used between
1750 and 1850 by members of the Copp family of Stonington,
Connecticut. The Copp family textile collection was presented in the
1890s to the United States National Museum by John Brenton Copp,
together with costume items, furniture, and related family pieces. The
variety of fabrics used in this quilt is a clear example of the enormous
selection of materials available to the American housewife during the
second half of the eighteenth century. As has been pointed out by Grace
Rogers Cooper in her excellent catalog of the Copp Family collection:

---

47. Dow, *op. cit.*, page 160.

The fabrics in the quilt. . . are quite unusual because of both their condition and pattern variety. Although they play an inconspicuous part in the overall effect, at least nine different white fabrics appear in the top— five dimities and two each of plain cotton and plain linen. There are three different woven silk and linen stripe patterns, in blue and white, red and white and yellow and white. The greatest treasure trove, however, is the variety of printed dress fabrics—at a conservative count over 150—dating from the 1770's–1790's. It is hard to believe that such a variety could represent the fabrics of a single household, even with many friends and access to a dry goods store, over a span of two generations. This goodly selection gives some idea of the great number of printed dress goods that were in use in a single community in eighteenth century America.[48]

With the greater number of fabrics available, it was also possible to piece or appliqué the top in predetermined patterns and designs, and patterns could be varied and elaborated upon. Equally important was the increase in leisure time. The quilt maker was able to stress more and more the decorative aspects of the quilt. Quilts no longer had to be exclusively utilitarian. Women devoted themselves to the laborious and time-consuming tasks of sewing thousands of stitches in quilted designs. Hours, days, and sometimes years were lavished in the making of a single quilt. The focus of household decorative attention during the seventeenth and eighteenth centuries often centered on elaborate counterpanes and quilts. It must be remembered that beds were probably the most important item of furniture in the home during this period and were accorded a special place of attention in the bedroom or living room.

Houses were generally small with rarely more than one or two bedrooms in earliest colonial America. "Many families of eight or more persons lived in houses only 18 x 20 feet in size, possibly with a shed attached."[49] Twelve to fifteen people in a family were common, although the mortality rate was extraordinarily high. Sarah Sedgwick Leverett, for example (see page 34), had fourteen children. During the seventeenth and eighteenth centuries, and as late as the beginning of the nineteenth century in some rural areas, the master bed for the head of the family was located in the parlor, or "best roome" (the living room) on the first floor of the house. Beds were also to be found in the halls and kitchen. Though

---

48. Grace Rogers Cooper, *The Copp Family Textiles*, Smithsonian Institution Press, Washington, D.C., 1971, page 5.
49. George Francis Dow, *Domestic Life in New England in the Seventeenth Century*, Benjamin Blom, Inc., New York, 1972 (first published by the author in 1925), page 2.

bedsteads were placed in upstairs chambers, there is evidence that in the seventeenth century no families or heads of families lodged on the second stories. Privacy was almost totally lacking.

For the more affluent, the most popular bedstead during the colonial period was the high post bed or four-poster. There were also simpler low four-posters, the field bed, the press bed (known as the "slawbank" in the Dutch colonies) or built-in bed, and bedsteads with rope netting on which mats were placed. Probably the most common type of bed was a pallet of homespun blankets or a tick filled with rags, straw, corn husks, or wood shavings. Quilts as undermats were also very likely used. Alice Morse Earle, in her book *Customs and Fashions of Old New England*, refers to an eighteenth-century almanac that contained advice as to the "easy rearing of children." The anonymous writer of the almanac recommends —as had John Locke in the seventeenth century—that it is best to have children sleep on quilts instead of feathers. Quilts as a form of sleeping mat have been used by New England fishermen aboard ship until recent times.

The youngest infants slept with their parents in the larger and wider four-posters. Other children slept in trundle beds kept during the daytime under the large four-poster and rolled out at night. Older children slept on mats or feather beds placed on settees or on the floor. The high post beds were fitted with elaborate bed hangings—valances, and long curtains that could be drawn for warmth and privacy and to shut out the light. By the mid-nineteenth century, beds without curtains were preferred. With its accessories of green or crimson harrateen or calico or camlet curtains, valances of chintz or richly embroidered linen, the bed often became the most decorative object in the room. As it was costly to furnish, the bed was considered a measure of a man's wealth in the community.

Women lavished great attention on the bed covers. There were palampores of rich color and design imported from India; counterpanes embroidered with soaring birds and carnations, roses and daisies, trees and strange animals; linsey-woolseys, dark blue and brown, quilted with flowing feather patterns and vines; elegant all-white quilts stitched in relief with baskets of fruit and symbols of friendship and hospitality; and the beautiful pieced and appliquéd quilts. Aside from the 1704 Saltonstall Quilt, the earliest surviving American quilts date, for the most part, from the mid-eighteenth century; but even these are rare. It is not until the last quarter of the century that quilts, especially pieced and appliquéd types, are found in any great numbers. Most textiles are particularly perishable. Exposure to light, moisture, dust, moths and mice, dyes that eat into the fabric, and, of course, constant use contribute to their

Plate 18.
Framed Center Counterpane, 1782. Appliquéd and embroidered linen and cotton, 94 x 90 in. Courtesy The Henry Francis du Pont Winterthur Museum, Winterthur, Delaware. The bird at the top of the tree and the pair of peacocks are cut from copperplate-printed linen and cotton cloth that dates from about 1765–75. Beneath the bowknot at the top the date is embroidered on either side of the applied initials "E.B." The coverlet is said to have been made in America from various English textiles.

deterioration. The loss of quilts over our history has been great. It is only within recent times that much attention has been paid to the scientific conservation of textiles.

Quilts made of sturdy materials—and "best quilts," used only on special occasions and considered important enough for special care— have survived. These best quilts frequently contained expensive imported materials and show the increased attention to design and detail characteristic of the period.

A lovely and historic bed covering thought to have been made about 1790 in Virginia is the Westover-Berkeley spread (plate 6). Neither backed nor quilted, it is included in this survey since the top combines the techniques of piecing, appliqué, and embroidery. It is in a formal design, the traditional framed center style of the period. A history of the quilt written in 1946 by an owner and descendant describes the making of the quilt:

My Son asked me to write down the history of the "Westover-Berkeley" spread which came to me on Mother's death. Her sister-in-law, my Father's sister, aunt Lucy McGuire, gave it to her before she died, and Mother always treasured it as one of her most valued heirlooms.

It was made somewhere before the time of the Revolution (because the beautiful Evelyn Byrd is supposed to have stitched one of the squares) by the ladies of Westover and Berkeley, the Byrds and the Harrisons. Their custom was to meet every "fortnight" under the "trysting tree" weather permitting, and sew on the spread. The trysting tree was situated somewhere on the boundary line between the two places, but in case of wet weather they met at one or the other of the "great houses."

The designs were cut from English chintz and appliqued in colored silks on to fine unbleached cotton, and each four corners which formed a square within a square were sewed together with strips of red and white calico. The colors are remarkably clear still and the sprays of pink roses caught with tiny blue bows—the pine-apples in four of the corners, the emblem of hospitality, and the cornecopias, or horns of plenty in four other corners are beautifully done. There are sprays of hops and tiny birds on trailing branches of flowers and a chipmonk, done entirely in embroidery. Around the whole there used to be a valance of hand crochetted lace but when that became tattered aunt Lucy cut it off, before she gave it to Mother. My grandmother, Mary Willing Harrison who was the daughter of the last Benjamin Harrison to own Berkeley (the 7th, I think) and the great granddaughter of Mary Willing, the second wife of Col. William Byrd third of Westover, from whom the spread descended, used it always on her own bed and aunt Lucy had it on her bed when Father brought

*Mother, as a bride, to visit her and Uncle Edward. To carry on the
tradition Mother had it on our bed when Taze and I returned from our
wedding trip! Ever since then it has been kept wrapt in a towel and put
carefully away in a chest. It is remarkably well preserved, though there are
some age spots, and some of the chintz has flaked off especially on some of
the rose leaves the embroidered vines and the appliquing only remaining.
Mary Willing Harrison was born at "Westover" the great granddaughter
and namesake of old Mrs. Byrd who was still living at that time. Her
mother, who was a daughter of Judge William Nelson of Yorktown, went
to Grandmother's to have her first baby as her own mother was dead.
Every summer when Mother and I visited Aunt Lucy and Uncle Edward
the spread would be brought out and Aunt Lucy would tell us it's history
but my children want it written down for them. Mother remembers seeing
the "Trysting Tree," just a stump then, but still pointed out, when Father
took her to Westover after they were married.*[50]

Some questions emerge concerning the accuracy of this history. For
example, the chintz fabrics appliquéd to the top are post–Revolutionary
War vintage and would place the making of the spread closer to 1790—
and, charming as the story may be, the tradition that the beautiful Evelyn
Byrd worked on the spread cannot be correct, as she died in 1737, much
too early a date to have participated. The spread, in excellent condition,
the colors lovely and faded, is in the collection of the Valentine Museum,
Richmond, Virginia.

The fortnightly meeting of the ladies of Westover-Berkeley is an
early instance of a form of sewing bee, that American institution that was
to blossom into the very popular "quilting bee" of the nineteenth century.
There were, undoubtedly, quilting bees during the eighteenth century as
well. Mrs. Earle, in her book *Homelife In Colonial Days,* refers to a quilting
bee in Narragansett in 1752 that lasted for ten days. More typical of the
everyday type of quilts of the period are those shown in plates 4, 19, and
43. The first, a coverlet, primitive in its construction and design,
beautiful in its simplicity, was made in Connecticut about 1750. The
background of the top is pieced of irregular squares and rectangles of
homespun wool. The maker was undoubtedly limited by the materials
available to her. Appliquéd to the ground fabric are cutouts of birds,
hearts, and fruit. A flowing vine zigzags over the top, and the shapes are
reminiscent of the tendrils, flowers, and stems found in crewel work of
the period. In one of the squares, a five-windowed building stands with

---

50. Records of Valentine Museum, letter from Susie McGuire Ellett, dated September
8, 1946.

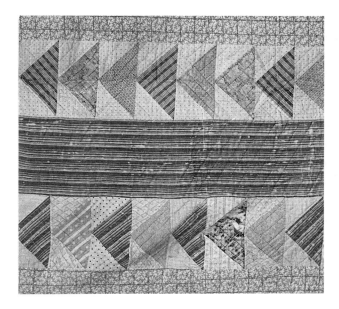 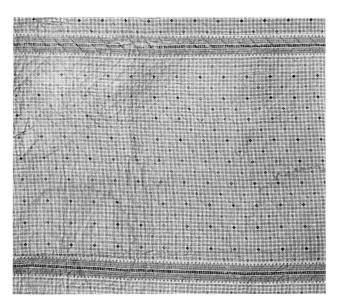

birds and stars in the sky above. The backing of the coverlet is green and white plaid homespun, which is tacked to the top with tan and brown wool knots. There is an overt attempt at design.

The second (plate 19) is a simple everyday quilt made for constant use. It is alleged to have been made in Frederick City, Maryland, at the end of the eighteenth century by a ten-year-old girl. The top is pieced with salvaged scraps of material in a common and popular pattern, "Wild Goose Chase." It is an early example of a repeated geometric pattern used in a quilt top. Although the quilt is now torn and frayed, it was in continuous use by six generations of a single family until 1912 and was brought to Nebraska from the east sometime during the middle of the nineteenth century.

The last (plate 43) is a linsey-woolsey, one of the earliest types of quilted bedcovers in the colonies. Sturdy and richly colored, the materials were probably spun, woven, and dyed at home.

By the time of the Treaty of Paris of 1763, England had gained political control over the colonies. Spain, France, and the Netherlands were no longer serious threats to England's complete domination of the New World. Years earlier, England had initiated a series of economic acts, starting with the Navigation Act of 1650, by which it sought to restrict trade with the colonies to English ships and to establish an economic system with the colonies in which they would supply raw materials in exchange for English manufactured goods. High duties were placed on goods whose production England wished to discourage; bounties were

Plate 19 (ABOVE LEFT). Wild Goose Chase Quilt (detail), Maryland, c. 1775–1800. Pieced cotton. Nebraska State Historical Society.

Plate 20 (ABOVE RIGHT). Wild Goose Chase Quilt (detail of back).

paid for the production of other items, such as tobacco and indigo; while still other manufactures, such as wool cloth, were prohibited from export from the colonies entirely. To discourage the development of a competing textile industry, equipment such as textile printing machinery was not permitted to be exported to the New World.

Acts were passed curtailing westward expansion and finally direct taxes were levied on the colonists: the Sugar Act of 1764; the Stamp Act of 1765; the Townshend Acts of 1767. The colonists responded by boycotting British goods. Boston, New York, and Philadelphia merchants banded together and refused to buy imports from England until the acts were repealed. "Buy American" campaigns were promoted everywhere. Stores specialized in "All American Manufactures."

Patriotic efforts were also made to stimulate the manufacture of domestic goods. Artisans and craftsmen increased the output of their shops. People from all walks of life patriotically and enthusiastically wore articles of clothing made at home. As early as 1718, a Boston official described the progress of manufacture in Massachusetts:

> Scarce a Country man comes to town, or woman, but are clothed in their own spinning. Every one Incourages the Growth and Manufacture of the Country and not one person but discourages the Trade from home, and says 'tis pitty any goods should be brought from England; they can live without them.[51]

It is estimated that by 1750 ninety percent of Pennsylvania's farmers fabricated their own wearing apparel. A poem that appeared in the *Massachusetts Gazette* is indicative of the tenor of the times:

> Young ladies in town and those that live around
> Let a friend at this season advise you.
> Since money's so scarce and times growing worse,
> Strange things may soon hap and surprise you.
> First then throw aside your high topknot of pride,
> Wear none but your country linen,
> Of economy boast. Let your pride be the most
> To show cloaths of your own make and spinning.[52]

---

51. James P. Baxter, ed., *Documentary History of the State of Maine*, Maine Historical Society, Collections (Portland: Le Favor-Tower, 1907), 2d ser., X, 122: Tyron, "Household Manufactures," pages 70, 76, 103–4.
52. Little, *op. cit.*, page 70.

As a token of support to home industry, the Harvard graduating class of 1768 appeared to a man dressed in black cloth made from Rhode Island wool.

By the end of 1769 imports from England were almost halved. During the War for Independence that followed, the Continental Congress encouraged the development of native industries to offset the cutting off of English imports. There was a new sense of nationalism. Colors were named Independence Green and Federal Blue. Names of Revolutionary War heroes and events were symbolically given to quilt patterns; "Burgoyne Surrounded" and "Washington's Quilt" are two examples of this practice.

Undoubtedly, the efforts at self-sufficiency gave added impetus to the quilt-making tradition in the colonies. Women of every class participated in sewing activities. The quilt, made up of scraps of precious material, warm and simply decorative, was a particularly suitable type of bed cover for a society conscious of conservationism and experienced in the reuse of its resources.

The war also forced greater movement and contact between all parts of the country. It gave an opportunity for settlers of different backgrounds to exchange cultural values and ideas. Dress, food, language, architecture, design were being assimilated and commingled. In time, there would be less dependency upon imitating European styles and a consequent rise of an indigenous American style and taste.

After the war, state governments took measures to aid and encourage business and industry. Grants of money and loans were made to promising new business ventures. One such loan was made in 1789 to John Hewson, an artisan of great importance in the history of American textiles. The loan, in the amount of 200 pounds, without interest, was made by the Pennsylvania State Treasury to enable Hewson to "enlarge and carry on the business of calico printing and bleaching in the state."

John Hewson was born in England in 1745. During one of Benjamin Franklin's visits to London, he met and befriended Hewson and encouraged his lifelong wish to settle in the colonies. In 1773, Hewson, his wife, son, and three small daughters sailed for the New World, arriving in Philadelphia in the fall of the year. By July 1774, Hewson had established his bleaching and printing business at Gunner's Run, Pennsylvania.

Life was not easy for Hewson in the New World during the next few years. In 1774 his wife died, and he married Zibiah Smallwood, an American. When the Revolutionary War broke out, he enlisted and fought with distinction as a commissioned captain in the Philadelphia County Militia. At the Battle of Monmouth, he was captured by the

British, but escaped. At war's end, though much of his equipment and many of his materials had been destroyed by the British, he reestablished his textile printing and bleaching business. Because of the fine quality of his work, his reputation grew. Martha Washington is said to have dressed in calicos printed by Hewson and "expressed a desire to have handkerchiefs printed with a representation of Washington on horseback." Hewson took for his model a miniature showing Washington on horseback in full military dress and sent the first examples of these prints, which achieved great popularity, to Mrs. Washington in Virginia.

During the great celebration in Philadelphia marking the adoption of the United States Constitution, Hewson was selected to represent the Pennsylvania Society for the Encouragement of Manufactures and the Useful Arts in the Grand Federal Procession. The Hewson float, twenty-ninth in the long procession, was thirteen feet wide and thirty feet long, and was drawn by ten large bay horses. It was described in the *Pennsylvania Gazette*:

> *Behind the looms was fixed the apparatus of Mr. Hewson, printing muslins of an elegant chintz pattern, and Mr. Lang, designing and cutting prints for shauls; on the right was seated Mrs. Hewson and her 4 daughters, pencilling a piece of very neat sprigged chintz of Mr. Hewson's printing, all dressed in cottons of their own manufacture; on the back part of the carriage, on a lofty staff, was displayed the callico printer's flag, in the center 13 stars in a blue field, and thirteen red stripes in a white field; round the edges of the flag was printed 37 different prints of various colours, one of them a very elegant bed-furniture chintz of six colours, as specimens of printing done at Philadelphia.[53]*

In 1789, the same year in which he received the state loan, Hewson was awarded a "plate of gold" or medal from the Pennsylvania Society for the Encouragement of Manufactures and the Useful Arts for the "best specimen of calico printing done within this state." The value of the medal was $20. Hewson continued to work, producing beautiful printed textiles until his retirement in 1810. He died in 1822 at the venerable age of seventy-seven.

Florence Montgomery refers to Hewson's spreads in her superb book *Printed Textiles, English and American Cottons and Linens, 1700–1850*:

---

53. Florence M. Montgomery, *Printed Textiles, English and American Cottons and Linens, 1700–1850*, A Winterthur Book, Viking Press, New York, 1970, page 96.

The importance of the Winterthur bedspread as a representative example of John Hewson's work is two fold. It is technically remarkable for its date in America, and is comparable to some of the most handsome English furnishing fabrics of the same period. It is (together with the Philadelphia Museum spread) the finest example of American textile printing. The bedspread is also of great interest for having been made by a patriot who served his adopted country well, both as a soldier and as a manufacturer. Hewson stands beside such loyal citizens as the silversmith Paul Revere of Boston and the pewterer William Will of Philadelphia, both of whom held posts of responsibility and leadership during the Revolutionary War. Like another manufacturer, John Frederick Amelung of the New Bremen Glass Manufactory near Frederick, Maryland, Hewson found it necessary to seek financial aid from the federal and state legislatures to carry on his enterprise. Many handsome pieces of silver, pewter, and glass made by these craftsmen are prized for their historic associations and excellent workmanship. The John Hewson bedspread rightfully belongs amongst them. John Hewson's startlingly sophisticated and handsome bedspreads and quilt centers have long been considered without parallel in eighteenth-century American textile printing.[54]

There are twelve known surviving examples of Hewson's work: two complete printed spreads, two printed handkerchiefs, and eight pieced or

Plate 21 (ABOVE LEFT).
Framed Center Quilt, 1848. Pieced and printed cotton, 92 x 92 in. Spencer Museum of Art, The University of Kansas, Lawrence. The center, block-printed by John Hewson, is surrounded by pieced star motifs. "Elizabeth Hart" is inscribed in ink to the left of the urn, and "Warwick Bucks Co. Penn. 1848" to the right.

Plate 22 (ABOVE RIGHT).
Detail of a Hewson center. Block-printed cotton. Courtesy collections of Henry Ford Museum and Greenfield Village, Dearborn, Michigan. This is the only center in all the known Hewson quilts that does not have the urn of flowers. For these less finely drawn bushes, birds, and butterflies, Hewson cut small single motifs that could be printed alone or joined in groups.

54. *Ibid.*, page 98.

appliquéd quilts (see plate 10). A ninth quilt owned by the Henry Ford Museum in Dearborn, Michigan, was unfortunately destroyed by fire (see plates 21–28). The quilts are distinguished by either a center printed panel having a stylized urn filled with flowers and surrounded by birds and butterflies, or by cutouts of the birds that have been appliquéd to the quilt top. The colors are generally pink, red, light brown, and sepia. Several of the quilts have borders or sections containing fabrics of a later date and not attributable to John Hewson. The one in the collection of the University of Kansas Museum of Art (plate 21) has "Elizabeth Hart" inscribed in ink at the left side of the base of the urn, and "Warwick, Bucks Co. Penn. 1848" on the right side. The stars surrounding the center are pieced of red calicoes of the period. Undoubtedly the quilter, Elizabeth Hart, salvaged a Hewson center from an earlier counterpane or availed herself of a center that had never been utilized before.

The quilt shown in plate 10 was discovered at a flea market in Massachusetts in 1971. Perhaps other Hewson textiles will be found to add to the treasury of American printed fabrics. The quality and beauty of his textiles rank him among the top craftsmen of the period.

Thus, by the end of the eighteenth century, America was producing textiles to compete with Europe—and in some instances, such as in the Hewson printed fabrics, of equal quality.

During the nineteenth century, quilt making flourished in America. The period from 1800 to 1900 was one of enormous creativity in the design of the quilt top. Quilt makers everywhere seemed to vie with each other in the creation of one geometric pattern more dazzling than another. They were unrestrained in their use of color and line, exorbitant in their expression, as if the energy and excitement they sensed in the expanding young country around them could not be contained. There was innovation in the types of quilts: the Pictorial Album Quilts, composed of repeating squares containing figures of people and animals and scenes of village life, pieced and appliquéd in calicos and chintz; the Victorian Crazy Quilts made into a collage of materials, spangles, beads, velvet, and satin ribbons; the Autograph Quilt.

Variations in quilt types and designs appear as endless as the numbers of men, women, and children who made them. Everyone seemed to participate in the making of quilts. Husbands or fiancés frequently drew complex patterns on a quilt top or cut out templates from which patterns were cut. Grandmothers and children threaded needles and cut out patches while the mother sewed pieces together and quilted the top. A quilt, in some instances, represented the creative efforts of an entire family.

Quilt making reached rage proportions during periods of the 1800s, particularly the second and third quarters. Even after industrialization brought a greater supply of inexpensive blankets, the needs of the average family were great, and the good old reliable quilt, decorative as well as utilitarian, could be made more economically using scraps and worn materials. It was still a period in our history when thrift was an essential part of the cultural attitudes.

Probably of equal importance in perpetuating the quilting tradition was the opportunity to socialize provided by the quilting bee. In city and country alike, it was an occasion as important as a church social or a barn raising. Except for such large cities as Boston, Philadelphia, New York, and Charleston, the population along the Atlantic seaboard was sparse and rural. With the movement and migrations west, the rural quality of life continued well into the twentieth century. In many isolated areas, the quilting bee was the only source of social contact that many women had with each other. The quilting bee brought people together. It was an opportunity to exchange news and recipes and quilting patterns, a time to have a party and to quilt.

The bee was also a way for neighbors to help each other. Dr. J.G.M. Ramsey described the spirit of frontier cooperation in Tennessee in 1853:

> . . . a failure to ask a neighbour to a raising, clearing, a chopping frolic, or his family to a quilting, was considered a high indignity; such an one, too, as required to be explained or atoned for at the next muster or county court. Each settler was not only willing but desirous to contribute his share to the general comfort and public improvement, and felt aggrieved and insulted if the opportunity to do so were withheld.[55]

The bee, symbolic of industry, is typical of the American philosophy that combines the practical with the social, industry with fun. During the first half of the nineteenth century, there were bees and "helping get-togethers" of all types: candle-dipping bees, corn huskings, wool shearings, barn raisings, trencher bees, apple parings, sugar boilings, and the quilting bee.

Of course, social activities were not all directed toward work and industry. People enjoyed hunting and riding and, in fine weather, picnic excursions in pleasure boats that sailed along the many rivers. Public balls were in vogue and there were concerts and lectures and painted panoramas of nature and historic events. The first colonial public "Concert of Music on Sundry Instruments" was performed as early as

---

55. J.G.M. Ramsey, *The Annals of Tennessee*, n.p., Charleston, South Carolina, 1853, page 725.

62 Quilts in America

Plate 23 (OPPOSITE, TOP LEFT).
Framed Center Quilt, c. 1780–1800. Appliquéd cotton, interlined, 86½ x 83 in. Courtesy The Henry Francis du Pont Winterthur Museum, Winterthur, Delaware. The familiar urn and the surrounding circular arrangement of birds in bushes, block-printed by John Hewson, were cut out and appliquéd to the center. The two borders of polychrome English chintz motifs are appliquéd to a plain-woven white cotton ground. Quilted in curving feather patterns and diagonal lines, the piece was probably made in America from English and American textiles.

Plate 24 (OPPOSITE, TOP RIGHT).
Framed Center Quilt (detail), Philadelphia, 1811. Cincinnati Art Museum. Center square block-printed by John Hewson; inner border appliquéd.

Plate 25 (OPPOSITE, BOTTOM LEFT).
Framed Center Quilt, 1809. Cotton, 116⅓ x 112½ in. St. Louis Art Museum. The block-printed center by John Hewson measures 29 x 30 in. Said to have been made by Fanny Glover of Springfield, Massachusetts, the quilt features two framing borders of printed chintz typical of those block-printed in this period specifically to frame and complete quilt centers. At the center top of the outer edge is a medallion with the quilted initials "F.G." and the date.

Plate 26 (OPPOSITE, BOTTOM RIGHT).
Framed Center Quilt. 96 x 98 in. Courtesy Herr Collection, Historical Society of York County, Pennsylvania. The center square, measuring 30 x 29 inches, is the only one in all the Hewson quilts that contains its own printed border. Four other borders surround the center; the outer one, 10½ inches wide, is of early 19th-century English origin. The piece is quilted in diagonal lines and a shell pattern.

Plate 27 (ABOVE LEFT).
Framed Center Quilt Top. Cotton, 65 x 65 in. Smithsonian Institution, Washington, D.C. The center was block-printed by John Hewson, c. 1800. The urn and birds have been appliquéd to the center block, and the corner motifs are appliquéd cutouts of English chintz, c. 1830. It was made by or for Mary G. Jessop of Baltimore County, Maryland.

Plate 28 (LEFT).
Framed Center Quilt, Philadelphia, c. 1800. 103 x 107 in. Philadelphia Museum of Art. This quilt, featuring a center and bird motifs block-printed by John Hewson, was said to have been made by his wife, Zibiah Smallwood Hewson.

1729 in Boston. At tavern shows and exhibitions, the curious might see an Arabian camel or a picture of a "HOG, bred in America—suppos'd to weigh near Nine Hundred Weight." People bought prints with views of New York and Boston and other cities. Book shops sold a wide selection of titles, and newspapers sprouted. For the women of the period, however, the quilting bee stands out as one of the most popular of all social activities.

Besides the quilts she made for herself, and the help she gave in making some of the quilts of her neighbors, the housewife might participate in as many as twenty-five to thirty quilting bees during a single winter. And the quilting bee was held only after long hours had already been spent in assembling the pieces of materials, cutting them into patterns, and then sewing them together to create the top.

Housewives kept remnant bags in which they saved pieces of materials to be used for piecing and appliqué. The bag, found in homes in community after community, was filled with scraps, often saved for years.

> *The good wives of New England, impressed with that thrifty orthodoxy of economy which forbids to waste the merest trifle, had a habit of saving every scrap clipped out in the fashioning of household garments, and these they cut into fanciful patterns and constructed of them rainbow shapes and quaint traceries, the arrangement of which became one of their few fine arts. . . . Collections of these tiny fragments were always ready to fill an hour when there was nothing else to do; and as the maiden chattered with her beau, her busy flying needle stitched together those pretty bits, which, little in themselves, were destined, by gradual unions and accretions, to bring about at last substantial beauty, warmth, and comfort.*[56]

Within a community, women exchanged choice remnants of prints and calicos from their scrap bags in order to achieve greater variety in color and design in their quilt tops. The length of time materials were accumulated and the fact that they were exchanged freely accounts for the astonishing number and variety of materials found in some quilts. There are quilts with as many as 60,000 pieces, and pieces measuring as small as $1/4$ x $3/4$ of an inch.

Women also exchanged pattern blocks of both pieced and appliquéd designs and passed them on from one generation to another. Though the piecing together of a top was most frequently done by the housewife

---

56. Harriet Beecher Stowe, *The Minister's Wooing*, James R. Osgood and Company, Boston, 1875, page 435.

alone or with the help of her family, there were "piecing bees" called to sew the top together. The medley surprise party, said to date from before the Revolution, was a bee at which each guest brought her own material to be pieced into a pattern. No two blocks were to be the same. When the blocks were completed, they were sewn together or to a set supplied by the hostess. In more recent years, women have been hired and paid to piece the quilt top or to piece the top "on the half": that is, for piecing a quilt top, the woman employed would receive half of the materials for her own use.

Girls pieced tops together for many years as part of their hope chests. By the time a girl was ready to marry, she had a collection of tops of her own. A proverb held that if a girl had not made a quilt before she was twenty-one, no man would want to marry her.

The "Thirteenth Quilt" was traditionally a bride's quilt, generally all white, stitched with hearts. Hearts were reserved for bridal quilts. If there was a vine or spray of foliage along the border, the belief was that it should not be broken, for fear that a broken vine foretold a life cut short by disaster.

> *Part of the entertainment provided for the feminine guests at a girl's wedding was the display of the quilts and coverlets she had made, the visible proof of her accomplishments as a needlewoman. But the bridegroom also brought to the new establishment a certain amount of similar gear as the contribution of his own family. Though perhaps somewhat lacking in fancy and in the intricate stitchery of twin hearts which the bride-to-be dreamily lavished on her best quilts, the dowry gift of quilts and coverlets furnished by the bridegroom's mother represented a tradition which was likewise never ignored. They too were always exhibited before the appraising eyes of the feminine wedding guests, equally expert needlewomen.[57]*

The announcement of a girl's engagement was frequently made at a quilting bee, at which time the tops were quilted or sewn together. Although tops had been pieced and saved in many instances for years, they were not quilted until a girl was ready to marry, as the real expense came when the wadding and back had to be furnished and sewn.

Quilting bees were occasioned also when a young man reached legal age, at which time a "Freedom Quilt" was sewn and presented to him; or

---

57. Frances Lichten, *Folk Art of Rural Pennsylvania*, Charles Scribner's Sons, New York, 1946, page 172.

an "Album Quilt" might be made as a gift for a departing friend or community leader. Most frequently the bees were called just to replenish a neighbor's household stock of bed covers. There were also public quilting bees to raise money for a church or a charity.

Sometimes quilting bees lasted for days. Catherine Fennelly, drawing from the journals of Ruth Henshaw Bascomb, written from the end of the eighteenth century until 1847, notes the length of time of various quilting bees as well as how long some quilting activities took a quilter alone.

> "This afternoon 21 young ladies paid us a visit and assisted us in quilting"—on this occasion on Mrs. Henshaw's petticoat. It took four days, with some assistance, to prepare and quilt a coat for Mrs. Scott. A printed India cotton coverlet had to have a backing made for it, then must be quilted. A patchwork coverlet was quilted in three days; "evening a large number of gentlemen." Another, made shortly before Ruth's marriage, was striped in plaid and plain "tea color" calico (dyed by Ruth herself), then quilted in two days; two piecework bed quilts took six days to complete, with outside help. One quilt was completed in two days, Ruth and a friend sewing during the day, six neighbors helping in the evening. At the same time one of these quiltings was taking place, the men of the family held a husking bee.[58]

In country areas, where long distances and difficulty of travel precluded easy contact, the quilting bee was an all-day event. Early in the morning, the women would arrive at the home of the hostess:

> Group after group, in calico or gingham dresses, with hair done up pyramidally on the apex of the head and fastened with a long glistening horn or tortoise-shell comb, came posting in until the room was full. . . .
>
> The floors were scoured and sanded, and things in general brought into perfect order. . . .
>
> The largest room in the house was cleared of all furniture, except the flag-bottomed chairs, the old eight-day clock with the half moon upon its face, and the antique looking-glass, which had reflected faithfully the beauties and deformities of at least five generations.[59]

Sometimes the guests would bring a pie or cake or favorite dish, or a

---

58. Old Sturbridge Village Booklet Series, Sturbridge, Mass., 1961, page 10.
59. Elias Nason, "A New England Village Quilting Party in the Olden Times," *Granite Monthly*, Vol. 8 (1885), page 235.

present. Usually one or two quilting frames were set up and the women would take their positions, two or three on each side and one at each end. The better quilters were always sought after for the quilting bees. The hostess was ready with thimble, scissors, or thread whenever anyone needed them. Women who were not quilting were assigned to help in the kitchen until their turn to take a place at the quilting frame. Younger women helped thread the needles. The least expert quilters were graciously kept busy at other tasks in the kitchen.

Discussion followed as to which quilt pattern was to be used— "straight," "diamond," the "clam." When the decision was finally made, the quilters would begin. Children often played under the quilting frame while the quilting was being done. An interesting description of a quilting bee that took place in southern Illinois about 1840 was written by Mrs. John A. Logan in her "Reminiscences of a Soldier's Wife":

> A patchwork quilt was generally prepared thus for quilting: The lining was first laced in frames made for the purpose, the cotton laid smoothly over the lining, the patchwork spread over and basted closely all around the edges. Then, with chalk and a line, the women marked out the designs for the quilting, fan-shaped figures being the most popular. After quilting one or two rows of fans, according to the size, the side frames were loosened, the quilted part rolled up, and the frame again fastened by placing a peg through the holes in the frames, thus allowing the quilters to reach another row nearer the center, repeating the process until the whole of the quilt was quilted.
>
> Among so many there were often drones, or unskilled needlewomen. These went into a kitchen and helped the housewife cook the dinner and supper, an indispensable feature of the occasion. The young people many times remained for dancing or games, according to the scruples of the persons giving the entertainment.[60]

Sewing methodically, rolling the quilt frame, talking to people of politics and the news, women would stop only for tea—"pies, cakes, preserves and Hyson tea, with large lumps of loaf sugar, were provided liberally for the occasion"[61]—and lunch. In comparison to our dainty tea sandwiches, these meals seem enormous. A hostess at a country quilting bee in Lancaster County, Pennsylvania, in about 1840 made provision for her guests at dinner and tea:

---

60. Thomas Hamilton Ormsbee, *Collecting Antiques in America*, Robert M. McBride and Co., New York, 1940, page 245.
61. Nason, *op. cit.*

Aunt Sally had her quilt up in her landlord's east room, for her own house was too small. However, at about eleven she called us over to dinner; for people who have breakfasted at five or six have an appetite at eleven.

We found on the table beefsteaks, boiled pork, sweet potatoes, kohl-slaw, pickled tomatoes, cucumbers, and red beets (thus the "Dutch" accent lies), apple-butter and preserved peaches, pumpkin and apple-pie, with sponge-cake and coffee.

After dinner came our next neighbors, "the maids," Susy and Katy Groff, who live in single blessedness and great neatness. They wore pretty, clear-starched Mennist caps, very plain. Katy is a sweet-looking woman; and, although she is more than sixty years old, her forehead is almost unwrinkled, and her fine fair hair is still brown. It was late when the farmer's wife came,—three o'clock; for she had been to Lancaster. She wore hoops, and was of the "world's people." These women all spoke "Dutch;" for "the maids," whose ancestor came here probably one hundred and fifty years ago, do not yet speak English with fluency.

The first subject of conversation was the fall house-cleaning; and I heard mention of "die carpet hinaus an der fence," and "die fenshter und die porch;" and the exclamation, "My goodness, es war schlimm." I quilted faster than Katy Groff, who showed me her hands, and said, "You have not been corn-husking, as I have."

So we quilted and rolled, talked and laughed, got one quilt done, and put in another. The work was not fine; we laid it out by chalking around a small plate. Aunt Sally's desire was rather to get her quilting finished upon this great occasion, than for us to put in a quantity of needlework.

About five o'clock we were called to supper. I need not tell you all the particulars of this plentiful meal. But the stewed chicken was tender, and we had coffee again.

Polly M.'s husband now came over the creek in the boat, to take her home, and he warned her against the evening dampness. The rest of us quilted awhile by candle and lamp, and got the second quilt done at about seven.

At this quilting I heard but little gossip, and less scandal. I displayed my new alpaca, and my dyed merino, and the Philadelphia bonnet which exposes the back of my head to the wintry blast. Polly, for her part, preferred her black silk sun-bonnet; and so we parted, with mutual invitations to visit.[62]

---

62. Phebe Earle Gibbons, *Pennsylvania Dutch and Other Essays*, J. B. Lippincott, Philadelphia, 1874, page 35.

Not all the talk was about quilting, food, recipes, babies, and the fashion of the day:

> The conversation, as well might be supposed—for the public library, lyceum, railroad, telegraph and telephone had not then appeared—was not very aesthetical, literary, scientific, or instructive. The women of that period, in the rural village I am thinking of, had but little time to read, or to think of much, except domestic and church affairs, together with the faults and foibles of their friends and neighbors. . . . So, as the busy needles pierce the quilt, the busy tongues, sharp as the needles, pierce the characters of the absent.[63]

By evening one or more quilts was completed. It was in the evening that there would be "a great supper and general jubilee, at which that ignorant and incapable sex which could not quilt was allowed to appear and put in claims for consideration of another nature."[64] And so, the husbands, sons, and suitors would arrive. The quilting frames would be put away and platters of chicken, vegetables, and pies placed on the table. After dinner, depending upon the inclination of the hostess, games and dancing would start. Harriet Beecher Stowe describes the festivities in her novel *The Minister's Wooing:*

> Unrestrained gayeties followed. Groups of young men and maidens chatted together, and all the gallantries of the times were enacted. Serious matrons commented on the cake, and told each other high and particular secrets in the culinary art which they drew from remote family archives. One might have learned in that instructive assembly how best to keep moths out of blankets, how to make fritters of Indian corn undistinguishable from oysters, how to bring up babies by hand, how to mend a cracked teapot, how to take out grease from a brocade, how to reconcile absolute decrees with free will, how to make five yards of cloth answer the purpose of six, and how to put down the Democratic party.[65]

It was the custom to place a cat in the center of a new quilt. The unmarried girls and boys held the edges of the quilt and tossed the cat into the air. The person closest to the spot where the cat landed would be the next to be married. The men and women joined in square dancing. Quilt patterns, which frequently reflect the everyday events and activities

63. Nason, *op. cit.*
64. Stowe, *op. cit.*, page 437.
65. *Ibid.*, page 460.

of the people who made them, were named after square dance calls, such as "Swing in the Center" and "Hands All Around." Or there might be singing, sometimes of a patriotic nature, as described in a quilting bee that took place during the sad days of the Civil War:

March 26 (1862).—I have been up at Laura Chapin's from 10 o'clock in the morning until 10 at night, finishing Jennie Howell's bed quilt, as she is to be married very soon. Almost all of the girls were there. We finished it at 8 P.M. and when we took it off the frames we gave three cheers. Some of the youth in the village came up to inspect our handiwork and see us home. Before we went Julia Phelps sang and played on the guitar and Captain Barry also sang and we all sang together, "O! Columbia, the gem of the ocean, three cheers for the red, white and blue."[66]

Late in the evening the party would end and, a few at a time, people departed.

Even this evening, so glorious, so heart cheering, so fruitful in instruction and amusement, could not last forever. Gradually the company broke up; the matrons mounted soberly on horseback behind their spouses, and Cerinthy consoled her clerical friend by giving him an opportunity to read to her a lecture on the way home, if he found the courage to do so.[67]

The following day, the threads of the quilt would be cut and the binding put around it.

Sometimes the quilting bee was held at a church vestry room or grange hall so that many women could participate. But, of course, not all quilting was done at quilting bees. Many women chose or were forced by isolation to quilt alone and at home. The quilting frame was set up in the kitchen or parlor and could almost be considered part of the permanent furnishings. In some houses, four quilting rings were set in the ceiling so that the quilting frame, quilt and all, could be raised out of the way when no quilting was going on. If a woman quilted alone, the work could take months depending upon the difficulty of the quilting design.

Women found time to quilt along with other activities and sometimes back-breaking amounts of housework. They did the washing for the family, cooked, knitted, weeded the garden, raised small stock, dipped candles in the spring and made soap in the autumn, pickled and

66. Caroline Cowles Richards, *Village Life in America*, Henry Holt and Company, New York, 1913, page 140.
67. Stowe, *op. cit.*, page 461.

preserved, as well as tending to the tasks of spinning, weaving, dyeing, and sewing.

A diary kept between 1825 and 1829 by a young girl living on Long Island, New York, makes repeated references to quilt making as it records other events and observations of her daily life:

> *Killed our ox today, had 84 pounds of fat—finished our candles, had 350—Sarah Baldwin, Frances and Jane Bergen, hear to help us quilt— clear and finished thrashing rye. Bleaching rye.—A man aged 21 years was married this day to a lady upwards of 40 years this being her nine husband—I began to spin wool—we got 2 swarms of bees today—Miss Jane Voorhees, Ann Bergen, Mrs. Frances Bergen, Margaret Emmons, the two Miss Van Dyke, the Miss Van Brunt, Ryme Van Dyke and I was over to Mr. Baldwin's to quilt—we put in and took out.*[68]

(The last phrase refers to putting a quilt into a frame, quilting it, and taking it out.)

As the settlers moved out over the land during the 1800s, they took their quilts with them. The country stretched open and unsettled in every direction; the scrubby barrens of Maryland and North Carolina; the Kansas and Dakota prairies; the great Smoky and Appalachian Ranges; "beautiful natural Meadows, covered with wild Rye, blue Grass, and Clover, [abounding] with Turkeys, Deer, Elks, and . . . particularly Buffaloes."[69]

Farm land had to be cleared, settlements founded, new cities created out of the wilderness. They left behind established conditions of living. All the hardships of work and the conditions of scarcity that the early colonizing settlers had endured were to be repeated again and again on the frontier. Once more there was the need to make do, once more the need to lend a helping hand.

Women continued to make quilts as they had at home in the East or as their mothers had before them. They used simple homespun and home-woven materials and worn dress calicos. They saved and sewed, making fresh and marvelous quilts. Proudly, women named quilts in celebration of the new land: "Ohio Rose," "Arizona Cactus," "Rocky Road to Kansas." Once again, the quilting bee broke the long days of loneliness and was a time to socialize and see friends.

A woman living in Ohio in 1841 wrote to a relative in Connecticut:

---

68. Florence Peto, *Historic Quilts*, American Historical Company, New York, 1939, pages 57–69.
69. Furnas, *op. cit.*, page 18.

February 7 . . . We have had deep snow. No teams passed for over three weeks, but as soon as the drifts could be broken through Mary Scott sent her boy Frank around to say she was going to have a quilting. Everybody turned out. Hugh drove on to the Center where he and several other men stayed at the Tavern until it was time to come back to the Scotts for the big supper and the evening. There were papers at the Tavern, and Hugh says they are full of the New Whig President (William Henry Harrison). . . . I took six squash pies for Mary's supper. My pumpkins all froze. She had two big turkeys and her famous bar le duc. What wouldn't I give to taste some real cranberry sauce again—and oysters. But of course we don't have anything like that here. . . . One of Mary's quilts she called "The Star and Crescent." I had never seen it before. She got the pattern from a Mrs. Lefferts, one of the new Pennsylvania Dutch families, and pieced it this winter. A lot of Dutch are taking up land here in the Reserve. . . . Her other quilt was just an old fashioned "Nine-Patch."[70]

Wherever American women went, as far as Alaska and Japan, they took their knowledge and love of making quilts. In the early part of the nineteenth century, wives of missionaries introduced piece work into the Hawaiian Islands and thus the genesis of the beautiful Hawaiian quilt.

On Monday morning, April third, 1820, the American Board of Missions held its first sewing circle in the "Sandwich Islands." The place of meeting was the brig Thaddeus, one hundred and sixty-two days out of Boston, as almost at her journey's end she sailed along the western coast of Hawaii, after a brief stop at Kawaihae. A group of eleven women were seated on lauhala mats on deck: Kalakua, mother of the young king, Liholiho; Namahana, her sister, another widow of Kamameha I; two wives of chief Kalanimoku—their ample figures wrapped in folds of tapa from waist to below the knees, their brown bosoms and shoulders bare; and seven young New England matrons, wives of the first missionaries to these islands, Lucy Thurston, Lucia Holman, Sybil Bingham, Nancy Ruggles, Mercy Whitney, Jerusha Chamberlain, Mrs. Elish Loomis—dressed in the tight-waisted, tight-sleeved garments of the day, their ankles no doubt tucked discreetly beneath their billowing skirts.

    Mrs. Thurston relates, "Kalakua, queen dowager, was directress . . . Mrs. Holman and Mrs. Ruggles were executive officers, to ply the scissors

---

70. Ruth E. Finley, *Old Patchwork Quilts and the Women Who Made Them*, Charles T. Branford Company, Newton Centre, Mass., 1970, page 37.

and prepare the work. The four women of rank were furnished with calico patch-work to sew—a new employment to them." The easterners had picked up only a few Hawaiian expressions from the four native boys travelling with their party, the Hawaiian women had learned but very little English, *but scissors, cloth, needles, and thread have their own language, and the sewing party progressed happily.*[71]

Quilts were also sent to the Islands as early as 1822. "We received from the Board by this conveyance [the schooner *Rover*] a box . . . and with the rest, a bed-quilt from the young ladies in Miss E. Dewey's school, Blanford, for Kaahumanu, which was very acceptable to this honored female ruler."[72]

The Hawaiian quilting bees that took place over the years were similar to the New England quilting bees, except that the stands for the quilting frames were made in two sizes: high for the missionary women who sat on chairs, and low for the Hawaiians who sat on the ground or the floor.

During the nineteenth century quilt making, along with all types of home crafts and domestic industry, was encouraged at the great country fairs that were held annually, generally in August and September around the country.

The first fair, the brainchild of Elkanah Watson, was held in 1808 in Pittsfield, Massachusetts. By the middle of the nineteenth century, regional and county fairs had gained wide popularity.

The Fair gave an opportunity for all of the town and country people to show off their talents and abilities to their neighbors. Livestock was brought in to be exhibited and judged, horses to be exhibited and raced. Handiwork and food were featured. These were usually housed in separate tents or buildings. There was much competition among the women, as prizes were awarded for the best in the various categories of food and handiwork. Most fairs had lectures on the various fads of the day and the larger fairs had acrobats or side shows, minstrels and other music. This was a big day for the children with so much excitement in the air, and even the stingiest father would loosen his purse strings for the special occasion.

The fairs were usually held for three days. The first day the exhibits were arranged and harness racing was featured in the afternoon. . . . The

---

71. Stella M. Jones, *Hawaiian Quilts*, Honolulu Academy of Arts, 1930, page 7.
72. *Ibid.*, page 13.

second day of the fair was the biggest, with the cattle exhibited and judged, and ribbons awarded. On the third day of the event, the horses were shown and horse racing went on all day.[73]

Women competed for prizes in bread baking, pickling, the growing of vegetables—and, of course, for the best quilt. Friendly competition between neighbors undoubtedly fostered a pride in the quality of workmanship in quilts of all types and inspired invention in design and the use of color. Year after year women strove to show their best, their most exquisite needlework, or an original pattern they had conceived, or a quilt displaying great beauty of design and composition. When they won a first prize, it was an honor that acknowledged their skill and expertise throughout the county. Prizes ranged from blue ribbons to dictionaries and encyclopedias and money. At a fair held in Pennsylvania in 1852, the Lehigh County Agriculture Society offered a premium of $1 for the best quilt and 50¢ for the second best. Honorable mention was given to a Miss Hewson of Coopersburg for an "elegant quilt, made of 14,000 pieces."[74]

The county fair also gave women a chance to exchange patterns and discuss quilting techniques. Patterns of appliqué and pieced designs were for sale, costing as much as $1.25 in the 1870s. County and regional fairs are still held in which quilts are entered in competitions and prizes given for excellence. The annual Kutztown Folk Festival at Kutztown, Pennsylvania, draws as many as 700 quilt entries in its competition.

A magnificent all-white quilt, made in 1856 by Virginia Mason Ivey of Logan County, Kentucky, depicts scenes from a county fair in Kentucky (plate 156). The center has the quilted legend "1856 A REPRESENTATION OF THE FAIR GROUND NEAR RUSSELLVILLE, KENTUCKY." The quilt brings vividly to mind in exquisite detail a county fair of the past, alive with people and animals and lovely trees and foliage.

While other homecrafts were rendered obsolete by factory substitutes and industrialization, quilts continued to be made throughout the nineteenth and twentieth centuries. In fact, industrialization—particularly after the middle of the nineteenth century—provided the housewife with a variety of goods and new devices that enabled her to lavish more time and effort on the making of quilts.

By 1850, huge quantities of textiles, manufactured and printed in

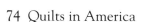

---

73. Floyd and Marion Rinhart, *America's Affluent Age*, A. S. Barnes and Co., So. Brunswick and New York, 1971, page 35.
74. Lichten, *op. cit.*, page 174.

the United States, were marketed throughout the country. They were inexpensive and readily available. In the cities, there were stores stacked with fabrics of all types. Particularly appealing to the quilt maker were the cotton calicoes, washable and soft to the touch, printed in hundreds of different designs.

For the housewife in the rural areas, the Yankee peddler plied his wares: tin pots and kettles, glassware and matches, washboards and household remedies—the inventory was seemingly endless. He supplied gossip and occasionally a quilt pattern or two, and he brought with him a wide assortment of soft goods. As Ms. Fennelly has pointed out: "There was no dearth of materials. The housewife could make herself or she could purchase almost anything she wished, provided she could afford it."[75]

Materials were bought specifically for the purpose of making a quilt. The housewife was no longer dependent solely upon the accumulation of scraps of different colors and sizes in her scrap bag to create a specific pattern or design. She was now able to repeat a pattern in a particular color or fabric or carry out a desired color scheme. "Cloth was cut to suit the quilt, not the quilt to suit the cloth."[76] Quilts were to become less a salvage art than they had been, though economy and thrift were too engrained in the American character to be totally forgotten.

With the discovery of aniline dye in Germany in 1856, a whole new range of colors was available in the weaving and printing of textiles. Colors produced by the new dyes were bright and generally fast in washing. The dyes were also inexpensive and easy to use. Quilters quickly adapted the new broader spectrum of colors to vary old and create new designs. It was a period of particular creativity, especially in the making of pieced quilts and the eye-dazzling geometric patterns popular during the second half of the century.

The sewing machine, too, influenced the habits and techniques of the quilt maker during the nineteenth century. Although there were primitive forms of sewing machines as early as 1818 or 1819, historians generally give full credit for the invention to Elias Howe, Jr., with the patenting of a sewing machine in 1846. It was not until 1856, when Howe and Isaac Singer pooled their patent interests, that there was an attempt at mass marketing of a family sewing machine. Between 1856 and 1860, over 130,000 machines were sold. The numbers increased rapidly thereafter. In 1867, the Singer Manufacturing Company sold

---

75. Fennelly, *op. cit.*, page 37.
76. Finley, *op. cit.*, page 39.

43,053 machines; in 1876, the amount had increased to 262,316 for the year; and this was the product of only one company.

The sewing machine actually became the first widely advertised consumer appliance, pioneered installment buying and patent pooling, offered interchangeable parts, and revolutionized the ready-made clothing industry. All types of attachments were made available to the home sewer: fellers, tuckers, binders, hemmers, rufflers, shirrers, puffers, braiders, and hem stitchers. There was even a combined sewing machine and parlor melodeon offered to the consumer.

A quilter attachment was invented by Henry Davis in 1892 that would enable the housewife to quilt "comforts, quilts, coat linings, dress skirts, and any other article which it is desired to have filled with cotton or wool."[77]

The editor of *Godey's Lady's Book* commented in 1860 about the sewing machine: "By this invention the needlewoman is enabled to perform her labor in comfort; tasks that used to require the midnight watches—and drag through perhaps 20 hours, she can now complete in two or three."[78]

The sewing machine made the quilt maker's work faster and easier. Some quilts combined hand-sewn and machine-sewn stitches. In the early years of mechanization, people took pride in the mechanical devices. To emphasize the fact that she was using a sewing machine, the quilter used threads of different colors to quilt and to give prominence to the quilting stitch as well as for decorative purposes. Quilts of the period frequently show white thread quilting on red, green, or brown materials.

The 1800s were also the period of the first women's magazines, such as *Godey's Lady's Book*, which printed fiction and advice on etiquette, style, cookery, beauty, gardening, interior decoration, and all forms of needlework. *Godey's*, first published in 1830, spanned much of the nineteenth century until it ceased publication in 1898. By mid-century, it had a circulation of 150,000 readers. There are frequent references in its pages to quilting patterns and advice on how to piece and appliqué a quilt top. As early as 1835, *Godey's* gave instructions for the making of a hexagon or honeycomb pieced quilt, commenting:

> *Little girls often find amusement in making patchwork quilts for the beds of their dolls, and some even go as far as to make cradle quilts for their infant brothers and sisters.*

---

77. *Scientific American*, March 18, 1892.
78. Ruth E. Finley, *The Lady of Godey's*, J. B. Lippincott Company, Philadelphia, 1931, page 150.

Patchwork may be made in various forms, as stars, triangles, diamonds, waves, stripes, squares, etc. The outside border should be four long strips of calico all of the same sort and not cut into patches. The dark and light calico should always be properly contrasted in arranging patchwork.

Children may learn to make patchwork by beginning with kettleholders and iron-holders; and for these purposes the smallest pieces of calico may be used. [79]

By 1851, the magazine recommended to its readers that "as a change from the accustomed routine of knitting, netting or crochet, the production of ornamental patchwork will be found an agreeable occupation." [80] In 1860, *Godey's* said: "Patchwork has especially established for itself the character of a winter industry, as it requires no additional light for its execution, the work which produces it being slight and easy. The only care which it exacts is a mathematical precision in the foundation shapes of which it is composed, and a knowledge of the laws of color: that is, light and shade, and contrast. When these two points are remembered and practiced in the arrangement of patchwork, the ornamental effects may be produced." [81]

For some women, the greater amount of leisure time, the variety of textiles, and the availability of the sewing machine gave added incentive for the creation of superb works of appliqué, pieced, and quilted quilts. Others simply copied the innovators.

T. S. Arthur, in "The Quilting Party," a story appearing in an 1849 issue of *Godey's*, commented:

Our young ladies of the present generation know little of the mysteries of "Irish chain," "rising star," "block work," or "Job's trouble," and would be as likely to mistake a set of quilting frames for clothes poles as for anything else. It was different in our younger days. Half a dozen handsome patchwork quilts were as indispensable then as a marriage portion; quite as much so as a piano or guitar is at present. And the quilting party was equally indicative of the coming-out and being "in the market," as the fashionable gatherings together of the times that be. [82]

By the second half of the nineteenth century, patchwork was in the full bloom of the Victorian age. Quilts were used not only in the bedroom

---

79. *Godey's Lady's Book*, Vol. 10, January 1835, page 41.
80. *Ibid.*, Vol. 42, March 1851, page 198.
81. *Ibid.*, Vol. 60, March 1860, pages 262–63.
82. *Ibid.*, Vol. 39, September 1849, page 185.

but also in the parlor as elegant slumber robes or lap throws. Pieced work was also used for piano covers and stools. In keeping with the Victorian love of knick-knacks and what-nots, the Crazy Quilt became a collage of silks, velvets, and fragments of ribbons fancifully embellished with spangles and beads and embroidered designs of flowers, fans, and figures. *Godey's* was to recommend: "The greater the diversity in stitches the better,"[83] and the preferred forms were curves and ovals:

> *It saves time if a few of the smaller pieces are joined by a sewing machine, but we would suggest only a little of this being done, as it gives straight lines. If, on completion, there are any angularities offending the eye, they can be hidden by the application of ovals or other curved forms of silk being put on the top and worked around.*[84]

The *Lady's Manual of Fancy-Work* of 1859 rejected the use of calico in favor of silk, velvet, and satin:

> *This is a favorite amusement with many ladies, as by it they convert useless bits of silk, velvet or satin, into really handsome articles of decoration. Of the patchwork with calico, I have nothing to say. Valueless indeed must be the time of that person who can find no better use for it than to make ugly counterpanes and quilts of pieces of cotton. Emphatically is the proverb true of cotton patchwork, Le jeu ne vaut pas la chandelle! It is not worth either candle or gas light.*
>
> *But scraps of the more expensive materials I have named, will really, with a little taste and management, make very handsome cushions, chair covers and ottomans.*[85]

In *Godey's Lady's Book*, January 1885, J. L. Patten, 38 West 14th Street, New York, advertised:

> *Crazy Patchwork. We send ten sample pieces of elegant silk, all different and cut so as to make one 12 inch block of crazy patchwork with a diagram showing how to put them together, and a variety of new stitches, for 35¢. We send a set of thirty-five perforated patterns, working size, of birds, butterflies, bugs, beetles, spiders and web, reptiles, Kate*

---

83. *Ibid.*, Vol. 106, April 1883, page 371.
84. *Ibid.*, Vol. 106, May 1883, page 462.
85. Mrs. Pullan, *The Lady's Manual of Fancy-Work*, Dick and Fitzgerald, Publishers, New York, 1859, page 95.

Greenaway figures, flowers, etc., with materials for transferring to the silk for 60¢.[86]

Crazy Quilts produced during the Victorian era are frequently criticized. Writers refer to them as degenerate and the beginning of the decline of quilt making in America. These views are difficult to understand. Quilt makers of the period showed a high degree of originality in the creation of appliqué collages and in the use of various needlework stitches. The work was produced in an era of esthetics different from the formalist geometric Bauhaus traditions of the twentieth century, but this should not inhibit our appreciation of the best work of the period, which shows humor and a rampaging use of color and textiles.

And although there was a sharp decline in the making of quilts by the end of the nineteenth century, this had more to do with Sears, Roebuck than Victorian style. Inexpensive blankets and bed covers within the economic reach of nearly all were to be found in abundance in stores everywhere. No longer did women find it necessary to spend long hours over a quilting frame or in piecing intricate designs cut of hundreds of scraps of material for a quilt top. People purchased and used manufactured goods with the same enthusiasm and pride as we do handmade objects today. It was also a time when more and more women were freed from the endless chores of the home and, in increasing numbers, took jobs and entered professions. The social and economic movements of the period gave women greater freedom and leisure than they had ever had before.

But the decline in quilt making was only temporary and during the twentieth century there have been periodic revivals of interest in the art. Such revivals frequently follow in the paths of war and economic recession. The terrible depression of 1929 brought in its wake national concerns for thrift and economy. A poignant letter written in September 1931 describes life on a farm in Minnesota during the depression and the comfort found in quilt making by one woman:

I have been real busy this summer, for farmers aren't hiring any help, only what was really necessary, for it was so hot and dry around here during July and August that crops are a failure. I never saw the like. We didn't have any garden, it all burnt up and our corn—we had to cut most of it with a grainbinder, could only use the corn binder for a few acres. Then the 22nd of July a fire from the railroad burnt up all our pasture of fifty-

---

86. Mildred Davison, *American Quilts*, Art Institute of Chicago, 1966, n.p.

two acres with eighteen acres of oats and twenty acres of meadow, so for nearly a month we had to keep all our cows in the yard and feed them hay and grain: in fact, we are still feeding them grain and corn fodder now. But we ought not to complain for a week ago in some places around here they had a frost, but we escaped it, and so many need help, what will it be before Spring? Last Monday a nine year old boy here in St. Paul died from eating rotten fruit that had been thrown in the city dump; his father had been out of work and they were destitute and felt too proud to ask for aid. I have done quite a lot of canning of what is left of our fruit and vegetables and for the winter I think I shall make a quilt to keep from getting lonesome, for some of the women around here are real interested in quilting again.[87]

Women everywhere were encouraged to sew. Magazines and newspapers of the 1930s carried advertisements for quilting kits and gave notice of quilting bee contests. Patterns based on those first printed in *Godey's Lady's Book* during the nineteenth century, as well as new patterns, were reproduced in newspapers and farm journals throughout the country. Themes were patriotic and emphasized new technology. A 1934 model airplane—"the airplane will take its place in historical quilts"—was the basis for a quilt pattern published in newspapers in the Midwest. It was to be pieced in orange and blue.

There were also patterns of state flowers and birds, scenes from history, and bright floral appliqués of orange blossoms, morning glories, and water lilies. Traditional patterns such as the "Dresden Plate" and "Fan" were done in Art Deco styles.

Women made scrapbooks of the patterns that were published weekly in local newspapers. Appliqué quilt blocks were sold in quilting kits. The ready-made blocks were numbered and the design stamped on color-fast patches ready to cut out and appliqué upon a quilted background block. A set consisted of twelve blocks, sufficient for a child's bed, or thirty-two blocks for a full-sized bed. A twelve-block set cost $1.20 plus 10¢ postage. The patterns available included "The Sun Bonnet Girl," "The Colonial Lady," and "The Romper Boy." There were also paper templates for appliqué and pieced quilts that sold for 25¢ each. Quilt making was becoming a mechanized craft. And, of course, there were ready-made manufactured quilts for sale for $5 and $10.

Quilting-bee contests sponsored by newspapers and magazines offered cash prizes of $50, $25, and $15 for first, second, and third place for the

---

87. Peto, *op. cit.*, page 208.

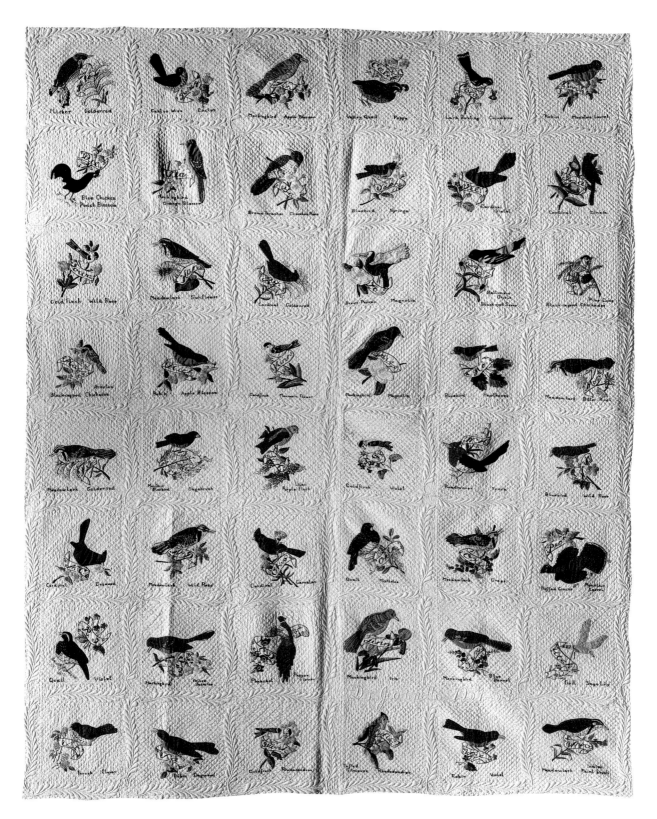

best designed and made quilts. In the larger cities and at regional fairs there were quilt shows displaying 700 to 800 quilts. Attendance ran high, sometimes attracting 20,000 to 25,000 people. Quilt contests were held throughout the country. Entries were grouped under the categories of antique quilts made before 1850, pieced, appliqué, unique, modern, and special categories for people over sixty and children under fourteen years of age.

In a Depression-worn country, efforts were made through the Work Relief Program of the Works Progress Administration to stimulate home crafts and develop community industries. The aim of the handicraft program was to create employment. It also recognized the importance of recording and preserving American handicrafts of the past and of "keeping weaving, handicrafts and sewing crafts alive."[88]

Eleanor Roosevelt used her enormous influence to spearhead craft training projects under the WPA. In Appalachia, the Carolinas, and the Midwest, women were taught quilt making, weaving, appliqué work, block printing, and textile production. By the beginning of World War II these programs were assimilated into projects for the war effort or dropped.

With interest aroused in handicrafts and our heritage, people bought quilts for their beauty and historical significance. An advertisement in the *New York Times* of May 1, 1938, announced Macy's "Second Annual Show and Sale of 115 Superb Hand-Made American Patchwork Quilts." Prices ranged from $19.98 to $64.54, depending upon the intricacy of the work. (Quilts commonly sold in 1974 in New York City for $350, with special quilts selling for as much as $10,000.00.) Patterns were the traditional "Delectable Mountain," "Pine Tree," "Hearts and Gizzards," "Grandmother's Flower Garden," and others. The Macy's advertisement cautioned that at the first sale all of the quilts sold out in the first few hours.

As in every period there were quilt makers of unusual talent and creativity: Rose Kretzinger of Kansas, Charlotte Jane Whitehill of Colorado, Dr. Jeannette Dean Throckmorton of Iowa, and Bertha Stenge of Illinois. Mrs. Stenge's quilts are of particular note. She created a series of quilts during the 1930s and 1940s that must rank among the most beautiful ever made. They combine superb craftsmanship with great originality and creativity. Mrs. Stenge adapted contemporary themes as well as themes having to do with quilting traditions. Months, sometimes years, were spent researching the subject matter of a quilt before she began the actual work of sewing. She won first prize at the New York

---

88. Andy Leon Harney, "WPA Handicrafts Rediscovered," *Historic Preservation* magazine, National Trust for Historic Preservation, Washington, D.C., July–September 1973, page 10.

World's Fair in 1939–40 for one of her quilts and the Grand National Award for an appliqué quilt, "The Victory Quilt," in a National Needlework Competition sponsored in 1943 by *Woman's Day* magazine. Patriotism combined with good design, dignity, and superlative workmanship were cited as winning factors. Mrs. Stenge created her own designs and executed them in superb techniques (see plates 13 and 14).

Plate 30.
Sunburst or Rising Sun Quilt, c. 1800–1825. Pieced and appliquéd cotton, 80 x 80 in. Courtesy The New-York Historical Society. Possibly made by Mary Totten, New York, this wonderful sunburst is done in varying shades of brown and orange. The border is appliquéd.

Quilting bees continued to be held as in days of old. Carlie Sexton describes a quilting bee she attended in the late twenties or early thirties in a little town in Iowa:

One morning the postman brought me an invitation to a real Quilting Bee. I was so thrilled for I knew many of the quilters in the little town in Iowa. The gathering was in honor of one of my dearest friends who had just celebrated her eighty-sixth birthday, and was breaking up her home in this town, to go back to her old home in Pennsylvania, then out to California. She was so keenly alive to all that was going on and had so many friends that they gave this quilting bee a few days before she left.

Two quilts, the Compass and the Wedding Ring, were in frames on the long screened veranda. The day was ideal and everybody came. Yes, and they all came with baskets filled with the good things that farm women know how to prepare. Each one tried to outdo the other, and I guess they did. Such a jolly, good time we had! Only the very best quilters were allowed to quilt—the others pieced or cut blocks for another quilt. The younger women threaded needles and helped with the dinner. There were women from two churches and from the farms around.

One little, dimpled, happy woman said she was not in the quilting mood so she would entertain the visitors—I was the only visitor, but not the only one to enjoy the show she put on. She sang some of the funniest old songs and chorded on the piano. She was past 80, too. She gathered her skirts and danced some of the quaintest dances until we cried with laughter. Some of the others did their bit by speaking pieces. One played the mouth harp; some told stories, or did whatever their talents brought forth. The men did not come to supper, otherwise it would have been like the quilting bees these women enjoyed when they were younger. No wonder these gatherings meant so much to the women in the earlier days.[89]

It was during the 1930s that the suggestion was first put forth that quilt making was useful as occupational therapy.

In making a quilt top the worker has the stimulus of color and she also has to concentrate upon her task of sewing the pieces together in order that they may join to form an accurate pattern. If the quilt block is not a pieced one, but patched, the maker must turn under the edges of the pieces and stitch them down neatly in order that the form of the appliquéd pattern shall be perfect. A task also requiring concentration of attention. It is

---

89. Carlie Sexton, *Yesterday's Quilts in Homes of Today*, Meredith Publishing Company, Des Moines, Iowa, 1930, page 10.

easily understood that a nervous lady who is concentrating on making a quilt block has no time to worry over her fancied physical ill health or even over wrongs or slights which may be real, so that she is cultivating a more healthy mental attitude and habit.[90]

So much for nervous women.

The 1970s brought a great renewal of interest in quilts. They have been reappraised and freshly appreciated as an important American antique craft, as well as for their strong contemporary visual qualities. An impetus to the new status of quilts was given by the Whitney Museum of American Art in 1971, in an exhibition of quilts from the collection of Jonathan Holstein and Gail van der Hoof called *Abstract Design in American Quilts*. The emphasis was on the visual characteristics of pieced quilts. Mr. Holstein has stated: "Quilt makers in effect 'painted' with fabrics, joining colors and textures, their pallets, the family scrapbags and those of their neighbors."[91] He further states that the body of work of pieced quilts "exhibits some particularly American design traits; a traditional, reductive approach to visual problems, which tended towards simplification of imported forms and the production of unfussy native ones; vigorous, innovative forms; the bold use of color."[92] The success of the Whitney show was repeated in 1972 in major museums throughout Europe. Europeans are enjoying and collecting American quilts as avidly as Americans.

In the United States, quilts are purchased and hung on walls in the same fashion as tapestries and paintings. The strong nonobjective compositions, the use of color, and the everyday subject matter all seem strikingly prophetic of the images of the avant-garde of contemporary art of the 1950s, 1960s, and 1970s.

Many people have found particular pleasure in the bold geometric and nonobjective designs of the pieced quilts, comparing them to works of art in contemporary movements. The unexpected similarity of expression found in quilt design that anticipates minimal, pop, and op art and color-field painting has astounded and excited followers of modern art. How could a mid-nineteenth century American farm woman, in piecing a simple utilitarian bed cover, anticipate the sophisticated art work of America over a hundred years later?

---

90. William Rush Dunton Jr., *Old Quilts*, privately published at Catonsville, Maryland, 1946, page 3.
91. Jonathan Holstein, *American Pieced Quilts*, Smithsonian Institution, Washington, D.C., 1972, page 14.
92. *Ibid.*

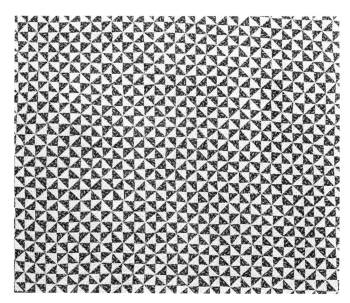

It is far-fetched to suggest that the creators of these quilts had the same artistic objectives as a contemporary artist or that they even came out of the same esthetic sensitivities. Nor do we believe it necessary to legitimize this original expression on the basis of present-day esthetics. Obviously, quilts are not paintings, nor were they meant to be. But they were created with a strong sense of beauty, and they were made to be used as we presently use art objects. Artist Robert Rauschenberg once said: "I think a picture is more like the real world when it's made out of the real world."[93] The artist David Smith said he wanted to create an art "that men could view as natural, without reverence or awe."[94]

The definition of what makes an object art is unclear, particularly in the field of functional objects, which are both utilitarian and decorative. With quilts the question is further confused by sentimental and historic associations, and the value placed on antique objects. "The line between the work of art and the antiquarian object is sometimes so obscurely drawn as to bewilder the ordinary observer."[95]

The quilt makers set out to make esthetic and functional objects with much less self-consciousness than we meet with today. And they possessed fully the capabilities necessary to accomplish their ends. In

Plate 32 (ABOVE LEFT).
Robbing Peter to Pay Paul
Quilt (detail), c. 1850–75.
Pieced cotton. Collection of
Tom Woodard and Blanche
Greenstein.

Plate 33 (ABOVE RIGHT).
Windmills Quilt (detail),
c. 1875–1900. Pieced cotton,
86 x 87 in. Philadelphia
Museum of Art. The quilt top
is made up of thousands of
minuscule pieces of material.

93. Calvin Tomkins, *The Bride and the Bachelors*, Viking Press, New York, 1968, page 193.
94. Jack Kroll, *"Dead or Alive,"* Newsweek, October 1, 1973, page 96A.
95. Dow, *op. cit.*, page xxxii.

those instances where a great esthetic sense expressed itself through the tools of textiles, the colors and shapes of materials, they did create works of art. What we find in quilts is a sense of color, balance, and harmony as quilters in each period knew it. This sense of color and composition was natural to them. We react with amazement, as if they were naive or as if their work was accidental, but it was their esthetic sense that we are now recognizing and accepting.

Today, shops specializing exclusively in the sale of quilts have opened around the country. Newspapers carry advertisements and notices for quilting classes, bees, and clubs. There are publications devoted exclusively to the subject of quilts, such as the *Quilter's Newsletter* of Denver with a circulation in the thousands. In Appalachia, to help employment, the state of West Virginia has encouraged needleworkers to organize cooperatives for the purposes of quilt making. A famous co-op is known as Mountain Artisans, Inc.

But the new attention to quilts is really only the reappearance of a continuing tradition of quilt making and collecting in this country. Fortunately, there have been collectors who have understood and appreciated the historical significance of quilts as a masterful expression of American craftsmanship and esthetic and who have saved outstanding examples of this art from forever being lost. It was not unusual, until the past few years, to find lovely examples of quilts used as ironing board linings, rug mats, and even rags. These early collectors recognized the importance of quilts in the same way that others have acknowledged achievements in ceramics, glass, tin, and woodwork. It is also a recognition of our historical roots and background represented in these works we have created over the years. As Moreau de Saint-Mery stated: "The true character of the Americans is mirrored in their homes."[96]

There has never been an interruption in the making of quilts. Even after the popularization of the sewing machine and the mass production of ready-made bed covers, women hand sewed and stitched quilt tops and quilts. It is one of the few handicrafts that has continued uninterrupted almost as it originally evolved. Unlike the great traditions involved with working in tin, glass, and wood, quilt making has never depended upon a professional class for its skills. It is a handicraft that requires only a needle, thread, material, a simple quilting frame, and the ability to sew. Women can take their skills with them and materials are readily available.

96. Charles F. Montgomery, introduction to *America's Arts and Skills*, Time-Life Books, New York, 1968, page 9.

Throughout the years women in Appalachia and the Midwest, in Kentucky, Tennessee, and Pennsylvania have continued to make their beautiful pieced and appliquéd and all-white quilts. A moving experience was described by Allen H. Eaton in the middle 1930s in the mountains of North Carolina:

> When night overtook me I had not reached my destination. . . . An old but beautiful cabin stood near the road and here I asked if I might spend the night. After a good supper and a visit around the fireplace, I was directed to my bedroom above the living room, commonly called the loft. When I had climbed the crude stairway the light of my candle revealed the whole sleeping apartment floor covered with beautiful patchwork quilts and, neatly hanging from the roof beams the entire length of the room and on both sides of my bed, were coverlets and quilts to afford additional protection from any drafts, or rain, or snow which might come, and also, it seemed to me, to give splendor to the scene.
>
> These people had no carpets for their floor nor curtains for their windows, but they had a rare collection of home-made quilts, some of which were old and worn, but all I thought very beautiful. . . . I could not walk over this carpet of quilts to my bed without first removing my shoes and by the candlelight that night I studied the designs and color combinations in perhaps ten or twelve of them. I doubt if I shall ever have the privilege of sleeping in such surroundings again, and if the sight of a patchwork quilt does not stir in me anything more than the recollection of the experience in this lovely scene it does quite enough.[97]

Some modern quilters have followed traditional patterns—the "Log Cabin," the "Goose Tracks," and the "Rose of Sharon." Others have created original designs and given a new look to the top. Materials such as plastic and canvas have been used and objects such as toy automobiles have been incorporated into the top. Rocket flights to the moon and contemporary events have been depicted in quilt-top designs. Other quilt makers have gone back to the earliest forms of quilt designs, such as the framed center or medallion.

Women have continued to make quilts and doubtless will in the future. They have made them for practical reasons. They make them as part of a sewing tradition handed down from generation to generation like family recipes and customs. A favorite pattern passes from mother to

---

97. Allen H. Eaton, *Handicrafts of the Southern Highlands*, Russell Sage Foundation, New York, 1937, page 130.

daughter. A family quilt once belonging to a grandmother or an aunt or some relative whose identity is lost in time is carefully kept and prized as an important family heirloom. Sometimes quilts are clung to as a reminder of the past and carried with a woman's belongings no matter how meager. Willa Cather, in her lovely book *One of Ours*, describes such a cherished possession:

> *The only possessions Mahailey brought with her when she came to live with the Wheelers, were a feather bed and three patchwork quilts, interlined with wool off the backs of Virginia sheep, washed and carded by hand. The quilts had been made by her old mother, and given to her for a marriage portion. The patchwork on each was done in a different design; one was the popular "log-cabin" pattern, another the "laurel-leaf," the third the "blazing star." This quilt Mahailey thought too good for use, and she had told Mrs. Wheeler that she was saving it "to give Mr. Claude when he got married."*[98]

Women have continued to make quilts because of their love of the beautiful colors and designs and materials they have worked with. They have found satisfaction and pleasure in making quilts. And they have created works of great evocative power as part of an endless struggle for expression.

98. Willa Cather, *One of Ours*, Alfred A. Knopf, New York, 1953, page 72.

2
The Quilt

It is interesting and instructive to divide a quilt into its many parts. Like a good drama, a quilt has, as it were, a beginning, a middle, and an end. While our examination here is technical and oriented to function, it is fitting nevertheless, for artists have indeed been as interested in technique as in the purely esthetic aspects of their work. One discovers in looking at backings, interlinings, and tops, for example, an inexhaustible solicitude for the machinelike aspects of the quilt. If Le Corbusier was correct in saying that a house was a machine to live in, perhaps one can suggest the utilitarian virtues of these quilts by saying a quilt is a machine to sleep under.

The basic elements of the quilt are the top, interlining, backing, and edges. The design of the top sometimes included border and sets. The top was made and decorated first, then the three layers of the quilt—backing, interlining, and top—were assembled and quilted together, and the edges were finished last of all.

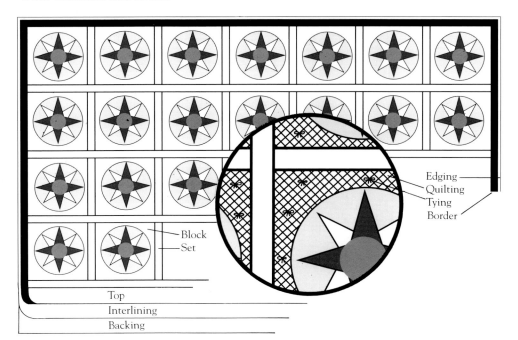

Plate 34.
The various parts of a quilt.

Plate 35.
Quilt back (detail), c. 1800–1825. Pieced cotton, 84 x 66 ½ in. Courtesy Mrs. R. MacFarlane. A repeated pattern of squares within minutely pieced frames, each square is also pieced of tiny fragments. The reverse side is a miniature LeMoyne star pattern.

Plate 36.
Album Quilt (detail), c. 1800–1825. Polychrome cottons appliquéd and embroidered on a white cotton ground, 72 x 78 in.
Collection of The Brooklyn Museum. Made by Mary Rosalie Prestmen Myers of Baltimore. There is another Baltimore quilt of
unknown origin made with identical motifs and arrangements, which suggests that the Myers quilt may have been purchased with the
designs already drawn. The border quilting is in a running rope pattern, and the edges are done in the self-binding technique of back
over front. Note the vertical sets.

THE TOP

The two principal techniques used in American quilt making are piecing and appliquéing. Piecing, or piece work, is the process of seaming small bits of fabric together to form an overall sheet. As has been pointed out by Irene Emery, pieced work is "a means of constructing a usable fabric out of fragments too limited in size for individual usefulness—but with proper selection, shaping and arrangement of the individual pieces, a highly decorative fabric may be put together."[1] Appliqué, from the French *appliquer*, meaning to put on or lay on, is the process of sewing small pieces of fabric onto a larger background piece. The pattern is produced by the cut-out sections of fabric that are laid on the face of a ground fabric and stitched to it. Both techniques have been popular in most times and places throughout the history of American patchwork, and frequently they are combined in a single quilt top or even a single block. Each genre includes an extraordinary range of style and quality of design and workmanship. Piece work, though it is sometimes used in a representational way, is usually composed of abstract geometric shapes; thus it is a graphic style. Appliqué, while frequently employing abstract as well as representational forms, is essentially a pictorial style, for virtually anything that can be drawn can be rendered in fabric with the appliqué technique.

To design an appliqué quilt top, the maker could either begin with a background fabric as large as was desired for the finished top and compose the entire design as a painter plans a canvas; or she could compose separate units of design on a number of small background pieces and sew the units together after each had been appliquéd. For each element in the design she carefully cut a piece of fabric the exact size and shape it was to be when finished, plus seam margins or hems all around. The hems would be pressed under before the piece was applied to the background. Obviously, the narrower the motif, the more difficult its execution, since two hems had to be concealed under each slender stalk; and the hems could not be too bulky, lest they ravel out from under the hemming stitches during use and repeated washings. When each piece was properly hemmed it was basted in place and then sewn down with invisible hemming stitches or slanted whip stitches.

There were a number of ways in which an appliqué pattern might have been developed. During the eighteenth century when imported printed textiles were prized and expensive, a popular style evolved from

---

1. Irene Emery, *Primary Structures of Fabrics*, Textile Museum, Washington, D.C., 1966, page 252.

Plate 37.
Flowering Tree Quilt. Cottons and linens, broderie Perse technique, 106 x 107 in. Shelburne Museum, Shelburne, Vermont. Made in America from English block-printed or Indian painted chintzes, this quilt has a foundation of homespun linen. Briars are embroidered in green onto the stalks of the flowers in the urns and latticed baskets. Both the flowering tree and the latticed baskets are late-18th-century motifs.

the practice of delicately cutting the printed flowers, birds, trees, and human figures (plus seam margins, of course) from a piece of printed fabric. These were then rearranged according to the taste of the quilt maker and appliquéd to the quilt top.[2] In this way a yard of costly fabric—or even scraps—could be made to cover an entire top. The areas between

2. This technique was sometimes referred to as *broderie perse*, French for Persian embroidery; but the phrase came to refer to the technique of cut-out chintz designs sewed to a foundation material. A definition of *broderie perse* from *The Dictionary of Needlework* (1882 edition) informs us: "in *broderie perse* . . . applied pieces of chintz . . . representing flowers, foliage, birds and animals . . . require no backing . . . and are simply pasted on a colored foundation . . . and caught down with a stitch. . . . Stretch your background upon a frame, and paste the chintz flowers into position upon it. When the pasting is finished and dry, take the work out of the frame and stitch loosely with as little visibility as possible, all around the leaves and flowers."

Plate 38.
Quilt detail. Broderie Perse
motif cut from a French
chintz appliquéd on a cotton
ground, with shell quilting
and knotted and tasseled linen
fringe. Courtesy Massillon
Museum, Massillon, Ohio.
This quilt was owned by
Isabel Hall Hurxthal of
Baltimore, who married Louis
Hurxthal of Massillon, Ohio.
Friends and relatives
autographed signatures in ink
or embroidery. The earliest
date is 1846.

appliquéd motifs were filled in with embroidery, piece work, fancy
quilting, or appliquéd shapes cut from humbler ginghams and calicoes.
The maker might emphasize particular lines of her pattern with
decorative embroidery, or outline the appliquéd piece with buttonhole
embroidery stitches.

Another form of appliqué found in quilts is reverse appliqué, widely
used in Central and South America, much rarer here. In this technique,
"the pattern is produced by applying the accessory fabric under a ground
fabric from which the areas have been cut out."[3] For example, the quilter
would trace a design on the ground material and cut it out. Then a
different color material was applied from the underside so that it could be
seen through the cut-out areas. The edges of the top material were turned

3. Emery, *op. cit.*, page 251.

Plate 39.
Quilt maker, West Virginia, 1972.

Plate 40.
Framed Center Quilt, late 18th century. Cotton and linen, 86 x 101 in. Shelburne Museum, Shelburne, Vermont. The vase, stems, buds, and leaves are of indigo blue printed calico. Hand-blocked linen is used for the inlaid blossoms, and a hand-blocked chintz is used for the applied flowers on the meandering vine border. The shell pattern is very finely stitched.

under and sewed to the patch with tiny, invisible stitches. An example of this that we have seen on a quilt was a watermelon in which the green rind was appliquéd on top of the background fabric in the usual fashion, but the pink was seen through cut-out holes.

Interesting effects could also be achieved by the use of the appliqué technique in combination with padding. On the appliquéd spread, when the needleworker chose to give a three-dimensional effect, or to

Plate 41.
Baltimore Album Quilt (detail), c. 1820. Reverse appliqué, closely quilted cotton. Maryland Historical Society.

Plate 42.
Urn of Flowers Quilt, c. 1790–1810. Cotton and linen, 104 x 84½ in. Courtesy The Henry Francis du Pont
Winterthur Museum, Winterthur, Delaware. Quilted in a diagonal pattern, this work was made in Connecticut from
various English textiles. The printed fabrics range in date from the mid-18th century to about 1810. The meander
border has been identified as a block print of the 1790s; some butterflies and flowers are copperplate-printed. A
number of motifs with shading in parallel lines are identifiable as floral patterns from 1808–10. The corner bouquets
and the flowering tree appear to be not-so-distant relatives of the motifs found on Indian palampores.

Plate 43.
Framed Center Variation Quilt, c. 1775–1800. Pieced linsey-woolsey and glazed worsted, 93 x 74 in.
Collection of Jonathan Holstein. Fragments of thirteen different linsey-woolseys as well as glazed worsteds are
found in the pieced center. Heart motifs are quilted throughout.

emphasize an important shape, she would add extra cotton or wool to the underside of the appliquéd piece before she hemmed it down. This caused the shape to puff up, particularly after washing. Like stuffed quilting, it was a tricky technique, because if she stuffed a space too tightly the batting would swell in the wash and burst the stitching. One frequently finds a stuffed bird sitting in a tree, a bowl of fruit in which the cherries are padded, or a vine border in which all the grapes stand in relief.

A quilt maker could draw appliqué patterns freehand, or copy forms from illustrated books, wallpaper, or practically anything flat enough to be traced. If the pattern was to be repeated she then made a paper or cardboard template around which she traced the pattern onto the fabric before cutting out, so that her leaves or grapes or baskets would be uniform. Before sewing, she pressed the hems in toward the wrong side of the fabric, often using the template centered on the back of the cut piece as a guide to insure taking even margins, for if the hems were turned under unevenly, the finished piece would be the wrong shape. For abstract and free-form patterns, she began by folding a square or circle of paper into quarters, then snipped out a design as one cut snowflakes or paper dolls in kindergarten. This technique is most often employed in quilts made in Hawaii and Pennsylvania.

A certain mystique dividing piece work and appliqué quilts has evolved in the literature on the subject, suggesting that piece work represents the meat and potatoes of quilt making and appliqué the dessert. We have found that, besides differences in technical execution, there is no other fundamental differentiation. Pieced quilts were not just used for "everyday" wear, and appliquéd quilts were not always put aside for the "best" bed or for show or for the bride's trousseau. Through the years the quilter has decorated her quilt with what she saw fit and with what was available. There are embroidered quilts, stenciled quilts, and quilts whose only design is their quilting (which will be discussed later).

If quilt making was a salvage art, then certainly what went into the quilt was determined by what salvage goods were available to the needleworker. In all probability most accomplished quilt makers were proficient in both techniques and used each at different times for different reasons. Some of the most extraordinary appliqué spreads turn out on close inspection to be composed of tiny scraps—as much a humble salvage endeavor as a child's first checkerboard quilt—and some of the apparently simple repetitive geometric pieced patterns were in fact enormously difficult to sew as in appliqué and required the purchase of special materials. Similarly, some piecework patterns that achieve optical effects as dramatic as much graphic art found in museums were in fact very simple to plan and sew. Both piece work and appliqué techniques were used in humble utility quilts and in spectacular projects requiring as much as forty years to complete. The maker's choice depended on local fashion and availability of materials, and our response to the finished quilts is now sometimes very different from the original feelings and intentions of the maker. We admire certain pieced quilts for the sophistication of design when at the time they were made they would have been dismissed at the county fair or by other needlewomen as badly sewn. Similarly, we sometimes underestimate certain highly stylized appliqué designs, because the symbolism employed is no longer potent in our culture, while we fail to understand how incredibly fine and difficult was the sewing involved in making such a pattern.

Pieced quilts may be composed of odd-shaped scraps of fabric or geometric forms—squares, triangles, and rectangles—which the quilt maker manipulated into arrangements of light and dark to create a pattern. In Europe the most popular form of piece work was and is the one-patch, in which thousands of pieces of a single size or shape—say a hexagon—are sewn together one by one until a sheet large enough for a spread is achieved. In America probably the greatest number of quilts are composed in sections, called blocks, that are assembled to make up the top.

The maker would begin with a square of paper which she might fold into quarters, forming a checkerboard called a four-patch; she might then continue to cut and fold the four basic patches until she had a design containing squares, rectangles, and triangles. Or she might fold the original square in thirds forming nine equal patches (a nine-patch), or, more rarely, into other modular systems known as five- or seven-patches. When she had finished designing the block, she made a template of each geometric shape in the pattern (templates were of paper, cardboard, or soft metal). She then very carefully traced and cut each piece of fabric, usually one at a time, even though this might require cutting out several thousand pieces. In piece work the success of the design depends upon great accuracy in cutting and sewing, for if the joints and corners of the pattern fail to meet the design falls apart—and perhaps the quilt does as well. Particularly in pieced designs of diamonds—like the enormous "Blazing Stars," which are master works of piecing, the tiniest error in measuring would be multiplied until it became impossible to fit the pieces together.

The simplest patterns are those that can be joined with straight seams. Setting angled corner pieces is more difficult, and most difficult of all is the smooth piecing of curved seams, circles, and arcs. The more acute the angle or the arc, the more difficult the piecing. Frequently quilts are found—particularly in Pennsylvania Dutch work—that appear

Plate 44.
Unfinished quilt top (detail). Pieced, 57 x 75 in. Connecticut Historical Society. Made from bolt ends that include the British stampings of the period, in some cases showing the date 1825.

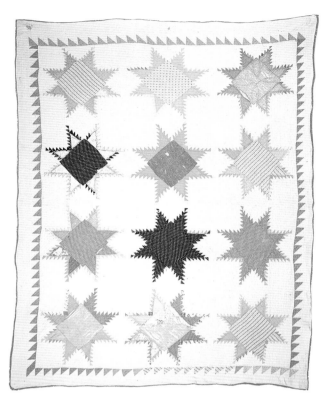

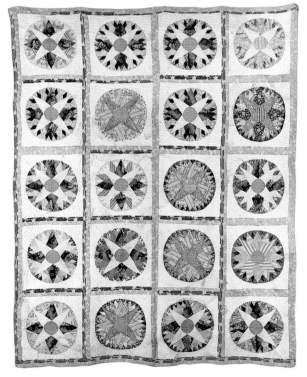

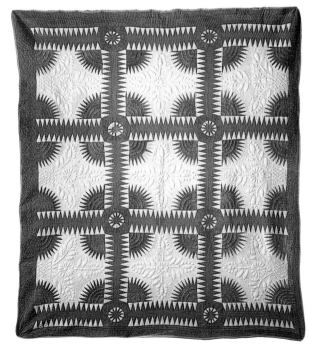

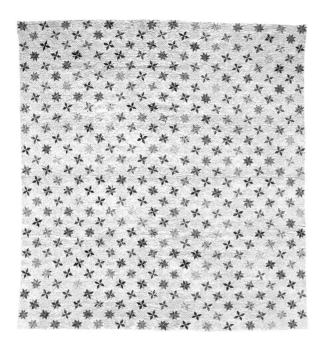

Plate 45 (OPPOSITE, TOP LEFT).
Cherry Wreaths Quilt, probably New Jersey, mid-19th century. Appliquéd cotton, 142 x 68 in. Collection of Mr. and Mrs. Ben Mildwoff. The wreaths display clusters of stuffed cherries that create a three-dimensional effect.

Plate 46 (OPPOSITE, TOP RIGHT).
Feather Star Quilt, c. 1850–75. Pieced cotton, 83 ½ x 65 ½ in. Spencer Museum of Art, The University of Kansas, Lawrence. The stars are composed of colorful calicos, and shell quilting designs fill the white squares.

Plate 47 (OPPOSITE, BOTTOM LEFT).
Chips and Whetstones Quilt, Kentucky, 1850. Pieced cotton, 108 x 78 ½ in. Spencer Museum of Art, The University of Kansas, Lawrence. Made by Susanna Richards Mosely. The top is made up of calicos, chintz, and rainbow roller prints. The back is homespun.

Plate 48 (OPPOSITE, BOTTOM RIGHT).
New York Beauty Quilt, Texas, c. 1875–1900. Pieced cotton, stuffed quilting, 74 x 88 in. America Hurrah, New York.

Plate 49 (ABOVE LEFT).
LeMoyne Star Quilt, c. 1875–1900. Pieced cotton, 80 ½ x 88 ½ in. Collection of Louise Emerson Francke.

Plate 50 (ABOVE RIGHT).
Emeline Dean Quilt, New Jersey, 1860–65. Appliquéd and embroidered cotton, 92 x 92 in. The Newark Museum; Gift of Katherine A. Righter. The center diamond, done in chain stitch, pictures the quilt maker, Emeline, and her house. The quilted border has stuffed grapes, and running vines with leaves are applied to the narrow sets.

Plate 51 (ABOVE).
Cradle Quilt, c. 1832. Appliquéd cotton, 43 ½ x 42 in. Courtesy Pennsylvania Historical and Museum Commission, Harrisburg. Made by Rebecca Kohler, Pennsylvania.

to be relatively simple appliqué patterns but on closer inspection turn out to be pieced. One wonders why they deliberately chose the more difficult technique when the final effect would have been the same.

Pieced quilts were sometimes organized in strips running the length of the quilt, instead of in blocks. Forms of the "Delectable Mountains" and "Tree Everlasting" are venerable examples. Such a strip pattern could also be used as the border to a block design, and, alternatively, border patterns could be pieced in strips to form an entire quilt top.

Another technique, called press piecing, amounts to a cross between piece work and appliqué; in this method the work is simultaneously pieced and appliquéd to a foundation layer of fabric. "Log Cabins" and all their variations and latter-day "crazy quilts" are made in this fashion. In the "Log Cabin" pattern, the center square is basted onto the center of a block of muslin or other backing, without turning under the raw edges. Then the first rectangle is pieced onto the center square, right sides together, edges matched, and sewn through all the layers. The rectangle is pressed to the right side, then the next rectangle is applied in the same way, and so on. Thus each raw edge is covered by the hemmed edge of the piece adjoining. The work is built up until the block is covered, and when all the blocks are finished the top is pieced together. This explains why many Victorian crazy quilts, though random in overall effect, are generally found to be divided by a grid of perfectly straight seams.

Finally, a special set of procedures is required for piecing enormous cumulative one-patch patterns such as hexagon mosaics, or diamond-based "Baby Blocks." In these patterns, each piece is fitted into an angle formed by two others. If measuring, cutting, hemming, or sewing is off by even a hair, the cumulative error again spells disaster; the pieces simply will not fit together. Additionally, at least two sides of any diamond or hexagon are cut on the bias instead of straight across the weave of the fabric, which means they will stretch and can throw off measurements even further. The following article from *Godey's Lady's Book* of 1835 explains the steps necessary to insure absolute precision:

> *Perhaps there is not patchwork that is prettier or more ingenious . . . than the hexagon or six sided; this is also called honey-comb patchwork. To make it properly you must first cut out a piece of pasteboard of the size you intend to make the patches, and of a hexagon or six-sided form. Then lay this model on your calico and cut your patches of the same shape, allowing them a little larger all around for turning in at the edges. Of course the patches must be all exactly of the same size. Get some stiff papers (old copybooks or letters will do) and cut them also into hexagons precisely the size of the pasteboard model. Prepare as many of these papers*

Plate 53 (ABOVE LEFT).
Urn with Flowers Quilt, Pennsylvania, early 19th century.
Appliquéd and embroidered cotton, 90 x 85 in. The New-
York Historical Society. The borders of this lovely Moravian
quilt are edged by an embroidered meandering vine of wool
with appliquéd flowers.

Plate 54 (ABOVE RIGHT).
Urns and Bouquets Quilt, mid-19th century. Appliquéd
cotton, 96 x 84 in. Courtesy The Henry Francis du Pont
Winterthur Museum, Winterthur, Delaware. Delicate handles
distinguish the urns. The quilting is done in a diagonal pattern.

Plate 55 (RIGHT).
Framed Center Quilt, Pennsylvania or Delaware. Pieced and
appliquéd; cotton backing, 101 x 91 in. Courtesy The Henry
Francis du Pont Winterthur Museum, Winterthur, Delaware.
The two birds in the tree and the two flowers in the corners of
the center block are cutouts from English block-printed
textiles of the 1780s. The honeycombed leaves out of which
the tree grows also appear to be block-printed. Quilted in an
all-over diagonal pattern, the border is another version of the
bowknot and swag design. The quilt was made by Margaret
Nichols for her sister, Hannah, at the time of Hannah's
marriage to Jacob Pusey in 1813. The initials "M.N." are
stitched above the upper bird.

Plate 56.
Centennial Flag Quilt, c. 1876. Pieced cotton, 72 x 72 ½ in. Mastai Collection of American Flags. Twenty flags have been pieced together to create a patriotic motif. The back (shown in the corner folded over at upper right) is pieced of international Centennial flags.

Plate 57.
Flag Quilt, Pennsylvania, c. 1875–1900. Pieced cotton, 80 x 80 in. America Hurrah, New York.

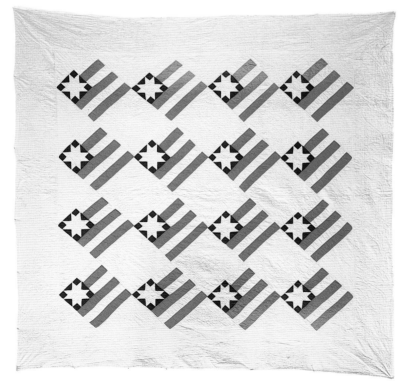

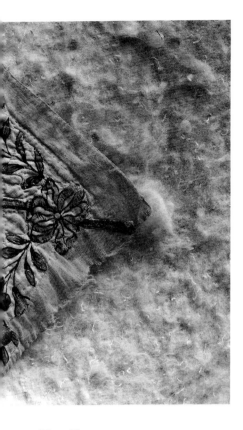

Plate 58.
Quilt interlining, c. 1790–1810.
Cotton, 100 x 86¼ in. Courtesy The
Henry Francis du Pont Winterthur
Museum, Winterthur, Delaware. Quilt
top appliquéd with block-, plate-, and
early roller-printed linens and cottons.

as you have patches. Baste or tack a patch upon every paper, turning down the edges of the calico over the wrong side. Sew together neatly over the edge, six of these patches, so as to form a ring. Then sew together six more in the same manner, and so on until you have enough. Let each ring consist of the same sort of calico, or at least of the same colour. For instance, one ring may be blue, another pink, a third yellow & c. The papers must be left in, to keep the patches in shape till the whole is completed.

When you have made a sufficient number of the calico rings, get some thick white shirting-muslin, and cut it also into hexagons, which must afterwards be sewed over papers like the coloured patches. Sew one of the white hexagons in the center of each ring of calico, which must then be surrounded with a circle of white, which will make three white patches come together at each corner of the coloured rings. In this manner, all the patches are put together till the whole is finished.

Prepare a lining of thick white muslin and lay bats of carded cotton evenly between after you have put it into the quilting-frame. In quilting you have only to follow the shape of the hexagons.[4]

INTERLININGS

A great range and odd assortment of formulae flourish for quilt interlinings. The interlining is the soft middle of the textile sandwich, the part that comes between the top and the backing. By far the two most important ingredients for filling a quilt were wool and cotton.

The warmth of the quilt depended upon the thickness of the interlining, and nothing provided greater warmth or thickness than wool. The quilter had many ways to procure the wool for the inside of her quilt. If she lived on a farm, the livestock might include sheep, and then, of course, a supply was readily available. At shearing time, odd clippings and less desirable parts of the fleece (like the underbelly and legs) and any wool left over from the amount that was to be sold or set aside for household spinning could be saved for interlining stuff. Lambswool was considered softest and most desirable. One could also obtain wool from a neighbor, perhaps in exchange for sugar or some other staple. A diary kept by Reverend Samuel Peabody in Atkinson, New Hampshire, at the turn of the eighteenth century records the exchange of a pound of wool for three pounds of sugar.[5] Anywhere from one to four pounds of wool

---

4. *Godey's Lady's Book*, Vol. 10, January 1835, page 41.
5. Fennelly, *op. cit.*, page 12.

were needed to fill a quilt, depending on the size. Surprisingly enough, a good deal of wool could be collected from hedgerows, wire fences, and briar patches, although it took considerable patience to gather enough to fill a whole quilt.

However the raw wool was obtained, the preparatory steps remained identical. First, it had to be washed and scoured in soapy water, then put through several rinsings, and laid out on the ground to dry in the sun with some kind of netted covering over it so that the wind would not scatter it. Among quilters there were two schools of thought about washing the wool. Some felt that the wool had to be washed thoroughly so as to be purged of its natural oils, which might deposit small brown stains on the quilt if allowed to remain, or give off an unpleasant odor when exposed to heat or damp. Others took care not to over scrub their wool filling, because some natural oils left in the wool would make carding easier and protect the quilt from omnivorous moths.

At any rate, after excess grease and all dirt were removed, it only remained to card the wool. This was done with wire brushes that fluffed and teased and combed the wool into shape and allowed one to spread it evenly throughout a quilt with no lumps and no thin places. A carding machine was invented in 1790 and consequently this tedious job could be done mechanically in the nineteenth century. In the first decade of the nineteenth century, a Litchfield, Connecticut, advertiser claimed that "the wool by running through the machine becomes thoroughly mixed, the rolls are even and clear of knots, and a woman will spin one third more for a day's task from these rolls, than from those which are carded by hand."[6] The invention of the carding machine did not mean all that much greater use of wool for such ends as quilt interlinings, however, because American wool during the eighteenth century and the first quarter of the nineteenth century was considered to be coarse and rough, and a quilter creating a special coverlet would have probably turned to cotton for a filler.

Bedcovers for use in temperate climates and those that were delicately quilted in intricate patterns usually required some form of a cotton interlining. Cotton was cultivated by the English on their plantations in America in the seventeenth and eighteenth centuries, and it was thought of mostly as a garden plant, except in South Carolina and Georgia where it was grown for domestic use. With painstaking effort, and many long hours of slave labor, it was possible to remove the cotton from the boll and disentangle the unsightly seed. But it was very unlikely

---

6. Fennelly, *ibid*.

that the farmwoman could or would devote her time to such a project. This did not mean that, without having slaves, you could not acquire a cotton interlining for your quilt. First, cotton grown in the South was purchasable in New England, and, second, and really of greater importance, England was exporting into her colonies large quantities of the cotton that was the staple crop in her other nearby colonies, the British West Indies (where slave labor similar to that of the South removed the seeds). As early as 1636, the first ship from Jamaica and the islands had already begun supplying New England colonies with raw cotton and "by 1700 Jamaica and her sister islands were supplying 70% of all cotton used by great Britain and her dependencies."[7] Also England was importing into America raw material for quilt battings. In the *Boston News Letter* of June 22, 1727, "Quilts, Ruggs, and Wadings" are listed as exciting purchases just off the latest ship from England.

But then the Revolution and Eli Whitney came along and changed everything. Whitney had observed slave women clawing the seed off the cotton boll with their fingernails, and he recreated this same principle out of a roller and the protruding teeth of a wire comb that, when placed close to the cotton, would claw away the loose fibers from the cotton bolls. The seed was caught by the sawlike teeth and dropped away from the fiber by a contrivance. The invention of the cotton gin, completed in 1793, revolutionized the tedious process of preparing cotton for use. This meant that during the nineteenth century the American quilter could have any grade of cotton for any use she wished—and, in fact, because of its multiformity and the fact that women seem always to have thought of cotton as a cleaner filler than wool, it has been the preferred interlining for quilts. Cotton quilt batting, already made up into a rectangular shape, was purchasable from the mid-nineteenth century on. Today it can be bought in a roll corresponding to your exact bed size and unrolled onto the backing of a quilt frame.

Flax, the plant fiber from which linen is produced, was also used in its raw state as a filler for quilts at a very early point. As early as 1286, tow (coarse, broken flax prepared for spinning) is mentioned as an item for stuffing quilted gambesons.

The demands made of an interlining are that it be soft, warm, and easy to sew through. Naturally, different ideas of what would be used came from different households. The family that had need for constant thrift found that rags did very nicely for the interlining. In the 1700s a diary kept by Ruth Henshaw Bascomb recounts "sewing rags together"

Plate 59 (OPPOSITE). Sunburst Bride's Quilt. Pieced roller-printed calicos; bound with braid, 114 x 84 in. Collection of Mrs. Robert Wright Northrop. Made by Cornelia Ann Schenck of Flatbush, Long Island, prior to her marriage in 1851. Planned for a high bedstead, the quilt was used the long way across the bed. It is now owned by the quilt maker's great-granddaughter.

---

7. Finley, *Old Patchwork Quilts and the Women Who Made Them*, page 134.

among her childhood household duties[8]—and she was the daughter of a prosperous farmer. There are other accounts of using cast-off woolen clothing whose seams had been picked clean of threads and pressed flat: woolen stockings split open were mentioned; and the use of odd lengths of old and worn woven materials, such as sheets or coverlets, laid tidily end-to-end, without any lumps, to become the interlining. Recycling was taken so literally by the very poor or very thrifty that there were even cases where both outer layers of an old tattered quilt were removed in order to reuse the interlining for a new effort.

Loosely woven woolen or cotton cloths like flannel and flannelette were also popular for interlining in the late nineteenth century. They were soft and warm and had the reputation of not shrinking in the washing.

An old, worn, or raggedy quilt or blanket often found its way in between the top and the backing of a new quilt. As a very last resort, even paper and newsprint were used for interlining. Caulfield and Saward's *Dictionary of Needlework* rather smugly indicates: "Quilts of paper are much used for charitable purposes,"[9] and Mrs. Colby recalls for us Oliver Twist's mother dying in the workhouse, "the patchwork quilt which was carelessly flung over the iron bedstead *rustled*."[10] There can be no doubt that the interlining of that charitable quilt was paper! There are other instances of paper substitutions for cloth in lean times. In a journal kept by Caroline Cowles Richards, an entry during the mid–Civil War period, 1863, reads:

> *War prices are terrible. I paid $3.50 today for a hoop skirt. All the girls wear newspaper bustles to school now, and Anna's rattled today and Emma Wheeler heard it and said, "What's the news from the front, Anna?" They both laughed out loud and found that the latest news from the front was that Miss Morse kept them both after school and they had to copy dictionary for an hour.*[11]

There are not too many other materials that could be used inside a quilt, because of the problem of sewing through them, but we do read of very unlikely things used as interlinings for comforters, bedticks, and pillows, none of which required quilting at small intervals. We have seen

8. Fennelly, *op. cit.*, page 10.
9. Sophia F. Caulfield and Blanche C. Saward, *The Dictionary of Needlework*, London, L. Upcott Gill, 1882, page 415.
10. Colby, *op. cit.*, *Patchwork*, page 87.
11. Caroline Cowles Richards, *Village Life in America, 1852–1872*, New York, Henry Holt and Company, 1913, page 149.

reference made to cornhusks, the feathers of geese and game birds, hair, silk-grass, leaves, string, paper, cattails, straw, and animal skins.

BACKINGS

Sometimes the best part of the quilt is the back. This is where you see soft, pale, faded, sprigged cottons, the startling chintzes and beautiful homespun linens turned ivory with age. It is always a surprise to turn over a quilt and see what the maker has chosen for the part that was not for "show." There is an unending variety, as diffuse and decorative as the patchwork on top.

There are many instances in which the backing fabric is one whole piece of cloth bought expressly for the purpose of backing and finishing the quilt. But very often, and particularly on the earlier quilts, the backing is a melange of pieced remnants just as the top is. The material thought suitable for the backing was often a sturdier material than that used for the top. And the size of the remnants differed. Whereas very tiny fragments can be found pieced into a top, the back would contain much larger scraps. Very likely the quilt maker wanted to save herself from too tedious a job when it came to the back.

The most popular backing material has always been a plain white fabric: cotton or linen, homespun or store-bought. The simply woven linen or cotton used for the backing on quilts of the eighteenth century and early nineteenth century often came from the stocks of household linens. Household *linen* received its name precisely because linen, not cotton, was the preferred material for most of the household needs. A large amount of plain linen of varying quality was woven for shirting, tablecloths, napkins, toweling, pillowcases, bedticking, grainsacking, curtains, aprons, undergarments, and, especially, sheeting. The finer grades of homespun linen were considered valuable commodities and were used as barter in the local village store, and they found a ready market in the urban centers for shirts, underclothing, and sheeting. In 1743, a Philadelphia merchant, Samuel Powell, commented:

> *A vast deal of linen and woolen is made within the Province; so much linen by the back Irish inhabitants that they not only hawk a great deal frequently about both town and country but they carry considerable quantities away to the Eastward by land, quite away as far as Rhode Island.*[12]

---

12. Carl Bridenbaugh, *The Colonial Craftsman*, Phoenix Books, University of Chicago Press, 1950, page 35.

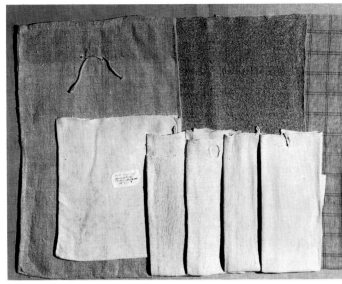

Plate 60 (ABOVE LEFT).
Checked and striped plainwoven
homespun linen fragments, mid-
19th century. Royal Ontario
Museum, Toronto. Such fabrics
were staple backing materials for
quilts.

Plate 61 (ABOVE RIGHT).
Bleached and textured homespun
in various shades, mid-19th to
20th centuries. Royal Ontario
Museum, Toronto.

This was true up until the nineteenth century in America, because
before this point cotton yardage had to be imported—which, of course,
made it more expensive. But linen could be processed on the farm and it
was amazingly durable. Its drawback of not taking dye easily was not a
problem for these household needs. Even in the first quarter of the
nineteenth century, when cotton did become available at more
reasonable prices, linen was still preferred to a great extent for household
usage.

This is not to say that cotton fabric was never used as a quilt
backing. Although no industry for the manufacture of cotton yardage
existed before the late 1700s in America, it was imported in large
quantities, particularly muslins and white calicos from India or England.
Neither was homespinning of cotton one of the thriving institutions of
the colonies, though there was a bit of home manufacture of cotton
goods.

In the south, where slave labor was available, plantation-grown
cotton was manufactured into cloth. Thomas Jefferson wrote in a letter in
1786:

> The four southernmost states make a great deal of cotton. Their poor
> are almost entirely clothed with it in winter and summer. In winter they
> wear shirts of it and outer clothing of cotton and wool mixed. In summer
> their shirts are linen, but the outer clothing cotton. The dress of the
> women is almost entirely of cotton, manufactured by themselves, except

*the richer class, and even many of these wear a great deal of homespun
cotton. It is as well manufactured as the calicoes of Europe.*[13]

However, this was the exception rather than the rule, and an all-cotton fabric used to back a quilt made before 1800 would in most cases be identified as imported cloth.

Any household article of hand-woven linen could be pieced together to create a backing for a quilt, but it was mainly the homespun linen sheeting that seems to have found its way into quilts. Probably because sheeting was more coarsely woven than the other articles (except for grain storage bags), it made particularly good backing. Hand-loomed linen sheets have a seam down the middle, the cloth having been produced on a narrow loom and then sewn together. However, because remnants as well as whole sheets were used for quilt backing, it is not always possible to tell whether or not there was originally a seam.

All linen homespun was used and reused. Its lifespan was exceptional. After it had outlived its usefulness as a garment, it spent a long life as patching material. Patches and repairs are often found on the backs of old quilts, and sometimes these repairs can even help determine the age of a quilt, since the earlier ones are very deftly mended with the use of homespun linen pieces. One additional trick employed in the reusing of household linens—and store-bought, too—was to give them a new life by dyeing them. *The American Frugal Housewife*, a book of household hints written in 1836, offers this helpful recipe:

A pailful of Lye, with a piece of copper as half as big as a hen's egg boiled in it, will color a fine nankin [yellow] color, which will never wash out. This is very useful for the linings [backings] of bedquilts, comforters, etc. Old faded gowns colored this way, may be made into good petticoats. Cheap cotton cloth may be colored to advantage for petticoats and pelisses [cloaks] for little girls.[14]

Another very frequently seen fabric used for quilt backings was a winter sheet, also called a summer blanket. These came in combinations of linen and wool, and of cotton, wool, and flannel.

The cotton and linen that is used on the backs of quilts appears in varying shades of whiteness. There are tints of gray, yellow, and beige. The

13. Perry Walton, *Story of Textiles*, New York, Tudor Publishing Company, 1925, page 144.
14. Mrs. Child, *The American Frugal Housewife*, Boston, American Stationers' Company, 1836, page 39.

color depends on the amount of bleaching and aging that has taken place. Linen, for example, came from the loom a dark gray color; this was its unbleached state. It grew lighter either by being processed at the bleachworks or throughout repeated launderings at home. Throughout the seventeenth and eighteenth centuries and even into the nineteenth, surprisingly enough, laundering was done infrequently. The household wash accumulated for up to three months, at which point there would be a large seasonal washing. (It was for this reason that a good stock of household linen was had by those who could afford it.) The fabrics were washed with a soft jelly-type soap created from all the refuse grease of cooking, butchering, and so on, and wood ash taken from the great fireplaces. After the washing, the women laid their linens on the lawn to dry in the sunshine, and the sun did its bleaching. Amazingly, this grass bleaching technique has never really been improved upon. Today it is combined with modern chemicals, but the natural process is still used as the basic ingredient. The reason for this is something that the early housekeepers could not have known: a perfect chemistry was at work— oxygen in the air and ozone given off by the grass were acting as the best bleaching agents known.

Until 1774, the only bleach was the sun. At this time, C. W. Scheele, a Swedish chemist, happened to notice that the cork in his bottle of chlorine had been bleached of color and deduced that chlorine destroyed vegetable colors. From about 1800 on, chlorine was used in America in the bleaching works, where it helped to shorten the time of the old method.

In order to print or dye fabric, it first had to be bleached; so the early printers set up bleaching yards to handle this. In 1774 John Hewson opened a printing manufactory and bleaching yard in Philadelphia. Here the dozens of necessary bleaching operations were performed in order to return the fabric to the customer within three weeks. These included souring in buttermilk and cows' dung and steeping in boiling-hot potash lye. The last step was the grassing, which meant sewing loops to the edges of the fabric, attaching the loops to pegs, and stretching the material out on the grass. This final process took two weeks or more, during which time the cloth was dampened several times a day and, of course, exposed to sunshine and rain. This work was principally done in the summertime, when the weather was accommodating. Occasionally we have seen the stamp from the bleachworks on a piece of linen backing a quilt. This is useful in dating a quilt if information is available as to when the bleachworks was in operation.

Whether the fabric achieved its different stages of bleaching over the years through constant use or at the bleaching meadow, the final white that was achieved was not the white of today. Because of a dyestuff called an "optical brightener" in our laundry products, we have become accustomed to a blueish whiteness that was not known in early textiles. What appears, then, to be discoloration of the backing of a quilt may in fact be the color the textile was meant to be. There may also be a yellowing or browning that occurred later as the result of age.

The backings as well as the tops were products of the salvage arts. The practice of recycling materials came not only out of necessity but of a mentality that proclaimed: "Thou shalt not waste." These women saved their useless rags and turned them into rag rugs, lined trunks and bandboxes with old newspapers, saved grease from their stoves for a whole year to make soap, rerolled their basting thread back onto the spool to use it again, and recycled their floursacking and feedbags into backing for their quilts. From the diary of Caroline Cowles Richards, December 11, 1865, comes this entry:

Plate 62.
Quilt backing, 1855. Cottons and linens, 84 x 168 in. Fall River Historical Society Collection, Massachusetts. Recycled flour bags alternate with other fragments, including "Pocaset Choice Family Flour" and "Bristol County Mills Superfine Flour."

> *I have been downtown buying material for garments for our Home Missionary family which we are to make in our Society. Anna and I were cutting them out and basting them ready for sewing, and grandmother told us to save all our basting threads when we were through with them and wind them on a spool for use another time. Anna, who says she never wants to begin anything she cannot finish in 15 minutes, felt rather tired at the prospect of this unexpected task and asked grandmother how she happened to contract such economical ideas. Grandmother told her that if she and grandfather had been wasteful in their younger days, we would not have any silk dresses to wear now. Anna said that if that was the case she was glad that grandmother saved the basting thread.*[15]

Martha Washington was also extremely frugal:

> *It is told of Martha Washington that she always carefully dyed all her worn silk gowns and silk scraps to a desired shade, unravelled them with care, wound them on bobbins, and had them woven into chair and cushion covers. To a group of visitors she at one time displayed a dress of red and white striped material of which the white stripes were cotton and the red silk from the General's worn out stockings.*[16]

Over and over again, when we look more closely at the backing material, we are delighted to see what the quilt maker salvaged: not only repaired

15. Richards, *op. cit.*, page 199.
16. Earle, *op. cit.*, page 237.

household linens and floursacking, but also old flannel petticoats and even premiums from the backs of tobacco pouches. *The Copp Household Textiles* mentions that a backing on a glazed worsted quilt was made of "two different natural wool fabrics, probably portions of old blankets."[17]

As textiles, particularly printed fabrics, became more affordable and accessible to all during the second quarter of the nineteenth century, it became quite common to use a whole piece of cloth more often for the backing. Because it was the underside, quilters were usually less concerned with making it decorative. Their concession to decoration was generally their choice of a pleasing fabric well loved.

The fabrics that were the most popular have been called "wash goods," an appropriate name. A material that will not withstand laundering is useless in an everyday quilt. From approximately 1825 to 1900, the wash goods used most often included calicoes, ginghams, chintzes, dimities, and challis.

Calico, of course, has been the mainstay of all quilt fabrics. The term generally refers to cottons printed with small-scale, sometimes minute, conventionalized patterns often in one or two colors, and has been used in America mostly for dress goods. The myriad different figured patterns are truly unending, and there are some so similar that it is only from an inch or two away that one discerns that they are actually different. There are also identical patterns that have been reproduced over a period of sixty or seventy years, which can make dating a quilt by them a guessing game.

The meaning of *chintz* may be confusing, but it is largely different from calico. Again, it is a cotton fabric printed with floral designs—but in five or more fast colors. Chintz is usually glazed and generally considered furnishing fabric rather than dress goods. A whole piece of striped floral chintz is seen as backing fabric on many quilts dating from the first half of the nineteenth century. Chintz patterns are usually thought of as larger in scale than those of calico, and the overall impression is a more colorful one. Chintz is more common in quilts in the first half of the nineteenth century, often without its luster, because the glaze on early chintz disappeared as the cloth underwent laundering.

Gingham is of cotton, generally checked or striped in two or more colors. It is not printed cloth; it obtains its design from the use of woven threads that have been dyed in the yarn. Gingham is about as universal and omnipresent a fabric there is, particularly on the backs of quilts. It would be nearly impossible to date a quilt by its gingham fabric. Furniture

---

17. Cooper, *op. cit.*, page 3.

check is the name given to a variety of woven linens[18] that were checked, striped, or plaid. In both, the sizes of the woven checks and stripes vary as do the colors used.

Dimity is a cotton fabric, ribbed or figured, commonly used in quilts; the construction is warp twill stripes in relief on plain weave ground. Challis is a thin, soft textile of silk and worsted, printed or woven with designs, and particularly used in the third quarter of the nineteenth century, although it existed somewhat earlier.

There are quilts whose reverse side is another pieced design, essentially a quilt on both sides. We have seen no more than a handful, and they have all dated after 1800. There is some evidence, however, to indicate that this may have been a rural southern tradition. Irene Smith, formerly of Burlington, North Carolina, recalls details of quilt making told to her by her grandmother, Mrs. Sallie Covington, also of Burlington, who died at the age of 104 in 1970. Irene recalls: "Both the top and bottom were pieced, so that it was like having a new quilt when you turned it over." One of five children in a black farming family, Irene remembers that, although blankets were available in the local general store (she even recalls the boxes they came in), they were terribly expensive for a family of seven. In any case, "Quilts were considered more homelike than store-bought blankets, as they were more decorative, and quilting was a social activity." In the summer, quilting was done by kerosene lamplight from about 6:30 to 9:30 in the evening. Some neighbors had a hoop that had a groove cut around the side. The hoop would be set up in someone's house and family and friends would gather around. Usually about six people quilted around the hoop. All hands began to stitch in the patterns, and Irene remembers that there seems to have been no leader in this activity, just a kind of communal knowledge at work. In the wintertime quilting was done during the day because it was too cold to work outside at farming chores. Someone would say, "I have a few quilts—come over," and they would gather. Coffee was served and a gingerbread cake called johnnycake. Old fabrics were not used; the neighbors would go down to the textile mills and buy the scraps they needed from the seconds. The quilts were not viewed as hand-me-downs, but rather as fine things for the house. Finally, the family would bind the edge of the quilt at their own leisure. The quilts were well cared for, kept

---

18. "The material was apt to be linen, but woolen check has survived, and the inventory of the estate of Nathaniel Thwing. Esq., of Boston, taken in 1768, mentions 'furnitr. Checkr. Cott [on] for a bed.'" So reports Cummings in *Bed Hangings*, Boston, Society for the Preservation of New England Antiquities, 1961, page 20.

Plate 63.
Star and Web Quilt (detail),
mid-19th century. Pieced
roller-printed cottons and
linens. Old Sturbridge
Village, Sturbridge,
Massachusetts.

for family use, and rarely sold. When they were, Irene remembers the prices in the early twenties to be 50¢ and 75¢.[19]

Documented here are a few representative examples of the unending variety of materials and techniques used to back a quilt. Seen in plates 19 and 20 is an example of a quilt backed with a calico not in evidence anywhere in the patchwork on the front of the quilt, but its decoration is still in the same spirit of those used on the top. The backing appears to have been laid out in three sections, the seams being covered over with a third ribbonlike calico. Plate 63 also shows the use of a harmonious but newly introduced printed fabric on the back. These examples illustrate what is probably the most common method of backing a quilt. Inevitably, there would be a shortage of materials after completion of the front of the quilt, and the quilter would either have to purchase new lengths of other materials for the back or just find scraps of materials that would finish the quilt in a consistent feeling.

A starred patterned fabric predominates as the backing material for the Centennial Quilt in plate 212. This same star fabric was also used to make up the set on the quilt top (see plate 211). The top is entirely composed of centennial textiles. Most interesting is a commemorative handkerchief (containing the text and the names of the signers of the

19. Irene Smith, personal interview, New York, April 30, 1973.

Declaration of Independence), which was saved for the center of the back.

Plate 132 illustrates a quilt backed with a boldly patterned fabric known as blue resist. Precisely how, where, and when these textiles were produced is still a subject under study (see chapter 6), but they are quite rare and extremely collectible.

The top and back of the quilt in plate 183 are identical. Small rose-colored meandering vines of flowers are block printed on the coarsely woven cotton material that is pieced in sections to create both the front and the back. It is also interesting that the fabric is of French manufacture and, because of the *chef-de-pièce*, the date 1785 cannot be doubted. We tend to minimize French textile importation into America, but this piece reminds us of the enormous French textile trade.

A most extraordinary and rare quilt backing is shown in plate 99. This is a hand-block-printed motif, crudely printed from a number of different blocks in blue and red, made in the first quarter of the nineteenth century in America. It would not be far-fetched to assume that stamping was done at home by the lady of the house, although there

Plate 64.
Eight-Diamond Star Quilt (detail), 19th century. Pieced gingham and calico cottons and linens alternating with solid beige blocks, 85 x 93 in. DAR Museum, Washington, D.C.

Plate 65.
Back of quilt shown in plate 64 (detail), possibly 18th century. Five stylized floral designs embroidered in three shades of blue wools on white linen background, 85 x 93 in. DAR Museum, Washington, D.C.

Plate 66.
Quilt back (detail). Sateen with velveteen binding, 76 x 76 in. Maryland Historical Society. Autographed by the teachers and scholars of St. Peter's Church, Baltimore, and presented to Mr. William B. Hurst, Sr., April 16, 1903.

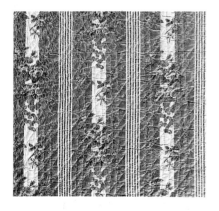

Plate 67.
Back of Sunburst Bride's Quilt shown in plate 59 (detail), c. 1825–50. Collection of Mrs. Robert Wright Northrop. Highly glazed roller-printed chintz showing large clusters of flowers on a striped background. Made by Cornelia Ann Schenck.

were professional counterpane stampers (see chapter 5). Certain newspaper advertisements from the mid-eighteenth century indicate that housewives stamped linen. Referring to another technique known as "china-blue," an advertisement in the *Boston News Letter* of 1761 stated: "The wife of John Haugen stamps linen china blue or deep blue or any color that gentlemen and ladies fancies."[20] We also know that, by the end of the first quarter of the nineteenth century, quilts and coverlets were being stenciled as well as stamped.

The provenance of the quilt in plate 64 attributes it to Tryphena Montague Hubbard of Sunderland, Massachusetts. She was born in 1757 and married Caleb Hubbard in 1780 at the age of twenty-three; he was twenty-six. Because the front of the quilt appears to be of a later style, it is our opinion that the back (plate 65) was of an earlier date. The needlework on the back is very definitely in the style of eighteenth-century crewel-work. Whether it was originally made as a bedcover cannot be known. This piece of crewelwork may have started its life as something else—possibly a panel from a bedhanging or a petticoat. If Mrs. Hubbard pieced the front in her later years—let us say at age sixty-three, in 1820— it might explain the pattern of repeating "LeMoyne Star" blocks on the front (which was in vogue in the first quarter of the nineteenth century) and her use of the much older piece of crewelwork as the backing. (There are also instances of quilt backings being added by a descendant. This, of course, results in a back of a much later date than the top.)

Today we have the practice of a group of friends and acquaintances all signing one card to accompany a gift. Plate 66 illustrates this very same sentiment—artistically autographed onto the back of a quilt. The quilt was presented to Mr. William B. Hurst, Sr., by the "Teachers and Scholars of the Infant Department, St. Peters Church, Baltimore," 1903. Each participant signed his or her name or saying, sometimes accompanied by a drawing. One drawing, for example, shows a lyre, representing the church choir, and all around this motif are the signatures of the members. Certainly this is a most personal way of backing a quilt, and in this case it is far more interesting and beautiful than the top, which is a design in satins and velvets with a "Maltese Cross" motif predominating.

It was not uncommon to back a quilt with four or five large alternating strips of fabric, or to use a striped chintz material as backing. It is a surprise to turn over Cornelia Ann Schenck's vibrating sunburst to find on the back a very fine, utterly contrasting, highly glazed, striped chintz (plate 67). You

---

20. Florence Pettit, *America's Printed and Painted Fabrics*, New York, Hastings House Publishers, 1970, page 106.

do see the underside of a quilt when it becomes rumpled on a bed or when you turn it back and this quilter didn't want the back to be disappointing. After the mid-nineteenth century, it is much less rare to find a whole piece of expensive chintz used as a backing. This is a direct result of the increased availability of all printed textiles and, specifically, the manufacture of American printed textiles.

Along with the glazed chintzes, we see bright paisleys, tiny printed bouquets of flowers, multicolored plaids, polka dots and checks of all sizes, and minuscule floral shapes of every conceivable type. And, of course, there are also solid-color backings. Particularly after the advent of the new dyestuffs in 1856 and the increased available color range, plain unfigured material could be bought in any shade. Plain backs are the preferred style of the Amish quilters.

It should be remembered that it is sometimes easier to see the beautiful and subtle quilting stitches more clearly on the back than on the front. In plate 66, brown and green threads were used to match the colors of the materials on the front; hence stitching is quite prominent. The lines of quilting follow the pattern of the appliqué motifs on the top.

BORDERS

Toward the end of the eighteenth century, counterpanes of all kinds were apt to be furnished with large single-piece borders that fell from the edge of the bed to the floor, hanging flat and smooth. About the beginning of the nineteenth century this large border tended to be gathered where it was joined to the quilt, hanging in a ruffle to the floor, hence a kind of a dust ruffle. These ruffles were often bound to the quilt by means of a narrow hand-woven tape. The flounce or ruffle was apt to be of the same material as the rest of the bed furniture; its approximate length was about twenty inches.[21] In the following news item from the *Boston Gazette* in 1736, the fact that such specific mention is made of the border leads one to speculate that the border was quite prominent on counterpanes at an early date: "COUNTERPANE Stolen, a Damask Counterpin of a Bed, one breadth, mark'd S. P. with a *red and purple chintz border:* from a Yard near Fort Hill, Boston."[22]

In plate 68, Mary Johnston has cut out and appliquéd her "swags and bowknots" to a huge ruffle. It is rare when the dust ruffle remains on an early quilt. There is conjecture that many of the early quilts and

21. Cummings, *op. cit.*, page 55.
22. Dow, *op. cit.*, page 157. *The Arts and Crafts in New England.*

Plate 68.
Framed Center Quilt. Pieced,
appliquéd, and embroidered cotton, 97
x 80 in. Courtesy The Henry Francis
du Pont Winterthur Museum,
Winterthur, Delaware. Made in
America from English textiles. The
bluebirds at the top and bottom of the
center section have been identified as
copperplate-printed cutouts from a
fabric engraving by Francis Nixon, c.
1765–75. Embellished with beige silk
embroidery, the center is appliquéd
and the inner borders are pieced. The
large ruffled border, appliquéd in the
bowknot and swag pattern, is edged in
beige fringe. The center panel is signed
and dated "Mary Johnston, 1793."

counterpanes that today are ruffleless may have once had them and lost
them to changes of fashion through the decades.

The needleworker, it seems, improvised more often on the border
than anywhere else on a quilt. It is possible that, since the border was
done after the rest of the quilt had been finished, the quilter had gained
confidence to experiment. Or sometimes the quilter would run out of
materials and have to create with makeshift scraps to augment the size of
the quilt. Or perhaps the difficulty of executing running designs and
corner treatments necessitated unusual solutions. And, since borders were
made to hang over the sides of the bed, the quilter looked at them
somewhat differently in terms of design.

The border frames the center portion of a quilt. In some instances a
quilt may be a series of borders. Borders can be pieced, appliquéd, quilted,
or a length of printed fabric that has been attached. In some cases there is
no border at all, usually when there is an overall design or the piece is a
whole-cloth spread. The border often repeats a motif from the main body

of the quilt (plate 72). The needleworker took the love-apples that she had used to form rosettes in the center of the quilt and marched them along the edges, creating a unique form of running vine.

Two of the most effective and popular border designs are running vines of all descriptions and the swag variations. Plate 69 shows a chunky

Plate 69 (ABOVE LEFT).
Oak Leaf Quilt with Bow and Swag Border (detail), 1841. 102 x 84 in. Schenectady Museum Collection. This bride's quilt by Mrs. William Snyder Miller uses two fabrics: one is a small stylized design of three-petal pink and blue flower heads and fine corallike lines on a medium blue ground; the other is a pattern of tiny wine-colored and yellow leaves on a slightly faded red ground.

Plate 70 (ABOVE RIGHT).
Laurel Leaf Quilt (detail), c. 1850. Appliquéd cotton with pieced Sawtooth border, 84 x 86 in. Courtesy Art Institute of Chicago. Made by Rebexy Gray Hamilton, Waynesburg, Pennsylvania, this quilt contains fifteen blocks with appliquéd motifs in green and tan alternating with fifteen blocks of plain white muslin. The quilting is done in diagonal lines and a variation of the princess feather design.

Plate 71 (LEFT).
Roses and Buds Quilt with Kissing Birds Border (detail), Pennsylvania German, mid-19th century. Appliquéd cotton. Philadelphia Museum of Art Collection.

Plate 72 (ABOVE LEFT). Love Apple or Budded Wreath Quilt (detail), mid-19th century. Appliquéd cotton in red and green, 79 x 80 in. Collections of Henry Ford Museum and Greenfield Village, Dearborn, Michigan. The background is quilted in a diamond and princess feather variation.

Plate 73 (ABOVE RIGHT). Full-Blown Tulip Quilt with Peacock Border (detail), c. 1800–1825. Pieced and appliquéd on handwoven linen ground, 90 x 99 in. Courtesy The Newark Museum.

Plate 74 (OPPOSITE). Nine-Patch Stenciled Quilt, Pennsylvania. Stenciled roses and pieced roller-printed cottons; cotton backing, 86½ x 73 in. Courtesy The Henry Francis du Pont Winterthur Museum, Winterthur, Delaware. Near the top is an inscription in ink: "Mary Ann Hoyt, Reading, May 15, 1834, no. 2."

primitive swag and bowknot border that is such an unusual interpretation of the usual flowing, graceful swag motif that it becomes almost the signature of this quilter. Plate 70 has a classic border treatment: the quilted border. The feather pattern is enclosed between two mini-borders of pieced saw teeth. The border was often a showplace for the maker's fine quilting skill.

Plate 71 is an appliquéd border of kissing birds. Birds seem to lend themselves to borders and a fascination with them abounds throughout quilt making: eagles, swans, doves, turkeys, ducks, other waterfowl, game birds such as partridges and pheasants, and especially peacocks—this last an omnipresent bird in American quilting. A chintz border (plate 73) is quite common, either as a whole strip of chintz or with motifs cut out from the chintzes and appliquéd onto the borders, as was done with three sides of this quilt. The fourth side of the border or top side is smaller here and on some quilts is nonexistent. This occurs on the earlier quilts since pillow covers or bolsters were used over the pillows, and the top edge of the quilt was concealed.

Plate 75 is an example of a full chintz border. In one of the most exotic fabrics to be seen in a quilt, rows of tall giraffes, head to toe, stalk around the quilt.

Plate 77 shows an elaborately worked appliqué border. The quilt is especially noteworthy for its primitive symmetry and its solicitude for particulars. The hunter behind the tree is accompanied by his dog and

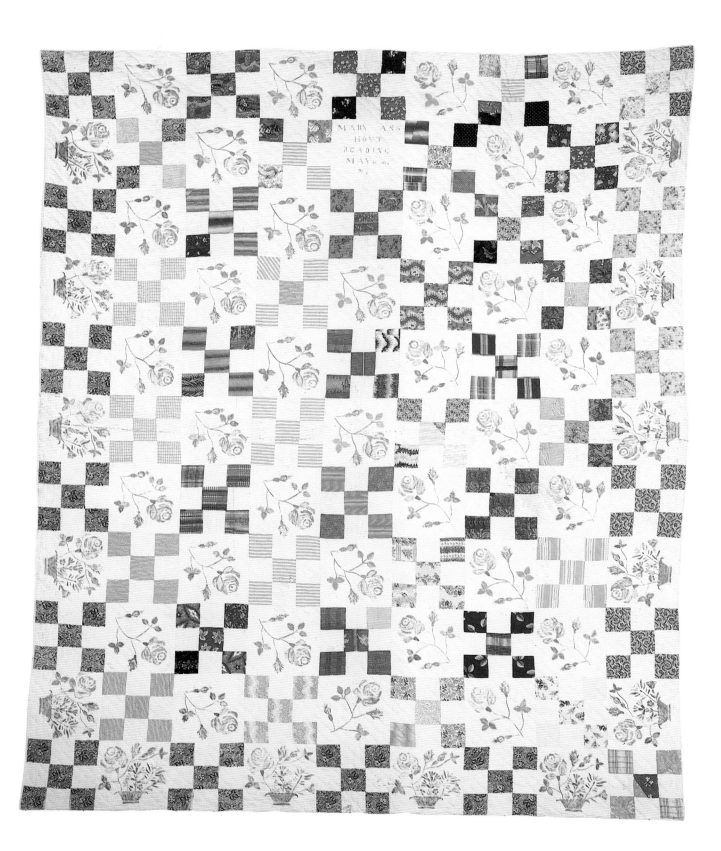

Plate 75.
Framed Mathematical Star Quilt
with Giraffe Border (detail), c.
1835–45. Pieced and appliquéd.
Maryland Historical Society.
Made by Catherine Mitchell.

Plate 76.
Pinwheel Star Quilt (detail), c.
1825. Pieced cotton and linen,
112 x 110 in. Courtesy M. H.
DeYoung Memorial Museum,
San Francisco. The border is a
floral strip block-printed in
madder colors on a brown
ground.

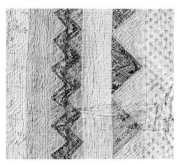

Plate 77.
Deer Hunting Quilt (detail), mid-19th century. Pieced and appliquéd cotton, 82 x 82 in. Courtesy The Ohio Historical Society. This elaborate version of a typical mid-19th-century repeat appliquéd quilt has a white ground with green trees and multicolored flowers, birds, dogs, and deer. The pieced inner border is yellow and orange. There is a green binding and a plain backing. The all-over quilting features hearts, flowers, and princess feather variations.

Plate 78.
Framed Center Quilt (detail), Virginia, c. 1750–1800. Cottons and linens; pieced border. Courtesy Pauline Pretzfelder Blumenfeld.

Plate 79.
Running Rose Vine Border (detail), mid-19th century. Appliquéd polychrome roller-printed cottons. Courtesy Mr. and Mrs. Ben Mildwoff.

scrutinized by birds in the branches. There are other birds in the border as well.

Plate 78 provides an example of a pieced border. The quilt itself is of the floral medallion type, and it is framed by a series of borders. The outer border is simply pieced with sprigged and figured calicoes from the last quarter of the eighteenth-century.

Plate 80.
Stenciled Quilt, Vermont, c. 1835–40. Unbleached muslin foundation cloth; cotton interlining, 88½ x 87 in. Courtesy Mrs. Robert Keegan. The stenciled geometric motifs are reminiscent of patchwork patterns.

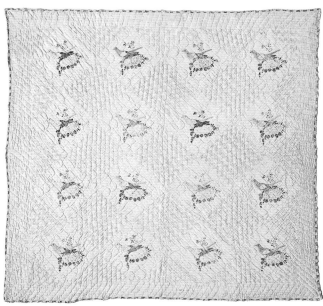

Plate 81.
One-Patch Stenciled Quilt, probably Connecticut, c. 1825–50. Stenciled and pieced muslin and homespun. Courtesy Mrs. Morton C. Katzenberg. A pink floral chevron motif printed on muslin alternates with stenciled homespun squares of birds.

Plate 82.
One-Patch Stenciled Quilt, Connecticut, c. 1825–50. Stenciled and pieced cotton; pieced linen backing, 90 x 88 in. Shelburne Museum, Shelburne, Vermont. A blue resist-printed calico (with hearts quilted in the corners) alternates with stenciled roses (quilted in a shell pattern). The quilt is bound in half-inch strips of two figured blue cottons.

Plate 83.
Stenciled Quilt, c. 1825–50. Pieced and stenciled cotton; homespun linen backing, 80½ x 81 in. (without fringe). Courtesy Historic Deerfield, Inc., Deerfield, Massachusetts. The top is pieced in ten-inch squares, the outlines of which are quilted in a trailing leaf design, with a quilted rosette at the juncture of each set of four blocks. The stenciled meandering vine is placed in long narrow sets surrounding each block.

Plate 84.
Lattice Flower Baskets Quilt, 1845. Pieced, appliquéd, and embroidered silk, velvet, and cotton, 94 x 87 in. Smithsonian Institution, Washington, D.C. Mrs. Mary Jane Green Maran of Baltimore made this quilt when she was a bride of eighteen. The appliquéd baskets have silk and velvet stuffed fruit and flower sprays embroidered onto white silk squares, which are attached to a cotton foundation with very fine quilting stitches. Supposedly 1001 skeins of silk thread were used in the quilting. A stuffed strawberry vine decorates the block seams, creating the sets, and an appliquéd running vine frames the quilt, which is backed with plain rose silk and finished with a knotted silk fringe.

Whether a border consists of simple bands of color, quilted designs, appliquéd motifs, pieced stars, scallops, or a flounce, it acts as a frame for the inner body of the quilt, and there is no question that a good deal of the impact of the quilt has to do with the effectiveness of its border.

SETS

The set is the name for the strips or blocks of material that are used to join quilt blocks or sections together. Not all quilts have sets. If a quilt has an all-over pattern that was pieced, the individual pieces were sewn directly to each other. If a quilt has an all-over appliqué pattern, the patches were sewn to a large foundation cloth. If the quilt was made up of blocks, the blocks could be sewn edge to edge, or they could be joined by a set.

A set might be of varying types. A block set (plate 86) is simply a plain square block, usually white and usually the same size as the

Plate 85.
Eight-Pointed Star Quilt (detail), New England, early 19th century. Pieced worsted. Old Sturbridge Village, Sturbridge, Massachusetts. Red stars on a green ground alternate with overshot woven squares with a fleur-de-lis figure, all with diagonal quilting.

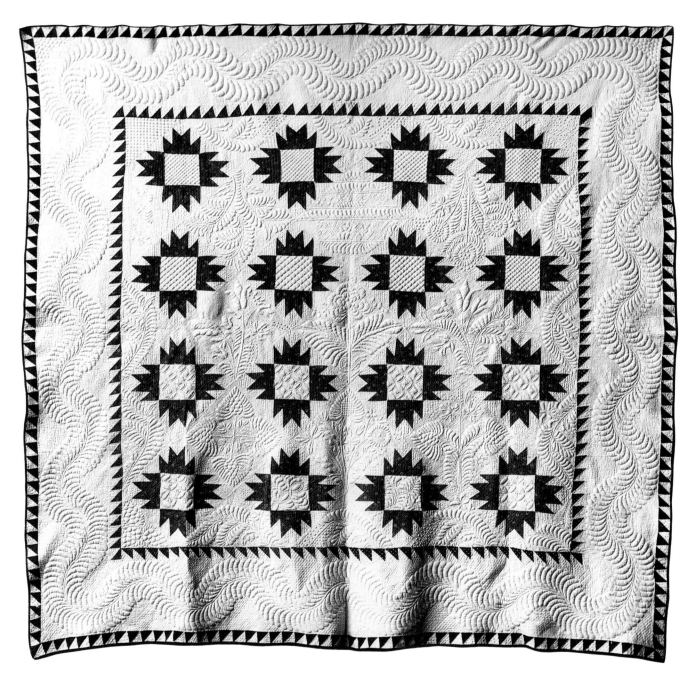

Plate 86.
Union Square Quilt, Indiana, 1866. Pieced red and white cotton, 88 x 88 in. Smithsonian Institution, Washington, D.C. The white squares are quilted with bouquet, leaf, feather, square, diamond, and teacup patterns, with stuffed running feather border. Made by Mrs. Mary Lawson Ruth McCrea. The middle block of the top row bears the quilted inscription "M.L.Mc May 18th 1866."

Plate 87.
Fort Dearborn Quilt, Detroit, c. 1825–50. Pieced, appliquéd, and embroidered silk, 77 x 77 in. Smithsonian Institution, Washington, D.C. Made by Mary Wilcox Taylor, this unusual quilt is enlivened with pieced and appliquéd vignettes of Fort Dearborn, two hunters with a dog, cows in a pasture, and a fruit-filled basket. The center depicts the sky with the sun, moon, stars, and a rainbow. The three-inch fringe was probably added at a later date.

Plate 88.
Victorian Album Counterpane, Washington, D.C., mid-19th century. Pieced cotton with crewel work (mostly chain stitch), 92 x 91 in. Smithsonian Institution, Washington, D.C. Made by Susan Adel Esputa, who copied popular pictures of the day and flowers from her first curtains after her marriage.

Plate 89.
Robinson Crusoe Quilt, Virginia, c. 1775–1800. Pieced and appliquéd cotton, 92 x 81 in. Valentine Museum,
Richmond, Virginia. Conjectured to have been made on the Hillsborough Plantation, King and Queen County, Virginia,
the quilt is said to depict Robinson Crusoe. Cutout chintz has been appliquéd with fine buttonhole and chain stitches.
The quilting is in a diamond pattern with areas of stuffed floral motifs.

Plate 90.
Geese in Flight Quilt (detail), c. 1875–1900. Pieced polychrome roller-printed cottons, 74 x 88 in. Collection of the authors. Knotting at intervals takes the place of quilting to hold the three layers firmly together.

decorated block and often quilted. It was placed between the decorated blocks to give space. Some old-time quilters felt that this block gave them a plain area to show off their quilting skills.

The term *strip set* refers to intermediate strips of cloth that cross the quilt horizontally, vertically, and sometimes diagonally, joining the blocks together. These sets not only covered up the seams, but sometimes they added interest to an otherwise pedestrian design. Of course, by cluttering up the pattern, they could also be the aesthetic ruination of a quilt.

Plate 36 is an example of the use of a strip set in contrasting material. On this quilt, as is the case in a great many of the Album Quilts, the strips were sewn between all the blocks and around the edges, creating a framework that appears to hold all the blocks. The set shown in plate 84 is exquisitely appliquéd with a continuous floral vine motif. Plate 91 shows sets created by complex pieced work. Decoration with sets can also take the form of double strips (plate 92), lattice work, cording, or quilting. Sets can sometimes assume such importance that they seem to engulf the whole quilt, creating their own pattern. Birds, hearts, or tiny squares or stars can be found as variations of sets in the corners of seams where the blocks were joined.

The term *set* should not be confused with the phrase *setting together*, which means sewing the finished blocks or sections into a whole quilt.

Plate 91 (ABOVE LEFT). Sawtooth Squares Quilt (detail), mid-19th century. Pieced cottons. Cincinnati Art Museum. Green, yellow, and red roller-printed calicos combine with white blocks containing quilting designs of stuffed flowers in pots or a princess feather pattern.

Plate 92 (ABOVE RIGHT). Sunburst in a Garden Maze Quilt (detail), Rankin County, Mississippi, c. 1874. Pieced cottons. Courtesy Mississippi Department of Archives and History. Green framing double sets surround sunbursts of orange, pink, and brown roller-printed cottons. The sunbursts were pieced with white material to fill in the areas between the rays, then the whole was pieced into a white background.

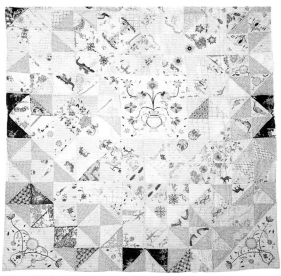

Plate 93 (TOP).
Framed Center Quilt, Maumee, Ohio, 1822. Pieced and embroidered cotton, 78 x 75 in. Smithsonian Institution, Washington, D.C. Made by Margaret Nowlan. The center is embroidered in wools and is dated 1822.

Plate 94 (ABOVE).
Framed Center Quilt, probably Massachusetts, c. 1800. Pieced and embroidered wools on a linen foundation with blue linen fringe; cotton interlining, 92 x 90 in. Smithsonian Institution, Washington, D.C. The border contains wool embroidered birds and flowers interspersed along a serpentine vine.

Plate 95 (TOP).
Crewel-embroidered quilt with pieced border, Connecticut, c. 1750–1800. Polychrome wools worked in twelve large sprays on homespun linen ground, 86 x 84 in. Courtesy Historic Deerfield, Inc., Deerfield, Massachusetts. The quilt has an all-over concentric lozenge quilting. The 10¾-inch border is composed of pieced stars on a linen background, and the backing is pieced of three large homespun fragments.

Plate 96 (ABOVE).
Pieced and Embroidered Counterpane, c. 1790–1800. Pieced cotton and linen cloth embroidered with wool yarns, 82 x 63 in. Courtesy Old Sturbridge Village, Sturbridge, Massachusetts. Found near Haverhill, Massachusetts, this quilt top is embroidered with imaginary birds and beasts and a variety of floral motifs. Some of the cottons are block printed. The crewel work, executed on linen, appears to be 18th century.

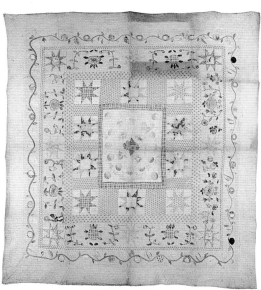

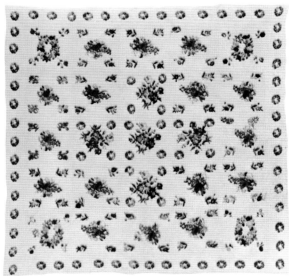

Plate 97 (TOP).
One-Patch Embroidered Quilt (detail), c. 1810–40. Pieced and embroidered wool; brown linen backing, 74 x 61 in. (child's bed size). Courtesy The Henry Francis du Pont Winterthur Museum, Winterthur, Delaware. Alternate squares are embroidered in polychrome wools; the quilting is diagonal.

Plate 98 (ABOVE).
Framed Center Quilt, c. 1800–1850. Pieced, appliquéd, and embroidered cotton; homespun back, 77 x 70 in. Courtesy The New-York Historical Society. The center is a printed handkerchief. The larger flowers in the border appear to be printed and motifs are outlined in embroidery. The quilting is in a cross-hatched pattern.

Plate 99 (TOP).
Block-Printed Quilt Back. 84 x 84 in. Formerly collection of New York State Historical Society, Cooperstown. Said to be designed and printed by Dan Pratt (1787–1813) in Connecticut or New York. There are few areas of solid color; shading is accomplished by hatching in delicate parallel lines in the block.

Plate 100 (ABOVE).
Berlin Embroidered Quilt, probably Virginia. Embroidered cotton, 98 x 98 in. Private collection. The heavily stuffed and quilted foundation appears to be earlier than the Berlin-work embroidery motifs characteristic of the third quarter of the 19th century.

The Quilt 141

BINDINGS

After the quilt is taken from the frame, the very last step is to bind up the edges. A palette of possibilities abound.

An early method was a self-binding technique in which the backing material was brought over to the front of the quilt, folded over and sewed down. To allow for this, the backing material was made an inch or so larger than the top and the interlining. Another early technique was to even off the edges of the top and the backing, turn them in toward each other, and then whip the edges together in an over-and-over stitch.

Throughout the second and third quarters of the nineteenth century, a popular method was to insert a piping of cotton cloth between the top and the fold that was brought over from the backing (see plate 126, left). Probably the most common binding method is that in which a simple length of half-inch-wide fabric, cut on the bias, is hemmed under and sewn down on both sides of the quilt. This leaves a binding about a quarter-inch wide all the way around the quilt (plate 126, right). When a quilt is bound in this manner, it may be a hint of a repaired edge.

Bindings were used not only for quilts, but for bed curtains and bed valances, as well, and they were available for purchase at an early date. An advertisement in the *New York Mercury* in 1766 offers:

> Richard WENHAM, *Upholster, in Little Queen's Street, opposite the New-York Arms, has to sell: A Parcel of live feathers, very cheap for Cash or short Credit; likewise has to sell, all Sort of bed Binding, of different Colours; he has likewise to sell, Tossels and Linen for Window Curtains.*[23]

Whatever the binding, the neatness of the edging was very important to old-time quilters. It was considered a mark of perfection to

Plate 101.
Left: Quilt binding on appliquéd quilt, mid-19th century. A piping of cotton cloth has been inserted between the top and the fold brought over from the backing. Right: Quilt binding on pieced quilt, c. 1850–75. A bias tape is hemmed under and sewn down on the front and back of the quilt to hide the unfinished edge. Both quilts collection of the authors.

23. Gottesman, *op. cit.*, page 141.

have the narrowest, most unobtrusive binding possible, with absolutely invisible stitches. On eighteenth- and early nineteenth-century quilts, the binding was usually no more than an eighth-inch in width.

There were two "fancy" techniques for finishing a quilt: tape and fringe. In the eighteenth and early nineteenth centuries, narrow linen and cotton tapes were frequently used as a means for binding off a quilt. The tape itself—also known as braid—was a rather important article around the house. It was used when a drawstring was needed, or a tie for a bonnet or a sewing pocket; it was the loop by which the bed curtain was hung on its rod, and it served as decorative trimming on bedhangings and curtains. It was even used for garters to hold up socks and suspenders.

Tape was both imported and made at home on a small hand-held loom. One finds repeated mention of these braid looms, tape looms, and garter looms in household inventories. The simplest handmade looms contained only the heddle board, a truly ancient contrivance (plate 102). The more sophisticated looms were simply carved wooden boxes, sometimes mahogany, that contained the heddle board, the frame, the cloth beam, and the ratchet (see plate 105). These boxes sat on a lap or on a table and sometimes adorned the drawing room. Work on these looms was deemed appropriate for a gentlewoman. Besides being a drawing room pastime during the seventeenth, eighteenth, and nineteenth centuries, making tape was a household necessity practiced in the plainest homes. It was simply an elementary weaving process. A child of seven or eight could weave a professional-looking tape. The design possibilities were limitless, depending on the skill of the weaver. Tapes one-eighth to one and a half inches wide were woven on these looms, and a housewife could weave a few inches a day as pick-up work in her spare time. They could be all white and of simple weave (plate 106), or they might be a pattern woven in many colors (plate 107). Not only were they used to form binding on quilts, but they could also be used as ornamentation, as in the Braid Framed Octagons Counterpane (plate 109).

The other "fancy" method for finishing the edge of a quilt was the addition of a fringe. Like tapes, fringes were made in complete lengths, in varying widths, to be added to the fabric of the maker's choosing. They were most popularly used to decorate quilts, other bed furnishings, and table covers. The earliest known American pieced quilt (plate 3) made in 1704, is edged with a handmade woolen ball fringe. The type that we see most often on quilts is the white linen or cotton woven or netted fringe that is found on the all-white quilts of the late eighteenth and early nineteenth centuries.

Two methods employed in making fringe were weaving and netting.

Plate 102.
Rigid heddle board, Quebec, 19th century. 27 x 8 in. Royal Ontario Museum, Toronto. A paddle-shaped tool for weaving narrow bands and tapes for household use. Two sets of warp threads are threaded through all the way across and from the same side: one set through a hole, the other through a slit. The threads through the hole remain stationary, those in the slit move above and below them. The weft was passed through and beaten into place.

Plate 103 (ABOVE).
One-Patch Stenciled Quilt, probably New Hampshire, c. 1830–40. Pieced, painted, and stenciled cotton and linen, 78 x 62 in. Courtesy Old Sturbridge Village, Sturbridge, Massachusetts. The pheasants and tree-trunk squares are cut from a roller print made about 1830. The motifs in the alternate squares have a shaded quality that suggests a stenciled technique touched up afterward with paint.

Plate 104 (LEFT).
Framed Center Quilt, possibly English, Irish, or American, c. 1775–1800. Appliquéd cotton and linen, 101 x 89 in. Brooklyn Museum; Dick S. Ramsay Fund. The storytelling design is worked in appliqué done with tiny cross stitches. Details of costume embroidery are worked in silk.

Woven fringes were made on tape looms with the addition of a device called a "fringe guide." Many woven fringes are attached first to a tape that in turn is attached to the quilt. Some woven fringes actually seem to grow out of a narrow tape band. They are apt to range from one to four inches in depth (plate 110).

A ship's invoice mentions fringe being imported from England in 1690:

> *Sundry Lotts of Goods:*
> *18 doz Narrow Fringe to sett on ye top of fringe*
> *18 yards White Corded Thred fringe*
> *13 oz. Silke fringe*
> *27 oz. best Narrow and Deep ditto*
> *18 oz. White Nar & Deep mixtd.*
> *21 oz. Culler'd blew and white Nar & Deep*[24]

The second method, netting, is an ancient craft; Egyptian mummies were buried in tunics of netting over 3000 years ago. The craft evolved over the centuries from its use in fishnets and bird-catching devices; it has been a drawing-room art in Europe and the British Isles since the sixteenth century; and Mary Queen of Scots even did netted work during her imprisonment in 1568. Instruments needed for netting are a needle to carry the thread and a smooth stick called the "mesh." The process is

Plate 105 (ABOVE LEFT).
Band loom with rigid heddle, Nova Scotia, 19th century. 12 1/2 x 7 1/2 x 20 in. Royal Ontario Museum, Toronto. When a rigid heddle is mounted in a frame the device becomes a band loom. These could sit on a lap or table for drawing room tape making.

Plate 106 (ABOVE RIGHT).
Quilt binding on pieced quilt, mid-19th century. Collection of the authors. The edge of the quilt is bound with hand-loomed tape of a simple weave.

24. Dow, *op. cit.*, page 47.

Plate 107.
Quilt binding on pieced quilt, c. 1825–50. Collection of the authors. The edge of the quilt is bound with a multicolored, patterned hand-loomed tape.

Plate 108.
Block-printed wallpaper, France, c. 1795–1800. Courtesy Nancy McClelland. Styles in wallpaper and printed textiles have often imitated or paralleled one another. Quilts have also incorporated such styles; in this case, the small medallions.

Plate 109.
Braid Framed Octagons Counterpane, early 19th century. Appliquéd and embroidered cottons, 91 x 94 in. Shelburne Museum, Shelburne, Vermont. Designs of birds, beasts, and flowers are cut out of imported chintzes and appliquéd to the quilt with a buttonhole stitch. Seventeen of the appliqué units have been framed in octagons of hand-loomed stripe braid.

simply a succession of loops secured in position by knots. The knots must be stretched while in progress, or the loops will come out all different sizes if the knots are not drawn tight. The stretching is accomplished by pinning the foundation loop of the netting to a lead cushion or weighted pillow (plate 111).

Netting, sometimes referred to as knotting,[25] was taught to young

25. There is another, unrelated technique also known as knotted work.

  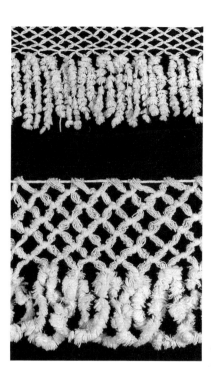

ladies along with the other needlecrafts. Knotted trimmings, tassels, and fringes of cotton, linen, silk, and wool were seen very frequently on curtains and bed furnishings throughout much of the seventeenth and eighteenth centuries and the first quarter of the nineteenth century. Scholars have noted "fringe averaging some two inches in depth during the 18th and early 19th century."[26]

Heavy fringes and elaborate knotted borders have been associated with bed furniture from the 16th century. They helped the curtains to hang well even in a draughty room, an important consideration when there would be candles burning within.[27]

An edging done by machine does not necessarily indicate that the whole quilt was done by machine, or that the quilt is of a late date. Since they were the first to wear, edgings were often replaced more than once in the life of a frequently used quilt. And, though the last repair may be contemporary, the quilt itself may be decades older. It is said that some

26. Cummings, *op. cit.*, page 57.
27. Therle Hughes, *English Domestic Needlework, 1660–1860*, New York, Macmillan Company, 1961, page 122.

(FROM LEFT TO RIGHT)

Plate 110.
Three woven fringes, 1 in., 1 ⅜ in., and 2 ½ in. deep. Smithsonian Institution, Washington, D.C. This was a popular method for finishing the edge of a quilt, particularly in the first half of the 19th century.

Plate 111.
Two netted fringes, 5 in. and 3 in. deep. Smithsonian Institution, Washington, D.C. This is a simple netting with additional tassels added by looping and knotting cut pieces to the bottom edge between the knots.

Plate 112.
Two netted fringes, 5 in. deep. Smithsonian Institution, Washington, D.C. Around the dangling cotton strings of the tassels were knotted short lengths of cotton yarns, producing a chenille effect.

quilters preferred to edge their quilts by strong machine sewing anyway, because the quilts were subject to so much wear and punishment and this would insure their long life. There were many early quilters who took exception to this, as they felt that nothing was stronger or more reliable than a seam hand-sewn by an expert. Prejudice for the hand predominates, often for good reason.

Thus we end our analysis of various parts of the quilt: top, interlining, backing, borders, edges. Just as a good drama often depends upon plot more than words or stage-setting, so the good quilt depends to an underrated extent on its structural elements. Not merely the colorful geometrics of cloth create the abiding value of this American art form, but the careful way in which the multiplicity of functional aspects has been handled. The quilt is not solely some dazzlingly decorative artifact, but a well-wrought structural entity, each part working in its crafted configuration.

3
Quilting

The contemporary eye is accustomed to looking at and appreciating a quilt in terms of its color and design. If one looks even more closely, however, it becomes apparent that the extraordinarily intricate stitchery that went into the quilting is where a great part of the art lies. In fact, fine stitchery rather than piecing was considered the highest accomplishment of the quilt maker during the eighteenth and nineteenth centuries.

One rarely sees examples of elaborate quilting made today. Its execution requires a mastery of needlework skills that comes from the kind of needlework training and background in hand sewing that has not existed in this country for many years. An old-time quilt maker

> used a needle as often, as easily, as casually as we use a telephone; it was her duty, her comfort, her companion, her mode of self-expression. And when she undertook a project of great magnitude, she was not just passing time or doing a bit of show-off needlework, she was making a statement about herself: about her skill, her patience, her ability to endure endless days of hard work and tedium for the sake of the pattern of the whole, and ultimately of her sense of her own value as a human being.[1]

And even during the time when a woman was expected to be highly skilled in all the needleworking arts, there was a considerable appreciation, if not awe, for the patience and technique required by the lavishly stitched quilts.

Quilting, the lines of stitching used to join the three layers of the quilt, was both decorative and functional. The function was to prevent the outer layers from shifting and to secure the inner batting that would otherwise have shredded and lumped and rolled off into the corners of

---

1. Beth Gutcheon, *The Perfect Patchwork Primer*, New York, David McKay Co., 1973, page 12.

Plate 113.
Quilting in running stitch (detail),
19th century. Cotton. Courtesy
Chester County Historical Society,
David Townsend House, West
Chester, Pennsylvania. Diamond
pattern background filler on all-white
quilt. The ends of the threads were run
under each other or lodged in the
interlining so they were invisible on
the top of the quilt.

Plate 114 (OPPOSITE).
Mariner's Compass Quilt (detail),
1834. Pieced polychrome roller-
printed cottons. Courtesy Mary
Strickler's Quilt Gallery, San Rafael,
California. In this quilt by Mary Royer
Strickler (1814–1890), minutely
spaced parallel lines form the ground
pattern, while graceful arches and
circles of princess feathers fill in
alternate blocks and adorn the borders.

the coverlet. In choosing quilting patterns, the maker first considered how her quilt was going to be used. If it was to be one of the many everyday quilts, she most likely chose the most straightforward possible pattern—outline quilting, which echoed the shapes in the patchwork, lines of parallel quilting, or a simple grid. If the quilt was for show or the "best bed," she generally combined filler patterns and decorative ones. Ornamental figurations were worked on the plain spaces formed by borders, sets, and blank blocks between patchwork areas, and the remainder was quilted with parallel lines or grids. An all-white quilt is often covered with ornamental patterns.

After the quilting design was decided upon, the top had to be marked for quilting. Marking meant tracing a design for quilting on the right side of the quilt top. Even expert quilters required lines to quilt by. There were two procedures for this: marking the design out all at one time before the quilt top was placed on the frame, or marking it after it was in the frame. On frames that required rolling, the marking would be done section by section as the work was rolled. This was quite a difficult method, for the stitcher was compelled to conceive of her pattern in its entirety while only being able to see and mark the relatively small section that was unrolled and nearest to her at that moment. Only the more professional quilters could properly employ that method because it required designing almost entirely by intuition. If all the figuring was to be intuitive, only a tremendous amount of practice could result in accuracy of measurement, marking, and quilting. Obviously it was to the advantage of most quilters to mark their pattern on beforehand, because then they had a chance to visualize the overall pattern and prevent mistakes later.

Marking was considered artwork, and as such intimidated even very proficient needlewomen. Consequently, from a very early period, it was possible to have someone else mark out your pattern for you. There are records of professional quilting pattern makers from the eighteenth century in England, and a specific reference to a tailor in the eighteenth century who gained a measure of fame not for his skill as a suit- or dressmaker, but because he drew quilting patterns on quilts for the local women.[2] It was a natural profession for a tailor's apprentice or even a portrait painter with a steady hand and a good head for design. Drawing a quilting pattern on material took from two to five days. (It was common to have an elaborately patterned waistcoat drawn up as well as a bedcover.)

Pattern drawing, marking, and instruction in quilting were services

2. Averil Colby, *Quilting*, New York, Charles Scribner's Sons, 1971, page 42.

available to American women as well. An advertisement in a Boston paper dated 1747 stated that "'Sarah Hunt' dwelling in the house of James Nicol in School Street, also stamped Counterpins, curtains, linens and cottons for quilting with Fidelity and Despatch."[3]

Another advertisement in the *Boston Gazette*, September 26–October 3, 1737, offered: "All sorts of Drawing for Embroidery, Children's quilted Peaks, drawn or work'd; Caps set for Women and Children; or any sort of Needle Work, done by Mrs. Mary Sewall, Widow, near the Orange Tree."[4] Still another ad, in the *New York Gazette* in 1731, was placed by a Martha Gazley, who taught, among other things, "Pencil Work upon Muslin." This might easily have been someone who would mark a quilt for others.

And of course there were needlewomen who did such work for others for a minimal fee. In a mid-nineteenth-century letter, Miss Rebecca Day of Jackson, Tennessee, writes that she had her "quilt marked for two dollars by the seamstress who lived down the street."[5] It was not too long after this that in the large cities one could purchase a stamped pattern of bowls of fruit, baskets of flowers, cornucopias, and groupings of birds for tracing onto a quilt top. These were probably the work of enterprising seamstresses.

It is probably safe to say that most women marked the quilting pattern themselves. There were many ways to put the pattern on the cloth. For the gifted, it could be done freehand with a pencil, or a cake of chalk or soap; for the less artistic a tracing pattern was needed. In many cases, a pattern, or template, was created in the desired shape and used again and again on successive new quilts. Templates could be made of cardboard, buckram, tin, wood, or a homemade conglomeration of whatever was available, such as starched fabric.

The quilter who wanted to pin her template to the quilt top would cut hers out of stiff cardboard or some other substance that would both be durable and pliable and would withstand many pinnings. Ruth Finley describes a template made from "mill-net" that belonged to her mother and grandmother. This was cut from a thick open-mesh material that had been stiffened with starch or glue.

Some women had their husbands fashion templates for them of wood or tin. Plates 115 and 116 illustrate two wooden quilting templates,

---

3. *Ibid.*, page 44.
4. George Francis Dow, *The Arts and Crafts in New England, 1704–1775: Gleanings from Boston Newspapers,* Topsfield, Mass., Wayside Press, 1927, page 274.
5. Collection of the authors.

carved of walnut, from the Memorial Hall Collection at Old Deerfield, Massachusetts. Inside the box in which they were found was a piece of chalk, which was probably rubbed on the raised areas so that a faint trace would be left when the block was pressed down on the fabric. Repeating this process over and over would quickly do the work of marking a quilt.

There was a wooden template in the collection of Mrs. Florence Peto that she called a quilting block and described as somewhat resembling a butter mold except that on the quilting block the design is in relief instead of incised. She noted:

Sailors from Nantucket Island and all along the New England coast carved such blocks from lightweight wood, presents for their quiltmaking

Plate 115 (TOP).
Wooden quilting template in shell pattern. Walnut, 6 x 5 in. Memorial Hall, Deerfield, Massachusetts.

Plate 116 (ABOVE).
Wooden quilting template in ocean wave pattern. Walnut, 11 x 3 x 1 in. Memorial Hall, Deerfield, Massachusetts.

Plate 117 (LEFT).
Top: Teardrop-shaped quilting templates of graduated sizes and fitted case, 19th century. Tin, 4 ½ x 2 in. Left: C-clamp with heart-shaped turning, 19th century. 4 ½ x 2 ½ in. Used to hold together a quilting frame where the two poles crossed. Lower right: Sewing bird with heart-shaped turning, c. 1750. 5 x 3 ½ in. Materials were slipped into the bird's beak by depressing its tail, which is worked by a strong spring. All collection of the authors.

womenfolk. The quilter would dust the face of the block with chalk and transfer the pattern to the material.[6]

Another mention of this type of early template seems to refer to the same type of template: "Some quilting templates have come down to us made of mahogany with tiny little knobs in the center for handles."[7]

Plate 117 illustrates a whole set of tin teardrop-shaped templates made in graduated sizes and fitted into their own teardrop-shaped tin case. Possibly these were dipped into a diluted solution of indigo or berry juice and then pressed onto the quilt. It is also possible that no accessory marking solution at all was used with these templates. One possible advantage of permanent templates such as these over paper ones might have been that these could be pressed down to leave an impression on the cloth, thus avoiding the necessity of having to mark quilting lines in pencil and ink. It is speculation that these were owned by professional quilters and wealthy women.

Another method of marking a pattern on a quilt top was the pricking and pouncing technique, which required not a template but a pattern-making aid of paper. There were two ways to do this: a particular pattern was outlined or traced onto a piece of paper, and the piece of paper was laid onto the quilt top; it was then pricked all around with the point of a pencil, leaving on the fabric the shape created by dotted pencil marks. The second was to prick the pattern all around with something sharp that would leave a small hole—an ice pick or upholstery needle—and then sift a dry powder through these holes, leaving a pattern of dots. A dead ember from the fireplace would provide a source of powdered charcoal to sift through the holes of the pattern. Cocoa and cinnamon mixed with cornstarch were also used. Some quilters joined the dots afterward with penciled lines.

The choice of a quilt-marking technique was an important one because in many cases the needleworker—especially when she had a very fine heirloom quilt in her mind's eye—had no intention of washing her quilt even once, and certainly not if it wasn't dirty. So the marking medium, if possible, had to be immediately fugitive. It was for this reason that the really finicky quilters would scratch closely around the template with a sewing, rug, or yarn needle or similar instrument, holding it almost parallel to the work surface with a slight but steady pressure kept on the pointed end. When the template was removed, the scratched line showed

6.   Peto, *op. cit.*, page 169.
7.   Elizabeth King, *Quilting*, Leisure League of America, 1934, New York, page 65.

clearly enough to be seen, and this indentation would last, it was hoped, until the sewing was finished. Sometimes a roweled dressmaking wheel, riding spur, or pie crimper was used to make the indentation.

Early-twentieth-century newspaper articles frowned on patterns stamped on or put on with transfer paper as being too hard to wash out and crude-looking rather than delicate. One warns: "Never use transfer patterns because many a quilt has been ruined by heavy marking that cannot be removed without washing."[8] Another advises: "Too much cannot be said about light marking. Old time quilters marked with their needles so that not a mark shows, or they simply pressed the template down hard enough to leave an impression."[9] When the sewing machine first arrived on the scene it was not readily accepted by all. There were some women who felt its only worth in quilting was as a marking tool. They ran the quilt top carefully through the unthreaded machine, leaving lines of perforations to use as quilting guides. But the sewing would be done by hand. Perforated patterns for pricking and pouncing were also made this way.

No template of any sort was required when the quilting followed the patterns of the pieced or appliquéd designs, and there was also no template required for the filler patterns. Straight lines were marked with a home-made ruler, yardstick, T-square, and a soft lead pencil or chalk or a charred, pointed stick, or a stretched and snapped chalked string. For this last method, a length of string is drawn repeatedly through chalk or powdered starch and stretched over the quilt and held tightly. It is then pulled up taut and let fly back onto the quilt with a snap, leaving a chalked image of a straight white line. This was usually done after the quilt was in the frame. It was, however, considered a primitive method by the experts because it was unscientific and usually made for very uneven cross-hatching. One can easily see that, for lines scarcely a quarter-inch apart (as on the more finely quilted pieces), this method could lead to serious trouble.

For circular motifs, necessity was again the mother of invention. If there was not a plate, cup, saucer, or wineglass of exactly the right size, a compass was improvised. This consisted of a pencil, a large pin, and a piece of twine. The pin was lodged firmly in the center of the proposed circle in a thin twine loop. The string was made as long as the desired radius and the pencil placed in an outer loop. Then the pencil was rotated around the pin to draw a circle. Cookie cutters were used for more elaborate motifs.

When a top was ready to be quilted it was placed on a quilting

8.   Prudence Penny, "Old Time Quilts," *Seattle Post-Intelligencer*, 1927, page 19.
9.   Marguerite Francis, "Quilting," *St. Louis Post Dispatch*, 1928, page 11.

Plate 118.
Quilting in sharecropper's home near Pace, Mississippi, 1939. The frame hangs from the ceiling and is stabilized against the bedstead.

frame. (Frames are described in detail in chapter 4.) This was done in different ways depending on the type of frame. With the old, full-size frames, the four poles that formed the frame were first clamped together to the exact size of the quilt top. The two longest bars had ticking tacked down on them with little nails all the way along. Then a sheet of backing was sewn with strong thread to the ticking. The interlining was spread carefully over this, and then the top was smoothed in place and the three layers were basted with gigantic stitches to prevent the layers from shifting while the quilting was in progress. Sometimes the basting stitches formed a huge grid, but more often they radiated outward from the center of the quilt. It was considered best to work from the middle outward to avoid a lump in the center. Generally the sides of the quilt were then stretched to the side beams of the frame with loops of tape. Because the quilt was then stretched very tightly, the stitching holding the edges to the frame was greatly strained, and usually the edges of the quilt were well shredded by the time the work was finished. This is why an extra strip of fabric was often needed to bind a quilt in place of self-binding techniques. After quilting, the raveled edges were considered unfit to be seen and had to be hidden in an accessory piece of cloth.

For rolling ratchet frames or quilting hoops, the three layers were laid out on the grass in the summertime, or on the floor in wintertime, and basted by hand. Then the bars of the quilting frame were removed and placed on the ground, one at the top of the quilt and one at the bottom, and with a heavy thread the edges of the quilt were basted to the bars. Two women would take hold of one of the bars and begin rolling, leaving about a two foot width or whatever the width of the frame was. Then the bars were carried to the frame and adjusted, the unrolled bar first. Pegs were inserted at either end to keep it in place and then the other bar was put in place and its pegs inserted. The quilter would then begin working on one side, rolling under after each section was completed until the full bulk of the quilt was transferred to the second stretcher. Or if she was working with her friends who were quilting at the other side of the frame, they would roll the quilt back until it was evenly distributed on each stretcher and begin quilting in the middle. Frames of this type were not more than two arm-lengths across so that the quilters on each side could reach to the middle. This was one of the reasons quilt making was considered the work of older folk; it required long arms, larger hands, greater strength.

American quilting has always been done using a running stitch, worked by simply manipulating the needle in and out so that each stitch is divided from the next by a space. The smaller the stitches, the more nearly the quilter created the illusion of an unbroken line. European quilters more usually employed a backstitch, which almost did form an unbroken line of stitching on the front and created alternate single and double stitches on the back. But the disadvantages of the backstitch were that, although it was stronger, it was far more time-consuming, and it required a third again as much thread as the running stitch.

Very fine American quilting prides itself on two things. First, the stitches and the spaces between should be absolutely even and as small as possible, and the stitches on the back should be as even as those on the front—a very demanding criterion because of the thickness of the material between. Second, it should be impossible to discover where each thread began and ended; the end must not be secured with knots or backstitching that will show. As nearly as we can discover without taking fine quilts apart, this was done one of two ways. The first was simply to run the end of the thread off into the batting under the next line to be stitched, so that the end would be caught and held (though it is hard to believe that this was really strong enough), and the second was to tie a single knot in the thread and jerk gently until the knot popped through the top and lodged in the interlining.

Whenever possible, the quilter began a line of stitching an armlength away and quilted toward her; to quilt away from the body forced her to hold her arm and fingers in an impossibly cramped position. But intricate patterns required her to quilt in all directions, especially since working at a frame prevented her from moving her work around to the most comfortable position as she would when embroidering or even working at a sewing machine. So some quilters simply ended the thread and began again from another direction whenever the line of stitching angled away from them; the best of them had several needles in the work at one time and learned to work equally well with both hands, so that if it was hard to maneuver with the right hand, the chair could be shifted to complete the line with the left hand.

The unending lines of the filler or background patterns were also done by keeping several needles in action at one time. When doing the diamond pattern, for example, instead of sewing one line as far as possible and then sewing on the next, quilters would stitch a little way along one line, then carry the next one forward with another needle, and so on.

The importance of tiny, even stitches was emphasized in an old saying that dismissed large, uneven stitches as "toenail catchers." The stitching of the quilting in some pieces is so even and perfect that it appears to be machine sewing. Don't be misled by this. Some women were nearly as proficient as the sewing machine; only perusal with a magnifying glass can show minute irregularities that confirm a handstitched piece. On the more elaborately quilted pieces the stitches were minuscule. Dr. William Rush Dunton, Jr., a Maryland researcher in the field of quilts, tells of a Baltimore quilt that had stitches so fine that three people and a magnifying glass were needed to measure them. The quilt was found to have five stitches to every three millimeters.

The actual quilting was done in some instances with a longer than average needle and in other instances with one much shorter. Among quilters there seemed to be two schools of thought. Some said that a fairly long needle should be used because the ordinary sewing needle was not sufficient to go through the three layers and take three or four stitches before running the thread through. Those of the shorter needle or "between needle" school swore by it because they said it encouraged shorter stitches. In fact, the "right" length of needle for quilting had to do with style and personal preference, because with the material stretched very taut on the frames it was impossible to push a needle in and out more than three or four times without the stitches becoming impossibly sloppy. One thing a great many old-time quilters were in agreement about, however, was the value of the needles that had become bent with use. Apparently a slightly curved instrument enabled them to do more intricate needlework because of the ease with which it could be pushed through a taut surface. It was a matter of taste; but the important point was to have all the stitches catch all the layers. It was for this reason that the quilter held one hand underneath the frame and grazed the tip of the finger with every stitch to be sure all three layers had been pierced. A veteran quilter had permanently pocked finger tips and eventually developed a hard callous. Less experienced quilters sometimes pricked themselves hard enough to bleed onto the quilt back, and though the spot was immediately dabbed with cotton dipped in cold water, the shadow of the stain often remained to damn even the finest quilt in the eyes of the judges at the county fair.

It is said that some quilters preferred to work standing up, especially if they were working from the center of the quilt out to the edges, though it is hard to see how this could be done and still keep a hand under the quilt to monitor the work, and it would have been most unorthodox to quilt without the hand underneath. But sitting at the frame long hours was enormously tiring to the back, and, perhaps to give relief from the same position all day, the sort of frame that was suspended from the ceiling might have been raised to the height of a standing worker.

Quilting was born of the discovery that two or three pieces of material sewn together were warmer and stronger than one piece. Quilting patterns must have come from a discovery that diagonal lines held woven material together more firmly than lines that followed the woven grain of the material, and circular lines were even better.

The sources of quilting patterns, like pieced and appliquéd design motifs, are infinite and universal. The strong geometrical form seen over and over again in the quilting is as ancient as the mosaic, as familiar as the cross-hatching in basketry. Similarly, flora and fauna have provided unlimited inspiration for naturalistic themes in quilting, ranging from formal representations to very primitive impressions. Pictures and symbols are quilted in the forms of ships' anchors, horseshoes, hearts, crosses, eagles, and houses, and there are freehand quilting motifs which include writing and experimental themes in contemporary quilts (see plate 123). There is also outline quilting, which follows the edges of the pieced or appliquéd motifs.

As we have pointed out, not all quilting patterns have come from the mind of the needleworker herself, but undoubtedly the great majority of patterns have evolved out of the creativity and imagination of the

Plate 119.
Rose of Sharon Variation Quilt (detail), mid-19th century.
Appliquéd cotton with diamond quilting. Courtesy Museum of
Fine Arts, Boston.

Plate 120.
Reverse of quilt (detail), mid-19th century. Cotton and linen.
Collection of Mr. and Mrs. Leonard Balish. The quilting
follows the outline of the appliquéd floral motif on the top.

Plate 121.
Delectable Mountains Quilt, detail of block quilting design of
urn with flowers. Courtesy Miss Louise Judson Cooke. Made
by Nancy Cooke Scovill in Waterbury, Connecticut, prior to
her marriage in 1821. Block quilting designs fill the spaces
between the pieced and appliquéd motifs.

Plate 122.
Roses and Buds Quilt, detail of block quilting design of
geranium with fern, mid-19th century. Collection of Bill
Pearson.

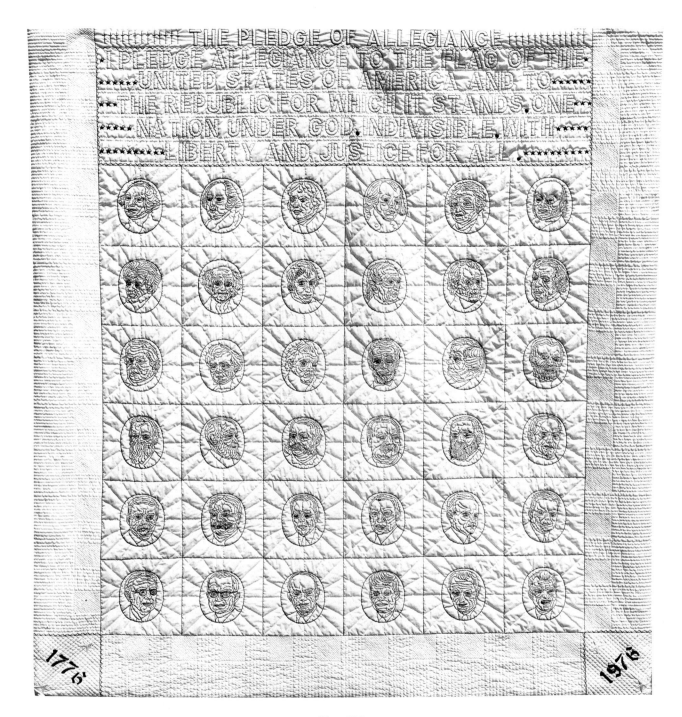

Plate 123.
President's Quilt, Dayton, Ohio, 1972. Red, blue, and black thread quilted on a white cotton
ground, 100 x 90 in. Made by Mary Borkowski, a contemporary quilt maker of great
originality. The images of thirty-six presidents—from Washington to Nixon—are quilted in
black thread in 12-inch squares. The Pledge of Allegiance is quilted and stuffed, and quilted
flags flank the borders.

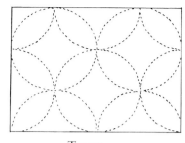

Teacup

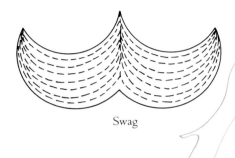

Swag

ordinary housewife and farmwoman. For a great number of these pioneer women, there were no schools of design, and they drew their inspirations from the things they saw around them, and from ideas handed down from past generations. There seem to have been no written records of the names of quilting patterns before the twentieth century, when people who wrote quilt books began to chronicle names that they either remembered or drew from the memories of older quilt makers who recalled what their mothers had learned from their grandmothers. Almost all of the history of design of American quilting and patchworking has come by word of mouth retelling of handed-down examples or, in more plain language, good memories.

Names of quilting patterns seem to have been very localized. Among women of a certain locality, there was a common understanding of what name fit what pattern. As in piecework patterns, one quilting design can have many names. For example, the rope design is also known as cable, twist, trail, plait, chain, and braid, and one woman called it the plate because that was what she used to make it.

There were three areas of quilting patterns: the fillings, or overall patterns; the block designs or single motifs for areas left blank in the patchwork; and running designs, used for borders and framing devices.

The fillings were used either for an all over design covering the whole quilt, or as a background to emphasize other quilting details. Shown are some of the standard patterns. These are all worked in small, close, running stitches.

The block quilting designs were single motifs used in a variety of ways, most frequently as a decorative technique on plain blocks, alternating with appliquéd or pieced blocks. These designs, however, are certainly not limited to this use. They are found in corners, in central medallions, and fitted in as an adornment wherever an open space was available. The following is a catalog of old standard block quilting motifs:

Bouquets—Of roses, lilies, daisies, sunflowers, tulips, or any garden favorites.

Leaves—Laurel, oak, ivy. One quilter recalls the fact that her mother and grandmother used to pick sprays of oak leaves, ivy, clover, and thistles, bringing them home to study in the evening, before making the decision of which should form the basis for a quilting design. Acanthus leaves were a much-used motif by early American craftsmen. Many late eighteenth- and nineteenth-century houses have acanthus carvings around their fireplaces and the inside of the front door.

Pineapple—Longtime symbol of hospitality. Seen in woodcarving over and over: pilasters on chests of drawers, mahogany and cherry mirror frames, clocks, and legs of candle stands and tables.

Weeping Willow—An early design.

Eagle—Dates before 1800.

Dove of Peace—Known to have been used before 1800. Dove was also a gentle slang term for woman, precursor of "hen."

American Harp or Lyre—This design is said to have been used in the north of England since 1600. It is found on very early American quilts, probably brought over by English immigrants.

Shell—Popular in England in the seventeenth century, used on armor, it is one of the oldest of all quilting designs.

Patriotic Motifs—Anchors, flags, Liberty Bells, log cabins, shields, sheafs of arrows, state shields or arms, banners containing *E Pluribus Unum*, and Miss Liberty.

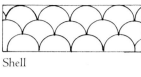
Shell

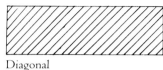
Diagonal

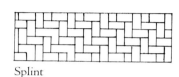
Splint

Cornucopia	Swirl or whorl	Fruit
Basket of flowers	Stars	Half moon
Flower spray	Heart	Ferns
Pot of flowers	Rosettes	Fan (peacock)
Feather wreath	Crescent	Birds
Feather circle	Persian pear (Paisley)	Bells
Spider web	Cross	Starfish
Ribbons and bows	Circles	

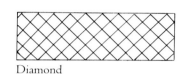
Diamond

The running designs were used for borders and framing devices. Most frequently seen were these motifs:

Herringbone

Serpentine	Rope, cable, braid, twist, trail, plait, chain
Ocean wave	
Running vine	Teacup
Princess feather (originally Prince's feather)	Laurel-leaf chain
	Hammock (cord and tassel)
Intersecting circles	Feather
Acanthus leaves	S-scroll or cyma curve

Basket Weave

Maverick designs—such as words or musical notes that trail or create borders

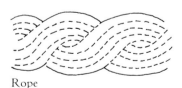
Rope

As in pieced and appliquéd designs, quilting designs also had their share of superstition stitched in. It was believed, for example, that if a cable or a vine was used for a border it should be unbroken by a spray of foliage or a heart or bell, because such a break foretold of a life cut short by disaster or a marriage marred by loss of love, or worse, by tragedy.

4
Tools and Equipment

Quilt makers had a variety of tools in common with other needleworkers, and some specific tools to their own trade, like the quilting frame.

THREAD

To begin with, there was hand-spun linen thread for sewing. While much of it was made in the home, it could be purchased in stores, and quite a bit of hand-spun linen was imported from England as well. Linen thread was commercially manufactured in the seventeenth and eighteenth centuries, even though it was a handmade product.

Silk thread was being imported by the eighteenth century. It was used as the marking thread on the household linens of the eighteenth century, and one sees it used with the all-silk quilts. There are also embellishments in silk threads on all types of quilts in the nineteenth century. It would be unusual, however, to find silk sewing thread used in the piecing or quilting of a quilt composed of cottons and linens.

It was not until late in the eighteenth century that cotton thread made its appearance. Until that time, cotton thread spun by hand was neither fine enough nor strong enough to be used very successfully as sewing thread. The story goes that in 1794 Hannah Slater of Pawtucket, Rhode Island, took some fine Surinam cotton yarns from her husband, Samuel, and twisted them onto her own home spinning wheel, thereby creating cotton sewing thread of a sort that could be used practically. However, it did not become a manufactured item at that point. Cotton thread as an industry originated in Scotland. The Clark Brothers built a factory in Paisley in 1812 and they sold thread in hanks in numbers from 12 to 60. About 1820, the thread began to be wound on spools. The spool cost the customer an extra half-penny, which was refunded if the empty spool was returned. This was a three-ply or three-strand thread. Another Paisley family, the Coatses, also manufactured thread at this time, and Andrew Coats brought the thread to the United States in 1840 and began to sell it.

Plate 124 (OPPOSITE).
Cherry Wreaths Quilt, Frankfort, Indiana, c. 1850–75. Appliquéd cotton, 68 x 83 in. Courtesy Art Institute of Chicago. Made by Kate D. Reed. Quilted in feather, circle, and square diamond designs, delicate cherry wreaths of red and green calico alternate with blocks of white muslin.

For approximately the first half of the nineteenth century, the United States imported this three-ply cotton thread and made a small amount domestically. In 1840 larger-scale industry began here. It was the invention of the sewing machine, however, and a six-ply cable thread to use with it, that really launched the thread industry in the United States, at mid-century.

Cotton thread, then, can be a general aid in dating a quilt. There was no cotton thread to speak of in the eighteenth century. The earliest cotton thread, three-ply, was used throughout the nineteenth century and into the twentieth century. The earliest examples of six-ply cotton thread date from 1840. This means that if the end of a loose thread on a quilt is untwisted and found to be made up of six strands (three branches of two threads), then the quilt can date no earlier than the middle of the nineteenth century.

As it is now, thread in the early days was always described by number. For example, a number 12 thread would be very coarse, a number 50 would be a medium weight, and a number 100 would be extremely fine thread. The general consensus is that a medium- to fine-weight thread is the answer for quilting, but it stands to reason that finer stitching with the finest thread will produce the most exquisite results.

Thread figured greatly in determining the cost when the quilting was worked by another person for a fee, but the most salient factor is the total lack of standardization during any period, even in one locality. And certainly there is no relation between price charged and quality of workmanship.

An ordinary spool of cotton thread such as was found in every dry goods store in the old days, and in every dime store now, contains about 200 yards of thread. It takes two and a half to three of these spools to quilt an average-size quilt. A record of quilting done by a church group in 1861 indicates that the price for quilting a quilt 7½ x 7½ feet in "cross bar" quilting with a "fancy feather border" was $2. One author writes that she was told that in 1875 quilting was a dollar per spool. This meant that to have had a whole quilt quilted in 1875 would have been approximately $3. In 1915 when she wrote her book the cost had climbed to $5 per spool or $15 to quilt a whole quilt.

Differing completely were the prices charged by the Dunkards Colony in the 1920s in Ohio. They had two charges: 50¢ a spool for ordinary quilting and 75¢ a spool for intricate quilting. This meant $1.50 and $2.25 respectively for working an entire quilt.

Still other guidelines applied to localities near Topeka, Kansas, in the 1930s. Here the going price was $4 a spool or $12 for a full quilt. Margaret Whittemore, who noted these prices, said that this represented

Plate 125.
Crib Quilt, New Jersey.
Appliquéd cotton, 39 ½ x 40 ¼ in. The Newark Museum. The quilting is done in the fan pattern, and there is an unusual scalloped effect in the petals and buds.

about ten days of fairly steady work. This averages out to about 12¢ an hour. She, too, noted: "This price varies in different localities and women who have reputations for neat or fancy quilting receive much more than that for their work."[1]

Thread may be natural or colored. Dyed threads used in quilting were common in the sixteenth century and were used in the fourteenth-century Sicilian Quilt. Threads of all colors are found in early quilts as well as very late ones.

Thread had to be handled a special way for quilting. The quilter had to choose the finest thread available that was also strong enough to withstand the strain of washing and hard use, for when a quilt became wet the batting grew very heavy, placing great strain on the quilting. Although quilting with ever tinier stitches became its own reward in many circles, it probably began because long, lazy stitches were more likely to snap than small, regular ones.

---

1. Margaret Whittemore, *Quilting*, Caper Publications, Topeka, Kansas, n.d., page 23.

Quilting was done with a single thread, except for occasional wool quilts in which the quilting is much coarser and the thread is doubled for strength: sometimes even yarn is used instead of thread. The quilter tended to use a rather longer thread than is usual in hand sewing, partly because the beginning and ending of each thread is likely to be the weakest point in the quilting and partly to save time in continually having to stop to rethread. However, the longer the thread, the greater the danger that it will knot, requiring the worker to remove the entire line of stitching and begin again. To guard against knotting, many quilters kept a lump of beeswax in their sewing pockets. After threading the needle they would draw the thread through the wax to give it a fine coating and enough stiffness to keep it from balling up. Beeswax cakes are still sold in most notions stores, but since World War II thread makers have offered a cotton thread coated with silicone to take the place of the wax process. It is sometimes marketed as "quilting thread."

NEEDLES

Different sorts of needles were used for different kinds of work. The standard sewing needle is a "sharp," which comes numbered in different sizes; the smaller the number, the fatter the needle. A needleworker generally chose the slimmest needle possible to leave the smallest possible hole, yet one strong enough not to bend or break. Thus the girth of the needle depends in part on the nature of the fabric—a stronger needle for coarse fabrics and the finest for silks and velvets, which retain holes from every needle and basting pin. But it also depended upon the skill and style of the worker. Children were usually taught to sew using blunt needles of the shortest size, which had also a strong tip that would not snap off when used clumsily. For quilting, many women preferred "betweens," also called "quilting needles," which are midway between sharps and blunts in length. Others preferred sharps or even longer needles, which develop a curve from being forced up and down through many layers of material.

Some quilt makers used size 8, 9, or 10 sharps for piece work, then lovingly set them aside for quilting when they began to curve. Others quilted only with straight new betweens, and, when they began to curve, threw them away. This was mainly a matter of style. Fans of the short, straight needle worked by manipulating the needle up and down through the material with the end of the thimble, scarcely using the fingers at all, while the long curved needle enthusiasts held the eye of the needle firmly with the thumb and the index finger. In this way they could prevent the curve of the needle from twisting off in the wrong direction; however, it caused the eye of the needle to bite painfully into the tips of the fingers, and such quilters would often toughen the sensitive areas by dipping their fingers into a solution of alum and water or even cover the area with adhesive tape. If the needle began to stick on hot days or to rust after many years of use, the quilter kept it sliding smoothly by dusting her fingers with chalk or talcum powder. One quilter, attached to her favorite needle and accustomed not to waste anything, used her needle "for 26 years and when the threads wore through the eye, she put it in a rose made of sealing wax and wore it as a stick pin."[2]

PINCUSHIONS

In the sixteenth century, needleworkers often wore pincushions hanging from their waists; these may well have been quilted or made of patchwork. Larger quilted and ornamented pincushions that remained on the dressing or sewing table have survived from the seventeenth and eighteenth centuries. In America patchwork pincushions filled with emery powder were popular; the emery powder served to sharpen and polish rusty needles that might otherwise snag or stain fine fabric. Garden-variety pincushions available in notions stores today very often have a small bag of emery dangling from the top. In the old days a quilter may have had several needles threaded with different colors and stuck into the emery strawberry to keep them sharp and bright and to save the bits of thread.

THIMBLES

For patchwork, many quilt makers favored tailor's thimbles, which leave the top of the finger exposed; this interfered less with their dexterity in picking up tiny patches or threading needles. However, for quilting, the short, straight-needle-style quilters needed a thimble that protected the end of the finger, and it was not uncommon for such a thimble to be worn right through by the pressure of the eye of the quilting needle.

BODKINS

In Alexander Pope's *Rape of the Lock* (published in 1712), the tiny spirits who were set to guard Belinda were warned that if they failed in their duty they would

---

2. Rose Wilder Lane, *Woman's Day Book of American Needlework,* Simon and Schuster, New York, 1963, page 57.

Plate 126.
Baskets Quilt, 1902. Pieced blue cotton and yellow calico. America Hurrah,
New York. Dated and signed "L.F.G.," the quilt displays highly successful use of
geometric forms.

Be stopped in Vials, or transfixed with pins
Or plunged in lakes of bitter washes lie
Or wedged whole ages in a bodkin's eye

In Pope's time a certain type of bodkin was an ornament much like a stickpin, worn in the hair. But the quilting bodkin is a kind of thick needle made of wood, metal, or ivory, used as a stiletto for punching holes or for picking out seams in clothing that was to be revamped. Before the days of the seam ripper not only was the cloth reused but the thread as well. The bodkin was also used to prod wisps of stuffing into padded quilting through a hole in the back of the work, and to draw yarn or heavy thread between parallel lines of stitching to form corded quilting.

TEMPLATES

Templates were made for every piece of a particular size and shape that was to be repeated throughout a patchwork design. In piecework, this meant a template for each size of square, triangle, circle, and hexagon, and, in applique, a template for every grape and leaf or other motif, unless each one in the entire design was to be different. The template was cut out of stiff paper, cardboard, or soft metal in the exact size and shape of the finished piece. The quilt maker laid the template on the wrong side of the fabric, traced around it with chalk or pencil, then cut the piece, allowing a quarter-inch outside the drawn line for a seam margin. Thus the exact line she was to sew was drawn on the back of the piece; nevertheless, the seam margins had to be precisely even to avoid mistakes in basting.

The tracing template was often used a second time as a pressing form in appliqué work, when the seam margins were turned and pressed to the inside before sewing. In some cases, a second set of templates was cut from such medium-stiff paper as letter paper or the pages of copybooks. The paper template was centered inside the appliqué piece, the seam margins folded over, and the thread basted in place through the paper. Sometimes these basting templates were dropped out after the piece had been sewn around all sides, as in such one-patch piecework as hexagon mosaics. And sometimes the paper was of necessity left in, forming an extra layer of warmth—though presumably such a piece could not be washed very successfully.

Patterns for quilting, in most cases, had to be marked on the quilt top before the three layers—back, interlining, and top—were assembled in the frames. There were several kinds of templates sometimes used in this process. See chapter 3 for a discussion of quilting patterns.

Plate 127.
Patchwork waistpockets, c. 1800
–1850. Pieced cottons and linens.
Tied around the waist and worn
under apron petticoats, the
pockets held various sewing
equipment. Left: Pieced of small-
scale stylized floral and striped
patterns block-printed in shades
of red, purple, and brown, some
with penciled blue. Right: Home-
woven fragments checked in
bleached and indigo blue linen.
Both Old Sturbridge Village,
Sturbridge, Massachusetts.

PATCHWORK WAISTPOCKETS

A colonial or pioneer woman would no more go about her daily business
without her sewing equipment than a modern woman would leave her
house without money for a phone call. To this end, the colonial woman
wore her sewer's pocket, which was commonly made of patchwork and in
which could be carried needles, pins, scissors, thimbles, thread, bodkins,
and so on. The pocket was a commodious pouch hung from a tape or cord
tied around the waist and worn *under* the skirt. They continued to be
worn until the high slim lines of the new dresses at the turn of the
eighteenth century raised the waistline for a time. Waistpockets were
made of linen, dimity, or frequently of chintz patches sewn together, and
they were often decorated with crewel embroidery demonstrating the
sewer's art. Since the pockets had to carry sharp needles and heavy
scissors, it is very likely they were quilted for strength as well.

Mrs. A. Ridgely of Delaware, in a letter to her sons attending
Dickinson College in 1796, disapprovingly describes a visit from a vain
young French lady to their home:

A young lady visited here last week who profess'd herself "astonished to find your sisters at work," and declared in a sweet simper, that she never had sizars, thimble, needle or thread about her, for it was terrible in a lady to wear a pair of Pockets—the French Ladies never did such a thing. What can such a poor vain piece of affectation and folly be worth? Nothing—and if she possess'd the wealth of the Indies and I was a man I would scarcely even pay her the compliment of a word.[3]

SEWING BIRDS

The sewing bird was a type of clamp in common use in home sewing until about the middle of the nineteenth century. It acted as a third hand to hold one end of a piece of material so that the needleworker could stretch the fabric taut with one hand while sewing with the other, to help in sewing long smooth hems and seams for curtains and bedding. The sewing bird was mounted on a C-clamp that could be screwed onto a table edge or the arm of a chair; the body was spring-loaded so that its beak opened and snapped shut on the fabric when the worker depressed and released the tail. It must have been invaluable during the final piecing of strips or rows or blocks in a quilt top; during earlier stages, it could have held patches ready for the worker, or kept lengths of thread at the ready. Caroline Cowles Richards describes how she used one to hold her quilt patches in 1860: "Aunt Ann gave me a sewing bird to screw on to the table to hold my work instead of pinning it to my knee."[4]

The example shown in plate 117 has a heart-shaped turning, suggesting that it was originally given as an engagement or wedding present— particularly appropriate because a girl's betrothal was a time of feverish sewing to prepare her trousseau and household goods, and her marriage committed her to a lifetime of sewing.

SCRAP BAGS

A household essential, the scrap bag was used to hoard all the odd-shaped bits of cloth left on the cutting table after garments had been cut out, and the areas of cloth still strong enough to use again after a garment was worn out or outgrown. Eventually all scraps too small for other uses would be employed as patchwork.

3. "The Ridgelys of Deleware and Their Circle, What Them Befell in Colonial and Federal Times: Letters, 1751–1890," edited by Mabel Lloyd Ridgely, *Antiques*, June 1973, page 1189.
4. Richards, *op. cit.*, page 126.

Plate 128.
Scrap bag, 19th century. Blue and white roller-printed cotton; handwoven tape drawstring, 10 x 8 in. Collection of the authors. Scrap bags were often hung on the back of a chair, ready for pick-up work.

QUILTING FRAMES

When the top of a quilt was completed, the three layers were assembled and stretched on a frame for quilting. Besides elevating the quilt and creating a work and stitching area, the purpose of the frame was twofold: to hold the three layers tightly so they could not shift during work and cause lumps and puckers, and to stretch the material tightly so that when it was released after quilting the interlining would puff up between the lines of stitching.

Every household, no matter how poor, could own its own frame. The only materials needed were four pine poles or pieces of board, 2 or 3 inches wide, 1 or 2 inches thick, and about 9 feet long (often they were as long as 12 feet). The poles could be held together at the corner with C-clamps (sometimes specially designed for quilting frames; see plate 117) or holes could be made for pegs to be inserted, or a slot could be made in the bar.

Even these things were not a necessity; one could simply tie the poles together at the corners with a length of twine, or drive a nail through if no twine was available. This simple frame formed a perfect square or rectangle, the size of the quilt top. A number of quilters could sit around all sides of this frame. When each quilter had completed the area within her reach, the frame was unfastened at the corners, the completed portion rolled under, and the frame clamped together again.

Another type of frame has two horizontal bars about 9 feet long and two cross bars about 4 feet long. A wooden ratchet at one end of each of the long bars enables the quilter to roll under the finished portion without taking the whole quilt from the frame and resetting it. This type may expose only about two feet of the quilt at one time.

The frame is always set so that the corners make true right angles. The frames were supported by trestles or sawhorses, or, more frequently,

Plate 129.
Quilting frame, 19th century. Pine, 98 x 27 x 30 ½ in. Courtesy Queen Anne's County Historical Society, Centreville, Maryland.

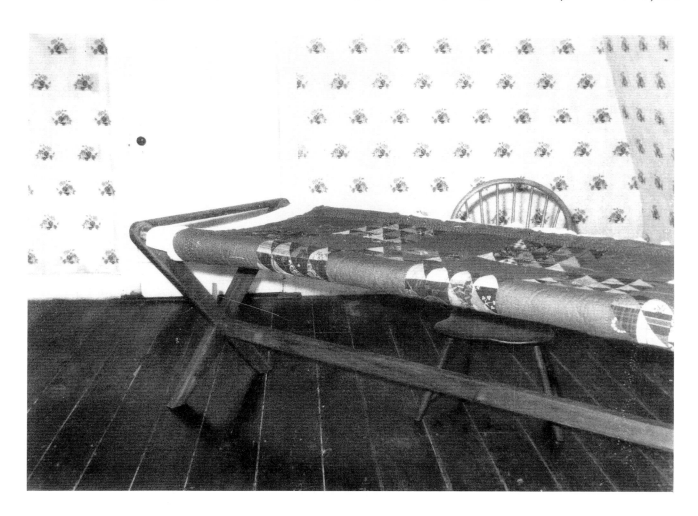

supported at the corners by matching low-backed or ladder-backed chairs. Many women prized certain chairs, not because they were valuable but because they were the right height for the quilting frame. Someone who quilted regularly was likely to have a frame with legs to bring it up to the correct height for her.

It was not unusual to see a frame fitted with a bar to stand on, for those quilters who preferred to stand at their work. On frames that rolled, standing up meant that the quilt did not have to be rolled so often, an advantage because each roll sent wrinkles through the cloth.

At the frame in which all the stretchers are the same length, workers sat around all four sides and all reachable space on each of the four sides was quilted. At the frame that rolls (which is long and narrow), the workers usually sat along one side of the frame with one at each end. As many as four could sit at one side at these frames and one at each end.

There is little doubt that the frame used for the quilting bee was a large one in which all the stretchers are of the same size, often from 10 to 12 feet, for it enabled all invited friends and neighbors to sit at the quilt and help sew. The rectangular frame could accommodate six or eight at most.

The beams or stretcher poles of the frame had to be very well sanded to prevent the snagging of material; then ticking or coarse homespun or other heavy cloth was tacked on and the edges of the quilt were basted to this material. In colonial times when houses were small and quilts were enormous, it was out of the question for a huge quilting frame to be left up until a single quilter could finish the work, which might take months or even years. Instead, customs and frames evolved in such a way that a great number of people—as many as sixteen—could work on a single quilt at once. In that way, one or even two quilts could be finished in a single day, and the frame taken down again.

When it was impossible for the quilting to be completed in a short period, the frame was sometimes removed from its supports and upended against the wall. But the most ingenious solution was to suspend the frame from the ceiling with pulleys, so that it could be reeled up out of the way and lowered again when needed. Since it was not unheard of for families to live in houses only 18 x 24 feet, a full-size quilting frame could very nearly fill a home. Mrs. Fitzrandolph tells this story:

Once in County Durham, I was examining a partly worked quilt in its frame which stood across the middle of the kitchen, reaching from one wall to the other, when there was a knock at the door and a man's voice called: "Can we come in?" The woman hastily swathed her quilt in an old sheet

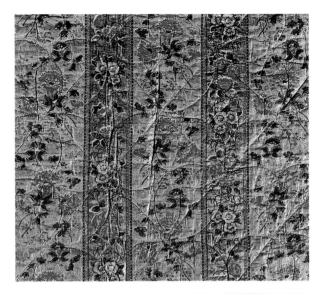

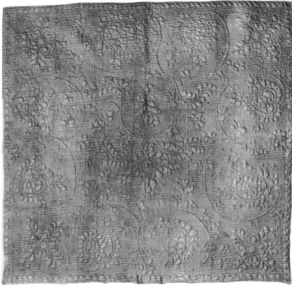

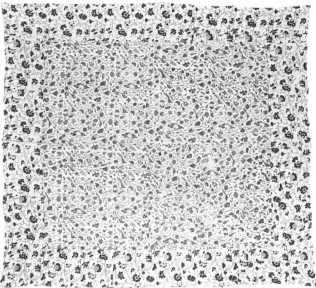

Plate 130 (TOP).
Chintz Whole-Cloth Quilt, c. 1825–50. Cotton, 82 x 72 in.
Collection of the authors. Roller-printed with vermiculate ground,
yellow and blue (for overprinted green); quilted in large diagonal lines
with rosettes in centers.

Plate 131 (ABOVE).
Glazed Worsted Quilt, c. 1750–75. Plain weave wool, 91 x 91 in.
Private collection. Two 45-inch widths of rose glazed wool have been
sewn together and quilted in running stitch in large scrolled vine
patterns with roses and other flowers. The binding is pink glazed wool
and the lining mustard brown wool. The quilt was probably made in
America from English material.

Plate 132 (TOP).
Blue-Resist Quilted Back, probably English, c. 1750–1800. Pieced
block-printed cotton, 85 x 82 in. Courtesy The Mattatuck Museum,
Waterbury, Connecticut. This cloth is the backing of a patchwork
quilt in the Wandering Foot pattern. It was not uncommon to make
whole-cloth quilts of blue-resist cloth both front and back. These
quilts are often pristine and appear to have been made from new cloth.
This particular pattern has been found pieced in part of a bed set along
with an English copperplate fabric that dates from 1765–75.

Plate 133 (ABOVE).
Quilted Counterpane, probably Massachusetts, c. 1790–1820. Cotton,
95 x 102 in. Old Sturbridge Village, Sturbridge, Massachusetts. The
12 ½-inch border is pieced of a roller print with overprinted color
added. The center is a more faded and more primitive woodblock
print. The reverse is an elaborately quilted all-white counterpane.

before calling in her husband and son, who black from the pit, crawled carefully under the frame and went on into the scullery for their baths.[5]

For a quilter working alone, there were quilting hoops made like large embroidery hoops, sometimes with their own legs. These gave the quilter a stitching space but were not very effective at preventing layers from shifting, since the whole quilt had to be moved every time a section was finished.

SEWING MACHINES

The sewing machine was the last major addition to the quilt maker's store of tools. For the woman for whom quilt making was not leisure-time fancywork but a necessary and time-consuming part of her daily household duties, the machine must have been an invaluable aid in the tedious business of piecing thousands of tiny scraps. It has been much less popular in appliqué, since the line of machine stitching cannot be made invisible as in handwork, but in the 1960s machine satin stitching and machine embroidery began to be used in appliqué and as pure decoration in contemporary quilts.

The reminiscences of Mr. R. E. Moody are interesting, pointing out the early use of a sewing machine for the making of quilts as well as the early training of a young boy. This letter, written in 1973, describes Mr. Moody's experiences almost seventy years ago:

As a very young lad, some seventy years ago, I learned to sew on the sewing machine. It was during a long convalescence from a serious accident one winter on the farm. My mother was always sewing when she was not cooking or keeping house, for she made most of the clothes for the younger members of our big family.

Besides this she found time to make patchwork quilts, and I believe she must have averaged one a year, for it seemed that every fall she had a quilting party when ladies from neighboring farms came in and helped to quilt a new cover.

With my mother's patient teaching, I really became adept in a few weeks at the sewing machine, pedaling away at a good rhythm while guiding the cloth under the needle. I was flattered when my mother let me help make the squares for her "patchwork" that winter. The pattern I did was a well-known one called "the bear's foot". It consisted of more than

Plate 134 (OPPOSITE). *Woman Quilting in Smokehouse,* Hinesville, Georgia, April 1941. Photograph by Jack Delano for the historical section of the Farm Securities Administration, part of the Department of Agriculture during the New Deal years.

---

5.   Fitzrandolph, *Traditional Quilting*, page 73.

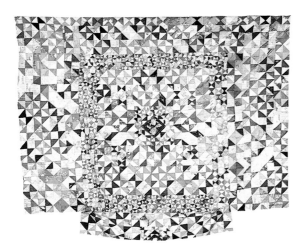

Plate 135 (TOP).
Framed Center Quilt. Pieced silks and cottons, including late-18th-century plain-weave silks, damasks, and brocades; glazed green plain-woven wool backing, 100 x 104 in. Courtesy The Henry Francis du Pont Winterthur Museum, Winterthur, Delaware. Some of the fabrics show embroidery and hand painting. Exposed newspaper templates show the dates "1788–89–90." The cutouts at the bottom of the quilt indicate that it was made for a four-poster bed.

Plate 136 (ABOVE).
Civil War Counterpane, New Jersey, c. 1850–75. Pieced and appliquéd cotton, 96 x 111 in. Shelburne Museum, Shelburne, Vermont. Made by a wounded Union soldier during convalescence. Within the framed center are appliquéd figures of soldiers on foot and on horseback, doves, and oak leaves (symbolic of continuing strength and life).

Plate 137 (TOP).
Framed Center Variation Quilt, New York, 1832. Pieced cottons and linens, 67 x 92 in. Collection of Barbara Ladd. Made by John W. Young at the age of seven.

Plate 138 (ABOVE).
Framed Medallion Quilt, 1795. Pieced and appliquéd cotton with silk embroidery. Collection of Mrs. John B. McIlhenny. Made by Jane Warwick Gatewood of West Virginia.

Plate 139.
Album Quilt, probably Baltimore, mid-19th century. Appliquéd cotton and velvet, 91 x 92 in. Smithsonian Institution, Washington, D.C.
There is a great deal of speculation about how and where these quilts originated. It is not known whether the separate motifs were drawn by a few people and purchased by many, or whether a whole quilt top was purchased with the motifs already drawn in. So many have turned up in Baltimore and the surrounding area that it is assumed that this is their source.

forty scraps, each cut in the shape of a triangle. We would cut a great number of these triangles and then begin putting them in the proper shape for the design. It was fascinating, and together with the thrill of operating the machine, was a Godsend to a shut-in.

The "Bear's Foot" was worked out like this: two triangles sewed together made a square which formed the sole of the foot. Then eight smaller triangles—a dark with a light one each time—made the toes, which were sewed on two sides of the first square. The space between the middle toes was always of the same color, so I put a small square there. The result was convincing.

Four bear's feet made up the big patchwork-square of the design and there were forty squares in the completed quilt. The scraps used were of varied hue and the final result was a creation of brilliant color, controlled and pleasing to the eye since each patch contributed to the over-all design. I soon became aware of how easily a mistake could be made in sewing together four bear's feet into the same pattern each time. I remember my quilt had all the "toes" pointing away from the center of each square—but there were many other arrangements possible. It was like the mathematical problem of "how many ways four equal squares may be arranged, four at a time, to make another square, when any one of them may be arranged in four ways"

After my job was done, the quilt was far from finished. It was composed of three layers, each made separately. The top layer, my forty squares, had to be sewed together with strips equal in width between them, and then a border surrounding the whole.

The bottom layer of the cover was the easiest. It was of strong cloth like homespun or "outing" and could be bought at the store.

The middle layer had to be a soft filling, like cotton, wool or down. In my part of the country it was usually a thin sheet of ginned cotton, the fibers made straight and smooth by the combing process called carding—a hard and tedious job done by hand. Not everyone can do it. I believe the only two people I ever saw carding were my mother and her mother.

When all the parts were ready, it was time to hold the party, or quilting bee. The ladies would set up a special wooden frame and carefully attach to it the three layers, making it possible to roll up the sides of the cover in order for the quilters to get nearer and finally reach its center. In one afternoon these expert stitchers would complete the quilting, or sewing together, at the same time having a fine talk-fest. Later they enjoyed good country snacks, or a light supper.

At our house the party was always in the daytime. However, there must have been nighttime quiltings for I used to hear one of my older

Plate 140.
James K. Polk Quilt, 1845. Pieced of cloth campaign flags and handkerchiefs from the 1844 campaign, 96 x 106 in. Collection of the White House, Washington, D.C. Surrounding Polk's likeness are flags, some bearing the names of James K. Polk and George M. Dallas, his vice-presidential running mate in 1844.

Plate 141.
Centennial Quilt, Pennsylvania, 1876. Pieced and appliquéd cotton, 77 x 83 in. Rhea Goodman, Quilt Gallery, Inc. The quilt maker's name appears in the border.

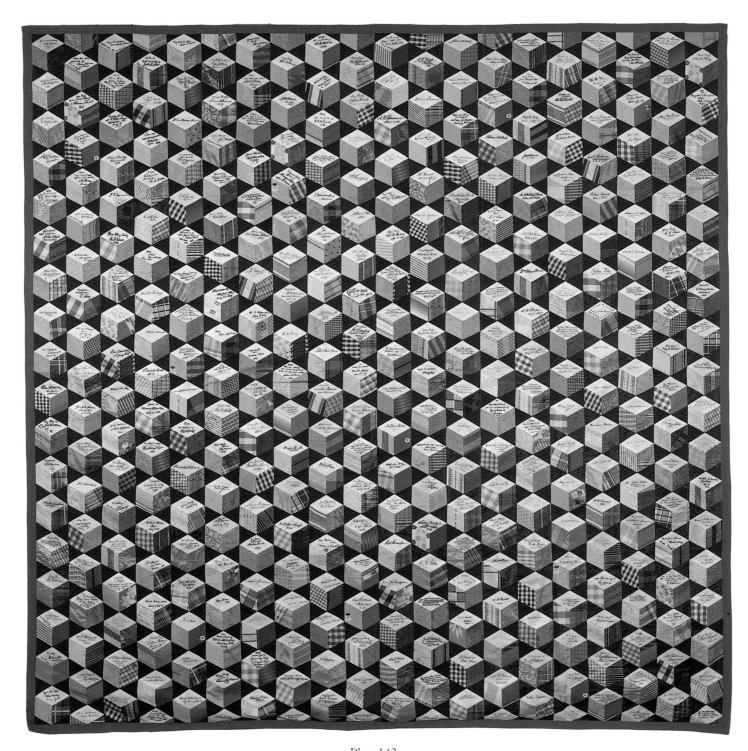

Plate 142.
Autograph Baby Blocks Quilt, Providence, c. 1863. Pieced silk, 72 x 72 in. Estate of Adeline Harris Sears. Made by Adeline Harris Sears, the quilt contains 360 blocks, each with the signature of a European or American notable of the period, including President Lincoln.

brothers softly strumming on his banjo and singing the following ditty, which to my mind always pictured a night-time adventure:

> *I was seeing Nellie home,*
> *I was seeing Nellie home—*
> *It was from Aunt Dinah's quilting party—*
> *I was seeing Nellie home.*[6]

Of all quilting tools the sewing machine has been used least. Since the presser foot tends to shift the three layers of fabric—the very thing quilting is meant to prevent—a quilt has to be basted so thoroughly before machine quilting can be undertaken that the work might as well have been done by hand in the first place. Furthermore, to execute angles and curves on a machine one is obliged to shift the whole quilt around instead of moving a single needle. Machine quilting was done relatively rarely, but that it can be done well is illustrated by at least one example of elaborate, flawless machine quilting dating from the third quarter of the nineteenth century made to celebrate the arrival of the first sewing machine "west of the Alleghenies."

---

6. "The Bear's Foot," by R. E. Moody, © 1973 The New York Times Company. Reprinted by permission.

Plate 143.
Floral Stenciled Quilt, c. 1825–50. Cotton, 90 x 86 in. The New-York Historical
Society. The stylized flowers and floral and vine border are stenciled in shades of blue,
rose, yellow, and green.

5
Stenciled, All-White, and Embroidered Quilt Tops

THE STENCILED QUILT

The stenciled quilt is rare. In fact, museum visits and considerable research have turned up fewer than twenty-five spreads, of which only a small percentage are actually quilted. They were all made in the early nineteenth century; most probably date between 1825 and 1835, although educated estimates have placed some as late as 1850 and as early as 1800. All the spreads are said to come from New York, Vermont, Massachusetts, and Connecticut, and one from New Hampshire. All have floral and more or less related designs.

There is plenty of evidence that a craze for stenciling existed throughout the second quarter of the nineteenth century in the decoration of various types of furniture, floor coverings, walls, and textiles. Stenciling on textiles was the least common of all these, but it would appear that there was a fashion in rural communities for stenciled bedcovers either as substitutes for the more elaborate embroidered spreads, or possibly as a means of approximating the effect of block-printed decoration.

The stenciled spreads were a product of the home and were not made commercially. Presumably, the household knowledge of stenciling was born of theorem paintings or stencil painting on velvet, which was a fad in the young ladies' seminaries that lasted for about twenty-five years

Plate 144.
Album Presentation Quilt, New York, 1853. Pieced and appliquéd cotton and linen, 89 x 82 in. Collection of Mr. and Mrs. John S. Walton. Each side of the border contains the legend "Presented to Richard H. Moser, Stanford, 1853, by his friends."

Plate 145.
Album Quilt, Ohio, 1890. Pieced cotton, 83 x 83 in. Collection of the authors. Each block in this Chimney Sweep pattern is made of material from a different state, with the name of the state inscribed in the center. It took Mrs. Jonathan Wood forty years to complete the quilt, primarily because the materials took so long to collect. Many pieces arrived by stagecoach as long as a year after they had been ordered.

Plate 146.
Sampler Presentation Quilt, probably New Jersey, 1842–44. Pieced and appliquéd cotton, 85 x 75 in. Smithsonian Institution,
Washington, D.C. Made for Mary H. Taylor, the quilt is dated and is signed in various places. It is a composite of traditional and
original pieced and appliquéd patterns.

Plate 147.
Four-Patch Variation Quilt
(detail), possibly Illinois,
c. 1850–75. Polychrome
roller-printed calicos, 65 x
65 in. Collection of the
authors.

in the first half of the nineteenth century. Interest in theorems seems to have died about 1840. The word *theorem* may have referred to the theorem or problem of arranging the single stencil units (consisting of a piece of fruit, a flower, a bird, or butterfly) into a pleasing still life on a plate or table. The stencil, then, was thought of as a means of guiding the hand of the less talented artist or achieving results quickly. The stenciled spread, however, was a different matter. Generally considered not to require much skill or patience, at closer look one finds that each part of the design is created by a different stencil pattern. For example, a many-petaled rose with leaves and a stem would be executed not with one rose cutout, but with a varying number. A different cutout would be used for the petals, another for the stamen, another for the leaves, another for the stem. This left the final arrangement entirely up to the artist. Understanding this procedure gives a little help in dating a quilt as well, because it is in the earlier examples of stenciling that so many forms were painstakingly put together to form a single motif. The later single stencil was more rigid and more limited. One finds in the later examples that a whole bouquet of flowers could be made from a single cutout. This method was quicker but tended to produce a slightly more manufactured look.

It is with the earlier technique, the use of many units, that the best results were produced, since they allowed variety and subtler shading. Examples may be identified by a slight irregularity, for instance, in the positioning of the leaves on two identical flowers. This irregularity of spacing (or a crowding or overlapping) indicates that the stencils were done individually leaf by leaf. It is important to remember that various parts were touched up freehand after the stencil was used. This practice added individuality to a craft that could produce a more or less stereotyped decoration. The potential for lack of individuality was increased about 1835 when stencils could be purchased from professional stencil cutters who turned out patterns by the hundreds for the theorem painters. In this way amateurs were spared the laborious job of cutting their own stencils. This is not to imply, however, that the later stenciled quilts were less beautiful. The primitive, delicate simplicity of stenciled quilts makes them among the most beautiful of all the early types.

The stenciling technique: Stenciling is the utilization of a cut-out pattern laid over an area to be decorated; the color is applied with a brush through the open spaces. This is an extremely old technique; Indian textiles show stencil printing over 2000 years ago, and Japan, too, has a long history of stenciling. Oriental craftsmen achieved extremely delicate results from finely cut stencils, some of which had hairs or silk threads separating the sections. The Eastern Europeans used the stencil to decorate their furniture, and French and English stenciled wall papers became very popular in colonial America and were the models for stenciled walls. Later, during the period of decorated tinware and painted furniture (the Hitchcock chairs), stenciling enjoyed a heyday.

The manner in which the home-crafted stencil quilt was done was not an exact science, as it would have been in the Hitchcock Chair Factory. Its methods were greatly determined by what was available in the household.

Plate 148.
Autograph Crazy Quilt, Missouri, 1884–93. Pieced and embroidered silks, velvets, and satins, 51 x 69 in.
Collection of Mr. and Mrs. Alastair B. Martin. Made by Sallie Yost, the quilt includes autographed
fragments of clothing sent by such notables as Oliver Wendell Holmes, Robert Louis Stevenson, Kate
Greenaway, and Mrs. Tom Thumb.

To decorate a spread using this technique, one first drew and then cut the design onto the stencil, which might be a piece of thick paper saturated in linseed oil, cloth dipped in beeswax, tin, or a thin piece of wood. The design would then be cut into this template by means of an ice pick, pocket knife, or scissors. A different stencil was cut for each color to be used. Then the foundation material, cut the desired size of the quilt, was laid out flat, preferably on some padding that would absorb the extra dye as it was applied, and the quiltmaker laid out her stencils and traced the patterns onto the cloth. The dye solution was mixed, either a vegetable dye mixed with gum arabic, cornstarch, and cream of tartar; or a ground-up pigment bought from the hardware store; or cakes of dye made in a dye factory. The dye solution was always very concentrated because the color was not being boiled into the fabric, and fading would occur almost immediately if the solution was not strong enough. Linen was the most resistant to accepting the dye, then cotton, then wool. The dye was applied through the holes in the stencils with a soft brush or ball of cotton covered in cloth. Each color was done separately after the previous color had been rinsed with hot steam to set the dye, and then allowed to dry.

Spreads that have been block-printed by hand are sometimes confused with stenciled spreads. It is not clear whether these block-printed pieces were done at home or professionally by unsophisticated printers and pattern stampers. There were advertisements for counterpane stampers in the mid-eighteenth century:

COUNTERPANE STAMPER *Whereas a certain Person, who followed the business of stamping counterpanes is going out of the Country, and has intirely dropt the Business here: These are to inform all Shopkeepers and others, that they may have Counterpanes and Curtains, &c. stampt after the same Manner and at the same Rates that the Said Person stampt them at the House of John Williams in King Street.*[1]

The block-printed spread is usually more compactly covered with design—that is, there is less ground showing than on stenciled examples, although there are few areas of solid color. Close scrutiny reveals that small individual blocks have been stamped next to one another to form the design of the printed covers. Another point of difference is that, in block printing, the paint is thick in the centers of the motifs and thin on the edges; the reverse is true in stenciling. There is almost invariably more intense color at the edges of the stenciled motifs, with a gradual

1. *Boston Evening Post*, November 16, 1747, from Dow, *op. cit.*, page 261.

lightening toward the center. In the block-printing technique, although the printing is coarse and crude, there is no smearing, the lines are thin and clear. The crudeness is particularly seen in border motifs that overlap or fail to meet, or clumsy mitering of corner motifs.

THE ALL-WHITE QUILT

In the last quarter of the eighteenth and the first quarter of the nineteenth centuries, a considerably more rarefied category of needlework skill produced the all-white quilt. The subtle, difficult, breathtaking stitching on these quilts is so fine that many spreads easily contain more than a million stitches. It is true that in most cases there has been no formal training or guidance in design, but the accomplishment was based on such flawless craftsmanship and so many years of familiarity with the needle that the final result is expert in both design and execution. The finest of the all-white quilts were done by extremely skilled women who must be considered professionals, creating an heirloom to be handed down, or a special counterpane for a dowry chest or for show on the best bed—purely as a decorative object. It is astounding to realize that a needle and white thread alone can change a simple piece of homespun into a masterpiece.

The foundation piece of the all-white quilt top was most frequently cotton or linen in a plain weave. It could also be a cloth that was a combination of cotton and linen threads. If a family could afford it, they chose a fine grade of plain-woven bleached homespun. The word *homespun* in this case denotes cotton or linen of domestic manufacture.[2] The homespun would be seamed together, since the looms produced only narrow goods, generally no larger than four feet across. A member of the family might have woven two or three lengths of cloth specifically for the making of the white counterpane, but it is more likely that most women, particularly in the eighteenth century, would not have enjoyed the luxury of owning three three eight-foot lengths of finely woven cloth that could be set aside for the counterpane. The alternative to this was a number of lengths and pieces, equally matched in texture and whiteness, which when pieced together created a suitable top ready for stitching.

Homespun, unfortunately, is unrecognizable to the naked eye of one unfamiliar with textiles, particularly because there are very fine as well as

---

2. That is, cloth that was spun and woven at home. A great deal of homespun is plain weave—a result of the need to conserve on both time and thread, particularly with household cloth for everyday usage, like sheeting.

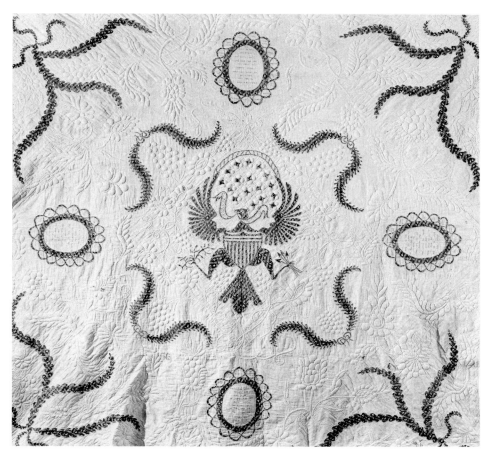

very coarse grades. But it does generally have a rougher, looser, more textured, and more uneven quality than machine-made goods. Widespread use of homespun became much less prevalent after the late 1830s and the 1840s. Store-bought textiles that had been available since the mid-eighteenth century were not yet universally abundant, but in terms of time, labor, and cost, were more economical than those made on the home loom. Of course there were always people who continued to spin and weave their own goods long after it became unnecessary; and those of little prosperity, as well as those who lived in rural and frontier areas, would continue to make homespun for decades to come.

Imported cloth purchased for a quilt top might have been cambric or muslin. Cambric[3] refers to a thin, very fine linen of plain weave. It was

Plate 149 (ABOVE LEFT). Rebecah Foster Quilt, Tennessee, 1808. Quilted and highly stuffed ground. Private collection. Around each oval are the names of the states, the last being Ohio (the seventeenth state to be admitted to the Union). The quilt is inscribed "Rebecah Foster Nashville, October 5, 1808."

Plate 150 (ABOVE RIGHT). Rebecah Foster Quilt (detail).

---

3.   It takes its name from Kamerjik, the Flemish version of Cambray, Flanders. From *The American Heritage Dictionary*, New York, American Heritage Publishing Co., 1971, page 192.

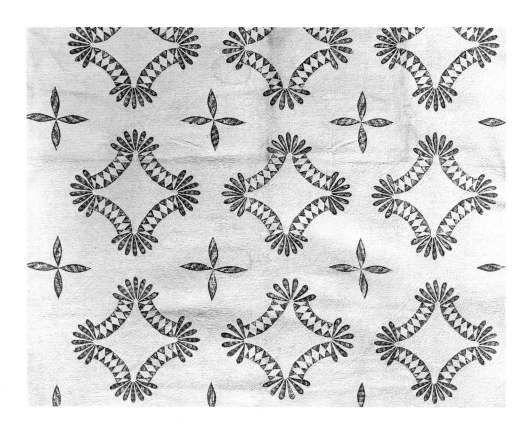

Plate 151.
Whig's Defeat Quilt (detail), probably Tennessee, c. 1825–50. Pieced and appliquéd cotton and linen, 94 x 75 in. DAR Museum, Washington, D.C. The intricate quilting pattern of running vine and wreaths took quilt maker Jane McKinney Walker almost a year to complete. The simple but elegant pattern is also known as the Sunflower, Broken Circle, and Indian Summer.

originally produced in Flanders and considered the finest white linen for bedding; but later there was an imitation in cotton also called cambric. Muslin[4] is a fine cotton of plain weave. Originally cambric and muslin referred to imported fabrics, but by the nineteenth century they were just "store-bought" fabrics.[5]

Whether the cloth was made at home or purchased in the store, there was no question that the quilt had to be made at home. There was

---

4. Muslin can be a misleading term because it is now thought of as any of a range of cotton fabrics from the sheerest batiste to the coarsest sheeting. Muslin traces its name to the French fabric Mousseline, which in turn derived its name from the town of Mosul in Mesopotamia. *Ibid.*, page 865.

5. The term *store-bought* should be enlarged upon. By 1750 there was a variety of materials available in stores, and, by the first quarter of the nineteenth century, an enormous range of materials was to be had in the stores: a vast number of imported fabrics from many countries, fabric manufactured in American factories, and excess home-woven goods that were sold to local stores. If a quilter could afford it, she could have almost any cloth of her choosing. At the same time a great many families were still depending solely on goods from their home looms, particularly when it came to bed linens and blankets.

no local dry goods store that sold such spreads, or tailor who could make one up and stay within a reasonable price range.

The interlining for the all-white quilt had to be chosen more carefully than for other quilts because it more greatly affected the final result. First, it had to be spread very thinly to allow for the tiniest and most elaborate background quilting; and, second, it had to be a thoroughly cleaned wool fiber or carefully picked cotton fiber so that no

Plate 152.
Primitive Garden Quilt, probably New Jersey. Appliquéd cotton, 95 x 92 in. Collection of Mr. and Mrs. Leonard Balish. This folk art quilt displays leaves and flowers in strong naive forms. The leaves are blue; the flowers lime yellow, ocher, orange, and tangerine.

look or feeling of coarseness would result. To our knowledge, all-white quilts are almost never heavily interlined. Many are just two different weights of material sewn together with no interlining.

The material used for the backing was very often repaired household sheeting of homespun linen, in various stages of bleached and unbleached condition. Before 1775,[6] launderable household needs were filled by the use of all linen cloth or cloth with a linen warp and cotton weft.

> *Linen was the fabric used for those items in the household that required frequent washing. Linen could be spread in the sun and bleached, it was stronger and more durable and more readily processed by hand. The sheets, pillow cases, bolster covers, mattress and pillow ticks . . . were all made of linen until the late 18th century.[7]*

After the last quarter of the eighteenth century, cotton became the most predominantly used fabric in the household.

The backing of the all-white quilt was often a coarser weave than the front—as, for example, a cambric for the top with a homespun linen for the back. Even when both the top and the backing were storebought in the latter half of the nineteenth century, it is interesting to find that a great many of the quilters continued to choose a finer fabric for the front and a fabric of coarser weave for the backing.

Various techniques were used to attach the layers of the all white quilt. Again, we are generally talking of a quilt with a very thin interlining or no interlining at all. On the all-white quilt, the decoration depends solely on whatever technique is used to join the layers. The most frequently used were quilting, cording, stuffing, embroidery, and candlewicking. On the white quilt these methods serve both to attach and to decorate. Some of these techniques are often found on single layer counterpanes as well.

Quilting: The quilting on the all-white quilt—white stitching on a white background—is usually characterized by close, tiny stitches creating an effect known as bunched, stippled, or pressed quilting. Thimble quilting, when the thimble is laid on the cloth and used as the template for the circular design, appears loose and puckered compared to the textured effect given by the stippled background.

---

6. Cotton was first spun by machine in the U.S. in 1775. It was only after this date that enough cotton yarn could be produced fast enough to warp a loom economically.
7. Cooper, *op. cit.*, page 25.

Plate 153.
Quilted Counterpane (detail), probably Connecticut, c. 1800. Fine white cotton surface; linen back,
180 x 105 in. Courtesy Wadsworth Atheneum, Hartford, Connecticut. The running feather vine
border and fruits and flowers are stuffed. The spacing between the lines of stitching on the
foundation is almost microscopic. Solid quilting often makes a heavy spread.

Cording: There are two methods of cording. The early quilters made very fine rows of running stitches, a quarter-inch apart, which formed little channels through which roving or yarn or candlewicking was carried by a needle (bodkin) that had a large eye and a blunt point. An average quilter took six or seven stitches per inch, although some fanatical quilters made twenty stitches per inch in backstitching to form the channels in such a way that no cotton cording could go astray. In doing the cording, the difficulty of too long a channel was met by bringing the needle through the backing, pulling up the roving, and introducing the needle again through the same hole.

The second method is a later technique and considered by old-time quilters the lazy woman's way. The pattern is drawn on top of the backing and the cording is tacked down or couched onto the lines. Then the quilt

Plate 154.
All-White Counterpane, Fairfield, Connecticut, c. 1750–1800. Corded and embroidered, 102 x 101 in. Courtesy Museum of Fine Arts, Boston. Made by Mrs. Thaddeus Burr. Embroidered stitches embellish and attach heavy cording on a white linen ground.

top was laid over this and the two thicknesses were quilted together with a double row of running or backstitch on either side of the cording. It is said that this latter method prevailed in England.

For both methods of cording, there was one thing that was of prime importance: stitched lines had to be exactly and evenly spaced. If they were too far apart, the cord would not fill up the channel, and if they were too close together the cording would not go through without pulling and stretching the material.

Like other forms of needlework, cording is centuries old. It appears on the Sicilian Quilt (plate 1) in the late 1300s. In England in the last half of the seventeenth and eighteenth centuries, cording was in great vogue for the adornment of men's linen and silk waistcoats, women's petticoats, babies' clothing and caps, bed hangings, and very large linen quilts. Much of the early corded work was characterized by elaborate all-

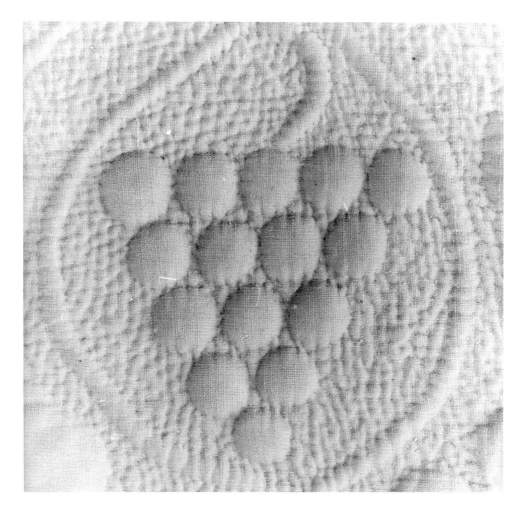

Plate 155.
All-White Quilt (detail), c. 1802. Quilted, stuffed, and corded linen; homespun linen backing, 82 x 94 in. Courtesy Chester County Historical Society, David Townsend House, West Chester, Pennsylvania. Said to have been made by a Quaker woman named Phoebe Parker Tucker, the quilt has an 8-inch gathered ruffle on three sides. Cotton is forced through threads in the back to create the three-dimensional grapes.

over designs, the result being that the cloth was "so closely covered with cord patterns that little space was available for ground pattern and even less for other additions to the general design."[8] There are examples of vases and baskets worked in outlines raised in fine cord on the early English counterpanes. These are surely the direct antecedents of the American quilts and counterpanes whose centers are these very baskets created from outlines of corded quilting. Ours date from a full century later: they are late eighteenth and early nineteenth century. In America at this time cording was rarely used alone. More often it is found complementing embroidery stitches worked in linen thread or as a component of stuffed work on quilts. It is the stem to a stuffed flower, the meandering vine for bunches of stuffed grapes, the border for the ubiquitous framed medallion of stuffed princess feathers.

Stuffing: The effect of stuffing, like that of cording, is to raise the design above the surface and provide it with a three-dimensional quality. It was done from the back of the quilt, which was usually a loosely woven material. This enabled the quilter to separate the loosely woven threads with a stiletto or bodkin and force in bits of cotton or wool until a thick padded effect was achieved in a leaf or petal or grape. Then the threads were pushed or scratched back together again, closing up the hole. After the quilt was washed there would be no evidence of the separation. Some quilters made a tiny slit in the back, then pushed in the stuffing, and then neatly sewed up the slit. However, this was a later practice and considered taboo by the expert quilters, because it violated their rule of thumb that the back should be as nearly indistinguishable from the front as possible. The old-timers prided themselves on being the only ones to discern which had been the under side in the frames and which had been the top.

There are many examples of stuffing in high relief on a background of very tight stippled or thimble quilting. In these instances, when there is quilting, the stuffing, like cording, is done after the quilting has been completed. There are also examples of stuffed designs on a ground that is not quilted but is decorated with French knots or other embroidery stitches (see plate 162).

Stuffing, too, dates back at least as early as the Sicilian Quilt and is in evidence in Europe and England all through the following centuries. In America the technique of stuffing was in vogue in the very late eighteenth century and was prevalent for a good half of the nineteenth century. It is difficult to date stuffed work precisely, since one cannot

---

8.   Averil Colby, *Quilting,* New York, Charles Scribner's Sons, 1971, page 75.

make an age determination based on, for example, heaviness or lightness of the padding. Very fine work was done during a period of fifty years or more. It was painstaking work, but in spite of this there is no dearth of stuffed white quilts in this country. One of the outstanding stuffed quilts in America is a quilt called "A Representation of the Fair Ground Near Russellville, Kentucky" (plates 156–58). Eliza Calvert Hall, the author of *Aunt Jane of Kentucky* and *A Book of Handwoven Coverlets*, writes of this quilt in 1931 in the *Handicrafter* magazine:

Plate 156.
A Representation of the Fair Ground Near Russellville, Kentucky, 1856. All-white quilted, stuffed, and corded cotton, 94 x 94 ½ in., including 4 ½-inch woven fringe. Smithsonian Institution, Washington, D.C. Made by Virginia Ivey.

Stenciled, All-White, and Embroidered Quilt Tops 203

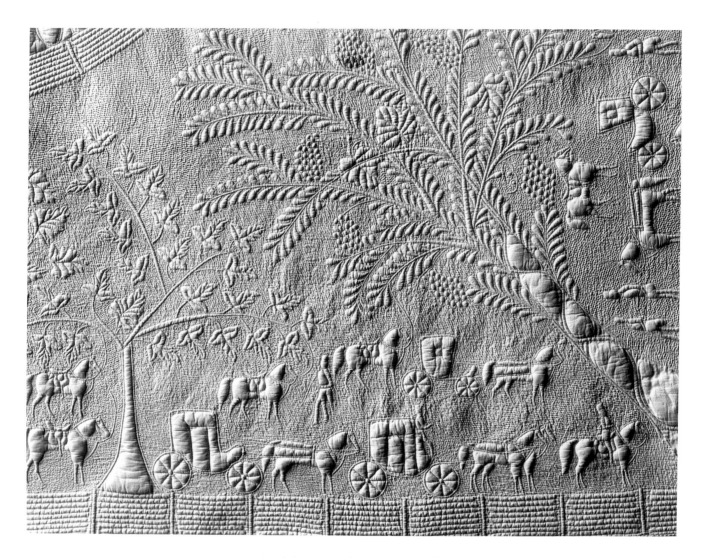

Plate 157.
A Representation of the Fair Ground Near Russellville, Kentucky (detail). Finely stippled background quilting makes the stuffed horses, carriages, and trees stand in high relief.

It is the delicacy and accuracy of the figures in this quilt which distinguish it from others of the stuffed variety. It is comparatively easy to quilt a design of large flowers and leaves, but it required more than a needlewoman's talent to outline these horses and other domestic animals that look as natural as life on the surface of the quilt. There are approximately 150 stitches in every square inch of the quilt. Make your own calculation of the total number of stitches.[9]

The answer is 1,200,600. The quilt appears to be a commemoration of a visit to the fair. It was made by Virginia Ivey, presumably in 1856 or soon

9. September–October 1931.

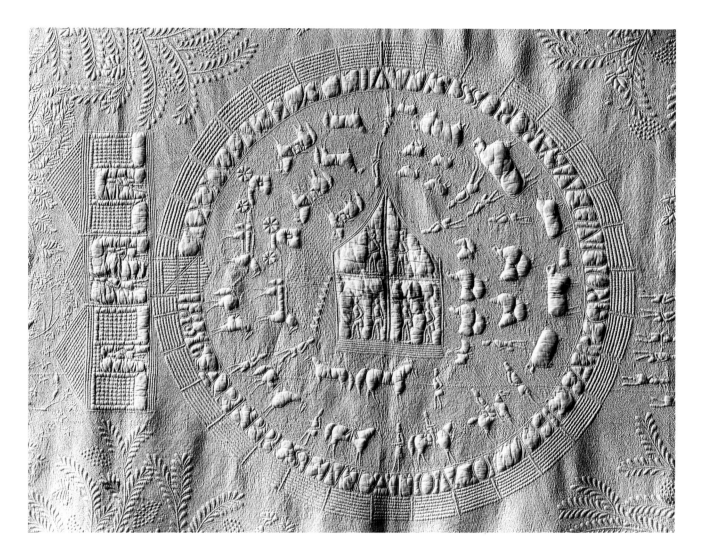

after as a pictorial record of a great event. It would not be unreasonable to assume that it was completed in one year despite the number of stitches. In the center of the quilt is the judging ring, encircled by its fence, with a gateway on the left side of the quilt. Directly inside the fence is a pair of concentric circles with the quilted legend "1856 A REPRESENTATION OF THE FAIR GROUND NEAR RUSSELLVILLE KENTUCKY." In the very center is the exhibition tent where judging is taking place on two levels. Parading within the ring are men, horses with riders, horses pulling buggies, cows, sheep, and pigs. On the edges of the whole fairground are beautiful, enormous trees, some appearing to be palms. Detail is so rich in the figures near the border fence that horses have saddles, buggies have reins, wheels have spokes, and coaches have windows.

Plate 158.
A Representation of the Fair Ground Near Russellville, Kentucky (detail), center section. A rail fence rings the quilted legend that gives the date and title of the quilt. The exhibition tent is seen in the middle; at left are two more pavilions.

Another astounding *tour de force* of quilting is the South Carolina "Secession Quilt" (plates 159–61) designed and made in 1860 by Mrs. Philip Drury Cook of Fairfield County, South Carolina. Mrs. Cook (Jemima Ann Thewitts Williamson) was born in Virginia and moved in early childhood to South Carolina with her parents. Her husband was a general in the Coast Artillery of the Confederate States of America. During the Civil War she raised her four children and managed the plantation with the help of an overseer. She gave the "Secession Quilt" to her granddaughter Sallie (Mrs. John W. Cunningham). She later made a similar but floral-designed quilt for her other granddaughter, Rebecca (Mrs. Jesse Robert Hix).

Mrs. Hix recalled seeing Mrs. Cook making the "Secession Quilt" from seamless, handwoven, fine white cambric, nine by nine feet in size. The sketching of the design and the quilting was done in charcoal on an "immense" frame that frequently had to be pushed out of the way to make room for other work. "Grandmother worked on it a long, long, time." The design was quilted with tiny stitches over very thin wadding to form the outlines; then cotton, picked seedless by hand and bleached to a snowy whiteness, was hand carded and stuffed with a bodkin through the sheer lining to raise the figures and give the quilt its striking appearance. Both quilts were said to have taken six months to complete.

The design of the "Secession Quilt" is historical and original. Mrs. Cook's zealousness for the cause of South Carolina and her ardent belief in secession manifested itself in the patriotic motif of this quilt. The central design is an eagle, its outstretched wings resting on cornucopias that spill over with fruits and flowers. From the eagle's beak floats a streamer with the motto "E Pluribus Unum"; the goddess of liberty stands on his back with a flagstaff in her right hand and cradling a sheaf of wheat in her left. To the left side of the quilt behind the flagstaff is the word *Secession* and the date *1860* above a starry ground. On the right side of the quilt is the name *Yancey* (William Lowndes Yancey, a Carolina proslavery secessionist). Above Liberty's head, *Washington* arches in large letters. Beneath the tableau and framed by the cornucopias is the name *P. D. Cook*, husband of the quilt maker. In a beautiful border of flowers and beadings that surrounds the centerpiece are four arches, each bearing the name of one of the four governors of the state during the nullification period (1830–37). *Butler* is above, *Hamilton* below, *McDuffie* on the quilt's right, and *Hayne* on its left. Around all this is a wide border of flowers and fruit flowing from two large cornucopias in each corner. Midway on the four sides is the state seal of South Carolina, a palmetto tree with two shields with figures on the faces.

As Sherman's army approached the Alston home (where the

Plate 159.
Secession Quilt, South Carolina, 1860. All-white quilted, stuffed, and corded linen, 108 x 108 in.
Courtesy Dr. and Mrs. W. Clough Wallace and Roberta Wallace, Boylston, South Carolina. Made
by Mrs. Jemima Ann Cook of Fairfield County, this masterful quilt has knotted fringe on four sides.

Plate 160.
Secession Quilt (detail), center section. Miss Liberty astride an eagle.

Plate 161.
Secession Quilt (detail), border. Cornucopias with trailing fruit and flowers.

granddaughters Sallie and Rebecca lived) to burn it, the family silver and other treasures are said to have been wrapped in the Secession Quilt, placed in a wooden box, and buried in the ground.[10] Later, when the box of valuables was finally dug up, the quilt was badly discolored and stained. Many washings restored its whiteness, but took their toll on the fabric by rendering the figures less distinct.

In 1902, when the quilt was displayed at the International Exposition in Charleston, South Carolina, the Committee on Awards noted: "The beautiful, handmade quilt surpasses anything in design and workmanship on exhibit." This quilt is also interesting in terms of dating. It is a perfect example of the consistency throughout domestic handicrafts of relying on the models of earlier generations for style in design and workmanship. It has all the elements of a late eighteenth- or early nineteenth-century piece. The quilting is of the early thimble-quilting style, the design is a framed medallion. The individual motifs of cornucopias spilling pomegranates, grapes, and roses, the eagle and Liberty are motifs that are seen well before 1800. There is stuffed and corded work. The interlining is homegrown cotton, picked, seeded, and carded by the maker herself, and a four-inch fringe has been netted and sewn to the edges. Only the date and the storebought fabric belie an eighteenth-century provenance.

Embroidery: White spreads were sometimes decorated with embroidery in different weights of white wool, white two-ply cotton, or white roving.[11] Almost all of the embroidery stitches were used on white spreads, particularly French knots and bullion[12] knots, but also chain, satin, stem, and seed stitch and couching. White embroidery on a white ground was known as "white work" in early America, and it was by no means confined to bedcovers. It was done in all weights of thread from silk to wool, and it was found to be particularly suitable for the decoration of frequently laundered costume accessories and household linens. Other white-on-white embroidery techniques that have been used for counterpanes include *Mountmellic work,* which originated in Ireland in the 1830s and is considered a style as well as a technique. The thread used for Mountmellic is a thick linen or cotton drill, white knitting

---

10. The floral quilt was not hidden, and it was cut into saddle blankets by Sherman's troops.
11. A white spread embroidered with white roving is often referred to as a white candlewick (embroidered) spread.
12. The yarn is rolled around the working needle, and this roll laid flat along the surface of the work instead of being raised up and knotted as in the French knot.

cotton, or strong white satin. It looks lighter than candlewicking, but heavier than most embroidery. It is on the bold and heavy side and is accomplished very quickly. It has been described as similar to Jacobean embroidery in theme, which would refer to patterns inspired by the Indian painted cottons, such as the flowering tree and natural leaf and petal shapes. *Drawn work is* the generic name for a kind of openwork; it includes drawn threadwork and drawn fabric work. In drawn fabric work, the threads are pulled aside, and gathered in clusters to leave holes and openwork patterns. In drawn thread work, threads are actually withdrawn entirely from the area, and other stitches are worked over the area where they have been removed.

Plate 162.
All-White Counterpane (detail), c. 1820. Stuffed, corded, and embroidered linen, 107 x 113 ½ in. Courtesy The Baltimore Museum of Art. The latticed basket is corded, the grapes and leaves are stuffed, and the ground is covered in French knots.

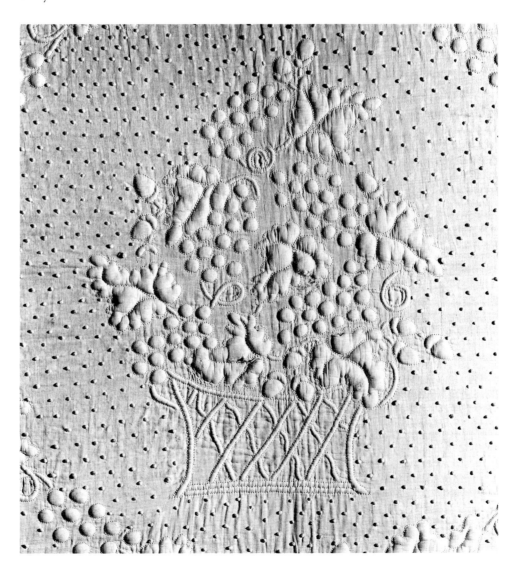

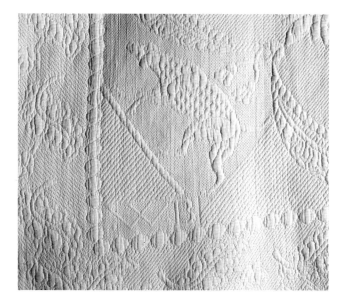

A white spread embroidered with white roving is often referred to as a candlewick (embroidered) spread. *Candlewicking* is a confusing appellation to many because it is applied to a number of very different-looking techniques. The term *candlewick*[13] refers to loosely spun yarn (or "roving" as it will be called), which can be employed in a variety of different ways. The easiest to recognize (because it looks like today's chenille bedspread) is the embroidered candlewick spread that has been *tufted*. This means the wicking is worked through the background material in large running stitches. The stitches are raised on the surface by passing the loop over a small twig. Then the twig is removed and the wicking is cut where the twig was, leaving strands sticking up in the air. After the piece is washed, shrinkable materials pull the strands tight and they fluff out to form a single puffy dot.

Another very popular method was *knotting*. The entire coverlet surface was decorated with French knots and bullion stitches, which were varied by using different weights of wicking and by increasing the number of strands. Another method was *couching*: when the needleworker wanted lines, she would lay the wicking on top of the material and sew it down at intervals with a finer sewing thread.[14] Naturally, other embroidery stitches were worked in candlewicking as well; satin stitch (cut and uncut),

Plate 163 (ABOVE LEFT). All-White Counterpane (detail), c. 1800–25. Candlewick-embroidered cotton, 103 ½ x 95 ½ in. Courtesy The Henry Francis du Pont Winterthur Museum, Winterthur, Delaware.

Plate 164 (ABOVE RIGHT). Marseilles Spread (detail). Illinois State Museum Collection. Said to have been made in England in the 18th century for Walter Buchanan, an ancestor of President James Buchanan. Note the initials "W.B." in the corner.

---

13. It takes its name from the length of loosely twisted yarn that was used as the wick in candlemaking of the eighteenth century.
14. "The use of cotton on the surface with linen used as the stitching thread is a good indication that it predates the machine." Cooper, *op. cit.*, page 12.

backstitch, stem stitch and outline stitch predominated. The embroidered candlewick spread could use up a great many yards of roving, which sometimes resulted in quite a heavy spread. There are counterpanes on which as many as five different weights of roving have been used. Details and lines were usually worked in a single strand.

Woven candlewick spreads should not be confused with the embroidered type described above. It is easy to tell whether the spread is a woven one or not because unlike all the other spreads that exhibit a use of candlewicking, the woven spread has a smooth reverse side.[15] These were done on large looms and were often without seams. The loom was threaded with fine white cotton, and the weft shuttle contained the loosely spun roving or wicking. The raised loops or bumps in the design are made by picking up the selected loops of roving from the flat web, and sliding a slender long reed through them. While the reed held the loops up, the weaver stepped on the treadle. The harnesses rose and fell and the loop was encircled and held tightly by the warp. Then the reed was pulled out and used to pick up the next row of loops.

The woven candlewick spread did not originate in America. The weaving technique using the pulled-up loop goes back to antiquity. The most immediate antecedents are Bolton Quilts, a cottage industry product in the late eighteenth and nineteenth century from Lancashire, England. Most were woven double width on wide looms, which meant no center seams. (There is one dated 1773 at Winterthur that does have a center seam.) Examples of these Bolton quilts are well known in Canada, but Canada has its own product, known as Boutonne Coverlets, hailing from the lower St. Lawrence area. There is some suspicion that they began to be imitated in America in the 1820s. It is very difficult to distinguish the English piece from the Canadian piece from the American piece—and therefore it is exceedingly difficult to know at what point they began to be made in the United States. They were all made of white cotton and had rigid geometric designs. It is said that those originating at Bolton are signed in the corner with initials and numbers. (It is not known whether the letters indicate the name of weaver or the pattern.)

There is another type of spread that has the appearance of an all-white quilt. The Marseilles spread made on a Jacquard-head mechanism in the last half of the nineteenth century in imitation of hand quilting

---

15. The word *woven* used in conjunction with candlewicking may be responsible for some confusion, because many of the embroidered candlewick pieces are done on a ribbed foundation material that employs candlewick warp threads at regular intervals in its weaving to create the ribbed pattern.

was so popular that old handstitched heirloom quilts were turned over on their backs to present their white side to the world in the hope that someone would mistake them for a Marseilles spread.

But this Marseilles spread of the nineteenth century has a venerable hand-stitched and quilted ancestor in the eighteenth century, also known as Marsala, Marsyle, or Marcella. Originally Marseilles quilting was probably stitched by hand in closely covered all-over ground patterns in the early eighteenth century, until the invention of the first loom that imitated it in 1758. The loom technique was so successful that twenty-five years later Marseilles quilting that had been produced on it was a thoroughly established British textile staple.

> When the proposition was first made in the Society, of offering a premium to encourage the making in the loom, an imitation of that Species of Needlework, long known by the name of Marseilles Quilting, it was almost rejected as visionary and impossible. . . . The manufacture is now so thoroughly established and so extensive . . . so greatly is it exported, [few] do not use it in some part of their cloathing. [1783] [16]

An example of the exports to America can be found in an advertisement in the *Virginia Gazette* in 1766: "Just imported to be sold by the subscribers at their store in Norfolk the following articles, viz. . . . counterpains, crankies, check furnitures; Marseilles quilting, etc." [17]

There is no real evidence as to the derivation of the name *Marseilles*. One authority on needlework has expressed the theory that it was first hand-stitched quilting, produced by the yard, in the south of France and then exported to other parts of Europe and England. Here is was sold by the yard for bedcovers, petticoats, and quilted vests and jackets. It came in colors, and examples of silk-faced Marseilles petticoats have been seen in cream, pale blue, and light and dark green.

By the first quarter of the nineteenth century, both early forms seem to have disappeared: "Her exterior garment was always quilted, varying. . . from simple stuff, or fine white dimity, or an obsolete manufacture called Marseilles, up to silk and satin" (1824). [18] The Victorian Marseilles spread is a product of the Jacquard-head mechanism. This loom-woven fabric is best described as a quilted or matelassé-weave: "There are certain loom-

---

16. *Marseilles Quilting, Society for the Encouragement of Arts, Manufactures and Commerce* (1783), *Transactions*, page 36: "Quilting in the Loom."
17. Balfour and Barraud, *Virginia Gazette*, 1766.
18. Miss Mitford, *Village*, Ser. 1, page 223 (1824), as quoted in *Oxford English Dictionary*, Vol. 6, Oxford, Clarendon Press, 1933, page 185.

Plate 165.
Whig Rose Quilt, c. 1850–75. Appliquéd cotton, 82 x 82 in. Smithsonian Institution,
Washington, D.C. Made by Matilda Kramer Whisler. The appliquéd patterns are outlined in
quilting and the spaces between are quilted in princess feather and diagonal lines. The colors
are pink, red, green, and yellow.

woven fabrics with a comparable appearance of being composed of layers of fabric being held together by lines of stitching (or being stuffed) that are sometimes designated as 'quilted weaves' (e.g. Matelassé)."[19] A great many of these survive.

Interestingly, there is a fairly common theme in the design of the all-white quilt. More often than not, there is a central motif, framed by one or a series of floral or geometric borders. The central motif is frequently a bowl, basket, urn, or pot of flowers; it may also be an abstract floral medallion, a sunburst, or an eagle.

The use of an important central design unit may be traced back through the eighteenth century to India, while the selection of moldings and the use of certain decorative elements in the white quilts appear to relate to the federal or classical style in architecture and the decorative arts that dominated the country from 1780 to 1820. "A beautiful variety of light mouldings, gracefully formed and delicately enriched," to quote Robert Adams, was a principal feature of this style. Another description of the qualities of this style of architecture also applies to the all-white quilts:

> Moldings and ornament are delicate and of low relief. Ornament is of a geometrical nature, even when composed of naturalistic or seminaturalistic forms; favorite types of ornament are the circular or elliptical patera, and the chain of husks. [A patera is a small, flattish, circular, or oval ornament employed in classical architecture.][20]

The method of working on the white quilt did not necessarily vary with the techniques used. In laying out the design for the quilt, certain basic steps were employed, perhaps in the following sequence. First the quilt was folded (without creasing) into four quarters, first lengthways and then from side to side. The center point was marked either with basting thread, charcoal, or chalk. Then the folds were marked in the same way, dividing the quilt into four sections. The quilter then chose her design units (princess feather, grape vine, fan, leaf, and so on) and studied the overall effect of her layout. Measurements had to be taken and place-ments were marked with long basting stitches, possibly in a circular motif for the central arrangement, and a large square that would mark out the distance that the surrounding border would be from the edges of the quilt. The truly skilled old-time quilters were so familiar with their favorite

---

19. Irene Emery, *The Primary Structure of Fabrics*, Washington, D.C., Textile Museum, 1966, page 252.
20. Marcus Whiffen, *American Architecture Since 1780*, Cambridge, Mass., M.I.T. Press, 1969, page 23.

Plate 166.
Eagle's Nest Quilt, Pennsylvania, c. 1850. Appliquéd cotton, 88 x 104 in. San Antonio Museum Association. Records say the quilt was made by Mary Van Voorhis between the ages of eighty-seven and ninety after recovering her sight. The predominant colors are red and green, with the eagles in brown calico. The cluster of blue eggs at the center is padded, as are the red cherries in the trees.

design units that they knew how many repeats of a unit would be needed for any given length or area. Over the years many quilters developed such tremendous expertise that a great many of the above steps were shortened or skipped altogether.

After the design was blocked out, details were filled in, either with the use of templates or freehand in the manner described in chapter 3. The last step on the quilted spread was the choosing of the tiny filler patterns. This sequence is recounted in a letter sent from Indiana to New Jersey in 1843:

> We all got together at Bessie Fuller's house for the quilting. The men did the husking while we worked Gracie's (daughter of Bessie) white piece. She'd begun it, but being taken with sickness through the Spring, had been unable to do much on't. Gracie looked quite comely and partook right up till we had in the last filling with the thimble by suppertime.[21]

---

21. Letter from Mrs. Willie Glover to Hulda Ward; collection of authors.

There is little doubt the very minuscule quilting was necessary on some quilts as a means of stitching the background without blurring the main theme of the design; but this was slow because it was very hard on the fingertips. After quilting continuously for several hours, fingers became sore and quilters learned to dip their hands in hot alum water, which toughened the skin. In drawing up the needle, the thread pulled across the upper side of the little finger, often causing a blister. This too, was soothed by the alum water.

One other problem in the working of these quilts was that they had to stay in one place until finished, while the pieced or appliquéd top could be carried anywhere to be worked on. This meant one had to have the extra room to be able to keep a quilting frame set up for a long time (unless of course, one had a frame on a pulley). The average completion time of these quilts was six months to two years.

THE EMBROIDERED QUILT

Embellishing the quilt with embroidery has been a method of decoration from an early point. As early as 1615, in Markham's *English Housewife*, instructions would seem to indicate that there was an attempt in quilting to achieve an embroidered effect: "Quilt it in a manner of a course imbroydery."[22] A century later, in 1718, Lady Mary Worley Montague describes a coverlet as having "Fine Indian quilting, embroidered with gold."[23]

Embroidery is simply defined as "enriching a flat foundation by working into it with a needle, colored silks and wools, gold or silver threads, and other extraneous materials in floral, geometrical or figure designs."[24] A quilt that has been embroidered would have its embroidery executed on the top layer of plain or pieced or appliquéd cloth before the other two layers were added and the quilting done, as is evidenced by the fact that the embroidery stitches do not go through to the reverse side of the finished quilt. Plate 96 shows a quilt top on which the embroidery has already been worked, although its interlining and backing are unfinished. Another method was to assemble the top layer from already existing pieces

22. Markham, English Housewife, II, i, page 12 (1615), as quoted in *Oxford English Dictionary*, Vol. 8, Oxford, Clarendon Press, 1933, page 62.
23. Lady Mary Worley Montague, *Letter to Contessa Mar*, March 10, 1718, as quoted in *Oxford English Dictionary*, Vol. 8, Oxford, Clarendon Press, 1933, page 63.
24. S. F. A. Caulfield and B. C. Saward, *The Dictionary of Needlework*, New York, Arno Press, 1972, page 171.

Plate 167.
Sprigged Quilt (detail), possibly English, late 18th century. Twill-weave cotton ground embroidered with wool yarns; cotton backing, 92 1/2 x 79 in. Courtesy Valentine Museum, Richmond, Virginia. Some of the blue and green wool has worn away over the years, exposing the ink outline drawn by the original designer. The entire stem of this sprig is ink. There is diamond quilting and a 1-inch tape border.

of embroidered material. Such items as dresses, petticoats, bed valences, or head cloths that had been used and worn were frequently recycled in this way. Sometimes they were fitted together with other pieced and appliquéd scraps to create the quilt top as in Plate 95.

Embroidery designs used on quilts obviously relate closely to other domestic embroideries and show a similarity to stylistic developments found in English pieces. Outlined broadly, seventeenth-century English designs, worked with twisted worsted yarns called crewels, utilized the flowering tree motif. Whole areas were filled with stitchery, flowering branches, hillocks and mounds, and various flora and fauna motifs. Eighteenth-century designs were often characterized by a general lightness. The motifs—delicate sprays, smaller-scale patterns—have more space around them. During this period, silk began to rival wool as a popular embroidery thread. A fashion for quilts embroidered in silk and for quilting in silk chain stitch developed in England.

The pattern sources for all these types were various: illuminated books of the fourteenth and fifteenth centuries, embroidery pattern books of the sixteenth and seventeenth centuries, printed volumes of botany and natural history, wallpapers, palampores (Indian interpretations of English designs), and chinoiserie (English versions of Chinese designs).

American embroidery was not merely derivative. Though an amalgamation of many styles, it was really a unique product. There is an economy of labor and thread that has left a distinguishing mark of simplicity and freshness on American pieces. Here the housewife often designed her own patterns and, if she could not buy imported materials, created her own. The wools often came from her own sheep and then were carded, spun, woven, and dyed in the indigo pot that stood on every hearth.

There are various embroidery styles used on American quilts. Not unusual in early examples are the overall patterns of sprigs sprinkled at random over the quilt. During the first half of the nineteenth century, embroidered motifs were used as further ornamentation in and about the patchwork pattern; or as in the case of the Moravian Quilt (plate 168) an embroidered motif served as the focal point of a pieced or appliquéd quilt. There are also examples in which repeated stylized embroidery motifs decorate the blocks of a quilt in lieu of appliqué designs (plate 97).

Embroidery on quilts was used to outline and emphasize details such as stems, stamens, and petals of flowers; or beaks, eyes, and tails of birds. A great many of the earliest quilts that have the chintz cut-outs are thoroughly outlined with silk and cotton embroidery threads. Later, about mid-nineteenth century, there is also a slightly more heavy-handed wool buttonhole stitchery and chain feather stitching on Pennsylvania and other quilts.

A fashion for Berlin work, a term that applies to various types of needlework on canvas produced during the Victorian era, began about 1850. The best patterns for it came from Berlin and the harshly colored worsteds were also of German origin—hence the name. Interest in this work thrived throughout the Victorian era, during which the prepared patterns of insipid designs reached an increasing peak of mediocrity. Plate 100 shows an all-white quilt embroidered in Berlin work. The embroidery appears to have been a later addition to the quilted and stuffed white cotton ground. Perhaps in an attempt to bring an old-fashioned quilt up to the latest fashion, the needleworker placed canvas on the surface of the quilt, withdrawing the threads of the canvas grid after the embroidery had been completed.

In 1895, two women founded the Deerfield Society of Blue and White Needlework. It was a decision to revive beautiful design as had been expressed in the early colonial blue and white embroidery of New

Plate 168.
Pennsylvania Wedding Quilt (detail), c. 1800–1825. Pieced and embroidered linen with wool-embroidered center motif, 90 x 99 in. Courtesy Moravian Museum of Bethlehem, Bethlehem, Pennsylvania. Made by Christina S. Kichline near Quaker Hill (northeast of what is now Bethlehem, Pennsylvania), for her marriage at age sixteen.

England. The blue and white crewel embroidery of the late 1700s and 1800s was sophisticated in its design and use of three shades of blue wools worked on a linen or cotton ground. The revival sought to produce simpler designs but identical colorations. To distinguish the early pieces from their revival counterparts, one would be well advised to look for a three-paneled or two-paneled ground, which would indicate early handloomed fabric. Fringes would be deceiving as they too were revived in the precise style of the early examples. Few of these pieces were quilted.

A late nineteenth-century embroidery fad was "etching on linen" or outline embroidery. Chiefly worked in one color of red, blue, or green cotton thread on a white linen background, these patterns of little children with pets and toys adorned pillow shams, towels, splashers for washstands, tablecloths, napkins, dresser scarves, and bedcovers. The most popular patterns to work in outline were Kate Greenaway designs of girls in bonnets with umbrellas and watering cans and fans and sprays of flowers with a pet lamb, cat, or other animal. Plate 169 illustrates some of these outline embroidery patterns interspersed with alternate blocks of a "Shower of Stars" quilt. Also used as designs were nursery rhyme figures, fruit, spiderwebs, cattails, and lily pads, and sayings like "Good Morning" and "Fast Asleep" accompanying the heads of children shown resting on their pillows. This was a phenomenon of the last quarter of the nineteenth century and it continued into the first decade of the twentieth century. Later pieces may feature Gibson Girls and phrases such as "Wireless Telegraphy." These outline embroidered coverlets are often accompanied by pillow shams, and both pieces are often ruffled.

6
The Whole-Cloth Quilted Spread

Decorative quilting on one large piece of fabric was an early form of bedcovering known in America. The whole-cloth quilted spread is, for the most part, made up of a single fabric. It may have a second fabric for its backing or a second fabric for its border, but the top is predominantly one material. It need not be created of one whole piece of the fabric. At close inspection it may be three lengths of the same fabric seamed together, or even a number of large-size fragments that have been sewn together to create a whole. But it is not pieced of hundreds of tiny scraps, nor is there any appliquéd work on it. The whole-cloth quilted spread is predominantly found in the following fabrics.

WOOLENS

Woolen stuffs found early use as bedcoverings in the colonies, no doubt largely because of the warmth they afforded. With increasing supplies of wool by the end of the seventeenth century, wools, flannels, and worsteds came into even greater use. Linsey-woolsey[1] spreads, a well-known and early type of quilted bedcover, home loomed and home dyed, utilized a linen warp and woolen weft. As cotton yarn became suitable for withstanding greater tension in the loom (around 1800), it rapidly replaced the handspun linen as warp. They were backed with similar homespun and home-dyed fabrics, and both top and backing were frequently in shades of indigo, although many other colors were used, such as reds, pinks, yellows, many shades of brown, and white. They were often interlined with wool. The quilting is elaborate, and the large,

---

1. Linsey, in Suffolk, England, was said to have been the original place of manufacture.

ornate floral and arabesque designs seem astonishing in view of the thickness of the three layers. They have survived in greater numbers than most of the early quilts, perhaps because they are quite sturdy and were produced in such numbers. Extant examples are rarely dated or initialed, and are considered to have been produced within the century from 1730 to 1830 only on the basis of circumstantial and stylistic evidence (see plate 131).

A large group of imported woolen stuffs was also available. Imported woolen textiles were quite fashionable among the well-to-do. "As domestic wools were coarse and not suited to fine spinning, the colonists had to rely on imports for fine wool furnishings."[2] The term "glazed worsted" is applied to a number of lustrous worsted textiles of various weaves. *Calimanco*[3] would be among them, but, because the names changed constantly, and as far as we know there is no definitive description of all the various woolen fabric names, the generic title *glazed worsted* is preferred. These textiles were imported in large numbers throughout the eighteenth century and are often listed in inventories and advertisements of the period. The high glaze they exhibited was produced by a process called "calendering," which involved running the fabric under a hot press that gave the wool a smooth and lustrous finish. In describing the appeal of calimancoes to the taste of the day, Mrs. Hazel Cummin gives us an insight into why these materials would have been chosen for quilts:

> *Their crisp texture and polished surfaces were well-calculated to satisfy the growing demand for lightness and cleanliness in household furnishings. Their cheerful stripes and unpretentious flower designs were welcome relief from the overpowering pattern of 17th century [imported] stuffs. The plain kinds came in beautiful, clear colors, dyed by secret processes. . . . It was the last and most effective effort of [England's] cloth weavers to stem the tide of cotton.*[4]

SILKS

Silk as a ground for quilting dates back to medieval times, and the quilted whole-cloth silk bedcover is known in the late sixteenth century. Mrs.

---

2. Anna Brightman, "Woolen Window Curtains," *Antiques*, December 1964.
3. *Calimanco,* a term that is sometimes bandied about, is "the name applied [in the eighteenth century] to a variety of satin weave wools from plain or simple striped fabrics to those with decorative floral patterns similar to the silks of the day." *Ibid.*
4. Hazel E. Cummin, "Calimanco," *Antiques*, April 1941, page 184.

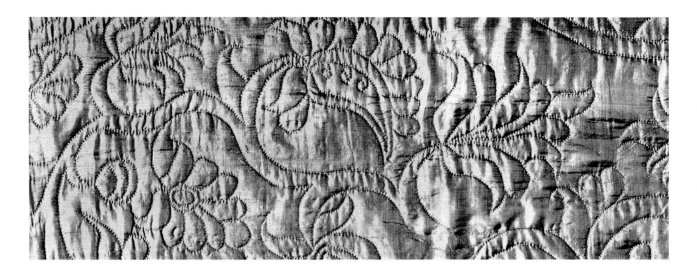

Plate 171.
Quilted petticoat (detail). Silk.
Courtesy Museum of Fine Arts,
Boston; Gift of Mrs. William H.
White. Worn by Mrs. John
Heath of Brookline,
Massachusetts, at her wedding in
1758. The form is typical of
both quilted silk petticoats and
silk whole-cloth quilts in the late
18th and early 19th centuries.

Averil Colby points out: "Lute-string—a corruption of lustring—was a lustrous silk material of which quilts were made, and quilts of taffeta . . . appeared in inventories, suggesting that it was of a quality suitable for upper-class households."[5] Quilts made of china silk were imported to England from the East in the seventeenth century.[6]

Decorative quilting began to be quite popular in England in the seventeenth century and by the eighteenth century it was a rage. A great deal of this was done on silk. Thomas Middleton, in his play "Women, Beware Women" (1626) mentions one such quilt: "Never a green silk quilt is there to cast upon my bed." Silk and satin spreads totally covered with quilting in backstitch were common, and quilted silk petticoats and men's vests did not escape either:

> *Nearly all silk embroideries, had backgrounds worked in imitation of [quilting] . . . and silk petticoats were frequently quilted in floral designs, and linen jackets, waistcoats, bodices and robes were adorned with the most elaborated designs worked in drawn fabric combined with Italian quilting.*[7]

In America, the silk quilted petticoat was totally à la mode too. A 1774 journal entry describes the dress of a lady: "She appears today in a

---

5. Averil Colby, *Quilting*, New York, Charles Scribner's Sons, 1971, page 26.
6. *Ibid.*, page 99.
7. Patricia Wardle, *Guide to English Embroidery*, Her Majesty's Stationery Office, Victoria and Albert Museum, London, 1970, page 20.

Chintz cotton gown with an elegant blue Stamp, a Sky Blue silk Quilt spotted Apron."[8] Often the petticoats were backed in glazed and unglazed worsted and interlined with wool.

The quilted silk bedcover was a type of whole-cloth quilt used in America and it is mentioned in eighteenth-century household inventories. Because of the extremely fragile nature of silk, few have survived intact, though some were cut up and used in pieced quilts that still exist.

PAINTED FABRICS

There are whole-cloth quilts of Indian mordant-painted cottons (or Indian hand-painted[9] chintzes). Bedcovers of these Indian "painted" and "dyed" chintzes already quilted were exported from India to England throughout the seventeenth century. "The early 17th century records show that at that stage, chintzes were sought mostly in the form of quilts—a term then used in its true sense of a padded coverlet."[10] And: "In the early period quilts were usually exported readymade but occasionally when delays threatened they were dispatched unsewn to be made in Europe."[11] These quilts have been found to be quilted in a variety of ways, all in a running stitch.[12] One, the quilting follows the outline of the main pattern; two, the stitches run in cross-hatched diagonal rows; and three, the quilting creates a decorative pattern of its own:

> [The quilting] in the center is a large 8-pointed medallion and there is a medallion segment in each corner. The intervening space is formed with diagonal lines of quilting forming a lattice pattern and the border [is quilted] in large flowers on slender, encircling stems.[13]

The painted designs of these seventeenth-century quilts had a characteristic style: the central medallion on a flowery field with corner motifs and a significant border.

---

8. Fithian *Journal*, Vol. 1, 1774, page 184, from *A Dictionary of Americanisms on Historical Principals*, University of Chicago Press, 1951, page 1342 (Mitford M. Mathews, ed.).
9. The word *painted* refers here to the process of applying the mordants and resists to the cloth freehand with a type of brush or pen, as distinguished from application by a wood block.
10. John Irwin and Katherine Brett, *Origins of Chintz*, London, Her Majesty's Stationery Office, 1970, page 26.
11. *Ibid.*, page 71.
12. It is interesting to note that the running stitch is employed. It is usually assumed that European quilting at an early date was done with the backstitch.
13. *Ibid.*, page 71.

Plate 172.
Sarah Furman Warner Coverlet,
c. 1800. Appliquéd and pieced cottons,
84 x 105 in. Collections of Henry Ford
Museum and Greenfield Village,
Dearborn, Michigan. The similarity
between this coverlet and the one
shown in plate 173 suggests that either
the mother of one of the two girls
(possibly Ann Walgrave Warner) made
both quilts, or the two girls themselves
helped make them when they were
living near each other. Sarah was from
Greenfield Hill, Connecticut, and was
first cousin to Phebe.

Plate 173.
Phebe Warner Coverlet, c. 1803. Appliquéd and pieced cottons
and linens, 90 ½ x 103 ¼ in. The Metropolitan Museum of
Art, New York; Gift of Catherine E. Cotheal, 1938. According
to family records, Ann Walgrave Warner made this coverlet for
her daughter Phebe, who married Henry Cotheal in 1803; it
was therefore most likely made in anticipation of the wedding.
Composed of various 18th and 19th century prints, the
coverlet has a backing but no interlining. Two of the birds and
roses in the center were cut out of a 1780s English block-
printed chintz of the type favored in England and France at
that time and very popular in American quilts in the late 18th
and early 19th centuries. Various other block-printed calicos
are appliquéd and outlined in a variety of embroidery stitches,
including buttonhole, chain, and stem stitch. The figures at the
base of the urn wear Regency costume, which is consistent with
the date. The hair of the figures is composed of colored silk
worked in French knots.

By 1687, England was requesting that no more quilts be sent in favor
of palampores,[14] a one-piece bedcover with no interlining or backing. A
palampore could of course have been quilted by its purchaser or owner
once it reached Europe or America. The characteristic designs of the
eighteenth-century palampore were the flowering tree and the all-over
floral repeats.

"Painted" and "dyed" chintz yardage with designs of repeating floral
motifs and arborescent branches was imported into Europe and America
and often found use as a quilt. Frequently a border of a French or English
block-printed sprig fabric was added.

Materials of all these types as well as printed textiles were used as
sources for the cut-out motifs on pieced and appliquéd quilts in the
eighteenth and nineteenth centuries. This chintz yardage surprisingly was
inspired by designs from European printed cottons.[15]

---

14. *Palampore:* The term is probably derived from a Hindu-Persian word meaning
    bedcover; it refers to an embroidered or mordant-painted and dyed cotton bedcover
    or hanging made in India and imported into England during the late seventeenth
    and throughout the eighteenth century. The palampore's exotic flowers stemming
    from trees provided sources of inspiration for many chintzes.
15. *Ibid.*, page 125.

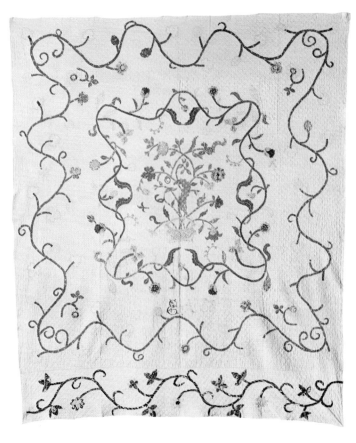

Plate 176 (ABOVE LEFT).
Young Girl in Landscape, New England, c. 1850–75. Appliquéd silk, 47 x 47 in. Collection of Jonathan and Gail Holstein. Though the scene depicts typically sentimental imagery of the period, the construction method of this quilt is highly unusual. Pieces of silk have been appliquéd, and in some places built up in layers and then ripped back, to give the effects of foliage, lichen on rocks, and so on.

Plate 177 (ABOVE RIGHT)
Bird Quilt, New England, c. 1825–50. Pieced and appliquéd silk, 77 x 64 in. Antiques on Peaceable Street, South Salem, New York.

Plate 178 (RIGHT).
Eliza Armstead Miller Quilt, late 18th century. Appliquéd and embroidered cotton and linen, 76 x 92 ½ in. The Metropolitan Museum of Art, New York; Gift of Frances T. Stockwell. Presumed to have been made by Eliza Armstead Miller, to whom it once belonged, the quilt has the embroidered initials "E.A.M." The vines and blossoms of English printed cottons are outlined in a white herringbone embroidery stitch. The foundation is of large pieced linen fabrics.

Plate 179 (OPPOSITE, TOP LEFT).
Trade and Commerce Quilt, Stockton, New Jersey, c. 1830. Appliquéd cotton, 103 x 91 in. New York State Historical Association, Cooperstown. Attributed to Hannah Stockton.

Plate 180 (OPPOSITE, BOTTOM LEFT).
Rising Sun Variation Quilt, Pennsylvania, c. 1850–75. Pieced and appliquéd cotton, 96 x 89 in. Collection of Bill Gallick and Tony Ellis.

228 Quilts in America

Plate 181 (TOP RIGHT).
Foundation Rose and Pine Tree Quilt, New Hampshire, c. 1850 – 75. Appliquéd cotton, 76 x 82 in. America Hurrah, New York.

Plate 182 (BOTTOM RIGHT).
The Indian Hunts a Stag, probably late 19th century. Appliquéd and embroidered cotton. Collections of Henry Ford Museum and

Greenfield Village, Dearborn, Michigan. In this whimsical folk art quilt, the maker has attempted to illustrate a story. At the bottom two Indians menace a figure identified as Buffalo Bill; in the center an Indian hunts a stag; at the top an angel is saying to a shepherd, "Behold, I bring you glad tidings of great joy." The star is labeled "The star which hovers over Bethlehem."

The Whole-Cloth Quilted Spread   229

Plate 183.
Quilted Counterpane
(detail). Cotton, 97 x 90 in.
Colonial Williamsburg
Collection. The coarse,
plain-woven fabric—
produced in Aix-en-
Provence, France—is block-
printed in rose on a white
ground in a simple, small-
scale pattern. The vines are
tightly arranged on a
picotage ground. The quilt
is made up of two 27-inch
strips in the center, flanked
by a 26-inch and an 8-inch
strip. The quilting stitches
are arranged in a simple
double-line diamond-lattice
pattern. The illustration
shows the *chef de pièce*, which
gives the name and location
of the manufacturer and the
date, 1785.

PRINTED FABRICS

Most of the whole-cloth quilts that were made of printed textiles seem to
date between 1785 and 1845. In the last quarter of the eighteenth
century there were increased numbers of printed textiles available to the
American market, and by the second half of the nineteenth century their
quality had declined and the idea of preserving a large piece of precious
printed fabric was not so appealing.

The textile industry frequently overlapped and combined printing
techniques, particularly in its transitional stages (for example, plate-
engraved designs can have colors added by brush, woodblock, or surface
roller), but for the sake of simplicity we will divide the printed quilts into
three large groups whose boundaries overlap: block printed, copperplate
printed, and roller printed.

The earliest printed whole-cloth quilts are block printed and
executed in a limited range of colors including brown, black, purples, and
reds. They are small-scale florals—dotted, diapered, striped, and sprigged
prints. The European prints bore a resemblance to the inexpensive
printed Indian cottons at that time. And the earliest American block
prints, which are slightly later (but still eighteenth century), have a more
open, uncluttered trailing vine or spaced sprig appearance. The
eighteenth-century block-printed whole-cloth quilts are rarely found—
and, when they are, they are usually not in good condition. In the
nineteenth century block prints became far more elaborate in color and
motif and included pillar prints and striped florals block-printed in
magnificent colors.

In the second half of the eighteenth century, copperplate printing

Materials Used in 18th- and 19th-Century American Whole-Cloth Quilts

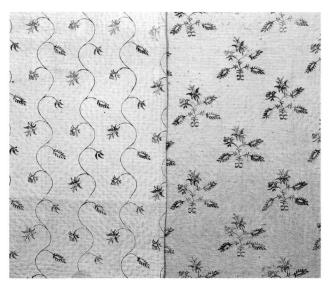

Plate 184.
Linen block-printed in red and black, Massachusetts, 1800–1815. Courtesy The Henry Francis du Pont Winterthur Museum, Winterthur, Delaware. The small-scale American sprigged patterns resemble late-18th-century English samples of the same.

Plate 185.
Cotton block-printed in red, brown, and blue, English, late 18th century. Colonial Williamsburg Collection, Virginia.

Plate 186.
Cotton woodblock-printed in red, damson, blue, and yellow, late 18th century. Colonial Williamsburg Collection, Virginia.

Plate 187.
Strip Quilt (detail), Nantucket. Pieced cottons, 98 ½ x 96 in. Courtesy Historic Deerfield, Inc., Deerfield, Massachusetts. Made by Eliza Howland (1783–1867), the quilt is marked "E.H." in cross-stitch on the back. Printed cottons often found in whole-cloth quilts have been cut into long strips and pieced together to form this quilt. The third stripe from the left is a blue roller-printed fabric dating to 1815–20.

Plate 188 (TOP).
Joseph and Deborah Wildman Quilt, Castile, New York, 1833. Pieced cotton, 76 x 72 in. New York State Historical Association, Cooperstown. A variety of blue and white roller-printed calicos have been used to create this unusual quilt, which was made for the Wildmans' marriage.

Plate 189 (ABOVE).
Rollins Family Record Quilt Square, c. 1825–50. Pieced cotton. Courtesy Abby Aldrich Rockefeller Folk Art Center, Williamsburg, Virginia. This unfinished quilt block flourished in pen and ink is inscribed in the center: "Father, Ebenezer Rollins, was born in Deerfield, N.H. March 22, 1791. He married Betsey Rollins in 1807. Moved to Grafton, N.H." Other inscriptions list offshoots of the family: brothers, cousins, and children.

Plate 190 (TOP).
Anna Tuels Quilt, Maine, 1785. Pieced and appliquéd linens, corduroy, cottons, silks, and wool; unbleached wool interlining, 81 x 86 in. Wadsworth Atheneum, Hartford, Connecticut; Gift of William L. Warren. The body includes plain, striped, printed, and damask-patterned linens. The wide border of pink glazed wool is quilted in floral and feather designs. The center square is inscribed: "Anna Tuels Her Bedquilt given to Her by Her mother in the year Au 23 1785," appliquéd in coarse red woolen cloth.

Plate 191 (ABOVE).
Ann Robinson Spread, Connecticut, 1813–14. Appliquéd cotton, 95 x 100 in. Shelburne Museum, Shelburne, Vermont. The quilt maker, Ann Robinson, cross-stitched her name and the dates she started and finished the quilt.

Plate 192.
Botanical Spread, Connecticut, 1868. Appliquéd cotton, 94 x 96 in. Shelburne Museum, Shelburne, Vermont. The colors of the calicos were specifically chosen to match the living counterparts of the flowers, fruits, and berries represented—roses, dahlias, tulips, pinks, wild cherries, and pears. There are also leaves, birds, and butterflies.

Plate 193.
Apotheosis of Benjamin Franklin and George Washington (detail), c. 1785. Copperplate-printed cotton or linen and cotton blend. Courtesy The Henry Francis du Pont Winterthur Museum, Winterthur, Delaware. This commemorative print, glorifying American Revolutionary War heroes, was made in England chiefly for the American market.

was introduced in both England and France. By this process, large-scale furnishing fabrics were printed. Often the quilts made up in these fabrics were from the newly purchased imported goods, bought expressly for the purpose of creating a quilt. Others were reused bed hangings or curtain materials that had faded or been ripped and sections were given new life and preserved through quilting. Copperplate fabrics were monochrome—that is, printed in one color—either red, blue, purple, or sepia. One entire group printed from copperplates are pictorial patterns: bucolic scenes, chinoiserie, classical ruins, historical views, battle commemoratives, and, after the American Revolution, themes glorifying American heroes (made in Europe for the American market). There were popular allegorical prints of the late eighteenth and early nineteenth century: "The Apotheosis of Benjamin Franklin and George Washington" and "America Presenting at the Altar of Liberty Medallions of Her Illustrious Sons." And there were commemorative prints eulogizing leaders of battles, patriots, and statesmen, such as "William Penn's Treaty with the Indians."[16] Some of these may have been of American manufacture.

At the beginning of the nineteenth century, the use of engraved metal rollers revolutionized the textile printing industry once again. Roller-printed fabrics were produced in monochrome schemes as well as in several colors and therefore can be easily confused with both copperplate- and block-printed textiles. One guide in distinguishing copperplate-printed spreads from the monochrome roller prints is to measure the size of the repeat of the design. Fortunately this is a possibility on the whole-cloth quilt. The repeat in the copperplate fabric is three feet, and the repeat of the roller is about one foot.

The great majority of the roller-printed fabrics, however, are polychrome, and these can be perplexing when one tries to distinguish them from polychrome wood-block-printed fabrics, particularly striped floral and pillar prints, which appeared in the eighteenth century printed by wood blocks and enjoyed a great revival through the use of the roller in the first half of the nineteenth century. Differentiating wood-block-printed textiles from roller-printed textiles is by no means an easy task even for the expert, but there are some clues that may aid in distinguishing them:

1. "Block-printed textiles are identified by pin points or registry marks (often carefully concealed), which indicate the size of the blocks employed, most frequently about ten inches long."[17]

2. Block-printed textiles sometimes show a break in a pattern line that is meant to be continuous.

3. In block-printed textiles the colors are overprinted, one on top of another—sometimes missing the outlines intended for them, like a child who goes outside the lines in a coloring book.

But even here caution is necessary, because there are instances of great exactness in the registry of wood blocks; and, even more misleading,

---

16. These scenic or "storytelling" copperplate-printed textiles are occasionally referred to as "toiles," from the French *Toiles de Jouy*. Handsome copperplate designs, many by Jean-Baptiste Huet, were produced at the famous Oberkampf textile print works at Jouy, France.
17. Florence Montgomery, *Printed Textiles: English and American Cottons and Linens, 1700–1850*, New York, Viking Press, 1970, page 111.

Plate 194.
A Military Encampment (detail), 1780–90. Fabric copperplate-printed in black. Courtesy Old Sturbridge Village, Sturbridge, Massachusetts. This engraving, on the back of a 19th-century American pieced quilt, was taken from a print by British caricaturist Henry Bunbury that satirized life in an army camp. The English inscription on the drum, "Royal Artillery G 3 R," was disguised by foliage, possibly for later import and sale to America.

Plate 195 (ABOVE LEFT).
Sunshine and Shadow or Trip Around the World Quilt, Amish, Pennsylvania, c. 1920. Pieced cotton and wool, 74 x 74 in. George E. Schoellkopf, Inc., New York.

Plate 196 (ABOVE RIGHT).
Bars Quilt, Amish, Pennsylvania, c. 1875–1900. Pieced wool, 78 x 96 in. Courtesy Rhea Goodman, Quilt Gallery, Inc.

Plate 197 (RIGHT).
Open Center Quilt, Amish, Lancaster County, Pennsylvania, c. 1875–1900. Pieced wool, 75 x 76 in. Collection of Jonathan and Gail Holstein.

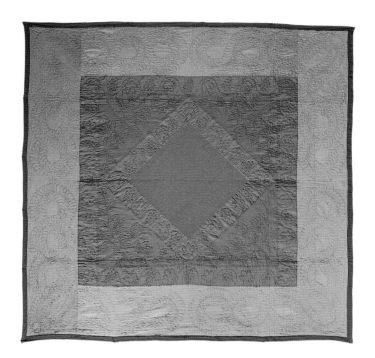

Plate 198 (ABOVE LEFT).
Crazy Quilt, probably Quaker, Pennsylvania, c. 1885–1900.
Pieced silk and silk velvet top; red wool backing, 73 ⅜ x 75 ¼ in.
The Metropolitan Museum of Art, New York; Purchase, Virginia
Groomes Gift, in memory of Mary W. Groomes, 1974. The quilt
contains a "crazy" pattern and includes hearts quilted into a
sawtooth border.

Plate 199 (ABOVE RIGHT).
Diamond Quilt, Amish, Pennsylvania, c. 1925. Pieced cotton and
wool, 74 x 76 in. Collection of Phyllis Haders.

Plate 200 (LEFT).
Roman Wall Quilt, Amish, Pennsylvania, c. 1900. Pieced cotton
and wool, 76 x 73 in. George E. Schoellkopf, Inc., New York.

The Whole-Cloth Quilted Spread 237

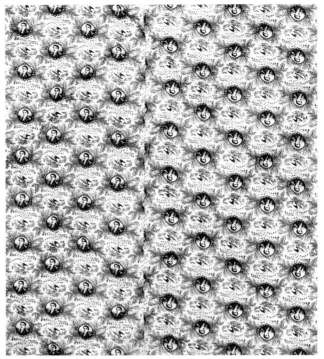

Plate 201 (ABOVE LEFT).
Cotton roller-printed in brown and red, possibly American, 1840. Courtesy Old Sturbridge Village, Sturbridge, Massachusetts. A repeated symbol of William Harrison's 1840 presidential contest with John Tyler is his North Bend, Ohio, log cabin flanked by cider barrels. The stippled ground also features cabbage roses.

Plate 202 (ABOVE RIGHT).
Roller-printed cotton featuring portrait of Lafayette, 1830–80. Courtesy The Henry Francis du Pont Winterthur Museum, Winterthur, Delaware.

Plate 203 (RIGHT).
Roller-printed cotton simulating patchwork, English and American, 1840–60. Courtesy The Henry Francis du Pont Winterthur Museum, Winterthur, Delaware.

sometimes roller prints were actually printed to look as if the color misregistered or went outside the outline. Recognition of the printing techniques used must be a composite of knowledge of textile production methods and familiarity with design and styles, which come with time, and with experience in handling and seeing fabrics.

The roller-printed striped floral and pillar prints that appeared in the first half of the nineteenth century are the ones most frequently seen in the whole-cloth quilt. About the middle of the nineteenth century a roller-printed fabric, best described as simulated patchwork, enjoyed great popularity in the whole-cloth quilt. During the third quarter of the century, we find American roller-printed historical, commemorative, and centennial patterns. A resurgence of George Washington, eagles, flags, drums, bells, liberty poles, the call to arms, peace scales, and scenes of the Mexican War like "General Zachary Taylor at the Battle of Resaca de la Palma" appeared.

There is one other group of eighteenth-century block-printed textiles that demands our attention: the blue resist-printed fabric,[18] often seen on whole-cloth quilts. There is a resist-printing process with woad or indigo "found in almost all European countries during the 17th and 18th centuries."[19] It is patterned in white designs reversed on a blue ground. But there is another group of blue resist cottons that are the subject of some controversy. These are all very much related and have blue designs on white grounds. Whether these latter are of American or English manufacture is not conclusively known, but in any case "the goal for resist patterns seems to have been large, effective designs in brilliant blues at low cost. All are printed on exceptionally wide, coarsely cut blocks, often badly registered or smeared."[20] They are often in more than one shade of blue and are enriched with distinguishing small white dots. Examples have often been found in the Hudson River Valley, and fragments are often found in patchwork quilts.

18. Resist printing: "Pattern application to a fabric by predetermining the pattern and by covering certain areas of the textile with either wax, paste or a chemical so that they 'resist' dyes and mordants when the fabric is dipped in a dye bath." Christa Mayer, *Masterpieces of Western Textiles*, Art Institute of Chicago, 1969, page 221.
19. *Ibid.*, page 187.
20. Montgomery, *op. cit.*, page 198.

Plate 204.
Hawaiian Quilting Bee. Courtesy Hawaii Visitors Bureau.

Plate 205.
Ke Kahi o Kaiulahi—The Comb of Kaiulahi, Hawaii, 19th century.
Appliquéd cotton, 88 ½ x 84 in. Honolulu Academy of Arts.
The entire quilt is covered with waffle quilting. The
Hawaiians associate red and yellow with royalty.

Plate 206.
Breadfruit Pattern Quilt, Hawaii, 19th century. Appliquéd
cotton, 83 x 78 in. Honolulu Academy of Arts. The quilting,
luma-lau, follows the outlines of the pattern.

7
Types of Quilts

Throughout the history of quilt making, fads and fashions for certain types of quilts have come and gone: Victorian Crazy Quilts and Baltimore Album Quilts, to name obvious examples, fit a distinct category, made during a certain period, using specific techniques, and suiting specific sensibilities. Some types of quilts are identified by the inclusion of unusual materials: pants quilts were made exclusively from discarded trouser materials; uniform quilts were pieced from the remnants of military and naval school uniforms; both types were notable for their weight and warmth.

Some types are made with unusual sewing techniques: button quilts are constructed pyramid fashion of circles of cloth, graduated in size, appliquéd to each other and then mounted or appliquéd onto a foundation cloth. There are Yo-Yo spreads, sometimes called Bon-Bon spreads, of shirred rosettes whipped together at the edges, and Postage Stamp Quilts pieced from hundreds of patches the size of postage stamps. (Both of these latter types were in vogue during the 1920s and 1930s.) One imaginative quilt maker created a quilt in which "Patches were hundreds of tiny, delicately curled, pink ostrich feathers mounted on a background of chiffon,"[1] though this type failed to achieve a vogue, probably for conservationist reasons.

Most special types of quilts are distinguished in the same way that a wedding cake is distinguished from an everyday cake—the materials are the same, the techniques are the same, but the intention is different. They were made for special reasons, or at special times in the life of the maker, or of the recipient, or of the nation.

Sampler Quilts, for example, are a potpourri of patterns, the idea being to show as many as possible. They are sometimes called Legacy Quilts, the work of a notable quilt maker in a community who wished to pass on a medley of her favorite or most difficult designs. Sampler Quilts

---

1. Peto, *op. cit.*, page 193.

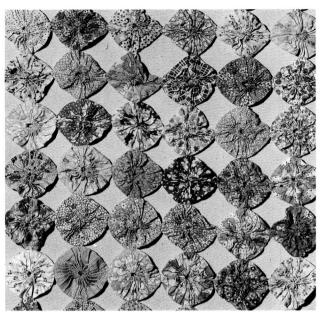

Plate 207 (ABOVE LEFT).
Shirred Dahlias Quilt
(detail), mid-19th century.
Appliquéd cotton and silk,
88 x 88 in. George E.
Schoellkopf, Inc., New
York. The delicate pink,
rose, and peach dahlias are
formed of shirred silk.

Plate 208 (ABOVE RIGHT).
Yo-Yo or Bon-Bon Spread
(detail), c. 1930. Cotton.
Collection of the authors.

were not only made by individuals, but very frequently as group project in which each person would be assigned a block in accordance with an overall plan—there are watercolors and drawings of such plans—or would make up her own favorite block that was then pieced into the overall top. Both appliqué and pieced patterns were used, though more often pieced. The blocks were then sewn to each other or to a lattice strip or sometimes to alternating blocks of a uniform pattern. This type of quilt can be found as early as the first quarter of the nineteenth century.

Another type, somewhat morbid in today's view, were Memory Quilts, made of pieces of material taken from the clothing of a deceased family member or friend. The pattern used was generally the Memory Wreath or Chimney Sweep, the white center of the block inscribed in ink or embroidered with the name of the deceased, the date of death, and sometimes a sorrowful verse.

One of the most bizarre of all Memory Quilts is the Kentucky Coffin Quilt (plates 209–10), done in tans, browns, and white. In the center of the quilt is a fenced-in cemetery containing caskets. Around the border of the quilt are coffins, each having the name of a member of the family inscribed on the coffin lid. As each person died, his or her casket was moved to the burial ground in the center of the quilt.

A rare type is the Mourning or Widow Quilt used by the bereaved during a period of mourning. Whether the quilts were made in anticipation of a death—and, if so, how long in advance—remains an

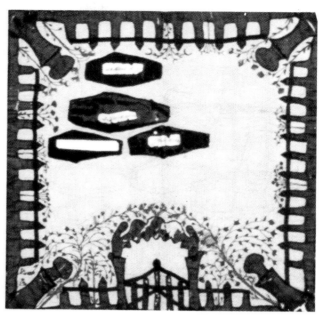

open question. Quilts of this type were said to be made during the Civil War. Colors favored were black and white and sometimes gray, usually with a black border. The patterns are simple, either a dart motif symbolizing the black darts of death or a Cross-and-Star design. Quilting patterns, usually stitched in alternating white blocks, may be a weeping willow, harp, or lyre.

Commemorative Quilts were made in patriotic observance of an event of national interest and importance: the admission of a state into the Union; the election of a president favored by the quilt maker; a historical celebration such as the centennial in 1876. The quilts are frequently distinguished by commemorative dates integrated prominently in the design (see plate 141) and the use of appliqué patterns of a patriotic character displaying symbols such as the Liberty Bell, eagles, liberty caps, and Miss Liberty, as well as likenesses of American heroes. Most telling, the quilts very often incorporate commemorative flags, banners, handkerchiefs, and printed textiles. There are Commemorative Quilts memorializing battles and campaigns (the Battle of Palo Alto and the Battle of Palma and the Civil War) and in honor of such war heroes as Zachary Taylor and Ulysses S. Grant. There are Commemorative Election Campaign Quilts incorporating campaign handkerchiefs, banners, and even broadsides, sometimes including slogans pertinent to the election, appeals for "Protection," "Home Industries," and Tippecanoe and Tyler Too." The James Polk Quilt (plate 142) is

Plates 209 and 210. Kentucky Coffin Quilt, Kentucky, 1839. Pieced, appliquéd, and embroidered cotton, 79 ½ x 80 in. Kentucky Historical Society. Made by Elizabeth Roseberry Mitchell of Lewis County, this highly unusual quilt contains coffins along the border bearing the names of family members. As the person died, his or her coffin was moved to the graveyard in the center.

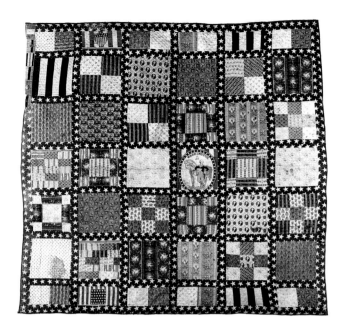

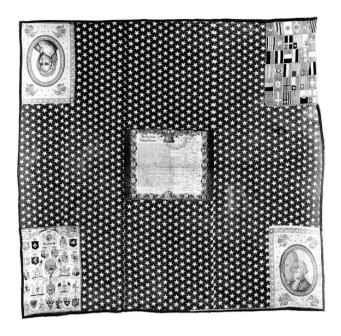

Plate 211 (ABOVE LEFT).
Bradbury Centennial Quilt, New Hampshire, 1876. Pieced cotton, 87 x 78 in. Smithsonian Institution, Washington, D.C. The quilt is composed of fabrics commemorating the first hundred years of the nation. The fabrics were collected by Mr. Bradbury, who was a merchant in the wholesale dry goods trade in New York and whose firm received samples from manufacturers. The quilt was made in Charleston by his wife, Emily; his daughter, Harriet, age twelve; and Harriet's grandmother Maria Selsby.

Plate 212 (ABOVE RIGHT).
Bradbury Centennial Quilt, back. The Declaration of Independence is printed on the handkerchief that forms the center. The corners contain representations of George Washington, Martha Washington, Arms of All Nations, and Flags of the World.

composed of printed broadsides and incorporates Polk's picture and name and the American flag. Most common are the Commemorative Quilts for the World's Fairs, and the most important World's Fair, the 1876 Centennial Celebration to commemorate the one-hundredth anniversary of the signing of the Declaration of Independence. The yard goods printed for this occasion feature flags, stars, eagles, Liberty Bells, and even scenes of bombs bursting in air, together with vignettes of Washington's life and the date of the Centennial celebration. A quilt composed of such fabrics is shown in plate 211 and even the back incorporates a commemorative handkerchief on which the Declaration of Independence is printed.

The Bride's Quilt has held a place of unusual importance in the history of American quilt making—and, indeed, in the lives of American women—for two hundred years. Made in every style, pieced, appliquéd, or all white, they have in common a wealth of superstition, sentiment, and symbolism, aspects illustrated in various ways in the design according to changing styles and tastes.

Since a girl spent her growing-up years making quilt top after quilt top until there were a dozen in the dower chest, by the time she began to plan a bride's quilt she had given a great deal of thought to style and design, and her bridal effort would surely be the culmination of all she had learned thus far. The needlework expended on a Bride's Quilt was the finest, most careful, most elaborate her friends and family were capable of—just as her betrothal represented the culmination of all their training and yearning on her behalf.

Many Bride's Quilts were made in the "Rose of Sharon" design; nearly all include heart shapes, either appliquéd or quilted. To use a heart lightly or prematurely was to court the disaster of a broken engagement, or of spinsterhood. Doves and lovebirds were almost as important, as symbols of conjugal bliss, and the swastika was often used as a symbol of good fortune and fertility.

Customs for the making of the Bride's Quilt varied. In some cases the bride designed and stitched the top herself but was not allowed to help with the quilting. In other instances, the prospective groom created an appliqué pattern for the quilt top. Sometimes the Bride's Quilt was

Plate 213.
Cherry Trees and Robins Quilt, c. 1820. Appliquéd cotton, 75 ¼ x 74 ½. Courtesy Art Institute of Chicago. The colors of this lovely quilt are shades of tan, red, and yellow. There are a variety of star, bird, and heart motifs in the quilting. The use of four large blocks on which the design is appliquéd is an early quilt construction technique.

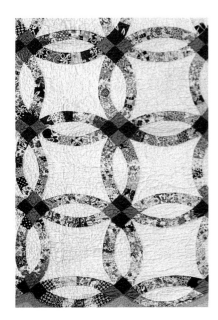

Plate 214 (ABOVE).
Double Wedding Ring Quilt (detail),
Maine, 1940s. Pieced cotton, 80 x
80 in. Collection of Marion Bennett.
Made by Lydia Keene McNutt Russell
of Vanceboro for her granddaughter
Marion Bennett.

Plate 215 (ABOVE RIGHT).
Eli Lilly Family Album Quilt,
Baltimore County, Maryland, 1847.
Appliquéd and embroidered cotton,
105 x 105 in. (each block, 17 x 17
in.). Collection of Louise Emerson
Francke. This Death Watch Quilt was
designed, sewn, and signed by friends
and family of Eli Lilly present at his
bedside during his final illness. Eli
Lilly signed the block with the lyre.
(See plate 271 for a detail of one of
the blocks.)

designed cooperatively by the women who were invited to help the bride
quilt the tops in her hope chest. In the Baltimore area, when Album
Quilts were in vogue, the Bride's Quilt was often composed of elaborate
blocks designed and quilted separately by each woman in the party. The
blocks in a Bridal Album Quilt often depict scenes of the bride's past and
future life, including perhaps a picture of her future home or symbols
representing the groom's profession.

For nearly seventy five years, from 1775 to 1850, the Bride's Quilt
was often a supremely elaborate all-white quilt. Late in the century a
pattern known as the "Double Wedding Ring" became popular, and has
remained so to this day, but without much symbolic significance; it is one
of the patterns most often mass-produced for sale in department stores.

In *Village Life in America*, Caroline Cowles Richards includes the
following passages from her diary, which illustrate the importance of the
Bride's Quilt as a wedding gift, a keepsake from girlhood companions, and

a blessing from the women of the community. When Ms. Richards was seventeen years old, in December 1859:

> *The young ladies have started a society, too, and we have great fun and fine suppers. We met at Jennie Howell's to organize. We are to meet once in two weeks and are to present each member with an album bed quilt with all our names on when they are married. Susie Dagget says she is never going to be married, but we must make her a quilt just the same.*[2]

And seven years later, in July 1866:

> *The girls of the Society have sent me my flag bed quilt, which they have just finished. It was hard work quilting such hot days but it is done beautifully. Bessie Seymour wrote the names on the stars. In the center they used six stars for "Three rousing cheers for the Union." The names on the others are: Sarah McCabe, Mary Paul, Fannie Paul, Fannie Palmer, Nettie Palmer, Susie Dagget, Fannie Pierce, Sarah Andrews, Lottie Clark, Abbie Williams, Carrie Lamport, Isadora Blodgett, Nannie Corson, Laura Chapin, Mary F. Fiske, Lucilla F. Pratt, Jennie H. Hazard, Sarah H. Foster, Mary Jewett, Mary C. Stevens, Etta Smith, Cornelia Richards, Ella Hildreth, Emma Wheeler, Mary Wheeler, Mrs. Pierce, Alice Jewett, Bessie Seymour, Clara Coleman, Julia Phelps. It kept the girls busy to get Abbie Clark's quilt and mine finished within one*

Plate 216 (ABOVE LEFT). Eli Lilly Plantation, Fairmont, Baltimore County, Maryland.

Plate 217 (ABOVE RIGHT). Five of the six Lilly sisters who worked on the Lilly quilt. Left to right: Mary Ann Seymour, Caroline M. Disney, Rachel Wolf, Emily Jane Milwand, Elizabeth Adeline Emmart. A sixth sister, Minerva Ann Lilly Crowther, is not pictured.

---

2. Richards, *op. cit.*, page 114.

Plate 218.
Baltimore Bride's Quilt (detail), 1851–52. Appliquéd cotton.
Woodlawn Plantation, Mount Vernon, Virginia.

Plate 219.
Friendship Quilt Block (detail), 1843. Appliquéd chintz. DAR
Museum, Washington, D.C. This floral wreath and peacock
block is inscribed in ink: "Aunt Eliza Moore, Trenton, New
Jersey, March 4, 1843."

Plate 220.
Album Quilt Block (detail), 1857. Appliquéd. DAR Museum,
Washington, D.C. The whole quilt was designed and made by
Cornelia Everhart Wissler in 1857 but not quilted until 1907,
when she was seventy-two. The basket of fruit includes a
pineapple, a symbol of friendship.

Plate 221.
General Washington Saluting Miss Liberty, New York, 1849.
Appliquéd and embroidered. Private collection. Made by Eliza
Conklin of Claverack.

During the 1840s, 1850s, and 1860s, Album Quilts of all types were particularly fashionable: Presentation Quilts, Friendship Quilts, Bride's Album Quilts, and Autograph Quilts. Some of the most beautiful Album Quilts of all were made in the Baltimore area and are referred to as Baltimore Album Quilts.

The Album Quilt is usually a cooperative quilt made up of blocks contributed by as many as thirty to forty different women and conceived to be presented to an honored recipient—a bride or teacher or popular community figure. By having the blocks individually made, each participant was able to exercise some form of independent expression as to preferences in color, pattern, and type of material used, and still participate in the collaboration of honoring a friend or acquaintance. The blocks were generally appliquéd and pictorial, though there are pieced, geometric Album Quilts. Some Album Quilts contain blocks appliquéd with floral and exotic bird chintz cutouts with the signature placed to one side of the block. When set together, the top is a series of

Plate 222 (ABOVE LEFT). Appliquéd detail of an unknown woman, mid-19th century. Private collection.

Plate 223 (ABOVE RIGHT). Appliquéd detail of General Zachary Taylor, mid-19th century. Private collection.

3. *Ibid.*, page 205.

Plate 224.
Album Quilt with Musical
Instruments (detail), 1846. The
Brooklyn Museum; H. Randolph
Lever Fund.

different pictures or patterns arranged in a horizontal or vertical grid. Blocks were inscribed with the donor's name and dated, and for that reason the Album Quilt is frequently of interest as a historical record. Men and women signed the quilts, though usually men inscribed in ink and the women embroidered their names. Where a man has signed a block, he may have made it himself or, more commonly, it has been made by a wife or fiancée or friend and presented to the man for his signature.

As a cooperative effort the endeavor was overseen and directed at the album party either by one thought to have great taste and discrimination, or the woman who called for the making of the quilt and the one who would present it. At the album party the donors met to display their blocks, to arrange and set them together and then interline, back, and quilt them. Sometimes they were quilted at a different time and the album party's function was simply to display and admire the work. There are some Album Quilt blocks in which each individual completed her block totally, even to the quilting. After she pieced or appliquéd her square, she cut a piece of padding for the interlining and then a piece of cloth for the backing. She then basted them together, drew lines for quilting, and quilted her individual square. They were then assembled by one person who joined the edges with a whip stitch.

Some Album Quilts were the work not of a group but of one woman who may have collected enough material for each block from a different friend. One can usually tell the quilt was the work of one person when there is great uniformity of workmanship (although sometimes irregularity could indicate that the maker had aged during the making of the quilt), when there are no signatures, or when there is repetition of the same design in all blocks. Over a period of years it may be that there was a change in the tradition of making of the Album Quilt. Although the earlier Album Quilts were comprised of blocks from a number of women, later it is more frequent to find that one individual made all of the blocks necessary for an Album top, then needed only to collect signatures from her friends—hence the name Autograph Quilt. The Autograph Quilt was the forerunner of the very popular Victorian Autograph Album Book of the 1870s.

Family Album Quilts may contain blocks made and collected over a period of years. The inscriptions to one person indicate the relationship of the donor, such as "To Mother," "To Aunt Eliza," "To Sister Jane." The date the quilt was finally presented to the fortunate recipient may be prominently recorded in one of the blocks. An early type of Album Quilt is the Presentation Quilt, a form of testimonial by members of a community—possibly to a doctor by his grateful patients, to an itinerant preacher by members of his church, or to a man or woman respected for

Plate 225.
Album Presentation Quilt, 1814. Pieced and appliquéd cotton, 66 x 90 in. Collection of Mr. and Mrs. James O. Keene. The predominant colors are red, yellow, green, and buff on a white ground. Intricate diamond and scrolled patterns are quilted around the block designs. An inscription in fine stitchery reads: "Presented by your scholars at Sunnyside, Ohio. 1814."

kindness and charitable deeds in the community.

The quilt shown in plate 225 is inscribed in fine stitchery "Presented by your scholars at Sunnyside, Ohio. 1814." The verse included on the quilt reads: "Accept our valued friendship, And roll it up in cotton, And think it not allusion, Because so easily gotten."

Women have continued to make Presentation Quilts. The Richard Dennis chapter of the Daughters of 1812 presented a quilt to Colonel and

Mrs. Charles A. Lindbergh on their wedding day. The motif on the quilt is in the form of overlapping ellipses that create the vague outline of an airplane. White and yellow sateen were chosen to represent air and sun. In more recent times an Ohio woman, Mary Borkowski, created Presentation Quilts for Presidents Johnson and Nixon while they were in office. The Johnson quilt is called "The President and the World," while the Nixon quilt pattern is called "Forward Together," taken from the president's first inaugural address.

An unusual form of Album Quilt is the Freedom Quilt, a memento made by friends and relations for a young man when he attained legal majority (twenty-one years)—or when he was no longer bound out as an apprentice. In early years, young men were under the legal jurisdiction of their fathers or legal guardians, who could take their wages, have them work without pay, and otherwise legally restrain them until they reached twenty-one. Young men of both humble and well-to-do families were apprenticed to learn a trade or occupation, and were bound out from four to seven years or until they reached twenty-one. As part of the indenture agreement, the "master" was to provide food, drink, lodging, clothing, and, of course, education in a particular trade. In turn, the indenture agreement provided that the apprentice:

> shall his said Master faithfully serve, his secrets keep, his lawful Commands gladly everywhere Obey; he shall do no damage to his said Master, nor see to be done by Others without letting or giving Notice to his said Master; he shall not waste his said Master's Goods, nor lend them unlawfully to any; he shall not Committ fornication nor Contract Matrimony within the said Term. At Cards, Dice, or any Other unlawful Game he shall not play, whereby his said Master may have Damage; with his Own Goods or the Goods of those during the said Term without Lycence from his said Master he shall neither buy nor sell. He shall not absent himself Day or Night from his Master's service without his leave, nor haunt Alehouses or Playhouses, but in all things as a faithful apprentice he shall behave himself toward his said Master, and all during the said Term.[4]

Small wonder that there was a freedom celebration, a party to which the young man's friends would be invited and at which time he would be presented with his Freedom Quilt. The quilts usually display patriotic symbols and subjects of masculine interest: Eagles, the Flag, Ships and

---

4. "Indentures of Apprentices, 1718–1727," *Collections*, The New-York Historical Society, 1909, page 113.

Plate 226.
Lafayette Quilt, 1829. Appliquéd and embroidered silk, 87 x 87 in. Maryland Historical Society. Made by Susannah Buckingham, the quilt has a military decoration appliquéd to the center. This badge of Lafayette was worn by Susannah's husband, Isaiah Buckingham, in a celebration of the War of 1812. The striped silk sets include state coats of arms and, in each of the four corners surrounding the center motif, the likenesses of Presidents Washington, Jefferson, Adams, and Jackson.

Anchors, Guns, Horses, and various insignia of fraternal orders such as the Oddfellows, Masons, and Foresters. The Freedom Quilt was generally put away by a young man until he married, at which time it was presented to his bride as a gift. Freedom Quilts went out of popular use during the first quarter of the nineteenth century.

The Friendship Quilt was a special token shared by women as their various lifestyles compelled them to sever their roots and leave their communities, and was their special way of showing affection to one another. Friendship Quilts were given to minister's wives who greatly aided parishioners, to the wives of merchants and schoolmasters who moved on in the constant resettling of the West, and to wives of missionaries returning to far-off places to continue their missionary work. It was a farewell token, a keepsake, a remembrance. In these quilts one

Plate 227.
Baltimore Album Quilt Block
(detail), c. 1825–50. Appliquéd.
Maryland Historical Society. The
structure is the Washington
Monument of Baltimore.

often finds that a woman has signed the names of her husband and
children next to her own so that the departing recipient would have a
record of the entire family. A Friendship Quilt might also be given
following the announcement of an engagement.

A Friendship Medley Quilt was often made at a farewell party.
Sometimes each guest brought favorite scraps and patterns; each vied
with the others to make the best and most unusual block she could,
always leaving a place for her signature; then the hostess provided set
materials, backing, and batting, and the work of quilting was planned and
done together. In other cases the Friendship Quilt was made by the
woman who wanted something to remember her friends by. She collected
enough materials for a block from each of them, made the patchwork
herself, then collected the signatures for each block. In such cases the
pattern of all the blocks was usually the same, while the fabrics varied.

Baltimore Album Quilts, frequently Bride's Quilts, enjoyed great
distinction and appreciation in and around Baltimore during the 1840s
and 1850s. The quilt blocks are elaborately appliquéd with traditional as
well as one-of-a-kind quilt designs: baskets and bouquets of flowers;
épergnes filled with fruit; wreaths of cherries and leaves; sprays of red and
yellow rosebuds; eagles, ships, buildings, and monuments; figures of men,

Plate 228.
Baltimore Album Quilt Block
(detail), c. 1825–50. Appliquéd.
Maryland Historical Society.

women, and children; hearts and doves, all set together in blocks of
dramatic colors (see plate 139). From the fineness and complexity of the
work and embellishments, and the exactness and similarity of some of the
more intricate patterns, we infer that enterprising seamstresses may have
supplied quilt block patterns much as needlepoint experts today. It is also
believed that a professional needlewoman living in Baltimore, Mary
Evans Ford, may have produced as many as twenty-six of these beautiful
Baltimore Album Quilts, possibly as bridal trousseau quilts. The heights
of workmanship found in the Baltimore Album Quilts were most
assuredly due to the spirit of competition that was a product of the
Album Quilt.

During the Victorian period, Autograph Quilts of various types
achieved great popularity. Some tops were composed of pieces of material,
usually silk, which had been sent to notables with a request for their
signature. The Autograph Baby Blocks Quilt shown in plate 142 is
constructed of 360 blocks containing signatures of scientists, statesmen,
churchmen, and generals and even included the autograph of President
Abraham Lincoln.

Another version of the Autograph Quilt incorporated pieces of
clothing belonging to famous people. Mrs. Robert Yost (Sallie Yost) of St.

Louis, Missouri, assembled the material for a quilt (see plate 148) from famous people, European as well as American, over a nine-year period from 1884 to 1893. Mrs. Yost wrote to a number of celebrities, particularly in the fields of music and literature, as well as officers of the Confederate Army and members of the Cabinet of Jefferson Davis, requesting bits of clothing for her quilt. The request to the women was usually for materials from a dress or, if an actress, a costume they wore. Ellen Terry sent swatches of her costumes as Beatrice and Olivia. The men were asked for materials from ties. Mrs. Yost frequently sent a small gift or souvenir with her request; jellies, a sachet, even a tie. The completed quilt contains velvets and silks and brocades from ties, handkerchiefs, wedding dresses, sashes, and ribbons on caps or uniforms contributed by such notables as Oliver Wendell Holmes, President Ulysses S. Grant, Kate Greenaway, Edwin Booth, Thomas Edison, and Julia Morrow. Robert Louis Stevenson, in response to Mrs. Yost's request, wrote a letter from Samoa, dated May 11, 1893:

Dear Madam:
I do not know that I have often been more embarrased than by the receipt of your amiable request. I have at the present moment two neckties in common, which I am vain enough to consider becoming. Earnest consultation with the ladies of my family leads me to believe that the colours of these neckties would not be found suitable for your enterprise. Besides which to part with any fragment of the two in question would inflict upon me a loss difficult to be retrieved. In these distressing circumstances it has been suggested that a portion of my sash might (if I might be allowed to express myself so trivially) fill the bill. I enclose accordingly a portion of this valuable fabric and I have the pain to inform you that in the act of separating it the sash (my only one) has been seemingly irrepairably damaged. I am, yours truly,

ROBERT LOUIS STEVENSON

President Grant contributed a necktie and Oliver Wendell Holmes sent a "summer necktie." The irregular patches in the quilt top have either the names of the donors embroidered on them or have signatures written in ink. There are also painted figures and two sections have stanzas of music, one with the inscription "Way Down Upon De Swanee Ribber, Far, Far, Away. Yours Faithfully, Jessee Foster."

Quilt makers continued to make Autograph or Signature Quilts, and in the 1930s quilts may be found that include the names of such figures as Eleanor and Franklin Roosevelt, Booth Tarkington, Mary Pickford, Jean Harlow, and many of the nation's ambassadors and Supreme Court justices.

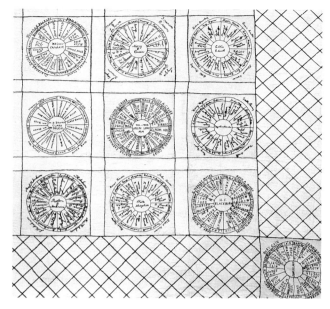

There are charming design variations in Autograph Quilts. Sometimes there may be rows of hands of different sizes with names signed or embroidered on the palm of each hand. More common are Autograph Quilts in which the names are embroidered on the top in a random fashion, thereby creating the design. They are frequently worked in red thread on a white background. Another variation will have the top made up of blocks. In each block, arranged in a circle, are the names either written in ink or embroidered. This was a type that frequently came out of Knights of Columbus banquets, Odd Fellow gatherings, lodge, or church and club meetings and was a way to raise money, with each signer paying a small fee, such as a quarter a signature. A great many of these date from the last decade of the nineteenth and the first decade of the twentieth century (see plate 229).

A variation of the Autograph Quilt was the Scripture or Bible Quilt. Included in these quilts, along with the signature of the donor, was a scriptural quotation, a favorite verse or passage from the Bible of the donor, or an adage, maxim, or proverb conveying religious or moral precepts such as: "Better it is to be of a humble spirit with the lowly, than to divide the spoils with the proud," or "Learn to be useful, not fanciful." The gathering at which the quilt was set together was apt to be less frivolous, more staid, with lots of talk about original sin.

The Quotation Quilt is still another version of the Autograph Quilt and enjoyed its popularity in the 1880s. This type of quilt seems to have

Plate 229 (ABOVE LEFT). Signature Quilt (detail), Indiana, dated 1893. Red embroidery on a muslin back. Vigo County Historical Society, Inc., Terre Haute, Indiana. There are over a thousand names embroidered on the double bed–size quilt top, which was made in Terre Haute.

Plate 230 (ABOVE RIGHT). Signature Quilt (detail), Pennsylvania, 1918–19. Embroidered cotton, 96 x 86 in. George E. Schoellkopf, Inc., New York. Signature quilts—which were usually embroidered in red or blue—were sometimes used to raise money for a local charity, with subscribers paying a small fee to have their names placed in the quilt. In this quilt are the names of men who served in World War I. The deceased are indicated by red stars.

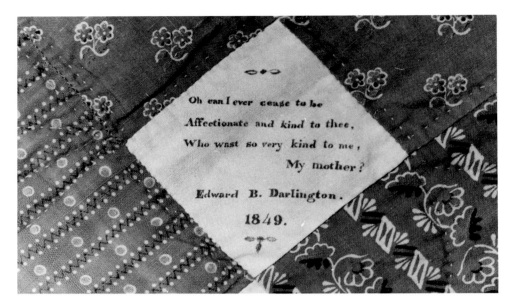

Plates 231 and 232.
Album Quilt (details). Lycoming
County Historical Society,
Williamsport, Pennsylvania.

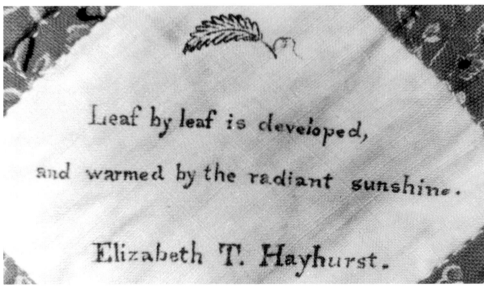

sprung from the Autograph Book craze of the 1870s. It is a quilt made up of clever sayings to dispel the boredom of the sick or old or even as a conversation piece for the parlor. Along with the quotation was the florid autograph of a friend or acquaintance.

Quilt makers have expressed a variety of sentiments, frequently in keeping with the social and political concerns of the time, in verses inscribed on quilts. It is not unusual to find inscriptions in French, German, and even Gaelic. Over and over again there were patriotic expressions of belief in Democratic principles:

From our green mountains to the sea
One voice shall thunder—we are free [1842]

Tis liberty alone that gives the flower of fleeting
Life, its lustre and perfume and
We are weeds without it [1842]

The Blessing of Government,
Like the Dew of Heaven,
Should be equally dispersed on the
rich and poor [1845]

Quoted, particularly on Bible Quilts, were passages from the Scriptures :

And as ye go preach saying the
kingdom of Heaven is at hand [1847]

There were moralistic lessons and simple maxims:

No spirit can be free under the fumes of tobacco [1842]

The Rain that wets the summer leaves
The Beam that dries, the Wind that heaves,
Each give a charm, and each receives [1842]

Many of the quilt sayings refer to sewing and, of course, to quilts:

Cousin Mary remember me though I am young
And let me to thy quilting come
Alice F. Wentworth, 1846

'Sleep sweet beneath this silken quilt,
O thou whoe'er thou art,
And let no mournful yesterday
Disturb thy quiet heart.
Nor let tomorrow scare thy rest
With dreams of coming ill,
Thy maker is thy changeless friend,
His love surrounds thee still.
Forget thyself and all the world,
Put out each feverish light,
The stars are watching overhead,
Sleep sweet, Good Night! Good Night!' [1822–23]

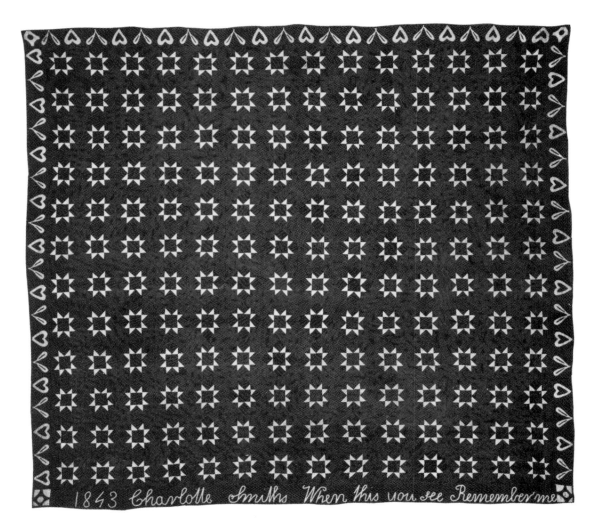

Plate 233.
Variable Star Quilt, New York, 1843. Pieced cotton with appliquéd border, 80 x 90 in. Collection of the authors. Made by Charlotte Smiths of Long Island. A quilt maker frequently broke the perfect symmetry of her design deliberately, following the superstition that she could thus avoid disaster that would befall someone trying to imitate God's perfect work. Note the imperfect star in the bottom row above the word "this."

If it were not for fair woman's eye,
This gift would useless be
No quilting needed but the sky,
Nor shade of Eden's tree [1845]

And time after time there are touching, simple sentiments:

1843 Charlotte Smiths When this you see Remember me.

8 Patterns and Pattern Names

Legends thrive concerning origins of quilt patterns and names; however, little documentary evidence emerges in letters, diaries, inventories, wills, and other historical records about sources of patterns and how or why quilt makers gave names to their patterns.

Early references to quilts are not descriptive, and there are no pattern or draft books, like those for woven coverlets or for embroidery work, describing and identifying patterns. Until the nineteenth century, quilt names were passed orally from one generation to another, their origins lost in time. To attempt a catalog of American quilt patterns and names, to insist upon a correct naming for this pattern or that one, is fruitless; thousands of patterns and names abound. Though there were probably no more than 300 basic patterns in use at one time, the variations are as numerous as the quilts themselves—and any change of color, the curving of a line, the addition or elimination of part of a design entitled the maker to assign the variation a new name. Collectors of quilt patterns—and there are collectors of pattern blocks and cut-outs as well as completed quilts—have assembled collections with as many as 4000 different designs. Patterns were changed and new ones created to suit the taste of the individual quilt maker. Some of the most appealing quilts are of maverick type: a single, unique design that no one copied and that displayed the individuality of the quilt maker and was named according to her whim.

Understandably, there is frequent confusion about what a pattern is called. Often a single name may be associated with a number of dissimilar patterns in diverse locales. And, most confusingly, the very same pattern can be identified by a number of names. For example, an early pattern usually known as "Indian Trail" (see diagram) has at various times and places been called: "Forest Path," "Rambling Road," "Winding Walk," "Old Maid's Ramble," "Climbing Rose," "Rambling Rose," "Flying Dutchman," "Northwind," "Storm at Sea," "Weathervane," "Tangled Tares," "Prickly Pear," and "Irish Puzzle."

One finds a beautiful paradox in the multiplicity of names for American quilts that are essentially products of an anonymous craftsmanship. While American women participated in an art that was largely anonymous, they gained some dominion over their products by giving them colorful names. In a sense, as in the parable of Adam in the Garden, to name something is to possess it. The names essentially have the true Whitmanesque flavor of America, delighting in the rooted, the real, the irreducibly factual. Even where the subject matter is sacred, the name and pattern may be as simple as a fact—a sun, a star, a delectable mountain. The names reflect regional folklore and religious enthusiasms, and the whimsy of the quilt maker.

The earliest patterns were most certainly identifiable as to particular localities and, perhaps, designers. In the first years of colonization, strong cultural ties continued with the mother country and decorative treatment reflected national differences. Women quilting in the same area used similar designs and incorporated common cultural themes in their quilts. Some patterns, such as those found in Pennsylvania-German and Hawaiian quilts, continue to this day to retain strong geographic and cultural characteristics. But, for the most part, there was an early assimilation of diverse ideas and traditions as the colonists moved freely from one section to another, intermingling and exchanging notions of fashion and culture.

Colonial and pioneer women were influenced by their contact with African and Indian cultures as well as with each other. American Indians used both appliqué and piecing techniques in the making of their clothing, and there are obvious similarities to such designs as the Sawtooth found in Indian baskets, weaving, and pottery. In the southern areas, many quilts were made by African women, who brought to quilt making the appliqué techniques of Dahomey and a rich heritage of design traditions.

Folk superstitions also carried over into design. For example, slaves believed that evil spirits followed straight lines. Their crafts, therefore, tend to display crooked, wavy lines.

How many of these cultural and folk traditions were assimilated into quilt design can never be known. It is impossible to determine at what date and place patterns and styles evolved. It is most likely that there was a beginning of an American design tradition at an early date, particularly

Indian Trail

in those areas removed from direct contact with the fashions of Europe. Russel Blaine Nye points out:

> . . . it was not always possible to continue to do, or to believe, the same things in the same way in the new World as in the Old. Placed in a new environment more than a thousand miles from the mother country, the American colonists were bound in time to reveal certain differences with the home population. By 1750, English customs, law, church, politics, manners, and even language in the Americas had been separated from the homeland for more than a hundred years. The colonies were English, of course; British life and institutions always provided a common central point for colonial culture. Yet their habits of thought and patterns of actions were not merely imitations of the originals.[1]

Patterns and their names changed in migrations from one part of the country to another. Designs were frequently recreated from memory, approximating as closely as possible a quilt that the maker had seen or known, perhaps as a young girl or before journeying to a new territory. Sometimes the maker was not successful in reproducing a pattern precisely, and, after a period of time, it was modified sufficiently to be a new design, though it continued to be called by its original name.

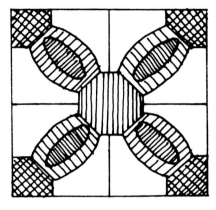

Job's Tears

Names were also changed over the years. For example, the "Endless Chain" has a long history, beginning with the original pattern name of "Job's Tears" (see diagram). Until the first quarter of the nineteenth century, the pattern was named after the seed of a plant used for decorative purposes in gardens. The seed is oval in shape, as is the quilt pattern. Originally the connotation of the name was religious, but by 1825, when the moral issue of slavery was on everyone's mind, the pattern became known as the "Slave Chain." At the time of the annexation of Texas in the 1840s, the pattern was renamed "Texas Tears"; and after the Civil War the pattern was known as "The Rocky Road to Kansas" or "Kansas Troubles." It finally ended up, during the period of great industrialization of the country, as the "Endless Chain."

Unfortunately, some quilt patterns have been lost. During the 1920s and 1930s, researchers on the subject were told by elderly quilters about certain patterns such as "The Candlelight," whose existence they remembered but whose precise designs they could not recreate.

Because of the great numbers of patterns, quilt makers most likely

---

1. Russel Blaine Nye, *1776–1830: The Cultural Life of the New Nation*, Harper Torchbooks, University Library, Harper and Row, New York, 1963, page 37.

gave names as an easy means of identification. (People in the United States are not alone in giving textiles imaginative names. For example, in India fine muslins are called by names such as "Running Water," "Woven Air," and "Evening Dew.") Quilt patterns were collected and exchanged not only within a particular community but between different communities. When a woman saw a quilt in a new design, she frequently made a sample pattern to be put away for future reference; it was a way of taking notes for one who saw and forgot many hundreds of quilts in a lifetime. Many of the quilt blocks we find today were sample pattern blocks never meant to be incorporated into a quilt top. There were also paper and metal cutouts or templates from which patterns could be traced. Some collections of quilt patterns were extensive and were handed down in families from generation to generation. Sometimes a pattern became associated with a particular family, and its construction was guarded as judiciously as the prized family heirlooms.

Patterns were exchanged at the great county fairs and carried by the itinerant peddlers who roamed the country. These merchants of all trade supplied gossip and entertainment as well as household wares. In remote areas they stayed overnight as the guest of a farmer and his family and, if they were as adroit with the scissors as with the tongue, would reproduce quilt patterns they had seen in their travels.

From the 1830s on, patterns for quilt blocks were reproduced in almanacs and women's magazines such as *Godey's Lady's Book*. In more recent times, the *Ladies' Home Journal* and *Woman's Home Companion* as well as numerous newspapers have printed patterns for copying.

Patterns for pieced and appliquéd quilts are both geometric and pictorial in character and many quilts combined geometric and pictorial forms in the overall design. Geometric patterns are particularly prevalent in pieced quilts. A form of geometric quilt top, not really a pattern at all, is composed of irregular pieces of material of all shapes, sizes, and colors, and the design appears accidental and random. This is the famous Crazy Quilt.

When families could afford to waste a snip of cloth here and there, American quilt makers developed more deliberate designs based on geometric shapes: squares, rectangles, triangles, diamonds, hexagons, and arcs. Patterns based on squares and triangles have always been especially popular because they are sewn together with simple straight lines.

As quilt patterns became more regular so also did the fabric palette; when she could afford to, a woman deliberately chose a set of colors to use in a regular repetitive way throughout the quilt top. These differed in intention and effect from quilts made of scraps left after cutting up the family aprons and overalls, and patterns traditionally made of scraps

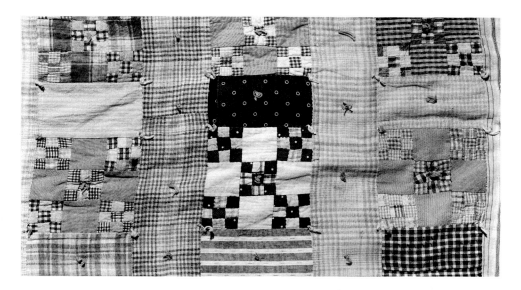

Plate 234.
Miniature Nine-Patch Quilt
(detail), New York, c. 1850–75.
Pieced and knotted cotton.
Collection of the authors. This
classic quilt for everyday use has
miniature nine-patches 1 ¼ inches
square.

rather than from a controlled palette were often named accordingly:
"Odds and Ends," "Old Scraps," "Economy," and "Home Treasure."
Names such as "Friendship Basket" or "Friendship Dahlia" meant that the
maker traded bits of cloth with her friends to supplement her own
assortment.

One-patch patterns, such as "Hit or Miss" and "Brick Wall," were so
named because the overall design was composed of a single geometric
shape, usually a square or rectangle, of a given size. The hexagon as a
one-patch was used in the designs of "Honeycomb" or "Grandmother's
Flower Garden" (the name changed according to how light and dark
fabrics were arranged). Diamonds form "Baby's Blocks" and various star
patterns.

There were also two-patch and three-patch, four-patch and nine-
patch patterns. The greatest numbers of pieced quilt patterns are derived
from variations of the four- and nine-patch design, so called because the
maker began the design by dividing a square of paper into four equal
squares, or nine, like a tic-tac-toe board. There are geometric patterns of
astonishing complexity, designed with mathematical precision, creating
eye-walloping optical effects, as well as tops composed of bands or circles
of color. The variations go on and on. Geometrics are used extensively as
all-over patterns and in repeat blocks in which the same pattern may be
varied as to colors and materials or repeated, depending upon the taste of
the quilt maker.

Pictorial patterns, most frequently appliqué, depict images of infinite
variety: flowers, trees, birds, animals, cups, fans, and schoolhouses. The
overall design may be a repeat of the same pattern or may contain blocks,

each with a different picture. Quilt tops are also composed of scenes or emphasize a single object.

There was a tradition of pictorial needlework in Europe found in elaborate embroideries, tapestries, clothing, and heraldic devices. Before literacy was widespread, needlework was used in much the same manner as illustrated manuscripts—to tell stories. The illustrated forms of trees and birds and the use of colors and symbols created a symbolic language which was read and understood by the illiterate. The use of pictorial symbolism is found in the hex signs on barns in Pennsylvania and in the use of painted signs in front of shops and buildings during colonial days as a form of advertising for the bootmaker, glovemaker, baker, and so on, aimed at a semi-literate clientele. Quilt makers included many symbolic forms in their quilts. In an age of exceedingly verbal mass media, it is difficult to comprehend how universally understood, and how potent, was the language of symbolism only a century ago. People knew that a pineapple on a best quilt or carved on a bedpost meant hospitality; a pomegranate meant abundance; and the swastika stood for good luck. Rings and hearts stood for love and specifically for marriage; in a society in which marriage was virtually a woman's only option, a heart motif was never used lightly. A pattern called "Wandering Foot" was thought to convey wanderlust. As such it was never used on a young person's bed for fear he or she would travel West and never be heard from again; eventually the block was renamed "Turkey Tracks" to break the jinx.

The tree was a symbol rich with levels of meaning. The tree motif is found in the early framed medallion quilts, cut out of a chintz fabric and appliquéd to the top. Indian palampores frequently had as a central motif the flowering tree. It is most likely that the Indian flowering tree motif was influenced by the English during the seventeenth century and commissioned as a design by English importers of textiles from India to satisfy the taste of the European market. In the Christian ethic, it symbolized a tree that grew in the Garden of Eden and also the cross representing man's fall and redemption.

The tree was not only used in quilts in a representational form but also in an abstract geometric form, as in the pattern called "Tree Everlasting." The pattern is a zigzag one, without an obvious beginning or end. It is also called "Arrowheads," "Herringbone," "The Path of Thorns," and "The Prickly Path."

There has been an attempt to give symbolic meaning to many of the geometric patterns, particularly as a result of the names by which they were identified. For example, the triangle is said to represent birds and we have many such patterns with names such as "Birds in Flight" and "Flying Geese." The geometric pattern "Burgoyne Surrounded," made up of dark blue rectangles, is said to be derived from the actual plan of the Revolutionary War battle. Whether the quilt makers created these patterns with a symbolic intent cannot be verified.

As has been pointed out, little is actually known about the derivation of quilt patterns and their names. A good number of patterns were probably the creations of individual quilt makers, who experimented with pieces of material or scraps of paper, creating variations of old patterns or entirely new ones. This required a great deal of imagination, particularly in the design of geometric patterns. The housewife had to conceptualize the overall effect—not only how the shapes would be integrated into a larger design, but also the effect of color combinations. She had to think in terms of the scale and size of the patterns and of the quilt. The dimensions of the quilt must have challenged the imaginations of women accustomed to dealing with samplers and theorems. The housewife had to visualize how the quilt would look lying flat on a bed, and the effect of looking on it from above as well as from the front and sides. We must not lose sight of the fact that the quilt was designed to be used on a bed and, very likely, a specific bed. There were always limitations placed on the design in a practical sense: the size of the bed; whether pillows were to be used at the top; how it would appear with folds; how the borders would look; where the lines would drape or fold.

Available as a source of design were patterns used as a weave or decoration in other textiles: elaborate geometrics of woven coverlets; embroideries, particularly lavish crewelwork found on counterpanes; and the patterns of printed textiles.

Household objects provided an endless source of inspiration for quilt patterns and names. Stenciled and painted patterns found on tinware of all types, decorative woodenware, pressed glass, and slipware plates were all used by the quilt maker. Additional visual stimulation was provided by carved and painted decoration on furniture, floor mosaics, and the inlay in paneling. Floors were frequently painted in bold geometric patterns that were copied.

Wallpaper styles were imitated, particularly the medallion patterns found in the late eighteenth-century Directoire designs. Floral patterns in the heavy black iron plates used to decorate stoves were copied, as was mantel ornamentation. No object seemed to escape the scrutiny of the quilter as a possibility for quilt patterns—even the elaborate carving on a tombstone was once reproduced.

As early as Revolutionary days, the art of papyrotamia—the cutting of paper to create ornamental designs—was popular in America. Elaborately cut paper work was used for valentines and very frequently framed as pictures, but more often it was simply a source of amusement

and entertainment. Quilters copied delicate cutouts of tulips and roses for border patterns and in some instances, particularly in the individual squares of album quilts, the symmetrical patterns of cut-out paper were copied to create lovely abstract patterns.

Masonic and Odd Fellow symbols were used, incorporated into overall patterns or set off in individual blocks. Thus we find the Masonic symbols of the Trowel, Pick and Shovel, and Horn of Flowers and the Odd Fellow symbols of the All-Seeing-Eye, Heart and Hand, and Globe (see plate 235).

Of course, nature was a constant source of inspiration. It has been suggested that the folk artist "turns the facts of nature into patterns."[2] The star is one of the most beautiful quilt patterns and one of the most frequently used. There are "Texas Stars," "Feather Stars," "Stars Without Stars," and the "Star of Bethlehem." There are central star patterns made up of a single star blazing in brilliant colors across the quilt top and quilt tops covered with dozens of tiny stars in different colors and fabrics. There are five- and six- and eight-pointed stars.

One of the earliest of all star patterns is the "LeMoyne Star," named after Jean-Baptiste and Pierre LeMoyne, who founded New Orleans in 1718. Through a gradual corruption of pronunciation, the "LeMoyne Star" became known as the "Lemon Star" in New England. The "LeMoyne Star" is the foundation for the tulip, lily, and dozens of other designs.

The "Star of Bethlehem" is a particularly important star pattern. In its original form it is a single central star made up of eight points, sometimes measuring as much as eight to nine feet from tip to tip. Variations may have smaller stars surrounding the large central one. The "Star of Bethlehem" is also known as the "Lone Star" or "Star of the East."

Like the "Star of Bethlehem," many quilt pattern names were derived from religious sources: "Hosanna," "The Star and the Cross," "Jacob's Ladder," "World Without End," and "Joseph's Coat" are a few. The early settlers were a religious people and they frequently turned to the Bible as an inspiration for quilt pattern names.

As there are star patterns, there are sun designs. One of the most difficult of all patterns to sew is the pieced "Rising Sun," which requires a great many extremely narrow triangular patches forming long rays radiating from the center sun, with an equally large number comprising the sun itself. Because it was difficult to execute, the pattern is rare. An easier form of the "Rising Sun" is appliquéd.

Plate 235 (OPPOSITE). Album Quilt, c. 1850–75. Appliquéd polychrome roller-printed cottons, 72 x 78 in. Courtesy The Brooklyn Museum.

---

2. "What is American Folk Art? A Symposium," *Antiques*, Vol. 57, No. 5, May 1950, page 356.

Plate 236.
Star of Bethlehem Quilt, c. 1840.
Pieced polychrome roller-printed
cottons, 103 x 104 in. Courtesy
The Brooklyn Museum.

All types of flowers and trees became the subject of patterns,
particularly for appliqué quilt tops. In some instances, the treatment is
representational, as where the flower is reproduced exactly; in other cases
it is symbolic.

In the years following the American Revolution, one of the most
formidable tasks facing the country was the collection and classification
of scientific information of American plants and animals. This was of
practical importance if the people were to develop their resources. Nature
was a part of the colonists' everyday existence; they were surrounded by
dense forests or lived at their edge. For the women, the use of tree names
and plants and flowers was one small way to commemorate their respect
and love for the world around them.

The "Pine Tree" is an early pattern and one that has not lost its
identity over the years or in its migration from one section of the country
to another. Probably the pattern had its inspiration in the great pine tree

Plate 237.
Pine Tree Quilt, possibly New York, c. 1850–75. Pieced cotton, 85 x 89 in. George E. Schoellkopf, Inc., New York.

of New England, though pine is found in every part of the country. The first coins minted in the country in 1652 in the Massachusetts Commonwealth had stamped on them the pine tree and the first war vessels of the new country flew a pine tree insignia. The tree is also used as a pattern in quilt borders. The tree pattern was adapted to the particular shape of tree growing in an area such as "Maple," "Palm," and "Weeping Willows."

The variety of flowers and plants used in quilt patterns is astonishing. There are "Daisies" and "Asters" and "Blue-bells" and "Forget-me-nots." There are "Tiger Lilies," "Prairie Lilies," "North Carolina Lilies," "Lily of the Valley," and meadow and mountain and water lilies. And, of course, there are "Peonies" and "Jonquils" and "Tulips." There are flowers from every section of the country—"The Prairie Flower" and "Mountain Pink" and "Sunflower." There are even "Botanical Spreads" (see plate 192).

Plate 238 (ABOVE LEFT).
Flower Garden Quilt (detail),
c. 1850–75. Appliquéd,
61 x 61 in. Wadsworth
Atheneum, Hartford,
Connecticut. The white
muslin ground is appliquéd
with plain red, yellow, and
dull green cottons, purple
poplin, taffeta, gabardine,
and printed cottons. The
background includes a variety
of geometrical motifs, a pair
of scissors, and two wine
goblets.

Plate 239 (ABOVE RIGHT).
Oak Leaf Quilt (detail),
c. 1850–75. Appliquéd blue
and white cotton, 75 x 84 in.
Courtesy Rhea Goodman,
Quilt Gallery, Inc.

So closely related to the actual plants and flowers around them were the flower patterns used that the type of flower can sometimes be helpful in dating a quilt. For example, the "Moss Rose" was not introduced into the United States until the 1840s. Although it could have been patterned from memory, it is unlikely, and the popular use of the "Moss Rose" after the 1840s would date a quilt from that time.

The quilt makers frequently made an effort to give the pattern a naturalistic quality similar to the color, tone, and texture of the flower or leaf they were copying. The "Tobacco Leaf" pattern is an appliqué made up of green and brown colors that capture the subtleties of the colors of the drying tobacco leaf. The pattern is common in Virginia and Connecticut.

Of all the flower patterns, the rose is probably the most frequently used and esteemed motif. Roses are intertwined in beautiful "Wreaths of Roses," or "Wreaths of Rosebuds," or set in bouquets in old-fashioned baskets; sometimes there is a single rose repeated in appliquéd squares across the quilt top. There is a "Texas Yellow Rose" pattern and a red "California Rose."

A rose pattern was even the subject of a political dispute in the 1840s between the Whigs (the "Whig Rose") and the Democrats (the "Democrat Rose"), with each party claiming it as its own. The dispute continued without resolution, but in the election of 1844, with the defeat of the Whig presidential candidate, Henry Clay, by the Democrat, James K. Polk, a pattern was named for which there could be no dispute— "Whig's Defeat."

The "Rose of Sharon" was invariably one of the baker's dozen of quilts that a girl included in her dower chest, and frequently it was the bridal quilt itself. The pattern is appliquéd and is made up of the rose flower buds, leaves, and stems. There are many variations to the design. The motif is of Biblical origin and the symbolism distinctly romantic:

Let him kiss me with the kisses of his mouth. For thy love is better than wine. I am the rose of Sharon and the lily of the valleys. As the lily among thorns, so is my love among the daughters. As the apple tree among the trees of the wood, so is my beloved among the sons. I sat under his shadow with great delight and his fruit was sweet to my taste. He brought me to the banqueting house, and his banner over me was love. Stay me with flagons, comfort me with apples; for I am sick with love. His left hand is under my head and his right hand doth embrace me. . . . My beloved is mine and I am his.

[Song of Solomon]

Although there were great numbers of patterns inspired by and named after trees, leaves, fruit, plants, and seeds, there do not appear to be any derived from vegetables. We do not find potatoes, radishes, or cabbages as subjects of quilt patterns. The "Golden Corn" pattern depicts a seed, as does "Corn and Beans" and the "Pumpkin Blossom." But

Plate 240.
Leaves Quilt Top, 1923.
Appliquéd cotton, 92 x 84 in.
Courtesy Spencer Museum of Art, The University of Kansas, Lawrence. There are 122 types of leaves in varying shades of green on the unfinished quilt top. The name of the species is carefully written behind each leaf.

quilters evidently resisted the use of the everyday garden variety—the carrot or beet—as a subject for quilts. The tomato as the "Love Apple" was used when it was a decorative flowering plant—but not as a commonplace vegetable.

Not all the flowers and fruits were reproduced from direct observations of nature. During the second half of the nineteenth century, commercial patterns were available. Flowers were also copied with an exact attention to detail from books of botanical plants or books on the art of flower painting.

Another pattern source was the printed images of exotic flowers, trees, and plants cut from English and Indian chintzes and appliquéd onto a quilt top. They might be applied at random or arranged in elaborate bouquets and wreaths or dramatic scenes. Fine stitches of wool or silk were sometimes used to emphasize the contour of flowers, stems, and leaves. One finds appliquéd gingham and calico butterflies embellishing the flowers, or small birds perched on the branches of delicate trees.

Quilters had no misgivings about mixing different objects in creating designs. They gave free rein to their imaginations and we find patterns made up of rose petals interspersed with stars, and roses with pine trees radiating from the center of each rose (see plate 181). Birds and animals were a frequent source of inspiration for quilt patterns and names, many of which are geometric. Patterns composed of triangles have particularly been identified symbolically with birds: "Birds in the Air," "Goose Tracks," "Hovering Hawks," and "Swallow's Flight."

Although there are few, if any, geometrics representing the eagle, it is the most frequently used of all birds in pictorial quilt patterns. Following the adoption by Congress of the eagle as the emblem of the Great Seal of the United States in 1782, a craze developed for eagles as a design motif. Silver, porcelain, furniture, mantel and post carvings—all were decorated with eagles. They were woven into textiles and appliquéd on quilts. Depending upon the particular skills of the needleworker, an eagle can look strangely like a chicken or turkey. The patriotic use of the eagle for decorative purposes seems to have gone out of fashion during the 1840s, to be revived fleetingly during the Civil War as the Union Quilt and in the period of the NRA in the 1930s.

The design of many quilt patterns was the expression of an individual whose motivations, sentiments, and feelings are now lost to us. Frances Garside tells of a touching experience in Tennessee at the beginning of this century:

From a press built in the wall at one side of the fireplace, the spinster had drawn down an armful of quilts, made by her mother a century before, the white background yellow with smoke and age.

. . ."*The Twin Roses*"*!* "*Mother,*" *said the spinster,* "*had fourteen children but only my brother and I lived. Some did not live long enough to be named; but there were two, twins, that lived a week, and she named them Rose and Roselle. I think she grieved for them more than for all the others. They were buried in coffins dug out of pine logs—I heard her tell many a time how she lined the coffins with oak leaves.*

"*The field was plowed up the next year and she lost track of their graves; they didn't have money for burying stones in those days, you know, and she wanted to keep them in mind somehow, so she made up the pattern of the twin roses. Her stitches are finer on this quilt than on any of the others, and she never let anyone use it, or touch a hand to it.*"[3]

Drawing of small leaf motifs in the border of the Sicilian Quilt. The design is strikingly similar to the "Wandering Foot" or "Turkey Track" pattern.

As has been pointed out, there are few geographic or cultural characteristics that can be detected now in the derivation of quilt patterns. Most have been lost or assimilated over the years. Undoubtedly, many original patterns were derived from design sources that were traditional in homelands of the settlers. Some go back to antiquity. For example, the narrow borders surrounding the quilted blocks of the Sicilian Quilt are decorated with groups of small leaf patterns. When these patterns are shown in detail and enlarged in scale (see diagram), they are strongly reminiscent of the popular "Turkey Track" pattern in America. Another example of a possible design origin that changed over the years is found in the palampore illustrated in plate 174. The hillocks at the base of the "Flowering Tree" could conceivably be the basis for triangle patterns such as the "Sawtooth" that we find later in American quilts.

However, there are some instances of strong cultural or geographic influences in quilt patterns. The Pequito Quilt found in New Mexico has a strong Mexican and Spanish flavor in its design. The quilt is constructed in squares, pieced out of fragments of cloth, folded in triangles and sewn in circular patterns that look like spinning discs. The influence is clearly Moorish, Spanish, and Mexican. And quilts found in many parts of the South reveal construction techniques strikingly similar to sewing techniques, both appliqué and piecing, used by African tribes.

Most particularly, strong cultural characteristics are found in Hawaiian and Pennsylvania quilts. Where there is a cultural quality retained and expressed in quilts, it is the result of a somewhat unusual ethnic or geographic separation from the mainstream of American cultural life.

Large numbers of Germans migrated from the Upper Rhine Valley— the Palatinate region of Germany, Swabia, and Switzerland—to the

---

3.   Frances Garside, "Patchwork Romance," *House Beautiful*, January 1919, page 24.

colony of Pennsylvania between 1683 and 1775. Families and individuals were encouraged to undertake the resettlement by agents sent to Europe by William Penn. Benefits to be found in the New World were publicized through pamphlets and word of mouth. The Germans responded, in large measure because of religious persecutions, bad economic conditions, and the political discontent in Europe at that time.

Many of the German settlers belonged to sects—the Mennonites, Moravians, Amish, the Brethren, Schwenckfelders, and the Church People—of strong religious convictions and practices. The great numbers of settlers, their concentration in specific areas, and their separatist attitudes enabled them to continue their European traditions and customs almost intact, aloof from their neighbors. They transplanted their native crafts to the New World. Traditional German forms of design and decoration continued to be used on furniture, in art, and in needlework.

Although the Pennsylvania German quilters used basic quilt patterns, it is the interesting variations in the patterns, the bright colors, the extensive use of traditional German symbols, and the exquisite workmanship that distinguish their quilts. There are unexpectedly dazzling color combinations discovered in the quilts—bright reds, greens, yellows, oranges, and pinks mixed with almost naive naturalness. The Amish quilts display particularly bold contrasts of color in geometric forms.

The use of symbolic forms—traditional to Pennsylvania German folk art and crafts—is found extensively in Pennsylvania German quilts. For example, hearts in a wreath are frequently found in Pennsylvania quilts and they signify a blessing and protection of the house; hearts in a wreath are frequently found painted under the eaves of barns. Also used extravagantly are the double rose, fuchsia, pomegranate, and tulips set in three lobes representing the Trinity. At some point in time, the actual significance of many of the signs and symbols was lost to quilt makers. The star and crescent painted on the side of a barn were meant to ward off harm to cattle and other livestock. In a quilt today, they have little symbolic meaning and the pattern is used for purely decorative purposes.

Hawaiian quilts are another type that remain distinctive both as to patterns and names. The technique of patchwork was introduced to the Islands during the first quarter of the nineteenth century by the wives of missionaries. The use of needle and thread was new to the women of Hawaii, and instruction in sewing became part of the curriculum in missionary schools. As the Hawaiian quilt evolved, it had no resemblance either in sewing techniques or design to the pieced quilts of the mainland, though it does bear a relationship to appliqué styles. There were no scrap bags for materials in the Hawaiian home. Clothing was cut in full widths of cloth, with nothing left as waste. The traditional forms of native bedding consisted of mats. Coverlets were "tapas," made from the beaten bark of the *wauke* plant and decorated with designs of many colors. Because of the isolation of the Hawaiian Islands, and a strong indigenous tradition, Hawaiian quilts took on a distinctive character that remains to this day.

The earliest Hawaiian quilts employed simple designs, usually with a strong central pattern of turkey-red color on a white background. The patterns are flat with the motif repeated without variations over the quilt top. Eventually, in addition to turkey red other colors were used, though the quilter continued to employ one color against a single color background, generally white. The quilting usually follows the pattern outlines.

The technique for cutting the pattern has been described as follows:

The material is first washed to make sure of fast color and uniform shrinkage. If that for the background and lining is not all of one piece, it is seamed lengthwise. The most common style, a square design with unbroken or slightly broken border, is cut from material folded diaperwise, eight-fold, the creases forming the corners of the border, the necessary seams falling at the middle of the sides. Thus, by cutting one motif, the entire border is produced at one time, and with exact repetition of the motif. This leaves a large, roughly circular piece for the medallion, which also is cut folded. Some women design free-hand with the scissors, others cut the pattern first in paper—in the old days tapa was used for this purpose. Both border and medallion are then basted on the background.

In another style of pattern, a motif is cut the entire length of the folded material, producing four repetitions which radiate from the center of the quilt to the corners.[4]

There was a proprietary interest in quilt patterns. The originator of a design had the pleasure of naming it. The quilt design and names were thereafter inseparable. Stella Jones wrote of the origins of Hawaiian quilt designs and names:

To one unfamiliar with Hawaii, no doubt many of these quilt names and their designs will appear far-fetched. This is due not to lack of logic on the part of the designer, but to the difficulty of interpreting in English the allegorical thought of the Hawaiian and the subtlety of his expression. Then, too, there is not necessarily any connection between the actual design and the theme. Many a woman, having worked out in her quilt some meaning known only to herself, gives it a name foreign to the subject

---

4. Stella Jones, *Hawaiian Quilts*, Honolulu Academy of Arts, 1930, page 19.

and keeps the interpretation secret. Nor are all quilts symbolic, any new design or subject that strikes the fancy may be reproduced on a quilt—the chandelier in the Palace when it was new was a favorite subject; the highly elaborate design in a stained glass window of the first "parlor car" on Hawaii was another; a vase or a basket of flowers in the house; any design seen in cloth or embroidery.

Any classification of Hawaiian quilt designs must of course be arbitrary; on the basis of theme, however, the following may be found acceptable and convenient: quilts with naturalistic motif; those associated with some place; historical themes. Such patterns as Saw pattern, Pile of lumber, Press gently, however, defy classification.

The Hawaiian woman drew upon her garden for many of her designs. The actual leaves of the breadfruit, of the pumpkin and papaia, fig leaves, and ferns she used as patterns. The wide-spread tentacles of the octopus, the outlines of the turtle, and Mahina (The crescent moon) were very old-time themes for quilt patterns. With the naturalistic designs also may be included; Lilia o ke awawa (Lily-of-the-valley); Fuchsia pattern; Lilia o Sepania Kepani (Japanese lily); Kaui o Amerika (American rose); Pineapple pattern, in many designs; Poni moi (Carnation); Grape-vine; Ohelo berries; Hibiscus flowers; Panini (Prickly pear); Pika pua waiohinu (Pitcher of dahlias); Popolehua (Round ball of lehua blossoms). The lei, or garland, which has so important a place in life in Hawaii, is amply represented in quilts: Lei mamo (Lei of the feathers of the mamo bird); Lei loke (Rose wreath); Lei o May (Lei of May, a woman's name); Lei ana kaui ika mokihana (With a wreath of Illokihana); Lei of Hawaii.[5]

Quilt pattern names are of interest for reasons other than identification. They are descriptive of the occasions of their day from literary to political (as are the names given to quilt patterns today) reflecting observations about the changes going on in the country, the day-to-day occupations, the places and people and trades, the entertainments and styles and events that occupied the thoughts of the people.

Great causes of the time—the Civil War, the Mexican War, the concerns regarding slavery—are commemorated in quilt names. The names give a lovely, almost naive description of life in the United States in the earliest days of the nation. There are pattern names descriptive of the trees and plants, the flowers and birds found in the land. As evocative as any picture, the short, graphic quilt names arouse a sense of the pleasures of the people and the customs of a different time. There are

Plate 241 (OPPOSITE). Crazy Quilt, Massachusetts, c. 1850–1900. Pieced, appliquéd, and embroidered silk and velvet, 74 1/2 x 57 in. Courtesy Museum of Fine Arts, Boston; Gift of Mr. and Mrs. Edward J. Healy, in memory of Mrs. Charles O'Malley. Made by Celestine Bacheller of Wyoma, the quilt is said to depict actual scenes of the neighborhood in which she lived.

---

5. *Ibid.*, page 24.

Plate 242.
Sailboat Quilt, New York, c. 1875–1900. Pieced cotton, 74 x 60 in. Courtesy Rhea Goodman, Quilt Gallery,
Inc. The initials "J.M.D." are embroidered in red in the lower left-hand corner.

references to which we have little association, but most are picturesque reminders of our past. Quilts were named "The Stone Wall," "Forest Path," "Country Farm," and "Fence Row." There are "Log Cabin" patterns, the "Courthouse Steps," the "Windmill," and the "Schoolhouse."

Perhaps more than any other quilt name, the one that most confirms the love of the land, the appreciation of the vast country, the peace and plenty and opportunity was the "Delectable Mountain." The name is derived from a passage in John Bunyan's allegory *Pilgrim's Progress*, published in 1678, which reads: "They went then till they came to the Delectable Mountains . . . behold the gardens and orchards, the vineyards and fountains of water."

Descriptive of the great westward expansion and migration of the nineteenth century are "Rocky Road to California," "Wagon Trail," "Arkansas Traveler," and "Wandering Foot." And the personalities: there were "Yankee Charm" and "Yankee Pride."

It was a time when people avidly played games and puzzles and named quilt patterns after them: "Leap Frog," "Follow-the-Leader," and "Merry-Go-Round." And there were "Farmer's Puzzle" and "Bachelor's Puzzle," "Old Maid's Puzzle," "Fool's Puzzle," and "Washington's Puzzle." And "Tic-tac-toe," "Puss-in-the-Corner," and "Domino." Quilts were named after square dance calls such as "Swing in the Corner" and "Hands All Around."

References were made to occupations and trades—"The Dusty Miller" and "The Water Mill." And the tools of a trade: "The Anvil," "The Carpenter's Square," "Double Wrench," "Chips and Whetstone," "The Reel," and "The Ship's Wheel." There were patterns named after household objects, such as "Flower Pot" and "Churn Dash."

The unhurried days of courtship and romantic fantasy supplied some quilt names—"Young Man's Fancy," "Cupid's Arrowpoint," "Friendship Knot," "Lover's Links," "Bridal Stairway," "Single Wedding Ring," and "Honeymoon Cottage." There were also the "Crib Quilt" and "Widow's Troubles."

And moral lessons to be gained from "The Drunkard's Path," a pattern that seems to swerve and meander across the quilt. For the more genteel quilt makers, it was called the "Pumpkin Vine."

There were literary references. Novels and poetry contributed a share of quilt patterns and names. An extremely beautiful quilt made in Virginia during the last quarter of the eighteenth century is known as the "Robinson Crusoe Quilt" (plate 89). Cut out of chintz and appliquéd to the top is a figure said to be Robinson Crusoe; he stands at the foot of a tree covered with giant rose, carnation, and sweet william blossoms.

A geometric quilt pattern with a literary reference is the "Lady of the Lake." The pattern is named after Sir Walter Scott's poem, which was

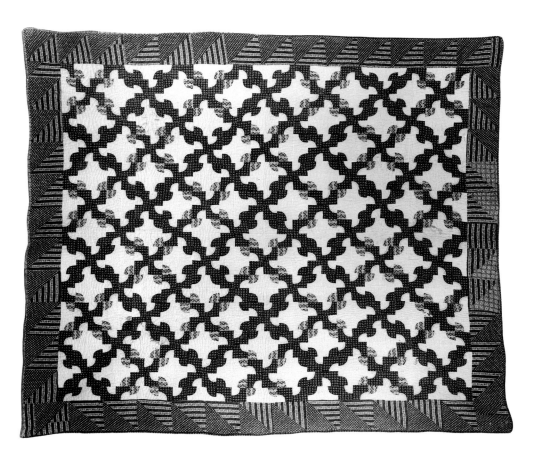

Plate 243.
Drunkard's Path Quilt, before 1884. Pieced cotton, gingham, and calicos, 84 x 71 ½ in. Spencer Museum of Art, The University of Kansas, Lawrence. The pattern is also called Fool's Puzzle, Wonder of the World, Country Husband, and other names.

published in 1810 and was a great popular success in the United States. Quilts with the "Lady of the Lake" pattern are found in every section of the country and, surprisingly, in its migrations the name has survived, being one of the few quilt patterns not known by other names. The pattern gained great popularity during the second quarter of the nineteenth century. Wallpaper patterns of the period were also named after the poem.

Quilt names were used to describe political and historical events and personages. We find "Martha Washington's Wreath," "Clay's Choice," "Garfield's Monument," "Jackson's Star," and "Lincoln's Platform." Political slogans became pattern names and we have patterns called "Tippecanoe and Tyler Too" and "Fifty-Four Forty or Fight."

And so the names go on and on—"Electra Amelia Hall and Her Twin Sister," "The Tonganoxie Nine-Patch," "Presidents and the World," "Aunt Eliza's Star"—new names and old, new patterns and old, all delightful reminders of our past and present. Like poems of Whitman, they serve as a witty catalogue raisonné of the "poem of these states." Naming and patterning showed the exuberance and imagination of their creators. Touches of creative genius, indeed!

9
Signing and Initialing

Quilts with names on them have a particular appeal. When there is an identifying mark: a cross-stitched initial, a name raised in the quilting, an inked signature, one feels that much closer to the source—a rare pleasure in an art form that is largely anonymous. Of even greater rarity is additional information found worked into a quilt. Sometimes the name of the town of the quilter is included, sometimes her age, sometimes the year of completion of the quilt, or the year it was begun, or a word defining the occasion for which the quilt was conceived.

The use of embroidered letters and numerals on needlework can be dated as far back as the tenth century in England, with the appearance of decorative lettering on the stole of St. Cuthbert.[1] The Bayeux Tapestry, worked in the eleventh century, displays an entire narrative in embroidered letters. The arms of the Wokyndon family, embroidered in colored silks, appear on the Marnhull Orphrey, which dates from 1315 to 1335;[2] and initials are seen as early as the sixteenth century.[3]

Quilt makers embroidered their names, gave dates, locations, and sometimes even added a word or two of descriptive phrasing as in "Sarah Kenedy Her Quilt" (plate 247), and "Ellen Dicus EX SLAVE Greenfield, Mo." (plate 246). Ann Robinson gave the date she began and the date she finished her spread, leaving us the startling information that this elaborate spread took no more than three months to the day to complete (see plate 191).

Embroidery used to sign quilts is quite common. The placement of

---

1. The stole of St. Cuthbert was embroidered around A.D. 909. Margaret H. Swain, *Historical Needlework: A Study of Influences in Scotland and Northern England*, New York, Charles Scribner's Sons, 1970, page 2.
2. Patricia Wardle, *Guide to English Embroidery*, London, Her Majesty's Stationery Office, 1970, Victoria and Albert Museum, page 30. (Orphrey refers to the band of elaborate embroidery found on ecclesiastical vestments.)
3. Mid-sixteenth century bed tester and chalice veil both display embroidered initials. *Ibid.*, page 31.

Plate 244 (RIGHT).
Lord's Prayer Quilt, Vermont, c. 1825–50. Pieced and appliquéd cotton; hand-woven linen backing, 85 x 94 in. Shelburne Museum, Shelburne, Vermont. Made by Samantha R. Barto Wing. Cross-stitched in light blue on the backing is "Samantha R. Wing" and "No. 11." The foundation is printed with tiny roses in faded tans and pinks on a creamy dimity. The pieced letters, appliquéd to form the words of Matthew 6:9–13, create one of the most unique folk art masterworks in quilt making.

Plate 245 (OPPOSITE, TOP LEFT).
Border of appliquéd quilt (detail), probably Indiana. Vigo County Historical Society, Inc., Terre Haute, Indiana. The signature reads: "Ann Maxwell 1861."

Plate 246 (OPPOSITE, TOP RIGHT).
Album Quilt Block (detail). Pieced cotton. Vigo County Historical Society, Inc., Terre Haute, Indiana. The embroidered signature reads: "Ellen Dicus, Ex Slave, Greenfield, Mo."

Plate 247 (OPPOSITE, BOTTOM LEFT).
Framed Center Quilt (detail), c. 1800–1825. Pieced block- and roller-printed cottons. Collection of the authors. The signature reads: "Sarah Kenedy, Her Quilt."

Plate 248 (OPPOSITE, BOTTOM RIGHT).
Appliquéd cotton quilt (detail). Collection of the authors. Signed and dated in primitive cross-stitch: "March 8, 1855, Matilda Cree." Note the quilted hearts.

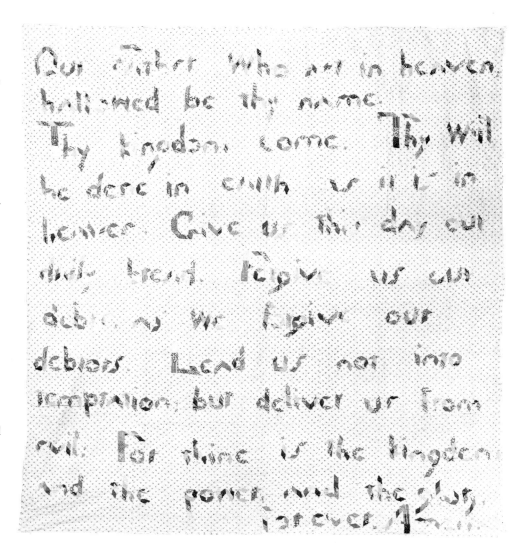

the signature and date can be anywhere, nestled in a corner of the appliqué border (plate 245), or prominently displayed, the focal point of the quilt (plate 249). There seems to be no standard pattern as to whether names are signed in full or initialed or accompanied by a date, and no customs emerge in terms of time or place. Signing was determined by the whim of each individual needleworker. No custom dictated to them. Two of the earliest known signed American quilts are the Mary Johnston Quilt in plate 68, which has the embroidered signature "Mary Johnston 1793," and the McIlhenny Quilt, which bears on the back the cross-stitched label "W.T.G. 1795" (plate 138).

The embroidered cross-stitch is probably the most common of all the

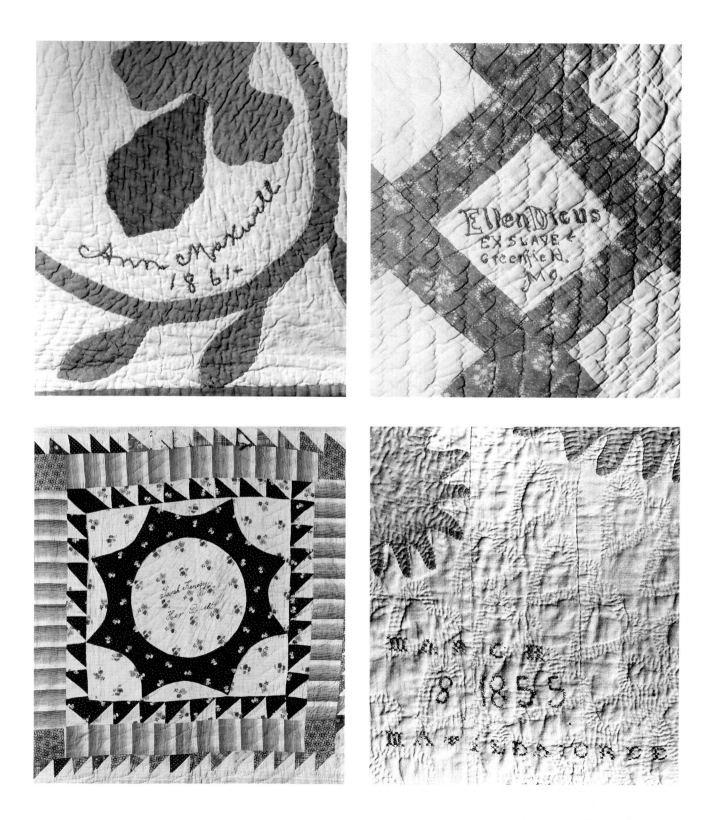

Plate 249.
Irene B. Forman Quilt, New York, 1853. Appliquéd and embroidered cotton, 80 x 90 in. National Gallery, Washington, D.C. Fifty-six appliquéd blocks—each quilted with individual designs—are stitched together with narrow strips of white muslin. Turkey red calico circles are placed at all the intersections.

methods of signing a quilt. This is very likely a carryover from linen marking, which originally consisted of initials and numerals done in cross-stitch. The practice of marking household linens made its appearance sometime in the early seventeenth century in England. Prompted by a greater affluence, stocks of household linen grew more plentiful. Numbers allowed the housewife to use her sheets in rotation, thereby enabling her to distribute wear and tear on the linens evenly. Initials facilitated the business of sorting the laundry after the large seasonal washings. As early as the sixteenth century, women were warned to take count of their linens at the washings:

Dry sun, dry wind, Safe bind, safe find,
Go wash well, saith summer, with sun I shall dry;
Go wring well, saith winter, with wind so shall I.
To trust without heed is to venture a joint,
Give tale and take count *is a housewifely point.*[4]

In 1836, *The American Frugal Housewife* cautioned: "Count towels, sheets, spoons, etc. occasionally, that those who use them may not become careless."[5] And in 1878, *The Useful Companion* counseled:

It should be bourne in mind, that too frequent washing is liable to wear out linen more than ordinary use; and therefore the process should not be repeated oftener than is absolutely necessary. It will also be found an excellent plan to have every article numbered and initialled, and so arranged after washing that each may be worn in its regular turn, and accomplish its proper term of domestic use.[6]

A precedent for the linen marking technique may be found in the use of engraved initials on metalwares.

Sometimes one notes a triangle of letters as on old pewterware, indicating a marriage, the surname initial at the top and husband and wife's Christian name initials to left and right below.[7]

Formulae for the placement of the initials and numbers varied. These are the instructions from *The Young Servants Friendly Instructor* (1827):

If only the initial of the surname is to be marked, place the figure directly under it; thus,

    O

    1

If the initial of the surname and the Christian name, place the figure below and in the middle; thus,   *P O*

        2

---

4.   This may also have been a caveat against thieves, who were apt to take linens drying unattended on the grass in the sun.

5.   Mrs. Child, *The American Frugal Housewife*, Boston, American Stationer's Company, 1836, page 8.

6.   Henry B. Allen, *The Useful Companion*, New York, H. B. Allen Publishers, 1878, page 295.

7.   Therle Hughes, *English Domestic Needlework, 1660–1860*, New York, Macmillan Company, 1961, page 161.

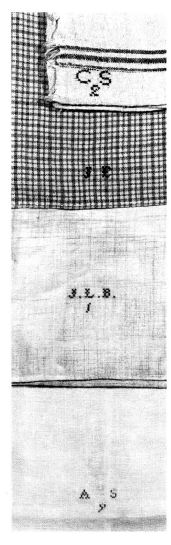

If there are two Christian names and surname for one person,

P K O

3

If it is to be marked with the name of a married pair, place the initial of the gentleman's Christian name to the left, that of the lady to the right, that of the surname at top, and the number below; thus,

   O

M P

   4

If the date is to be added, let it be placed below all; thus,

   O   P K O

M P   *or*   1827

   4

1827[8]

The custom of marking household linens[9] with initials and numbers is of particular interest to us because very often, on the back of an early quilt, usually along the edges, one will see small letters and numbers stitched into the fabric. Presumably the appearance of these markings indicates that a piece of household linen was used in the making of quilt, and the section with the initials was included.[10]

This is not always the case, however. Women did mark quilts with their initials and numbers, intending the number to reflect the accumulation of quilts for their marriage chest. These would eventually number thirteen, a baker's dozen. Plate 252 illustrates this marking system used on a home-woven Canadian blanket. "The initials stand for Rebecca Barker, and the number means that this was the sixth blanket for her trousseau . . . one blanket a year was woven, and each one put aside in preparation for her marriage."[11]

The Rebecca Barker blanket is accompanied by the precise information necessary for translating the ciphers, but decoding the numbers and initials found on the fronts and backs of anonymous quilts

8. Esther Copley, "Marking Linens," *The Young Servants Friendly Instructor*, London, page 85, as quoted from Copp Family Textiles, page 25.

9. Linens included grain bags, sheets, pillowcases, bolster covers, bureau covers, table linens, toweling, handkerchiefs, and often undergarments such as chemises, shifts, camisoles, petticoats, and even girdles.

10. Often sheets were numbered in pairs, which would explain why the same set of initials and numbers may be used twice on the back of one quilt. As many as twenty-five pairs of sheets might be found in a nicely stocked linen cupboard.

11. Harold B. and Dorothy K. Burnham, *'Keep Me Warm One Night': Early Handweaving in Eastern Canada*, Toronto, University of Toronto Press (in cooperation with Royal Ontario Museum), 1972, page 110.

Plate 251.
Bride's Quilt Top, New York, 1858–63. Silk, wool, velvet, and cotton appliquéd on cotton, 87 x 71 ½ in. George E. Schoellkopf, Inc., New York. Made near Poughkeepsie. Appliquéd templates cut out of newspapers establish the date. A boy with a jaunty hat was planned for the block to the left of the girl.

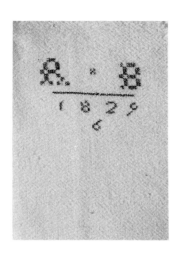

Plate 252.
Cross-stitched initials and marking numbers on hand-woven woolen blanket. Royal Ontario Museum, Toronto.

Plate 253.
Cross-stitched signature on quilt back: "E. A. Scofield, Darien, Conn., 1850." Darien Historical Society.

can be a misleading task. For example, someone deciphering the letters and numbers on the back of an appliqué framed medallion spread from the Brooklyn Museum (plate 104) for *Antiques* magazine in 1942 wrote:

> *On the reverse side of tile spread worked in tiny cross-stitches appears the letter S and directly beneath it, the numerals 17. One might conclude that S was the initial of the maker and that 17 stood for 1817 following a practice occasionally exemplified in the marking of old spreads. The materials used and the details of the design, however, suggest that this quilt may be earlier than that date. Possibly, then, 17 was the age of the young lady in whose dower chest it was to go.*[12]

It seems more likely that the number referred to a linen marking number or a trousseau-counting number than to the date of the quilt or the age of the maker. A date was usually expressed in four numbers (or at least three, omitting the "1"), and when the maker's age was included, it was often indicated by the word *age* preceding the number. Yet, two digits can express a variety of intentions: "14," for example, might refer to 1814, or it might be the maker's age, or the fourteenth quilt she made.

Plate 253 illustrates a name, date, and place of origin cross-stitched on the back of a quilt. The meaning here is perfectly clear. In plate 250 four different pieces of household linen are shown, cross-stitched by four different people with initials and linen-marking numbers. On the reverse side of the Lord's Prayer Quilt (plate 244) the maker has cross-stitched "SAMANTHA R. WING NO 11." The number obviously refers to the eleventh quilt in her bridal chest.

Marking was done either in cross-stitch or ink. Cross-stitch was learned on samplers; so much so, that by 1828 we find a sampler defined as "a marking alphabet wrought by girls at school."[13] Cross-stitching taught children to use a needle skillfully and was easy to learn because it was just two stitches crossed at their middles. If they were precisely crossed stitches, of precisely equal length, laid exactly on the straight lines of a fabric's warp and woof, a very tidy embroidery stitch was achieved, fine enough to adorn a gift:

> *I presented my teacher, Mr. Chubbuck, with two large hemstitched handkerchiefs with his initials embroidered in cross-stitch in a corner of*

---

12. *Antiques*, June 1942, pages 354–55.
13. John Walter's *English and Welsh Dictionary*, 1828, as quoted by Hughes, *op. cit.*, *Needlework*, page 157.

each. As he is favored with the euphonious name of Frank Emery Robinson Chubbuck, it was a work of art to make his initials look beautiful.[14]

A text in 1846 gave these instructions for school children:

Every letter or figure should be begun separately and the threads cut off on the wrong side. Leave two or four threads between each letter or figure of a sampler; but when marking shirts, cravats or houselinen, eight or ten threads will be necessary.[15]

It is said that the older version of cross-stitching is one in which the stitch looks exactly the same on both sides of the material. Ink was also used for linen marking at an early date. In 1750, *The Family Pocketbook* gives this recipe for an indelible marking substance:

Whatever Linen or Woollen, is marked with this Juice, such letters or Marks, are not to be discharged by any Means whatever. Tie 3 ounces of the powder of burnt horse-beans in a piece of Linen, and boil it half an Hour in a pint of the said Juice, and it makes a Writing-lnk, in all respects

Plate 254 (ABOVE LEFT).
Autograph Album Quilt (detail), probably Pennsylvania, 1848–49. Pieced cotton. Lycoming County Historical Society, Williamsport, Pennsylvania. The signature "John Darlington" is stamped from an ink metal die. These dies were commonly used in the signing of quilts during the 19th century.

Plate 255 (ABOVE RIGHT).
Signature Quilt (detail), Kansas. c. 1875–1900. Pieced and appliquéd cotton. Spencer Museum of Art, The University of Kansas, Lawrence. The center is inscribed in ink: "Reverend G. M. Alrod and Mrs. Mehitable Williams."

---

14. Caroline Cowles Richards, written when she was seventeen in 1859, *Village Life in America, 1852–1872*, New York, Henry Holt and Company, 1913, page 115.
15. *Needlework and Cutting Out*, Dublin, Commissioners of National Education in Ireland, 1846, page 21.

Plate 256.
Wild Goose Chase Quilt (detail), c. 1825–50. Pieced cotton. Collection of the authors. Printed on the alternate cotton strips in an all-over pattern are portraits of the first seven presidents of the United States. The pattern was based on an earlier French toile entitled "Les Présidents des Etats-Unis." The later textile, printed in brown, blue, and pink about 1830, is an English roller print made for American export. The frigate *Constitution* and the portrait of President Andrew Jackson with the legend "President of the United States from March 4th 1829 to ——— Supreme Commander of the Army and Navy" were added to make the print more contemporary.

Plate 257.
Scripture (Bible) Quilt (detail), Easton, Pennsylvania, 1845. Pieced and appliquéd cotton in peony pattern, 102 x 102 in. Courtesy Mrs. Frank J. Brazel. A sample of the staple quilt-making fabrics of the mid-19th century, this quilt incorporates an extensive collection of the numerous variations of 1840s calicos.

Plate 258.
Tumbler Quilt (detail), Milford, Connecticut, 1876. Pieced cotton, 74 x 82 in. Collection of Mrs. William B. Gillette. Made by Susan Buckingham Gillette and initialed "S.B.G.," the quilt uses textiles typical of the third quarter of the 19th century.

Plate 259.
Log Cabin Quilt, Courthouse Steps Variation (detail), New England, c. 1850–75. Pieced cotton. Collection of the authors.

Plate 260

Peacocks and Peahens Quilt, Charlottesville, Virginia, c. 1875–1900. Appliquéd and embroidered cotton, 103 x 109 in. Shelburne Museum, Shelburne, Vermont. Made by Dorothy Baker, the quilt uses thirty patterns to fashion the appliquéd birds, horses, and human figures. The mounted horsemen are made with tremendous attention to detail, down to the boots, ribbon-tied perukes, and embroidered reins and stirrups.

Plate 261 (ABOVE).

Eagles Quilt, possibly New Jersey, c. 1830–50. Pieced and appliquéd cotton, 96 x 94 in. The New-York Historical Society. Made by Ann de Groot. The eagle border is an English roller print, c. 1830–40. Eight-pointed stars pieced of calicos are scattered over the body of the quilt. The central eagle motif, cut from the roller print, is appliquéd. Fine cross-bar quilting completes the decoration.

Plate 262 (LEFT).

Irish Chain Quilt, 1822. Pieced and appliquéd cotton, 80 x 76 in. The New-York Historical Society. Made by Ann Maria Warner. Blocks of cutout chintz motifs alternate with nosegays fashioned of small-patterned calicos and floral chintz. Cross-stitched in black is "AMW 1822."

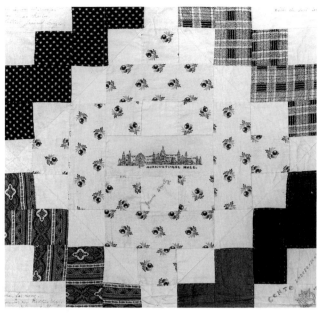

Plate 263 (ABOVE LEFT). Scripture (Bible) Quilt (detail), Maine, 1850. Pieced cotton. Baltimore Museum of Art. The ink inscription reads: "Be thou thankful and rejoice in all the beauty God has given but beware it does not win thee from the work ordained from heaven. Helen Duchamp, May 1, 1850."

Plate 264 (ABOVE RIGHT). Centennial Autograph Quilt (detail). Cottons pieced in Chimney Sweep pattern. Schenectady Museum Collection, Schenectady, New York. Made for Louise Howe, Hadley, Massachusetts, the quilt features a pen-and-ink rendering of the Agricultural Hall, a building in the 1876 centennial exhibition in Philadelphia.

far superior to any other, not being to be discharged by Art, or defaced by time. In regard to Needlework, it is evident more may be done in one Hour, by the assistance of this Juice, than could be accomplished with a Needle in many Days: You are to take Care the Linen is dry; and use this Juice with a Pen, in the same manner you do Ink. When washed, the Marks on the Linen are of a fine Purple Colour, and has this very great Advantage above marking with a Needle, that there is no other Way of removing whatever marks are put on, but by cutting out the Piece.[16]

The *New York Gazette* in 1771 advertised metal dies for linen marking to be used with ink: "cut gentlemen and ladies names, with numbers for numbering linen, and books, wherewith they give either red or black ink which will not wash out and may be used by any person without trouble or inconveniency."[17] By 1846 it would appear that ink had substantially replaced cross-stitch: "Marking in cross-stitch, though latterly very much superseded by the use of marking ink, is yet sufficiently useful."[18]

The use of ink for signing quilts was popular throughout the

---

16. Peregrine Montague, *The Family Pocketbook: or Fountain of True and Useful Knowledge*, London, eighteenth century, pages 49–50.
17. Gottesman, *op. cit.*, page 199.
18. *Needlework and Cutting Out*, Dublin, Commissioners of National Education in Ireland, 1846, page 21.

Plate 265.
Scripture (Bible) Quilt (detail),
Easton, Pennsylvania, 1845. Pieced
cotton. Courtesy Mrs. Frank Brazel.
On the right is an ink inscription from
John 14:27. On the left is an ink
rendering of the Holy Bible and the
signature of the artist, Mrs. Mary
Lehn.

nineteenth century. We have not seen it on quilts made earlier. It is quite possible that for many years ink was not a completely trusted mixture for cloth. As late as the 1830s ink was still homemade by individual families. An ink recipe from an encyclopedia published in 1798 calls for pieces of rusted iron in the mixture "to make it lasting" but too much iron in the solution had the effect of rotting the cloth.[19]

Plate 189 shows a quilt square with an entire family record flourished in pen and ink, inscribed in the second quarter of the nineteenth century. The fine art of penmanship has been considered integral to learning throughout the history of American schooling. In New England in the Colonial period, despite the lack of adequate schooling for girls, approximately sixty percent of the women could at least sign their names.[20]

---

19. 3 ounces of galls; one ounce of powdered logwood; one ounce of vitriol (sulphuric acid); 1 quart vinegar, white wine or water and ½ ounce gum arabic for each pint of liquid (gum arabic makes the ink adhere to the surface). Shake well 4 or 5 times a day. In 10 or 12 days the ink may be used, but it will get better with time. Strain before using. To make it lasting, add coarse powder of galls, from which dust has been sifted, plus pieces of iron rusted. *A Dictionary of Arts and Sciences* (1798 encyclopedia).

Old ink recipes are plentiful and extremely varied. The resulting products ranged from feeble and pale to longlasting, clear, black India ink. It is our impression that the quality of the original concoction has more to do with the legibility of signatures on century-old quilts than with the number of washings or hard wear.

20. Elaine Kendall, "Beyond Mother's Knee," *American Heritage*, June 1973, Vol. 24, No. 4, page 15.

Plate 266 (TOP).
Fans Quilt, c. 1875–1900. Pieced and embroidered cotton and wool, 70 x 80 in. George E. Schoellkopf, Inc., New York.

Plate 267 (ABOVE).
Grand Army Quilt, Connecticut, 1885. Pieced, appliquéd, and embroidered silk, satin, and velvet, 72 x 72 in. Mattatuck Museum, Waterbury, Connecticut. Made by N. W. Carswell. The center is formed of 49 blocks, with likenesses of Lafayette, Washington, and Fort Sumter. The satin sets contain 150 stars, and the border has Revolutionary flags. On the edge are the names of the U.S. presidents.

Plate 268 (TOP).
Album Quilt, Virginia, c. 1900. Pieced, appliquéd, and embroidered wool, 67 ½ x 67 ½ in. Smithsonian Institution, Washington, D.C. Made by Miss Pocahontas Virginia Gay of Fluvanna County, the quilt contains squares with likenesses of Andrew Jackson, Jefferson Davis, and Robert E. Lee.

Plate 269 (ABOVE).
Victorian Album Quilt, New Jersey, c. 1875–1900. Pieced, appliquéd, and embroidered wool, cotton, velvet, French ribbon silk, and satin, 78 x 78 in. Collection unknown. Signed "S. J. Buell." The maker is said to have been a relative of Sara Josepha Buell Hale, editor of *Godey's Lady's Book*.

Plate 270.
Matterhorn Quilt, 1934. Pieced cotton, 85 ½ x 104 in. Denver Art Museum. Made by Myrtle M. Fortner, the
quilt is pieced of 1-inch squares of plain and printed cottons, depicting the Matterhorn Peak in the Swiss Alps.
Threads of various colors were used to create the impressionistic effect. The maker's name and the date are
quilted in the upper left-hand corner.

Plate 271.
Album Quilt Block (detail of plate 215). Appliquéd cotton. Collection of Louise Emerson Francke. The ink inscription reads: "Emily Jane Lilly, Baltimore County," a typical form of signature on an album quilt.

Later, roaming instructors visited homes far afield in the countryside and held their own classes or flourished calling cards and Bible pages for people. It is very likely that it was such a man who was called on to pen this quilt square for posterity in lieu of a page in the family Bible. Penmanship classes, often advertised and given outside of the public schools, seminaries, and adventure schools, were known and popular from the 1750s on.[21] By the 1830s most states had begun a program of primary public education and by 1848 Platt Rogers Spencer had published his book launching the Spencerian method. Although flourishing was in use long before Spencer, he is credited as the originator of a style of penmanship that became an important influence on American handwriting. It was characterized basically by ornate, rounded letters slanted to the right, and it was taught in schools up until 1900. Throughout the Album Quilts, we see tiny examples of calligraphic flourishes in the poems, sayings, and signatures.

Leaving a signature that is barely discernible in the quilting stitchery

---

21. One important reason for penmanship classes was so that women, even if not wholly literate, would have at least the barest essentials to conduct some of their own affairs—if widowed, for example.

Plate 272.
Album Quilt (detail). Appliquéd cotton. Maryland Historical Society, Baltimore. An ink signature reading "E. A. Addison" is surrounded by a flourished wreath. The quilted hearts suggest that this was made on the occasion of a marriage or betrothal.

is an intriguing quilter's whim. Sometimes the signature was so concealed that few but the maker could find it. Plate 278 depicts a snowflake (on the right) with a date of 1852 camouflaged and practically hidden by the quilting motif. It remains a secret to all but those who study the quilt under a magnifying glass. Plate 86 illustrates an example in which Mrs. Mary Lawson Ruth McCrea has quilted "M L Mc May 18th 1866" upside down into the middle block between the top rows of patchwork blocks.

Often the lettering was done with cording or stuffing, particularly on the all-white quilts. This created a more prominent signature, because it was raised. The earliest known quilt, the Sicilian Quilt, has words raised in stuffing throughout the quilt, so this idea is centuries old. Plate 279 shows a corded "SARAH M." on a pieced quilt. In some cases, after many years, when the stuffed areas flatten considerably, the message can become indecipherable.

Of course, piecing and appliquéing, the basic quilt making techniques, were also employed by the maker for signing her quilt. Plate 188 is a pieced quilt whose complete design concept is a signature, and it is interesting that the letters are giant replicas of cross-stitched lettering. A similar quilt, also made in the same town (Castile, New York) but by another person fifteen years later, raises all kinds of questions as to how

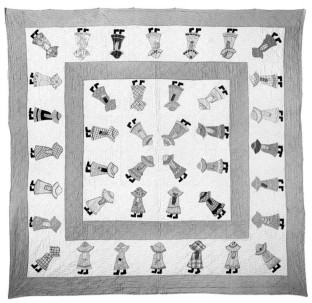

Plate 273.
Sunbonnet Girls Quilt, Pennsylvania, c. 1900–1925. Appliquéd and embroidered cottons, lace trim, 88 x 88 in. Collection of Tom Woodard and Blanche Greenstein. Some of the girls have embroidered purses, hats, and dresses, as well as shoelaces.

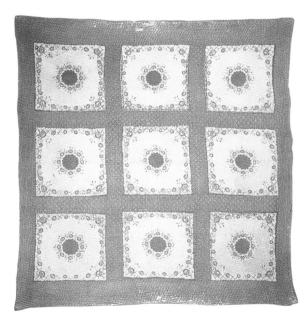

Plate 275.
One-Patch Quilt, c. 1800–1850. Pieced cotton, 79 x 70 in. Spencer Museum of Art, The University of Kansas, Lawrence. This unusual quilt is made of nine bandanas quilted with feather wreaths and separated by strips of red cotton.

Plate 274.
Flower Basket Quilt, c. 1825–50. Appliquéd cotton, 77 x 77 in. Denver Art Museum.

Plate 276.
Album House Quilt, New Jersey, c. 1850–75. Pieced and appliquéd cotton, 69 x 92 in. Courtesy John and Jacqueline Sideli. Each of the nine front doors contains the signature of the maker: Flint, Ames, Levy, LeClear, Strong, and so on—a classic American melting pot neighborhood. The edges are embroidered with feather stitching and the top is knotted with plain-weave hand-loomed tape. The sky and grass are calico.

Plate 277.
Indian Quilt, Crow Creek Reservation, South Dakota, c. 1900. Appliquéd cotton, 78 x 70 in. Collection of Mr. and Mrs. George Anderson. This unique quilt was made by an Indian. Follow the arrows to read the story, which starts and ends with the same motifs—the peace pipe and the tomahawk. The sacred animals of the Sioux are all depicted: the deer, buffalo, and wolf. The quilt is in the shell pattern.

Plate 278 (BELOW RIGHT).
Lily Quilt (detail), 1852. Pieced
cotton. Collection of the San
Antonio Museum Association.
The pattern is also known in vari-
ous parts of the country as North
Carolina Lily, Mountain Lily,
Prairie Lily, and Mariposa Lily.
The date is almost invisibly quilt-
ed into the center of the
snowflake on the right.

Plate 279 (BOTTOM).
Quilt with sawtooth border
(detail), c. 1850–1900. Pieced
cotton. Cincinnati Art Museum.
The signature "Sarah M." is raised
in corded work above the quilted
background.

the pattern traveled. Were the makers members of the same family? Did someone tell one maker about the other's quilt? Was there a needlework instructor in Castile who suggested this design? Both quilts are quite unusual and captivating. Plate 280 is another variation of this idea. The maker pieced her husband's initials prominently into the center of the quilt: a patchwork monogram.

Charlotte Smiths (plate 233), after finishing her pieced star quilt, appliquéd around the edges a border with a name, date, and startling refrain. "When this you see, remember me" was a common inscription for autograph books, quilts, samplers, and even tombstones, and yet it has the power to hurtle one back in time.

One last method of signing found on quilts—sometimes the most informative and personal but not always the most reliable—is an ancient paper with a fragmented history sewn onto a corner or the back of the quilt.

Plate 280 (BELOW LEFT). Initial Quilt, Texas, c. 1860. Pieced cotton and cotton sateen. Log Cabin Village Museum, Fort Worth, Texas. Made in Jefferson by Mrs. Gustav Frank for her husband, whose initials appear as the central theme. He began working in America as first violinist for P. T. Barnum on a Mississippi riverboat, where he accompanied such singers as Jenny Lind.

Plate 281 (BOTTOM). Flowers and Fruit Quilt (detail), 1847. Appliquéd and embroidered cotton, 91 x 93 in. Courtesy Art Institute of Chicago. Embroidered in the upper right-hand wreath is "C. Susan Thomas, Sept. 1847." A meandering flower border and bands of feather quilting surround the green, red, yellow, and purple calico appliquéd motifs with their embroidered tendrils. By the middle of the 19th century, there was a noticeable trend toward naturalism in quilt design, seen especially in the addition of embroidery to create more realistic renderings in appliquéd motifs.

Plate 282.
Log Cabin Quilt, Pineapple Variation, Pennsylvania, c. 1850–75.
Pieced wool and cotton, 86 x 86 in. Collection of Bill Gallick and
Tony Ellis.

Plate 283.
Dachau Quilt, Germany, 1945. Pieced wools and cotton,
77 x 70 in. Collection of America Hurrah, New York.

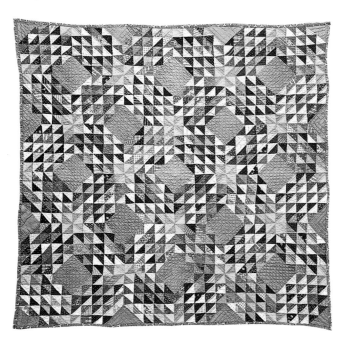

Plate 284.
Ocean Waves Quilt, c. 1875–1900. Pieced cotton, 86 x 90 in.
Courtesy Rhea Goodman, Quilt Gallery, Inc.

Plate 285.
Sampler Crazy Quilt, Vermont, c. 1875–1900. Pieced cotton; no
interlining, 76 x 76 in. Collection of Tom Woodard and Blanche
Greenstein. This quilt is a wonderful melange of patterns in Crazy
Quilt fashion.

10

The Age of a Quilt

The dating of a quilt is both tantalizing and frustrating. In a way it seems incredible that such a compelling body of work should have descended to us in so utterly anonymous and undocumented a fashion. We respond to quilts not only esthetically but also emotionally: they speak to us of the minds and lives of their makers, and the sensibilities of the culture that formed their making. We want to know where they came from and when; yet specific information is scanty. The few references to quilts in early writings are almost totally devoid of description except for an occasional mention of color, types of materials, and, very rarely, a pattern name. Quilts pictured in drawings, paintings, etchings, or photographs that would confirm that a style or pattern was in use during a particular period are, for the most part, nonexistent until nearly the second half of the nineteenth century.

The truth is that the process of quilt dating is frequently never more than a series of highly educated guesses. Unless a quilt is actually dated, there is rarely any single, irrefutable proof of its age or even period, but rather a string of possible clues, all of which must be assessed and balanced against one another. Frequently the clues are inconsistent or even contradictory and the amount of information needed to properly identify what one is looking at would—and has—filled many volumes. Accurate dating requires a detailed knowledge of two hundred years of textile production and of social, industrial, and economic history. Perhaps most important, it requires a sort of sixth sense developed from examining many quilts of many periods: looking at them, feeling the fabrics, and recognizing the techniques characteristic of certain periods, as well as the subtle change in color and texture that comes with age. Since a detailed explanation of all of these subjects is clearly beyond the scope of this volume, what follows is a guide, rather than an answer book of dating methods. There are specific answers to dating questions (and we have also provided dating information throughout the text), but much more often we have set forth a description of the kinds of questions that must be asked, of the kinds of evidence that may be inferred from different aspects of the quilt—its style, design, materials, construction, and condition. Although it often appears that consideration of each aspect separately raises as many questions as it answers, taken all together they amount to a method, and if you are not rendered an expert in your own right overnight, you may, at least, understand how dating is accomplished.

Trying scrupulously to describe the method of quilt dating without oversimplifying, we have found, to begin with, that it is almost more useful to tell about what you can't deduce for certain than what you can. For example, it is very difficult to discern the influence of the decorative styles of a period as expressed in quilt patterns and designs, particularly in the case of the nineteenth-century geometric patterns. The readily recognizable influences of the Victorian and Art Deco periods form exceptions to this rule. Many quilt patterns and styles remained fairly standard from the end of the eighteenth century to the present and there is an enormous overlapping of styles and types of quilts in use from period to period. Whole-cloth quilts were made at the same time as pieced and appliquéd quilts; after 1800 there is no period when pieced quilts were more in vogue than appliqué, no time when geometrics had more appeal to the quilt maker than pictorial. Quilt makers of all periods have copied quilt patterns and styles of earlier date, so it is not uncommon to find an early motif used in a much later quilt. Framed Medallion Quilts were made in the eighteenth and nineteenth centuries, and they are made today. There were, of course, periods when particular types of quilts and patterns gained wide popularity. Album Quilts were the rage in the Baltimore area in the 1840s and 1850s, while almost no American home seemed complete without a Victorian Crazy Quilt during the 1870s and 1880s. And, over and over again, the individuality of the quilt maker continued to express itself in unusual designs, combinations of styles, and variations of patterns. However, for the purpose of dating we are seeking the predominant style and design elements that mark a pattern and design of a particular period, that "elusive character which stamps it [the quilt] for a period, a people, a school, or a philosophy of life."[1]

Oddly enough, the condition of a quilt may not always be significant in determining its age. A very old quilt frequently will be found in pristine condition, while one made recently may be in tatters. Many quilts, such as the beautiful all-white Bride's Quilts and the magnificent

---

1. Marie Knorr Graeff, *Pennsylvania German Quilts*, Home Craft Course, Vol. 14, 1946, page 9.

Plate 286.
Oak Leaf Quilt, mid-19th century. Appliquéd cotton, 80 x 80 in. Collection of Bill Pearson. Reds and greens are used to create a geometric pattern of oak leaf motifs.

Baltimore Album Quilts, were considered "best quilts"; they were made for ceremonial or decorative purposes. These special quilts were brought out of storage only on important occasions, and when they were not being used they were carefully kept in camphor and chips, protected from light and dirt.

Most quilts were used on a day-to-day basis and the majority saw hard wear; they were washed and exposed to the sun and to all the natural wear and tear of daily family life. And it must be remembered that the fabrics in many quilts were salvaged and had already gone through a long life. A housewife saved fabrics for years—sometimes as many as thirty or forty years—before they were made into quilt tops. The quilt illustrated in plate 145 was made in 1890 and is composed of fabrics gathered from all the states and territories of the Union between 1850 and 1890.

While some quilts were made from salvaged scraps, others were fashioned from unused, unwashed cuttings from dresses and household

Plate 287.
Sun, Moon, and Stars Quilt, Vermont, c. 1850–75. Pieced cotton, 82 x 88 in. Collection of Tom Woodard and Blanche Greenstein. The quilting is in a diamond pattern with scattered motifs of concentric circles.

textiles. With the increase in availability of fabrics during the first quarter of the nineteenth century, many quilts were constructed with newly bought textiles purchased for the sole purpose of making a quilt. This gives an infrequently used but old quilt a pristine new look. Thus, the appearance of wear may be a most undependable indicator of the real age of a quilt.

There are, however, significant details that indicate a quilt's age and are useful in its dating. Each part of a quilt offers dating insights if carefully scrutinized; the top, interlining, fabric, binding, stitching, pattern, color—each tells something of the technique used in its making, or period of style, or type. There are stylistic differences and methods of construction of quilts peculiar to particular periods, and these trends in design appeared almost simultaneously in widely diverse sections of the country. We can only guess how this efficient, almost miraculous

exchange of ideas in quilt making and design was accomplished before the advent of women's mass media magazines and rapid communication. For the quilt collector, these style variations and methods of quilt construction, which we shall discuss later, offer interesting differences helpful in determining age.

Most quilts found today will date after 1800. Many beautiful, outstanding quilts are of very recent vintage, made during the 1920s and 1930s when there was a great revival of quilt making throughout the country. There are considerable numbers of quilts from the first half of the nineteenth century.

Why are there so many quilts available? It must be remembered that quilts were made in fantastic quantities in every section of the country, with the greatest number probably made between 1800 and 1880. The American family during the early part of the nineteenth century was large, sometimes with as many as twelve to fifteen children. Each girl in the family was expected to make a minimum of thirteen quilts by the time she was married. In a family with three daughters, at least thirty-nine quilts would be made. Women continued to make quilts after marriage, some quilting as many as several hundred in a lifetime.

Of course, many quilts have been lost through wear and neglect. Quilts were used until they were in tatters; then the materials were salvaged for use as filler or scraps. It is not unusual to find an old quilt used as an interlining in a quilt of more recent date. Many quilts were cut up and used for other purposes, and, of course, the natural enemies of textiles—dirt, sun, moths, and wear—often caused deterioration beyond preservation. They have been put in attics, and damp cellars, allowed to rot, fade, and mildew.

Plate 288.
Pair of Robins in Tulip Tree Quilt (detail), probably New England, c. 1850–75. Appliquéd cotton, 80 x 78 in. George E. Schoellkopf, Inc., New York. Red, brown, and green, with white clam-shell quilting.

The Age of a Quilt 309

But that is not to suggest that there are not excellent eighteenth-century and very early nineteenth-century quilts to be found. In fact, this is one of the few areas of antique collecting in which it is possible to obtain fine examples of early Americana and folk art as well as finely crafted textiles at fairly reasonable cost. How do we determine the age of a quilt? In many instances the quilt itself may be dated (see chapter 9). Frequently it is necessary to search for the date, which may be incorporated into the stitching patterns or overall design, found on the back of the quilt, or made a part of a verse or saying written on the quilt. It is also possible to find the underside of the quilt top dated and signed. Backs will sometimes have an initial and number cross-stitched in the material. This is not necessarily the date, but may be a household linen inventory marking.

If a quilt is signed, the method used to inscribe the maker's name will give a hint as to the age of the quilt; the earlier quilts were usually cross-stitched while the later ones were more apt to be signed in ink.

Though ink made with an iron-gall base was long in use, indelible ink was introduced into the United States during the 1830s. From that period quilts were more frequently inscribed in ink alone rather than with cross-stitch, although quilts combining cross-stitch and inked signatures continued to be made. (Characteristic of the 1840s and 1850s are quilts combining appliqué, embroidery, and drawing in ink). Between 1840 and 1870 stencils or stamps were popularly used to imprint names on quilts and for marking household linens. The earlier stamp will sometimes have a design such as a feather, quill, or plume with a space left blank for the name. Later stamps are block lettered and less delicate. In the late nineteenth century, human hair—blond, brunette, and red—was used in cross-stitch to mark initials on quilts. Written material incorporated into the quilt top may provide clues to its date. Pattern forms, over which the quilt material was basted, were frequently cut out of newspapers, letters, or dated lessons. When the material is worn or pushed back, it frequently reveals a date on the written or printed paper beneath. The Saltonstall Quilt (plate 3) incorporates fragments from a Harvard College catalogue of 1701, while the quilt top shown in plate 135 contains bits of newspaper dated 1788.

The age of a quilt may be established through a reliable provenance. You are fortunate if any notes are pinned or sewn to the quilt that tell when and where it was made or give personal information about the maker. Sometimes histories will be written on the quilt itself by a descendant of the maker in much the way records are inscribed in old family Bibles. A quilt in the New York State Historical Association collection at Cooperstown has written on the back in faded brown ink:

Plate 289.
Prairie Flower Quilt (detail), early
19th century. Appliquéd linen
and printed cotton. Courtesy The
Metropolitan Museum of Art,
New York. This pattern is also
called the Rose Tree and
Missouri Rose.

Made by Anna Maria Slackman Miller born 1786 in Barbadoes, West Indies. She married Joseph Dottin Husbands, Colonial Secretary of Barbadoes. They came to the United States in 1810. Settle in Hartwick, N. Y. about 1815. Presented in memory of their granddaughter, Mrs. Elizabeth P. D. ——— of Rochester, N. Y. in 1939.

Generally it is safe to rely upon dates of births and deaths, but handed-down histories of travel and residences tend to get more exotic with time.

Most frequently there is an oral history concerning the quilt, particularly if it has remained in a family—"It was grandmother's, or Great Aunt Caroline's." Figuring twenty to twenty-five years to a generation and always allowing for exaggeration, an approximate date can be established.

If you purchase a quilt from a descendant of the quilt maker, try to elicit as much information as possible about the quilt and quilter, the name of the pattern, where it was made, and when. It will increase your pleasure in the quilt to know something about it and, in years to come, it may prove to be a valuable record.

The age of a quilt may be ascertained if the quilt was left in a will or is described in the inventory of an estate. As quilts were usually made at home, it is extremely rare to find a bill of sale or other purchase records of the sort sometimes found for furniture or silver.

George Washington's mother, Mary Ball Washington, provided in her will:

Fredericksburg, V. 1778.
In the name of God, Amen.
I give to my son, Gen. George Washington, all my land in Accockeek Run, in the County of Stafford . . . to him and his heirs forever, also my best bed, bedstead, Virginia Cloth curtains (the same that stand in my best bedroom) and my quilted blue and white quilt, and my best dressing glass.[2]

As has been pointed out, the techniques used in constructing the quilt, the overall design, the materials used, and each separate part of the quilt itself are extremely important in its dating. The size of the quilt, for example, will provide an inkling as to its age. It is frequently suggested that quilts dating from the eighteenth century to the early part of the nineteenth century were almost always three yards square, but careful study indicates that during the eighteenth and nineteenth centuries there were no standard sizes of quilts. In fact, it is exceedingly rare to find two quilts of identical dimensions.

The earliest beds tended to be large—six or seven feet wide to accommodate several members of the family, and high enough to permit a trundle bed to be rolled under it. During the day, mounds of pillows and sleeping mats were piled high on the bed to be hidden under a supersized quilt. To accommodate a large-sized bed, and cover piles of mats and pillows, quilts were made large. From 1750 to 1830 quilts were square or near square in appearance and generally eight to nine feet in size, with a greater number being closer to nine feet. There are early quilts over ten feet square. The worsted and worsted combinations, such as linsey-woolseys, as well as other whole-cloth quilts, were apt to be smaller, between seven and eight feet square. From 1830 to the end of the century, the trend was toward smaller-sized quilts and a greater frequency of rectangular shapes. The three-quarter bed, smaller than the large four-posters of pre-Revolutionary days, gained in popularity during the second quarter of the nineteenth century. Popular quilt sizes were between six feet and seven-and-a-half feet square. When they were rectangular in shape, the length was six to ten inches longer than the width. During the twentieth century, quilts again increased in size with seven feet to eight feet square dimensions being commonplace.

Certain types of quilts tend to have a common size; the Log Cabin

2. Peto, *Historic Quilts,* page 81.

Plate 290.
Nine-Patch Doll's Quilt, mid-19th century. Pieced cotton, 20 x 20 in. The New-York Historical Society.

Quilt frequently measures five feet to six feet square. Crib quilts were made three to three-and-a-half feet square. Some of the small quilts we find today were not crib quilts at all but were made for doll's beds. There are also small-sized pieces that are quilted shams or bolsters.

It is sometimes startling to find a quilt with all the attributes of an early quilt, but small in size. Very likely it has been cut down to fit a modern bed, or to allow the cut-off section to be used as matching curtains with the bed cover. The method used in constructing the quilt top, and the overall design style, are helpful in quilt dating, particularly until the second half of the nineteenth century. In some quilt tops, the construction techniques and design are interdependent—that is, the design is a manifestation of the method used to construct the top.

It has frequently been suggested that the earliest and most common style of American quilt was the Crazy Quilt, constructed of scraps of irregularly shaped materials, pieced together at random to form the top,

Plate 291.
Framed Medallion Quilt, c. 1825.
Appliquéd cotton; coarse white
linen lining. Courtesy Charleston
Museum, Charleston, South
Carolina. The center medallion
may have been printed expressly
for use as a quilt center. The
trophy of arms, surrounded by a
floral wreath, was block-printed.
There are also appliqués of chintz
birds scattered around the
medallion, and three- and six-inch
framing borders. The white
cotton field is geometrically
quilted.

without any attempt to create a formal design. However, this is
conjecture. There are no existing examples of this type of quilt known to
the authors dating before the nineteenth century. Nor are there written
descriptions or illustrations that would confirm the existence of the Crazy
Quilt at an earlier date. Surviving eighteenth-century quilts indicated a
conscious effort at design and, in some instances, highly sophisticated
design. In the Saltonstall Quilt of 1704 there is an awareness on the part
of the quilt makers of the framed center design concept; a central section
of the quilt made up of horizontally placed squares is framed by a series of
blocks placed in a vertical direction. The Westover-Berkeley Coverlet
(plate 6), the Robinson Crusoe Quilt (plate 89), and the Anna Tuels
Quilt (plate 190) are all elaborately planned and designed. These are
quilts of the last quarter of the eighteenth century. And the pieced
worsteds and worsted combinations of this early period incorporate highly

intricate and geometric designs. However, the assumption that some early pieced quilts were of the Crazy Quilt type is not without merit. It is probable that the technique evolved from the patching of worn sections of a bed cover until the whole top was a random, irregular pattern of appliquéd patches. The next step would be to piece a quilt top of saved scraps of materials of all sizes and shapes—the Crazy Quilt.

An early construction technique that was popular during the eighteenth century—and which directly affected the design—was to construct the quilt top in a series of frames or borders emanating from a central panel or medallion. The quilt top is actually built up of borders. Quilts of this style of design are referred to as Framed Medallion or Framed Center Quilts.

The placement of a central point around which a pattern is symmetrically arranged is characteristic of the eighteenth century. We find a comparable form in eighteenth century American Bed Ruggs and in the palampores imported to Europe from India during the seventeenth and eighteenth centuries. Irwin and Brett have pointed out: "The characteristic 17th century palampore and quilt designs comprised a central medallion and four related corner motifs on a flowery field surrounded by a wide border."[3]

The center sections may be square, circular, oval, or diamond-shaped. They generally consist of a plain ground onto which birds, trees, or flowers cut out of printed textiles have been appliquéd or a segment of printed fabric, as for example "Penn's Treaty with the Indians." Often each corner of a center square contained a design element such as a star. Surrounding the center are borders in varying widths and numbers. These framing bands were sometimes elaborately pieced or appliquéd in geometric and symbolic patterns including diamonds, saw-tooth chains, or stars. In other instances the band was simply a plain or printed fabric strip.

The diamond-shaped central section (a square tilted to stand on one corner) is seen at an early point in quilt design. The Westover-Berkeley Spread is an example of this style in the eighteenth century. Amish quilts of the nineteenth and twentieth centuries also have this style as one of their classic design units. The origins of the Amish designs are not known, but they may have derived some inspiration from the framed center types. The popular all-white quilt is also commonly based on a framed center design.

In one variation of the framed center design the body of the quilt is

---

3. John Irwin and Katharine Brett, *Origins of Chintz*, London, Her Majesty's Stationery Office, 1970, page 27.

elaborately appliquéd with cut-out figures, buildings, and animals, depicting scenes of farm or village life. A single framing band forms a wide border (see plates 172 and 173). The framed medallion or center quilt is probably the most representative type of quilt top of the eighteenth and early nineteenth centuries.

Quilts continued to be made in the framed center style during the first half of the nineteenth century, but the quilt maker was able to vary the construction techniques. More frequently the framing design, usually cut-out patterns of exotic birds, flowers, and trees, was applied directly onto a ground of whole cloth instead of being made up of a series of borders. Sometimes the flowers and birds were pieced of a number of different fabrics and then appliquéd to the top in the frame design. By the second quarter of the nineteenth century there was continuing elaboration of the frames with bands of vines, rosettes, or bowknots interlacing the frame. In the 1840s and 1850s a Marseilles spread was sometimes used as a ground. The framed center quilt of the 1820s, 1830s, and 1840s is also characterized by a wide four- to six-inch outside border, generally of floral chintz patterns.

Because of the popularity of the framed center type of quilt, printed panels designed especially for use in quilts were produced during the early nineteenth century. The printed motifs often include flowers, a trophy of arms usually with a shield containing a sun emblem drawn on it, or an epergne filled with fruit, framed by a floral wreath or an oval scrolled border. Bunches of flowers may be seen in each corner of the panels, which vary in size from 18 x 20 inches to 21 x 21 inches. The beautiful panels of urns, flowers, birds, and butterflies printed by John Hewson were probably produced for this use.

Printed handkerchiefs and kerchiefs were also used as quilt centers. They were religious, patriotic, or educational in theme and usually highly moralistic. "Virtue," "good," "mercy," "sobriety," "self-denial," and "temperance" were extolled; while warnings against "gluttony," "evilspeaking," "envy," "gaming," "atheism," "ill-nature," and "vanity" were issued. Patriotic handkerchiefs of the period depict scenes from the life and death of General Washington and eulogize him. These handkerchiefs were printed in black, brown, red, or blue, and sometimes contain the name of the printer and the date of the printing. In some instances, entire quilt tops were constructed of commemorative handkerchiefs pieced together. Also used as centers were cut-out sections of printed fabrics such as "William Penn's Treaty with the Indians" and the "Apotheosis of Washington." Like the commemorative hand-kerchiefs, these fabrics are printed in monochromes of blue, red, brown, and black.

Although the formal framed center quilt went out of popular fashion after 1850, there is a continuation of the style with a pieced or appliquéd floral center, generally oval in shape, and a single or double row of vines containing flowers, fruit, or leaves framing the center. It is sometimes referred to as "Martha's Vineyard" pattern.

A second style of quilt of the period before 1800 is composed of vertical subjects as a focal point with symmetrical designs on either side. The emphasis is on a central design element such as a flowering tree, rising from the ground and flowing as it moves upward. The design unfolds in an upward movement. On either side of the main subject and in a symmetrical fashion are stylized flowers, fruit, or garlands of flowers. The overall composition is highly balanced. The background is plain and the feeling is uncluttered. An example is the Flowering Tree Quilt (plate 37) in which the whole design is a single pictorial element bordered by symmetrical designs. The technique used is appliqué.

In quilts made before 1800, appliquéd patterns are more likely to be sewn directly onto the foundation cloth rather than to block units that are then sewn together to create the quilt top. Appliqué and piecing techniques were equally common in the eighteenth-century quilt.

Still another type of eighteenth-century quilt top displays a dispersed design in which cut-out sections of printed fabrics are appliquéd in a scattered fashion over the quilt top. Though the placement appears random, there is a subtle grid of vertical and horizontal lines formed (see the Elk and Fawn Counterpane, plate 292). The cut-out appliqués (sometimes themselves pieced together) are of birds, flowers, animals, trees, and sometimes geometric shapes. The Levens Hall Quilt is surely a precursor of this type of design.

Appearing toward the end of the eighteenth century, but more common during the first quarter of the nineteenth century, are the large single star and sun quilts in which a pieced sun or star radiates from the center of the quilt. (The sun pattern can generally be distinguished by a round center motif.) Interspersed between the points of the sun or star are appliquéd wreaths or bouquets of flowers cut out of chintz fabrics. Generally there is a four- to six-inch-wide border of chintz material or a border composed of a series of pieced stars.

The use of a single, large, bold geometric element, such as a sun or star, as the focal point of the quilt top with smaller design units enriching and elaborating on the central motif is a particularly representative style between 1800 and 1830. During this period there is often an outside border of chintz or homespun, six to eight inches in width.

After 1830, the large star increasingly floats alone on a plain background without any designs placed in the corner square or angle

Plate 292.
Elk and Fawn Counterpane, late 18th century. Appliquéd linen, 91 x 100 in. Shelburne Museum, Shelburne, Vermont. Designs cut from polychrome blocks have been appliquéd over the quilt top, seemingly at random. The central flowering tree motif is surrounded by exotic birds, pomegranates, Persian pears, and an elk and fawn.

spaces between the points of the star. Nor is there usually a border. Frequently the areas between the points of the star will have highly quilted designs interspersed.

There are eighteenth-century American quilts pieced in geometric patterns. These geometrics are particularly common in the pieced linsey-woolseys and worsted quilts. Patterned geometrics also compose the borders of the framed medallion quilts. Surviving patterned geometric quilts before 1800 are rare, doubtless because they were used extensively as everyday quilts and wore out.

There is a form of pieced geometric that approaches a framed-center type of quilt. It is usually constructed of a series of small single-patch, two-patch, or other simple variations to form a geometric center

surrounded by larger geometric squares generally arranged in a different direction or in a band. There is usually a quilted outside border (see the Framed Medallion Quilt, plate 5).

Other examples of eighteenth-century quilts are the quilted worsteds and the quilted whole-cloth spread (see chapter 6), as well as a maverick type of quilt true of all periods that expresses the personal whim, esthetic, and skill of the quilter (see Peacocks and Peahens, plate 260).

Common to eighteenth-century quilts is a highly pictorial quality. Centers display objects or scenes as a focal point, sometimes illustrative printed sections of fabrics, or cut-out chintzes of flowers, garlands of leaves, or exotic birds. There are also pieced and appliquéd flowers, baskets, and scenes of village life. Symbols such as hearts and stars are

Plate 293.
Palm Tree Basket Quilt, possibly Maine, c. 1850–75. Appliquéd cotton, 92 x 76 in. Courtesy Mrs. Gemmell Jainschigg. The pattern for the red trees in baskets was made with a folded-paper cutout.

frequently used (see the center of the Anna Tuels Quilt, plate 190).

Most of the eighteenth-century designs carried over in some form to the nineteenth-century; in fact, quilt makers at the present time are creating lovely designs going back to the earliest form of the Framed Medallion Quilt.

By the end of the eighteenth-century there is a change in the construction techniques used in making quilt tops. It has been suggested in earlier writings on the quilt that the pieced framed center types, as well as the tops composed of appliqués sewn on to a large whole or pieced foundation, were cumbersome to handle and could not be carried easily from place to place. At the same time, greater quantities of materials of all types were available to the housewife, which enabled her to expand and vary quilt designs as well as repeat patterns in the same materials and colors. These factors led more and more frequently to the top being constructed in blocks, either four large blocks each containing an element of the overall design, or a series of smaller blocks that, sewn together or to strips, created the design. The quilt maker could carry the units with her and work at any time. The blocks are pieced and appliquéd, the patterns geometric and pictorial.

The overall effect of the design in the early nineteenth-century quilt top is still formal and geometric, but with the repeat of pattern squares there is no longer the strong orientation toward a center, nor is the design as rigidly contained by vertical or horizontal grids; rather, much in keeping with the neoclassical taste of the early nineteenth century, small repeat rectangles, circles, and ovals formed the basic pattern for a great number of quilts. The shift in style is reflected in woven and printed textile and wallpaper designs of the period, in which design motifs were framed in small octagons and ovals.

The series of repetitive blocks containing pieced or appliquéd designs became the mainstay of quilt construction during the nineteenth century. By the beginning of the nineteenth century most of the basic quilt patterns had evolved. As the predominant number of quilts that have survived from the period are not of the everyday but of the special type, there are not whole quilts of every pattern once in common use; however, Presentation and Sampler Quilts of the period preserve a record of the broad range of designs.

A Presentation Quilt (see plate 225) made in Ohio and dated 1814 displays a variety of both geometric and pictorial patterns, pieced and appliquéd. Such patterns as the "Oak Leaf," "Wandering Foot," "Pine Tree," "Double T Block," "Love Apple," "Variable Star," "Evening Star," "Cherry Basket," "Eagle," "Old Maid's Puzzle," "Windmill," "Double Peony," "Lily," "Court House Square," "Spice Pink," "Hollyhock

Wreath," and "Wreath of Carnations," as well as "Crosses and Losses" and "Cactus Basket," are sewn in random fashion without any apparent attempt at a formal design across the quilt top. There are also simple variations of the single patch, double patch, and "Roman Squares."

It is very difficult to date a quilt by its pattern or pattern name. Records are totally lacking as to times of origin; some patterns and names are said to date from Revolutionary days, but any attribution to a period can only be valued as hearsay.

As the nineteenth century progressed, less attention was given to quilting detail and more to piecing and appliqué designs. Quilts displayed geometrics in overall patterns that appear to begin at the center of the quilt and proceed outward to the corners and borders without beginning

Plate 294.
Star Quilt, Georgia, c. 1800–1825. Pieced silk. The New-York Historical Society. This quilt is an unusual variation of the star pattern.

The Age of a Quilt 321

Plate 295.
Harriet Powers Bible Quilt (detail), Georgia, 1886. Appliquéd and pieced cotton; cotton interlining, 88 ½ x 73 ¾ in. Smithsonian Institution, Washington, D.C. The appliquéd figures were stitched by machine. The quilts in plates 295–96 were made by Harriet Powers, a black farm woman who lived on the outskirts of Athens, Georgia. This quilt was exhibited at the cotton fair in Athens in 1886. The maker later sold it for five dollars.

or end. Although most were in fact constructed of repetitive square or rectangular design units, stress is placed on the overall balance of the design rather than on the presence of the grid. Examples are the "Drunkard's Path" and "Robbing Peter to Pay Paul."

By the second quarter of the century the designs of quilt tops become more complex; they are richer in the use of materials and more varied. In addition to the scraps that were saved, materials were purchased for the making of the quilt in order to carry out a color scheme or complement a design. The geometrics are no longer confined; they move in every direction across the quilt top, sometimes creating the effect of diagonal strips, at other times, strong vertical and horizontal effects. In the naturalistic patterns, there is elaboration of the flowers, stems, and leaves and a greater variety of color and texture.

There is also movement created by repetition of patterns with contrast of color creating optical illusions and effects. Patches of color alternate in light and dark shades. Patterns vary in shape and scale.

During the second, third, and fourth quarters of the nineteenth century, geometrics became particularly complex and varied, more

original in their conception. They exploded onto the top of the quilt in eye-dazzling designs: jagged red lines slashed against greens, stars and suns of a hundred calico colors, hexagon kaleidoscopes of orange and purple and blue. Innovative combinations of colors and patterns, each bolder and more striking than the last, evolved from the imagination of the quilter. Fabrics, in turn became more varied each year. There is an intensity of colors and abstract design not equaled, except perhaps in the dazzling Navajo blankets of the West, until the art of the abstract expressionist almost a century later.

Through the nineteenth century, the quilt top continues to be used to tell stories and commemorate events; charming primitive pictures were composed out of fabric, tales from the Bible, of Adam and Eve and the creation unfold across the quilt top; a day at a Kentucky Fair in elegant white; animals and Indians, fantastic calico birds and whales and blue indigo skies; checkered houses with plaid roofs; elephants made of flowered cottons. There are fans embroidered with delicate lilies of the valley and violets; there are hearts and half-moons and wild stuffed cherries; doves fly with branches of delicate leaves carried in their beaks;

Plate 296.
Harriet Powers Bible Quilt, Georgia, 1895–98. Appliquéd and pieced cotton, 105 x 69 in. Courtesy Museum of Fine Arts, Boston; Bequest of Maxim Karolik. Here again, Harriet Powers depicted scenes from the Bible: Job, Adam and Eve in the Garden of Eden, Moses, Jonah, two animals of each kind, the angels of wrath—all are represented in original appliquéd squares. Mrs. Powers wrote descriptive captions for each scene; one reads: "Cold Thursday, 10 of Feb. 1895. A woman frozen while at prayer. A woman frozen at a gateway. A man with a sack of meal frozen. Icicles formed from the breath of a mule. All blue birds killed. A man frozen at his jug of liquor."

The Age of a Quilt 323

sad, patriotic, religious impulses plead in words to be remembered; divine eagles and flowers, baskets and crosses and ships at sea vie for attention.

They are created with a great deal of charm and humor. It was a time of confidence, of nationalism, of a country moving and growing, of creativity and experimentation, and the quilts made were part of that experience— individual, confident, joyous. In their independence from the formal arts of the time, the quilts are the unconventional expression of a people who did what they liked and liked what they did. Looking at the quilts one is awed by the continuous improvisation of the quilt maker, quilts that, in their finest forms, go beyond decoration and become folk art, craft, art.

During the 1830s we find the first instances of appliquéd and pieced word quilts containing large block letters used to spell out names, places, and the alphabet. This type of quilt is rare.

Stencil quilts were made for a brief period of time and the predominant number date from 1825 to 1835. While there are rare examples of stencil quilts that contain fabrics of a later period, the 1850s and 1860s, the stencil squares are generally earlier, with the printed fabric squares replacing earlier worn-out sections or being made with later fabrics.

The 1840s, 1850s, and 1860s were the heyday of the Album Quilt, discussed in detail in chapter 7.

Presentation, Sampler, and Freedom Quilts exist as early as the first quarter of the nineteenth century, though Freedom Quilts went out of vogue by the 1830s. At a later date, in 1876, makers would again turn to Freedom Quilts, but not to celebrate a young man's coming of age. With great patriotism and pride, quilters used their quilts to commemorate the anniversary of one hundred years of American Independence.

The 1876 Centennial Quilts are usually of an original overall design containing familiar patterns and with the dates 1776 and 1876, a patriotic saying, and the quilter's name, sometimes in bold appliquéd or pieced letters across the quilt top; or they may be repeats of American flags. The most common types are made up of commemorative fabrics or handkerchiefs printed with patriotic motifs, including eagles, George Washington, flags, and Liberty Bells. Other commemorative events can be used to date quilts made to celebrate state and national events—for example, the Centennial of Texas Statehood.

Liberty quilts displaying an eagle as subject matter were made from Revolutionary days until the late 1830s. The eagles are usually stylized and found in the center of the quilt surrounded by a wreath of stars. The number of stars may represent the number of states in the Union and thereby provide some indication of the quilt's age. The eagle motif may

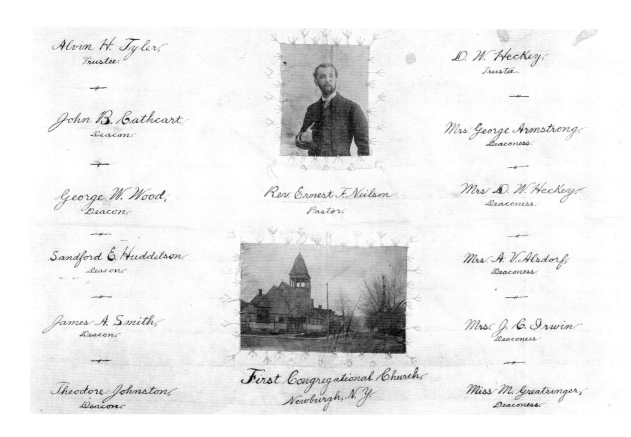

Alvin H. Tyler,
Trustee.

John B. Cathcart,
Deacon.

George W. Wood,
Deacon.

Sandford E. Huddelson,
Deacon.

James A. Smith,
Deacon.

Theodore Johnston,
Deacon.

Rev. Ernest F. Neilson
Pastor.

First Congregational Church,
Newburgh, N.Y.

D. W. Heckey,
Trustee.

Mrs. George Armstrong,
Deaconess.

Mrs. D. W. Heckey,
Deaconess.

Mrs. A. V. Alsdorf,
Deaconess.

Mrs. J. C. Irwin
Deaconess.

Miss M. Greatsinger,
Deaconess.

be cut out of printed fabric and appliquéd to the center, and the type of fabric used will be helpful in dating the quilt. The Eagle Quilt made by Ann de Groot (see plate 261) employs an English chintz eagle material for the central medallion and its wide border, the design on the material printed from about 1830 to 1840.

Union Quilts employing eagles as subjects, but arranged diagonally across the corners of the quilt and having stars or other geometric designs as a central decoration, were highly popular during the 1860s. The Union Quilt design was used primarily by quilt makers in the North during the Civil War, with the greatest numbers of Union Quilts apparently being made in Pennsylvania. During the NRA days of the 1930s, there is again a flurry of popularity for the eagle in quilts, complete with stars, stripes, and patriotic slogans.

The number of stars in a Flag Quilt, unless they express a particular whim of the maker, will offer some revelations as to the period of its making. Flag Quilts were frequently made by a patriotic quilter upon the admission of the state in which she lived into the Union. It was a time of rejoicing.

Plate 297.
Presentation Album Quilt (detail), Newburgh, New York, 1880–1905. Appliquéd cotton, 84 x 84 in. Courtesy Jolie Kelter and Michael Malcé. Among college girls and other women in the late Victorian era and early 20th century, the vogue for amateur photography produced blueprint images on cloth such as these, often appearing on pillows and quilts. These two photographs are appliquéd to the red ground with feather-stitch embroidery. Inscribed around them are the names of the quilt's presenters, parishioners of Reverend Ernest F. Neilson.

Album Quilts, Bride's Quilts, and Presentation Quilts that depict representational scenes may give clues to both date and location. Monuments, buildings, people, events are often depicted in exact likeness. (The Baltimore Album Quilt block shown in plate 227 is of the Baltimore Washington Monument, so the quilt could not have been made before the monument was completed in 1829.) Portraits of Presidents printed in the textiles (see plate 256), drawn in ink or embroidered, will date a quilt after a certain period. The style of clothing and uniforms, the type of hairstyle, the facial adornment of the men (are they bearded? do they have sideburns?) must be closely examined for the variety of information they give, and can establish the era in which the quilt was made, if one is familiar with social history. The activities of the people (what type of carriage are they riding in? what games are they playing?) are all informative as to the period of the quilt. So, too, with slogans or quotes written or stitched on the quilt. They may evidence a popular political or social movement—NRA in the 1930s, temperance in the early 1800s.

Sometimes the spelling of words or names of locations will suggest a period for the making of the quilt. For example, Dr. Dunton refers to an Album Quilt containing blocks with the old form of spelling of Charlestown, West Virginia—Charles Town—and the modern form of spelling, Charlestown.[4] The quilt is interesting also as indicating Charlestown, Virginia, and would indicate the quilt was made before 1863, the year West Virginia was admitted into the Union. Dated police and firemen's badges or military ribbons appearing in a quilt also provide evidence. The Grand Army Quilt, for example (see plate 267), includes badges of troops that fought in the Civil War from both the North and South.

Masonic and other fraternal organization symbols are sometimes found in quilt designs and are an aid in dating. For example, the Odd Fellows organization was established in the United States about 1819 and quilts incorporating Odd Fellow symbols will date from about that time.

During the 1850s occurred the flowering of one of the most popular of all American quilt types—the Log Cabin. In the following years, thousands of Log Cabin Quilts were made throughout the country in a burst of creativity and originality in dozens of pattern variations: "Windmill Blades," "Barn Raising," "Courthouse Steps," "Pineapple," "Sunshine and Shadows," "Straight Furrow." Although most of these quilts date between the 1850s and the 1880s, the Log Cabin is a quilt classic made to the present day.

---

4. William Rush Dunton, Jr., *Old Quilts*, Catonsville, Maryland, privately published, 1946, page 9.

Plate 298.
Log Cabin Quilt, Barn Raising Variation, Pennsylvania,
c. 1850–75. Pieced cotton and wool, 79 x 79 in. Collection
of Bill Gallick and Tony Ellis.

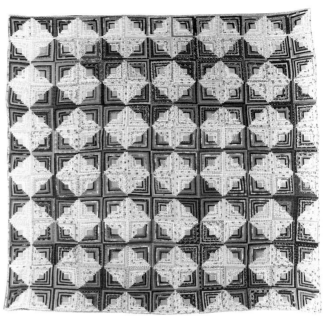

Plate 299.
Log Cabin Quilt, Light and Dark Variation, Pennsylvania,
c. 1850–75. Pieced cotton and wool, 72 x 72 in. Collection
of Bill Gallick and Tony Ellis.

Plate 300.
Log Cabin Quilt, Diamond with Four Squares Variation,
Pennsylvania, c. 1850–75. Pieced cotton and wool, 84 x 87 in.
Collection of Bill Gallick and Tony Ellis.

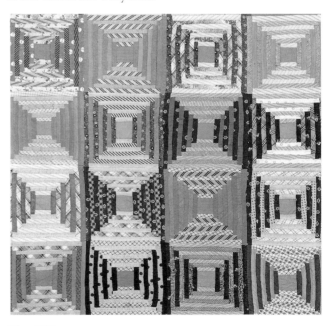

Plate 301.
Log Cabin Quilt, Courthouse Steps Variation, Pennsylvania,
c. 1850–75. Pieced cotton and wool, 71 x 82 in. Collection
of Bill Gallick and Tony Ellis.

In the Log Cabin it is the fabrics we must look to for dating. Mrs. Peto points out that the earliest Log Cabins were made of "mohairs and other sturdy woolens; the intermediate era used a wide variety of cotton prints and challis; the lush Victorian decades flaunted silks, satins, brocades, velvets."[5]

In the 1870s, 1880s, and 1890s there are the Victorian Quilts. Together with the fascination for the Crazy Quilt, there was a return to popularity of the Roman Square pattern, a three-patch block made up of three oblong strips of different colors, usually in wool and silk materials.

The Victorian Crazy Quilts are distinguished by irregular patches, the types of materials used (silks, velvets, and satins), decoration of the patches with elaborate collages of beads and other materials and a variety of fancy embroidery stitches, with as many as a hundred different types of stitches on a single quilt. The Victorian quilts were often decorated with appliquéd and embroidered figures of animals, birds, fans, horseshoes, and flowers. Sometimes there are hand-painted motifs, such as flowers on a satin or plush ground.

Quill Quilts and quilts evidencing Japanese-style motifs were also much in vogue during this period. Quill quilts were made of small, multicolored scraps of fabric, about two and a half inches wide by one inch deep, folded into pointed shaped "quills." The "quills" were then sewn in overlapping rows, frequently in circular patterns, to a ground material until the whole foundation was covered.

Autograph Quilts were the craze starting in the 1850s when famous people were asked to sign blocks or send pieces of their clothing to be incorporated in a quilt top. Bits of dresses, wedding gowns, and scarves were all included in quilts of the period. Some were autographed. If the identity of the person who has contributed the swatch is known, the autograph can be a key to the quilt's age (see chapter 7).

Beginning in the late 1860s and reaching vogue proportions by the 1870s and 1880s were pictorial silhouette repeat designs, representational and illustrative. There are fan, flag, little red schoolhouse, horseshoe, and butterfly quilts. There are realistic flowers and leaves and, of course, houses—red, yellow, green, black, and pink houses, complete with chimneys, door knobs, green calico grass, and blue calico skies (see plate 276). Botanical spreads in which flowers and leaves of great verisimilitude were appliquéd at random over the quilt top were also in vogue.

Between 1880 and 1900 pieced quilts were made up of wool patch

---

5. Florence Peto, "New York Quilts," *New York History*, New-York Historical Association, July 1949, page 331.

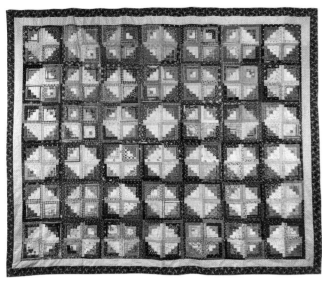

Plate 302.
Log Cabin Quilt, Light and Dark Variation, Connecticut, c. 1875–1900. Pieced cotton, 82 x 73 ¼ in. Collection of Mr. and Mrs. Michael Plisko.

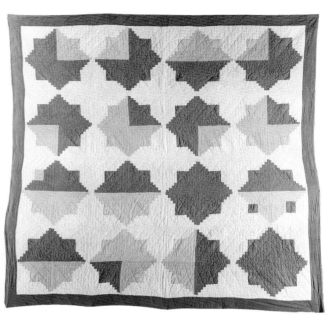

Plate 303.
Log Cabin Quilt, Clocks Variation, Pennsylvania, c. 1900. Pieced cotton, 86 x 90 in. Collection of Rhea Goodman, Quilt Gallery, Inc.

Plate 304.
Log Cabin Quilt, Zigzag Variation, Pennsylvania, c. 1850–75. Pieced wool, challis, and cotton, 86 x 80 in. America Hurrah, New York.

Plate 305.
Log Cabin Quilt, Barn Raising Variation, Pennsylvania, c. 1920. Pieced cotton and wool, 86 x 90 in. Collection of Rhea Goodman, Quilt Gallery, Inc.

Plate 306.
Log Cabin Quilt, Barn Raising
Variation, Pennsylvania, c.
1850–75. Pieced wool and
challis, 78 x 80 in. America
Hurrah, New York.

pictures given as premiums with the purchase of tobacco. The pictures may be of flags of various nations, American Indian rug designs, and scenes of Indian life. There are quilts made of cigar bands sewn together in Log Cabin patterns, as well as from labels from tobacco pouches.

During the last quarter of the nineteenth century, we may find Kate Greenaway–type figures—processions of children, or little boys and girls with umbrellas—worked in outline embroidery in quilt squares (see plate 169).

The interest in pictorial designs for quilt tops continues to the present time. During the 1920s and 1930s automobiles, boats, and airplanes became the subject matter for quilts, together with lily pads and trolley cars—and more little figures holding umbrellas. There was a revival of interest in patriotic scenes such as Penn's Treaty with the Indians, Washington Crossing the Delaware, the Signing of the

Declaration of Independence. Newspapers serialized patterns of a patriotic nature suitable for Album Quilt tops. And in the 1960s and '70s, rockets and subjects relating to outer space appeared on quilts.

Throughout all periods we must look to the characteristics of the sewing techniques for significant clues. An important indication of the age of a quilt is the quality of the quilting. Generally the finest quilting is found on the earliest quilts, although there are quilts with beautiful stitching made even at the present time. It is more difficult to discern fine stitching in the piecing and appliquéing techniques, but there can be

Plate 307.
Victorian Picture Quilt, Irish or American, c. 1860. Pieced, appliquéd, and embroidered silks, satins, and velvets, 70 x 82 in. Collection of Pioneer Museum and Haggin Galleries, Stockton, California. Made by Mrs. Edwin Hardman, this Victorian folk art quilt is filled with wonderful scenes that include ships at sea, cowboys roping steers, giraffes, and little girls jumping rope. The house in the center has lace curtains in the windows and a lawn of fake fur. A meandering floral vine makes up the border.

The Age of a Quilt 331

little hints there too. The stitching on the appliquéd pieces of the earlier quilts tends to be totally invisible, hidden under the piece that is sewn down or, when it does show, identical in size and slant.

Quilting found on the earlier pieced and appliquéd quilts will also display a greater expertise and concern for tiny, close, perfect stitches than is generally found in later quilting. In the earlier part of the nineteenth century, for example, the alternate blocks and borders are profusely quilted and very often include cording and stuffing.

The quality of the stitching is an important clue to the date of an all-white quilt. Those of the first quarter of the nineteenth century commonly have a background stitched so minutely that a stippled, textured effect is achieved. Thimble quilting, another technique, in which a thimble was placed on the cloth and traced around for the filler quilting pattern, is also seen much less frequently after the mid-nineteenth century. The use of such enormous quantities of stitchery in the background of the all-white quilts almost totally disappeared after 1850.

Cording and stuffing techniques can be helpful. Cording done with an unbleached or coarse roving tends to indicate homespun and therefore an early date. Stuffing with wool may indicate an earlier rather than a later period, since wool was available before cotton in most areas. Closely worked cording and stuffing is found on American quilts of the eighteenth century, but it is rare after the middle of the nineteenth century probably because of its painstaking and time-consuming nature.

Another thing to look for on an early white quilt is a top created from three widths of cloth sewn together, or a number of fragments pieced together. This is an indication of an early narrow loom, or a time in which cloth was less abundant.

Machine stitching obviously cannot predate the invention of the sewing machine, which was patented in 1846 and in common use by 1865. It is from this period on that greater numbers of quilts will be found with machine stitching. Beware! There are some instances where an early quilt top has been quilted at a later date on a machine. There are also examples of beautiful quilting done on some of the early machines of the 1860s that appears to have been done by hand until one looks closely. At the same time, some of the earliest nineteenth-century quilts have stitches of almost machine-like precision and regularity. During the 1870s and 1880s some quilters proudly emphasized machine quilting by using thread in a color contrasting with the quilt top, particularly white stitches on dark solids.

The type of thread used in the quilt can be a general aid in dating. An eighteenth-century quilt would contain handspun linen thread, as

there was virtually no cotton thread in the eighteenth century. The earliest cotton thread, three-ply, was used throughout the nineteenth century and into the twentieth, while the earliest examples of six-ply cotton thread date from about 1840. This means that if the end of a sewing thread on a quilt is untwisted and found to be made up of six strands (three branches of two threads each), the thread dates no earlier than the middle of the nineteenth century.

Plate 309.
Cockscomb, Rosetree, and
Pineapple Quilt (detail), c. 1840.
Appliquéd red, green, and yellow
calico, 77 ½ x 85 in. Courtesy
Art Institute of Chicago.

Threads were dyed at the earliest date. This can be seen in
counterpanes of early European origin. The color range of the thread on
the earliest quilts is generally limited to browns, blues, yellows, and reds.
Because of the iron mordants used in the dyes, some of the earliest quilts
have threads that have partly deteriorated.

In addition to quilting, the maker had the option of fastening the
three layers of the quilt together with knots, the technique called tying.
Tying is most apt to be found on everyday quilts, particularly those in
which the maker used interlining too thick to be quilted through. It may
have originated on bed ticks that were filled with thick, unruly
interlinings. There is nothing to indicate that either quilting or tying
predates the other as a fastening technique.

Embroidery in colored silks and wools has been used throughout the history of quilt making. There are examples of quilts that contain embroidery in eighteenth-century motifs. They are characterized by an openness and delicacy with light crewelwork florals sparsely placed on the background. Also, embroidery appears outlining and emphasizing shapes such as stems and petals of flowers, beaks, eyes, and tails of birds, particularly in silk. Later, about mid-nineteenth century, cotton and wool predominate and silk is not uncommon. Dr. William Rush Dunton, Jr., researched in detail this particular aspect of woolen embroidery in quilts and made the following comments:

> *The presence of so much embroidery would indicate that the quilt was made after 1850 and as so much wool was used the date would probably be moved forward, possibly into the sixties.*[6]

The Album Quilts often have motifs enriched with silk and wool buttonholing stitches. Frequently, on quilts of Pennsylvania provenance, there is an extra embellishment of bright wool outlining tulips, roses, animals, and birds.

The Victorians displayed an unending variety of stitches. By 1870, on the Crazy Quilts, there is a universal use of feather stitching for seaming, and hundreds of varying embroidery stitches are found ornamenting the crazy patches of silk, velvet, satin, and taffeta.

Introduced to America in the last quarter of the nineteenth century was a popular type of needlework known as Outline Embroidery. A great number of quilts are worked with the red and blue outlines of boys and girls with fans and umbrellas, and animals and such phrases as "Good Morning." Objects were drawn in needlework on the quilt top in Kensington stitch.

Interlinings, backs, sets, borders, and bindings all yield valuable information that tells something about the quilt's age. For example, sometimes the wadding is a used quilt or scraps of material that can be identified. Newspapers and letters, which also serve to insulate, may be dated or give information from which a date may be determined. The thickness of a quilt may be worth noting. Later quilts often have more wadding as it became a manufactured product and was therefore more easily available. Seeds in the interlining indicate unginned or poorly ginned cotton, which was on the market until about 1830 or 1840.

The backs of quilts should be examined for valuable hints. Printed cottons of American manufacture became available in abundance around 1840 and after that time, more and more quilts used printed cotton as a

---

6. Dunton, *op. cit.*, pages 9 and 167.

backing. It is sometimes possible to see a stamp from a bleaching works with a date of establishment on the back of a quilt, or stamping on flour or feed sacking. An attempt to identify these places of business might establish the quilt's origins as well as its date.

The design of the set offers dating information. With the use of repeat blocks in quilt construction during the first quarter of the nineteenth century, the set took on greater importance as a design element. Piece work or appliquéd blocks set with lattice strips or alternate plain squares date generally after 1800, as do designs composed of vertical or diagonal strips.

Borders can indicate certain facts about the age of the quilt. A border consisting of a gathered flounce approximately twenty inches deep indicates an early nineteenth-century date. An elaborately quilted border was prevalent in the first half of the nineteenth century. A border on three sides with a smaller border or none at all across the top of the quilt also points to a date before 1850.

Look carefully at the binding of a quilt, as it can be extremely informative in gathering dating clues. Hand-loomed tape was used in the eighteenth and early nineteenth centuries to bind off a quilt; woven and netted fringe suggest either a late eighteenth or early nineteenth-century date. Trimmings, fringes, and tassels of cotton, linen, silk, or wool are usually employed in the period before 1850. In fact, any kind of trimming, fringes, and tassels suggests compliance with an earlier fashion that ends in the second quarter of the nineteenth century. Laces and scallops, sometimes even thickly embroidered with pearls and intertwined with ribbons, very often accompany the Victorian quilt. Edgings, however, can be removed—and frequently are, often confusing the issue.

Probably the single most important clue in dating is the age of the materials used. However, estimating the age of materials in quilts, front and back, can be confusing and difficult for the beginner.

First of all, textiles of all types were used in quilts. As we have mentioned, almost any fragment of material was considered worthy: ties, bits of men's shirts, flags, pieces of calico dresses, cigar bands, remnants of furnishing fabrics used for curtains and slipcovers, commemorative handkerchiefs—ad infinitum. Textiles are designed and printed with specific uses in mind, and printed designs can be as distinct for fabric used in various types of clothing as they are different for clothing and house furnishings. All types found their way into quilt tops.

This variety in textile design requires an ability to recognize printed textiles "across the board" for furnishings and clothing for the periods they were in vogue. Easy recognition is complicated, as the quilt top may contain only a tiny fragment of a given fabric. Furnishing-fabric designs are generally larger in scale and wider in the area of repeat than clothing fabric designs, and it is difficult to identify them when only a small section is available for study.

We are also concerned with textile designs covering approximately a 285-year period (i.e., from the Saltonstall Quilt of 1704 to the present). In addition, textiles, particularly until the second quarter of the nineteenth century, were imported from all parts of the world. Though the major imports were from England, there were French toiles, Italian brocade, damask from Sweden, and cottons from India. The variety of design from a single country is enormous. The amounts from the United States alone were prodigious. During the nineteenth century, the textile industry developed in the United States with increased vitality. It began to boom after the first quarter of the century, encouraged by protective tariffs, an abundance of cotton and water power, and innovations in the use of textile machinery to produce inexpensive goods. More and more the home market was supplied with calicos and cottons made in the United States. During the second half of the nineteenth century and thereafter, a growing measure of textiles found in quilts are of American origins and reflect American taste and design. To be sure, there was never a time when European influences ceased, but increasingly Americans looked to their own industry and taste.

Further complicating the easy identification of textiles by period is the problem of different levels of technical development that may have produced both primitive and sophisticated textiles at a single time. As the settlement and development of the country progressed at different stages, advanced textiles were produced in the urban areas while the rural interior areas produced more primitive types. Fabrics were probably home woven in the West at the same time that the most beautiful printed textiles were manufactured in the East. Thus, in one section of the country wood blocks were used, and, in another, roller plates; manufactured goods in the East, homespun in the West.

Fabrics to be used in quilt tops and backs were saved over long periods of time and were exchanged within communities. For example, the quilt top shown in plate 5 contains over 150 different dress fabrics. In many instances the fabrics may be representative of a period that predates the actual making of the quilt by many years. Textiles were sometimes saved in the inventory of a shop from ten to fifteen years and could have been used in the making of a quilt at the time of their purchase. There is no set rule. However, for the most part, we must assume the materials used in a quilt generally date about the same time as its making. It is sometimes suggested that a quilt should be dated by the period of the last material used in the quilt. We believe that a better way to date using

Plate 310.
Sunbursts Quilt (detail),
probably Pennsylvania,
c. 1830. Pieced cotton.
Courtesy Cincinnati Art
Museum. The quilt employs
an intricate piecing
technique, as well as
diagonal quilting that
incorporates stuffed cherries
on trailing vines.

materials is by the period or age of the predominant number of materials found in the quilts. Quilts were frequently repaired throughout their life and it is not unusual to find a quilt of extremely early vintage with pieces of material of a much later date, perhaps even twentieth century.

Thus, a knowledge of textiles and fabric design is invaluable. Learning about textile designs can, in itself, be enjoyable and educational. Examples of period textiles can be seen in costumes, especially in museum collections, textile swatch books, furnishing fabrics on antique furniture, and, of course, quilts. We have come across wonderful examples of swatches of materials in schoolgirl lesson books, in which small pieces of calico were cut out and pasted in a notebook with a date. Dated quilts themselves are a goldmine of representative examples.

Most of all, knowing the age of textiles requires looking until you acquire almost a second sense of what types of printed designs were fashionable, what colors were in vogue at certain periods in our history, how old material feels. To illustrate fabrics or representative examples of printed textiles of all periods is not within the scope of this book, but in selecting dated quilts we believe we have presented fine examples of materials used during particular times or periods.

There are certain clues that give valuable information about materials used and may be helpful in placing them in a particular period. Obviously, we cannot date textiles only by recognizing the designs in patterns, we must also know something about the fabrication and the printing and dyeing techniques used—and even the import-export regulations of a country. For example, three blue threads in the selvage of cotton cloth dates the material between 1774 and 1811 and marks it as an English export.

The types of materials used and how they were fabricated give important insights into their dating. For example, if the material is a synthetic, it is, obviously, of a comparatively recent vintage. If wools and linens were used, are they hand woven? A hand-woven fabric suggests an earlier dated material than a manufactured one. What are the printing techniques used on the textiles: wood-block, copperplate, or roller printing?

The wood-block technique in which the design is cut or raised in relief on a flat block of wood, color applied to the raised portion, and the impression created by stamping the block, usually by hand, onto the cloth to be printed, came into common use in Europe at the end of the seventeenth century and remained a popular form of textile printing until it was rivaled by the use of copperplates from about 1750 to 1820. Copperplates broadened the range of textile printing with finer detail of engraving, larger repeat patterns than obtained with wood blocks, and more delicately blended effects of shading over small spaces. It, too, was finally outmoded by the roller-printing technique, which was faster, cheaper, and enabled a number of colors to be printed almost simultaneously with accurate register. Invented in 1783, the roller-printing machine was in general use by 1850 and was used almost exclusively thereafter. It was stated that the roller-printing machine in one day could turn out the equivalent of the work of forty men using copperplates. In copperplate and roller-printing, plates are incised with the design, color dyes applied, the excess dyes removed from the surface of the plate and, finally, the plate pressed onto the cloth, which forced the ink to be drawn out of the lines onto the material to be printed and thus caused the pattern to be transferred to it. In the United States there seems to have been a progression from wood-block prints to roller-printed textiles without very much development of the copperplate technique. Wood blocks were also used until a fairly late date in the nineteenth century in the United States.

There are certain clues as to the different techniques used. Mrs. Montgomery, for example, points out: "The patterns of copper plate printed textiles measure about 36 inches square. The repeat of roller printed textiles, almost entirely printed on 28 inch wide cloth, is governed by the size of the roller, commonly about 12 inches."[7] She also states: "Block printed textiles are identified by pin points or registry

---

7.   Montgomery, *op. cit.*, page 111.

marks (often carefully concealed) which indicate the size of the blocks employed, most frequently about 10 inches long."[8]

Are the dyes used in the textiles natural or synthetic dyes? Until the middle of the nineteenth century, textile printers were almost entirely dependent upon the use of dyestuffs obtained from minerals, plants, woods, insects, and shellfish. By the 1820s a new range of harsh mineral dyes—antimony orange, manganese bronze, chrome yellow, and "solid" green—brought about a transformation in the printing palette, which coincided with the development of roller printing. In 1856, William Henry Perkin opened up the vast field of synthetic dyes with his discovery that a lavender (or mauve, as it was popularly called) dye could be derived from coal-tar. The progressive development of new chemical dyes produced a new range of colors that were also standardized.

Natural dyes, particularly if not applied properly, can cause corrosion and fading in textiles. Brown colors found in early fabrics are frequently faded blacks and purples. Iron salt mordants used with some natural dyes rendered the materials brittle; iron spotting, produced from a concentration of iron salt mordant, could produce holes in the cloth before any noticeable deterioration in the rest of the material. As pointed out by Rita J. Adrosko: "This effect can be noted in some early printed textiles in which one colored figure, usually brown, or black, has been completely disintegrated because of the corroding effects of its iron mordant."[9]

If there is a solid green color, pieces of material date after 1810. Before that time, greens were produced by an overprint of blue and yellow. Careful scrutiny will point up the technique: usually some of the color lines do not overlap exactly.

Styles and pattern types are also useful in giving an indication of a printed textile's age. What follows is a summary of the characteristics of the textiles to be found in American quilts from the last quarter of the eighteenth century up to the twentieth century. We have not attempted to describe here earlier textiles because of the rarity of quilts prior to 1775.

The same basic materials appear throughout the years. Wools, and variations such as challis; cottons of all different weights and types; linens, and cotton-and-linen combinations; silks, in combinations with linen, silk plaids, damasks; and also velvets and satins.

Styles in printed textiles, which appear so frequently in quilts,

---

8. *Ibid.*
9. Rita J. Adrosko, *Natural Dyes and Home Dyeing,* New York, Dover Publications, 1971, page 49.

often followed the lead of high-fashion silks and patterned woolens. Eighteenth-century block-printed designs are usually small-scale florals, floral sprays in the manner of Indian cottons, floral stripes, trails, and meanders. They appear in reds, purple, and brown, with yellow and blue added and sometimes combined to produce green. Dark-ground floral patterns were also popular with purple or plum color used for the background.

After the introduction of copperplate printing about 1755, large-scale furnishing textiles in a single color—red, blue, black, or purple—were produced. Delicately detailed rural and classical scenes, floral and bird designs, and subjects derived from literature, the theater, and American history were portrayed.

In the first quarter of the nineteenth century, bold color schemes and new fashions in subject matter combined to create a great variety of fresh designs. Polychrome chintzes printed from wood blocks were extremely popular. Patterns in the "drab style" employed shades of yellow and brown. In discharge printing, developed about 1800, details are "reserved" in white on a dark ground; prints in the "lapis style" (c. 1808) exhibit reds and blues printed side by side, without an intervening white background. Patterns in the Indian, Chinese, and classical tastes appear, and about 1815 a fashion for palm trees and game birds emerged.

By about 1815, roller printing, which had been invented in 1783, began to be used for furnishing textiles as well as dress goods. This continuous printing process was less expensive and many times faster than copperplate printing; methods were perfected by which several colors could be used to produce a polychrome pattern. (As has been previously pointed out, monochrome roller prints are similar in appearance to copperplate examples, while those employing more than one color may be confused with block prints. Some roller prints have extra colors added by woodblock. See chapter 6.)

From about 1825 to 1835 roller-printed pillar motifs were extremely popular. Fancy machine grounds were much used, a result of the mill and die process which made it possible to engrave background rollers completely filled with fine repeating patterns. Varieties of these background patterns produced many different materials inexpensively. Other typical designs of the first half of the nineteenth century are "rainbow style" prints (1820s), in which several stripes blend into each other at the edges, and naturalistic floral patterns (1840s–50s), some of which are in the full-blown Victorian chintz tradition. Paisley motifs continued to be seen.

Red, green, and yellow calicos with tiny floral designs in yellow, blue, green, or black appear in hundreds of variations, and seem to date extensively and successfully that by 1840, one mill alone was producing yearly one-quarter million yards of goods dyed or printed with this color called turkey red. These cotton calicos came to be known as "oiled calico," because the color was obtained by soaking the cloth in oil and then boiling it in madder root. In the 1830s, 1840s, and 1850s, one sees many quilts in which the only fabrics that have been used are the reds, greens, yellows, and combinations. Often these were especially purchased for quilt construction. One reason for this may have been the belief that only oil red, oil green, and oil yellow were considered reliable enough to use. Sometimes indigo blue was admitted to this favored colorfast group. Today the black figures are often eaten away on these cloths, the green is faded to a pea-green shade, and the red has turned to a mellow rose.

About 1850 there was a fashion for textiles printed in imitation of patchwork. During the 1850s patterns were exceptionally eclectic, and before the appearance of well-known designers like William Morris in the 1870s both designs and printing were at a low point.

Dating from the end of the third quarter of the century are centennial prints, featuring patriotic motifs in commemoration of the events of 1776. Small patterned designs of dots or geometric figures printed in white, yellow, or red on navy blue, or in red, black, brown, or blue on white are seen, and continue into the twentieth century. In this century strong colors, then pastels (by the late 1920s) were preferred; "Bauhaus" geometrics, large-scale floral designs, and representational patterns have succeeded in fashion.

Textiles of different periods may be seen and studied in period costumes, upholstery, curtains and bed furnishings, fashion plates, sample books, magazines of home decoration, schoolgirls' work books, and, of course, quilts. Although it is impossible to illustrate representative examples of all types of textiles in this volume, photographs of dated quilts have been selected for inclusion in an effort to present evidence from specific periods.

1775–1800

Block prints found in quilts:

    Small-scale stylized florals, printed in brown, purple, and red
    Floral trails, some with pin-dot or picotage shading
    Flower sprays suggestive of the Indian painted cottons
    Dark ground prints
    Resist-dyed fabrics in one or two shades of blue
    Floral stripes printed in red and black with penciled third color
        (yellow, blue, or the two together for green)
    The Hewson centers—printed in madder colors with

overpainting of other colors
    Full chintz style—printed and then overpainted in a large
        number of colors (five or so), thus achieving quite a large
        variety of shades and hues
Copperplate prints (English and French) found in quilts:
    Only monochrome colors used—red, blue, black, or purple
        (Over the years the purple can change to a brown or sepia tone.)
    Floral and pictorial themes:
        Bucolic scenes, classical ruins, nursery prints, farmyard and
        rural scenes, exotic themes, chinoiserie, indiennes, theatrical
        performance designs, themes of American Independence and
        America's heroes
Solid colors: worsteds, druggets, twill woven linens, silks, and so on
Checks and plaids

1800–1825

Block-printed fabrics continue to be used in quilts.
    Polychrome striped florals
    Pillar prints with flowery capitals
    Lapis prints: red, blue, yellow, and green used together (Reds
        and blues are next to each other for the first time without
        intervening areas of white.)
    Pompeian prints: red, yellow, and black
    Drab-style prints: absence of reds and purples in favor of yellow,
        buff, brown, and olive. Designs are frequently acorns, oak
        leaves, thistles, bunches of little clustered flowers, and hops.
    Shawl prints: little repeat prints in imitation of the embroidered
        motifs on the popular Indian and Paisley shawls
    Palm trees and wild game birds
    Chinoiserie designs
    Discharge prints: indigo grounds and minute pinwork white dots
Roller printing emerges: designs proliferate enormously, new palette of
    harsh shades.
    Appearance of antimony orange in 1817 and manganese brown in
        1823.
    The earliest roller-printed fabrics are a single color with extra colors
        added by wood block (1815); then two rollers (red and black)
        inked together (1835); then many colors inked together (1840).

1825–50

Roller printing in full swing. Roller-printed fabrics continue to be used in
quilts.

Rainbow roller prints: variety of colors printed in vertical
     stripes; sometimes one color goes from dark to light.
     There are also motifs printed on top of the shading.
Fancy machine grounds: the mill and dye technique provided
     background rollers that produced the following grounds:
     all-over trellis ground
     all-over pin ground
     all-over vermiculate (wormlike) ground
     all-over dotted, diapered, netted, and honeycombed grounds
     "cracked-ice" ground
     grounds for block-printed patterns
Designs are small scale, active, in reds, blues, greens, browns. All
     these designs seem to be printed on elaborate subsidiary ground
     patterns. Many of these prints are characterized by a stylization
     rather than naturalization.
     corallike and seaweedlike forms
     little sprays and much use of dots
     curly leaves with tattered edges
     sprigs with berries
     finely engraved jagged forms in eccentric geometrics
Victorian ornamentation (particularly in the 1840s and 1850s):
     meandering scrollwork
     arabesques, cartouches
Addition of new fussier color combinations:
     pistachio, lavender, lime green, blue green
     heavy use of brown and brown shades; rose, green, and purple
Continuation of:
     shawl prints
     checks and plaids
     floral stripes
Polka dots: orange background with black dots. (Dots are both
     large and small; of both sparse and crowded composition.)
Pillar prints reappear (1825–30), roller-printed this time.

1850–75

Enormous variety of roller-printed fabrics now begin to appear. The
aniline chemical dyes are discovered, producing a broader range of
brighter, sharper colors. Emergence of one design printed in many
different color schemes.
     Orange-toned imitation paisley prints of the 1870s:
          coppery-red, orange, brown, white, and black together in the
          same design

Printed copies of fancy woven goods, plissés, matelassés, moirés
White grounds with minuscule printed designs of tiny triangles,
        squares, circles, printed in red, black, brown, and blue. These
        continue into the twentieth century.
Other popular designs on white grounds:
        Pins stuck in cloth
        Small horses' heads, fox heads, stirrups
        Nail and sledge hammer
        Ants and flies
        Dominoes
        Small crescents, persian pears
        Little girls and boys
Small patterned flowers, less likely to have stems and leaves
        defined by bold black outline
Simulated printed patchwork
Centennial prints:
        Liberty bells, shields, flags, eagles, Washington
Extensive use of challis
Navy blue grounds with minuscule patternings in white, red, or yellow
Purple grounds and soft grays printed in white or black
Continuation of checks and plaids

1875–1900

Still greater proliferation of roller-printed fabrics. The printed patterns in
shirting and other cottons are not so detailed, minute, or fussy. Slightly
larger-scale motifs.
        Continued use of navy blue, white, and red: anchors, bells, grids,
                sprigs, bubbles, concentric circles, interlocking circles, larger
                horses' heads, horseshoes, riding whips, fox heads, stirrups
        Continued use of commemorative fabrics
        One design comes in a number of colors: gray, mauve, blue,
                rose, rust, and so on

Twentieth century

Roller-printed fabrics show pastel colors, and many of the designs appear
to have been influenced by the Bauhaus architectural movement; there is
an Art Deco quality to many of the geometrics.
        Brighter colors: fuchsia, peach, coral, aqua on a white ground
        Representational objects, much less detail, larger-scale designs
        Continuation of many of the calicos from the nineteenth century,
                but with less delicacy

11
Care

There is a great deal to know about textile conservation and restoration and there are extremely worthwhile, scholarly books on the subject if one is interested in specialized, procedural information.[1] But there is a rather great distinction between the conservation efforts of a trained textile curatorial staff and the general care that can be successfully handled in a household.

In the home, a certain amount of caution must be exercised, no matter what the cleaning project. Laundering a quilt that receives everyday use (and its share of wear) necessitates knowledge of how to prevent undue damage through the cleaning process. A preservation effort of a fragile, early quilt should attempt to protect existing materials and preclude or arrest further deterioration. This work should be done by a professional conservator, someone who has worked with historic pieces.

One is tempted to think of the washer and dryer as the best solution to laundering problems. And indeed some sturdy (particularly twentieth-century) quilts may withstand steady punishment from these appliances, especially when the gentle cycles are used and bleach and harsh detergents are avoided. However, we would never advise this method for the great majority of quilts. It is altogether too great a possibility that the result will be a dryer full of puffy shreds. By the same token, hanging a quilt out on the line to dry has been a common custom for years, but the lack of proper weight distribution damages the fibers, and if the quilt is buffeted around by wind, there can be enormous weakening of the stitching.

Before the quilt is cleaned it must be determined whether it is wool, silk, cotton, or linen or a combination thereof. Generally wool and silk

---

1. *Textile Conservation*, edited by Jentina E. Leene, D.Sc., International Institute for Conservation of Historic and Artistic Works, London, Butterworths, 1972; Smithsonian Institution Press, Washington, D.C.

should be dry cleaned and cotton and linen wet cleaned or washed if the dyes are fast and if the filling or padding does not cause problems. Dry cleaning or wet cleaning should be handled by firms or individuals who have worked with large pieces and are familiar with cleaning perishable materials.

CLEANING A STURDY QUILT

First, one must test to see if the dyes are fast (that the colors will not run). Put a few droplets of water on an unobtrusive section of the quilt and then blot with a white blotter. If none of the dyes have come off on the blotter, repeat the test with a solution of detergent and water. It is a good idea to try this on more than one spot on the quilt and on any repaired areas. With the earlier dyes particularly, there is not the uniformity of today, and some fabrics may be colorfast while others may run. *If the dye is not fast, do not attempt further wet cleaning.* Explore the possibilities of dry cleaning.

If there is no problem with the dyes, take the quilt to a bathtub[2] or some other large tub that will allow the quilt to be unfolded as much as possible. The more folds you put in the quilt the more you will have to rinse it. In warm water with a neutral detergent,[3] gently agitate the quilt without taking it out of the water. Textiles become surprisingly heavy when wet, and when weighted fabrics come out of the water they tear more easily. The bathtub is quite a good solution in this respect, because the water can drain out without the quilt being picked up, and new rinse water can come in. Repeat this process as many times as you feel necessary to remove all traces of the cleaning agent. When the final rinse water has been let out, hand squeeze excess water out of the material and the quilt is ready to be lifted out. If you possibly can, recruit another pair

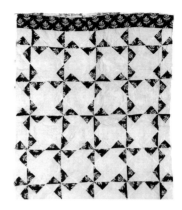

Plate 311.
Pinwheel Pillowcase (detail), Pennsylvania, c. 1830. Pieced in red and brown, 24 ¼ x 17 in. Collections of Henry Ford Museum and Greenfield Village, Dearborn, Michigan.

2. A caution about the bathtub: it may not always be the ideal size for wet cleaning a textile the size of a quilt, and there is always the danger of tearing and splitting as a result of crampness in the cleaning process.
3. Generally a half-full bathtub takes approximately twenty gallons of water. This would require about 1½ cups of detergent. Consider the light-duty, mild-sudsing, synthetic detergents: Dreft, Vel liquid, Ivory liquid, and Joy liquid (as listed in Isabel B. Wingate, *Textile Fabrics and Their Selection*, 5th edition, Englewood Cliffs, N. J., Prentice-Hall, 1964, page 399). A longer list is provided by the U.S. Government: Woolite, Palmolive liquid, Dove, Chiffon liquid, Octagon liquid (U.S. Department of Agriculture, Home and Garden Bulletin No. 139, *Soaps and Detergents for Home Laundering*. Prepared by Southern Marketing and Nutrition Research Division of the Agricultural Research Service, page 4). Avoid the use of such soaps as Ivory Flakes, Ivory Snow, or Lux Flakes; they can cause yellowing of the fabric. And by all means stay away from detergents described by their manufacturers as "heavy-duty."

of hands to help you. The more evenly the weight is distributed, the less tearing and stress on stitching and fabrics will result. Gently place the quilt onto big absorbent towels or clean cotton mattress pads and lightly press out as much water as you can. When most of the excess moisture has been removed, the quilt should be dried as flat as possible. Drying may take place outside on bright days with low humidity (away from exposure to direct sunlight). Spread the quilt out on a clean sheet or mattress pads on the grass. If there is no clean, grassy spot available, a raised grid of clothesline will support and distribute the weight of the wet quilt. If the quilt must be dried indoors, fans blowing across the surface of the quilt will expedite drying; if you don't own a fan, keep rolling the quilt—unfolded—in dry towels, absorbing as much moisture as possible each time.

CLEANING A WHITE QUILT

The basic washing steps are the same for the white quilt, but there is the added element of bleaching. Bleaching is definitely a weakening hazard and should be omitted entirely on rare and delicate fabrics. *In any case, be forewarned: damage can result from overzealous use of bleaches.* When used, bleaches should always be in a considerably diluted form, and most important, they should be *rinsed out thoroughly* as their residuals will continue to weaken the fabric.

Bleach is added after the first detergent bath. Which bleach to use? Not Clorox. It is difficult to rinse out completely and it is much too strong. It is a great whitener but it will exhaust the fibers. "A *3-percent* solution of hydrogen peroxide is safe for all fibers; it acts slowly on stains. Test all dyed fabrics for color-fastness. Do not use in metal containers."[4] Two quarts in the tub water will help to whiten yellowed fabrics. Another mild bleaching solution is sodium perborate: $1\frac{1}{4}$ pints added to the bathtub will help to whiten. Both 3-percent hydrogen peroxide and sodium perborate are available in drug and grocery stores.

STAIN REMOVAL

Often individual stains will be more unsightly than the overall yellowing or tan color that comes with age. Small brown stains and usage soiling (for example, a rather large area of prominent tan coloring) can be

---

4. U.S. Department of Agriculture, Home and Garden Bulletin No. 62, *Removing Stains from Fabrics, Home Methods*, prepared by Consumer and Food Economics Research Service, page 16.

Plate 312.
Ohio Star Quilt (detail),
Maine, c. 1800–1825. Pieced
cotton, 80 x 87 in. Courtesy
Baltimore Museum of Art.
Miniature pieces make up each
triangle of each star; each block
is only 3 x 3 inches.

treated if extreme care is taken. First, be advised of the dangers. There is the possibility of uneven lightening, ringing, and bleaching affecting the padding underneath, and the possible breakage of the fibers and threads of the quilt top.

The U.S. Department of Agriculture recommends the following procedure:

> *Moisten stain (apply with cotton balls) with a few drops of 3% solution of hydrogen peroxide. Expose stain to direct sunlight. Add hydrogen peroxide as needed to keep stained area moist until stain is removed. If above treatment does not remove stain, add a few drops of household ammonia to about 1 tablespoon of hydrogen peroxide. Moisten stain immediately with this mixture. Keep damp until stain is removed; it may take several hours or more. Rinse well.* [5]

The authors have tried this method with great success, but be advised that textile curators fear exposure of fabric to sunlight because not only may it fade the colored areas of the quilt but the fading process may continue after the quilt is removed from the sunlight.

---

5. *Ibid.*, page 16.

Plate 313 (OPPOSITE). Baltimore Album Quilt (detail), c. 1825–50. Appliquéd and embroidered. Courtesy Maryland Historical Society. The gentleman's suit shows signs of deterioration, so it was imperative that gauze netting be placed over it to protect worn areas during washing.

Another method that is safe and effective is a solution of sodium perborate:

> . . . add $\frac{1}{2}$ ounce of sodium perborate to $\frac{1}{2}$ gallon of distilled water heated to 85 degrees. Soak the fabric (or the stain) in this solution from one to four hours and then rinse thoroughly in distilled water of the same temperature.[6]

Mildew: Mildew spots should be treated, if possible, while they are fresh, before the mold growth has a chance to weaken the fabric. Wash the mildewed article thoroughly.

> Strong soap solutions and sunlight are best to remove new mildew stains from white cotton. (Again, be cognizant of danger by exposure to sunlight.) A bleaching agent must be used on old stains if the fabric is white. Stains on dyed fabrics should be covered with a paste made from powdered chalk and then exposed to sunlight.[7]

For linen there is a different recipe: "Soak the mildewed cloth in chloride of lime until the mildew disappears. Follow with a thorough rinsing with clear water."[8] Once again, if the quilt is fragile or delicate or more than fifty years old, these methods should be omitted entirely, for serious damage to fibers may result.

CLEANING A DELICATE ANTIQUE OR HEIRLOOM

This is an almost indefinable category. What is an heirloom to one family is a white elephant to another; what looks delicate to some may appear sturdy to another. However, if your quilt is over fifty years old; if it is showing signs of wear, such as stuffing beginning to come out or stitching beginning to give way; if fabrics have torn or deteriorated; if there is embroidery, cording, stuffing, or extremely fine stitching, it will fare badly with washing unless great care is taken. It is advisable to have a person trained in textile conservation carry out the cleaning and repair of a fragile quilt.

This is a multistep procedure and should be done outside in the summertime, with (1) a container of molded fiberglass, like an inexpensive child's wading pool, and (2) two large pieces of fiberglass or

---

6. Maureen Collins, *How to Wet-Clean Undyed Cotton and Linen*, Information Leaflet 478, Textile Laboratory, Smithsonian Institution, Washington, D.C., page 8.
7. Isabel B. Wingate, *op. cit.*, page 409. Strong soap solutions as listed by Wingate would be Duz, Rinso, Instant, and Fels Naptha.
8. *Ibid.*, page 410. Available at drug stores.

plastic screening. The first three steps can be done inside on a work table.

1. Lay the quilt out flat, place a large piece of screening over it, and run a low-power hand vacuum cleaner over it to remove all surface dirt particles.
2. Make the test to see if the dyes are fast.
3. All weak fabrics should be sandwiched between two pieces of screening for protection during the laundering process. (The screening can be tacked together with needle and thread at intervals, as in plate 313.)
4. Place the quilt, sandwiched between the two large pieces of screening, out flat, and lower it into the large bath of lukewarm water and a product called Orvus W.A. (made by Procter and Gamble). The fabric should never be squeezed, beaten, scrubbed, or agitated.
5. Watch the water. The quilt should be removed before an hour if a lot of soil comes out. Lift the quilt out of the bath and allow it to drain through the screen.
6. Lower into clean water, rinse at least five times (changing the water each time), and lift out. "Never pour or run water on top of an antique fabric; instead lower the article into the container of water."[9]
7. Last, place the quilt, still supported by the screens, between blotting pads or toweling. Remove all excess moisture. Dry as flat as possible on an additional stretched screen support, avoiding contact with the wooden or metal frame. Drying may take place outside away from exposure to direct sunlight on a bright day with low humidity, or inside with fans blowing across the surface of the quilt.

This set of instructions presents problems that will have to be dealt with at the outset. The water must be lukewarm, which means the hose will have to be attached to an indoor faucet in order to warm the water for the fiberglass pool. Also, the difficulty of changing the water and lifting the screen out at the same time will require the help of another person. Most wading pools do not have any built-in drainage.

If there is writing on your quilt (signatures, sayings, or drawings), wet cleaning of the piece should not be attempted. Only experienced persons should work on such pieces.

The stuffing swells when it gets heavy with water and may break through the top layer if the surface has been weakened by mishandling,

---

9.   Collins, *op. cit.*, page 7.

mechanical action, light damage, bleaching or other deteriorating factors. Gently push it back with a bodkin; when it dries it will be tightly enclosed again.

One other caveat: there is almost no way of arresting the disappearance of black lines and figures originally made by iron tennate black dye, since it oxidizes and eats away the fabric remorselessly. Consider cleaning such a piece only under extreme circumstances and, again, have it done only by an experienced person.

MENDING AND OTHER REPAIRS

First, get a good seamstress. If you judge you can't do the necessary work yourself, seek the help of a talented needleworker. On a hand-sewn quilt, all repairs should be done by hand. Mending tears, replacing missing pieces, darning, and reweaving lost areas—all these will help to support and strengthen an antique textile.

There is a limit to how much repair is actually beneficial, however. If pieces of the fabric are so badly worn that they need replacing, or pieces that are missing altogether, only replacing them with fabrics that are their contemporaries and that resemble the originals will actually improve the appearance of the quilt. It is a perfectly natural thing to mend and repatch a quilt. Repair, even after a period of many years, is very much a part of the life of a household textile. However, a great many fabrics today look crude compared to their ancestors and should not be used in an early quilt.

Edges, too, are often in need of recovering. It is a long job to hand stitch around all four sides of a large quilt and many are loathe to do it. Re-cover the frayed edges, but don't machine stitch them. Keep the original edge for documentation purposes.

Darning areas in which the dyes have eaten away a small line or blossom on a sprig of calico can be attempted if one is really expert, but it is a tedious, time-consuming job. Reweaving in large areas of single color can be attempted by an expert. This usually appears as very acceptable repair.

STORAGE AND DISPLAY

The quality of storage facilities in the home naturally will not approach the space or specifications of museum surroundings, but there are important things to keep in mind that will give a longer life to quilts.

Don't store quilts in plastic bags. Wrap them loosely in clean cotton pillow cases or sheets. Textiles need to breathe. Keep them out of direct sunlight and out of contact with wood surfaces.

Refold the quilt every couple of months to keep it from getting permanent creases. It can be an unpleasant surprise to find that a quilt has deteriorated even while it was carefully folded away in a blanket chest or closet. After a few years, a piece that is very old or has material that has become brittle will begin to wear away at its own folds. There are, however, times when just the process of folding and unfolding will leave tears where your fingers have held the quilt. Since repair of this sort is vexing at best and basically impossible, handle very old or deteriorated quilts as little as possible. Fingers contain natural oils that can leave remarkably unsightly stains after a while.

Single-layer spreads or pieces finely quilted may be rolled onto cardboard mailing tubes; first apply a protective wrapping of Permalife ledger paper to serve as an acid barrier. The quilt can be covered with washed cotton sheeting.

To fend off insects, there is a medicinal herb, long used in closets and pantries, to keep away moths and other insects. It is called southernwood (*Artemisia abrotanum*). A bunch of it hanging in the quilt storage area will do its job.

Small museums and historical societies that find themselves with some undesignated space can have a fine textile storage plant without much trouble or expense. Fluorescent light fixtures should have ultraviolet filter sleeves placed over the tubes. Lights should be kept off except for relatively short periods of time for examination and usage access. A CO_2 fire extinguisher nearby is a wise safety precaution. Humidity should be kept at approximately 50 percent, the temperature

Plate 315.
Hattie Klapp Brunner, *The Quilting Bee*. Oil painting, Reinhold, Pennsylvania, 1973. Courtesy Kate and Joel Kopp.

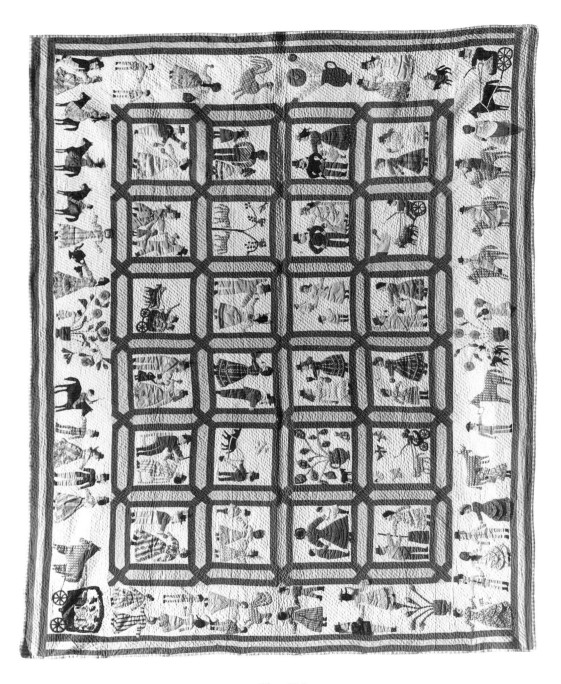

Plate 316.
Phoebe Cook Quilt, Ohio, dated 1872. Appliquéd polychrome roller-printed cottons, 75 x 94 in.
Ohio Historical Society, Columbus. The people represented are members of the quilt maker's
community. The clothing is detailed with ruffled dresses and free-hanging purses, and a few bonnets
and accessories are made of silk. The hair and beards are also quite detailed.

about 60 degrees. If there is space, bedcovers can be hung free from folds over aluminum or wooden poles or tubes protected by a Permalife paper wrapping and a washed muslin sleeve; this prevents creasing. As mentioned above, unlined or finely quilted bedcovers can be rolled on heavy cardboard tubes that are protected with Permalife paper. The rolled spread can then be covered with washed cotton or an inert plastic film, tied loosely with $^1/_4$-inch or $^1/_2$-inch cotton twill tape.

The exhibition of quilts takes considerable advance planning. The most important precaution in hanging an antique quilt is to see that the pull of its weight does not tear or weaken it. There are several methods of mounting to make sure that weight is evenly supported throughout. A piece of cloth, preferably unsized cotton, the same width of the coverlet but longer at one end can be sewn into a long, narrow sleeve and basted with small penetrating stitches all along the top edge of the back of the quilt. Through this sleeve or pocket a wooden or metal rod can be inserted into already prepared supports on the wall. Hook-and-loop tape can also be fastened to the back of the sleeve and pressed to the wall.

If the textile is extremely delicate and/or old, it may be necessary to baste on a layer that acts as another backing. Lining material should go all the way to the edges, and correctly applied linings (basted subtly and liberally in strategic places all over the quilt) should not pucker or wrinkle. There are some quilts that have no business being hung because they are just too heavy or too fragile. Unless some other display method can be worked out, the rare, weak pieces should be left out of exhibits.

The greatest hazard to quilts in an exhibition is that of curious hands, which, if the exhibit is well attended, can take their toll. Precautions should be taken in front of the display area to keep wall hangings out of the reach of visitors. (A rope railing is not necessarily the best guarantee.) Quilts should not be exhibited in a place where sunlight can beat down on them to fade and weaken them. Fluorescent lighting should be filtered; incandescent lighting should be a great distance from the fabrics. Quilts should not be on display for more than six months at a time.

Bibliography

Adrosko, Rita J. *Natural Dyes and Home Dyeing*. New York: Dover Publications, 1971. (Originally published by Smithsonian Institution Press.)

"All-White Quilted Coverlet." *Antiques* 51 (April 1947): 236–37.

Allen, Henry B. *The Useful Companion and Artificer's Assistant*. New York: H. B. Allen and Co., 1878.

"American Quilts on Exhibition." *Antiques* 53 (April 1948): 301.

Beard, Charles, Cecil Willett Cunnington, and Phillis Cunnington. *A Dictionary of English Costume*. Philadelphia: Dufour Editions, 1960.

Beer, Alice Baldwin. *Trade Goods: A Study of Indian Chintz*. Washington, D.C.: Smithsonian Institution Press, 1970.

Birrell, Verla. *The Textile Arts*. New York: Schocken Books, 1973.

Bolton, Ethel Stanwood, and Eva Johnston Coe. *American Samplers*. Massachusetts Society of the Colonial Dames of America, Thomas Todd Printers, 1921.

Boorstin, Daniel J. *The Americans: The Colonial Experience*. New York: Vintage Books, Random House, 1958.

———. *The Americans: The National Experience*. New York: Vintage Books, Random House, 1965.

Born, W. "Early American Textiles." *Ciba Review* (Basel, Switzerland) no. 76 (October 1949).

Bowen, Helen. "The Ancient Art of Quilting." *Antiques* 3 (March 1923): 113–17.

———. "Corded and Padded Quilting." *Antiques* 6 (November 1924): 250–53.

Brazer, Esther Stevens. *Antique Decoration*; twenty-seven articles reprinted from *The Magazine Antiques*. The Historical Society of Early American Decoration, n.d.

Brightbill, Dorothy. *Quilting as a Hobby*. Sterling Publishing Co., 1963.

Brightman, Anna. "Woolen Window Curtains." *Antiques*, December 1964, pp. 722–27.

Bridenbaugh, Carl. *The Colonial Craftsman*. Chicago: Phoenix Books, University of Chicago Press, 1950.

Burnham, Harold B., and Dorothy K. Burnham. *'Keep Me Warm One Night': Early Handweaving in Eastern Canada*. Toronto and Buffalo: Toronto Press, in cooperation with Royal Ontario Museum, 1972.

Callister, Herbert J., and William L. Warren. *Bed Ruggs, 1722–1833*. Hartford, Conn.: Wadsworth Atheneum, 1972.

Carlisle, Lilian Baker. *Pieced Work and Appliqué Quilts at Shelburne Museum*. Shelburne, Vt.: Museum Pamphlet Series, no. 2, Shelburne Museum, 1957.

Cather, Willa. *One of Ours*. New York: Alfred A. Knopf, 1953.

Caulfield, S.F.A., and B. C. Saward. *The Dictionary of Needlework*. New York: Arno Press, 1972. (Facsimile of 1882 edition.)

Channing, Marion L. *Textile Tools of American Colonial Homes*. Marion, Mass.: Published by the author, 1969.

Chase, Judith Wragg. *Afro-American Art and Craft*. New York: Van Nostrand-Reinhold Co., 1971.

Child, Mrs. *The American Frugal Housewife*. Boston: American Stationers' Co., 1836.

Christie, Archibald H. *Pattern Design*. Dover, 1969 (1910).

Clouzot, Henri. *Painted and Printed Fabrics, 1760–1815*. New York: Metropolitan Museum of Art, 1927.

Cobbett, William. *Cottage Economy*. New York: John Doyle, 1833.

Colby, Averil. *Patchwork Quilts*. New York: Charles Scribner's Sons, 1965.

———. *Patchwork*. New York: B. T. Batsford, 1958.

———. *Quilting*. New York: Charles Scribner's Sons, 1971.

Comstock, Helen, ed. *The Concise Encyclopedia of American Antiques*. New York: Hawthorn Books, 1958.

Cooper, Grace Rogers. *Invention of the Sewing Machine*. Washington, D.C.: Smithsonian Institution Press, 1968.

———. *The Copp Family Textiles*. Washington, D.C.: Smithsonian Institution Press, 1971.

Corbin, Thomas J. *Hand Block Printing on Fabrics*. London: Sir Isaac Pitman and Sons, 1945.

Cummin, Hazel E. "Calamanco." *Antiques*, April 1941, pp. 182–84.

Cummings, Abbott Lowell. *Bed Hangings*. Boston: Society for the Preservation of New England Antiquities, 1961.

———. *Rural Household Inventories, 1675–1775*. Boston: Society for the Preservation of New England Antiquities, 1964.

Davis, Mildred J. *Early American Embroidery Designs*. New York: Crown Publishers, 1969.

———. *The Art of Crewel Embroidery*. New York: Crown Publishers, 1962.

———. *Embroidery Designs, 1780 through 1820*. New York: Crown Publishers, 1971.

Davison, Mildred. *American Quilts from the Art Institute of Chicago*. Chicago: Art Institute of Chicago, 1966.

Dow, George Francis. *The Arts and Crafts in New England, 1704–1775: Gleanings from Boston Newspapers*. Topsfield, Mass.: Wayside Press, 1927.

———. *Domestic Life in New England in the 17th Century*. New York: Benjamin Blom, 1972. First published by the author in 1925.

Dunham, Lydia Roberts. "Denver Art Museum Quilt Collection." *Denver Art Museum Quarterly* (Winter 1963).

Dunton, William Rush, Jr., M.D. *Old Quilts*. Published by the author at 33 N. Symington Avenue, Catonsville, Maryland, 1946.

Earle, Alice Morse. *Costume in America*. New York: Macmillan Co., 1903.

———. *Child Life in Colonial Days*. New York: Macmillan Co., 1899.

———. *Customs and Fashions in Old New England*. Rutland, Vt.: Charles E. Tuttle Co., 1973. First edition published 1893 by Charles Scribner's Sons, New York.

———. *Home Life in Colonial Days*. New York: Macmillan Co., 1899.

Eaton, Allen H. *Handicrafts of the Southern Highlands*. New York: Russell Sage Foundation, 1937.

Eberlein, Harold Donaldson, and Abbot McClure. *The Practical Book of Early American Arts and Crafts*. J. B. Lippincott and Co., 1916.

Edwards, Ralph, and L.G.G. Ramsey, eds. *The Early Victorian Period, 1830–1860*. New York: Reynal and Co., 1958.

Ellet, Mrs. *The Practical Housekeeper: A Cyclopaedia of Domestic Economy*. New York: Stringer and Townsend, 1857.

Emery, Irene. *The Primary Structures of Fabrics: An Illustrated Classification*. Washington, D.C.: Textile Museum, 1966.

Endacott, Violet M. *Design in Embroidery*. New York: Bonanza, 1964.

England's Happiness Improved. London: St. Dunsten's Church, 1697.

Fennelly, Catherine. *The Garb of Country New Englanders, 1790–1840: Costumes at Old Sturbridge Village*. Sturbridge, Mass.: Old Sturbridge Village Booklet Series, 1966.

———. *Textiles in New England, 1790–1840*. Sturbridge, Mass.: Old Sturbridge Village Booklet Series, 1961.

———. *Town Schooling in Early New England, 1790–1840*. Sturbridge, Mass.: Old Sturbridge Village Booklet Series, 1969.

Fikioris, Margaret A. "Neoclassicism in Textile Designs by Jean-Baptiste Huet." *Winterthur Portfolio 6*. Charlottesville: University Press of Virginia, 1970. Henry Francis du Pont Winterthur Museum.

Finley, Ruth E. *Old Patchwork Quilts and the Women Who Made Them*. Newton Centre, Mass.: Charles T. Branford Co., 1970.

———. *The Lady of Godey's*. Philadelphia: J. B. Lippincott Co., 1931.

Fisher, Theo Merrill. "Some Early Pattern Blocks." *Antiques*, April 1928, pp. 285ff.

Fitzrandolph, Mavis. *Traditional Quilting*. London: B. T. Batsford, 1954.

Fitzrandolph, Mavis, and Florence M. Fletcher. *Quilting*. Woodridge, N.J.: Dryad Press, 1972.

Floud, Peter. "Copperplate Floral Designs." *Antiques* 72 (May 1957): 460–63.

———. "The Dark-Ground Floral Chintz Style." *Connoisseur*, May 1957, pp. 174–78.

———. "Pictorial Prints of the 1820s." *Antiques* 72 (November 1957): 456–59.

———. "The Pillar Print." *Antiques* 72 (October 1957): 353–55.

"The Frontispiece: Mixed Motifs in Appliqué." *Antiques*, June 1942, pp. 354–55.

"The Frontispiece: Patchwork Bed Quilt (1876)." *Antiques*, May 1934, pp. 168–69.

"The Frontispiece: Secession Quilt, 1860." *Antiques*, February 1929, pp. 108–9.

Furnas, J. C. *The Americans: A Social History, 1587–1914*. Vol. I. New York: Capricorn Books, 1971.

Gammell, Alice I. *Polly Prindle's Book of American Patchwork Quilts*. New York: Grosset and Dunlap, 1973.

Gibbons, Phebe Earle. *Pennsylvania Dutch and Other Essays*. Philadelphia: J. B. Lippincott and Co., 1874.

Giffen, Jane C. "Household Textiles: A Review." *Historical New Hampshire* 22, no. 4, 1971.

Glassie, Henry. *Pattern in the Material Folk Culture of the Eastern United States*. Philadelphia: University of Pennsylvania Press, 1968.

Goodrich, Frances Louisa. *Mountain Homespun*. New Haven: Yale University Press, 1931.

Godey's Magazine and Lady's Book. 1830–98. Philadelphia.

Gottesman, Rita Susswein. *The Arts and Crafts in New York, 1726–1776: Advertisements and News Items from New York City Newspapers*. New York: J. J. Little and Ives Co., 1938. New-York Historical Society.

———. "The Charm of Old Cotton Prints." *American Collector*, December 1935, pp. 7ff.

Graeff, Marie Knorr. *Pennsylvania German Quilts*. Home Craft Course, Vol. 14. 1946.

Grimes, J. Bryan. *North Carolina Wills and Inventories*. Raleigh: Trustees of the Public Libraries, 1912.

Groves, Sylvia. *The History of Needlework Tools and Accessories*. London: Country Life Books, 1966.

Guldbeck, Per E. *The Care of Historical Collections*. Nashville: American Association for State and Local History, 1972.

Gutcheon, Beth. *The Perfect Patchwork Primer*. New York: David McKay Co., 1973.

Haas, Louise Krause. *Quilts, Counterpanes and Related Printed Fabrics*. Santa Monica, Calif.: Coromandel House, 1956.

Hackenbroch, Yvonne. *English and Other Needlework Tapestries and Textiles in the Irwin Untermyer Collection*. Cambridge: Harvard University Press for the Metropolitan Museum of Art, 1960.

Hake, Elizabeth. *English Quilting Old and New*. London: B. T. Batsford, 1937.

Hale, Lucretia P. *Art-Needlework for Decorative Embroidery*. Boston: S. W. Tilton and Co., 1879.

Hall, Carrie A., and Rose Kretsinger. *The Romance of the Patchwork Quilt in America*. Caldwell, Idaho: Caxton Printers, Bonanza Books, 1935.

Hall, Eliza Calvert. *A Book of Handwoven Coverlets*. New York: Little, Brown and Co., 1912 (1925 edition).

———. *Aunt Jane of Kentucky*. A. L. Burt Co., 1907.

Harbeson, Georgiana Brown. *American Needlework*. New York: Bonanza Books, 1938.

Hawkins, Mary, ed. *Textile Handbook*. 4th ed. Washington, D.C.: American Home Economics Association, 1970.

Hedlund, Catherine A. *A Primer of New England Crewel Embroidery*. Sturbridge, Mass.: Old Sturbridge Village Booklet Series, 1963.

Hemphill, Herbert W., Jr. *Fabric of the State*. New York: Museum of American Folk Art, 1972.

Higginson, Francis. *New England's Plantation*. London, 1630.

Hinson, Dolores A. *Quilting Manual*. New York: Hearthside Press, 1970.

———. *A Quilter's Companion*. New York: Arco Publishing Co., 1973.

Historic Preservation. January–March 1972.

Holstein, Jonathan. *Abstract Design in American Quilts*. Whitney Museum of American Art, 1971.

———. *American Pieced Quilts*. Washington, D.C.: Smithsonian Institution Press, 1972.

Hornung, Clarence P. *Treasury of American Design*. Vols. 1, 2. New York: Harry N. Abrams, 1972.

Hostetler, John A. *Amish Society*. Baltimore: John Hopkins Press, 1963.

Howe, Florence T. "A Block-Printed Counterpane." *Antiques*, October 1929, pp. 286ff.

———. "Three Stenciled Counterpanes." *Antiques*, March 1940, pp. 120ff.

Howe, Margery B. *Deerfield Blue and White Needlework*. Vol. 47, nos. 1 and 2. Deerfield, Mass.: Needle and Bobbin Club, 1963.

———. *Early American Embroideries in Deerfield*. Deerfield, Mass.: Heritage Foundation, 1963.

Hughes, Therle. *English Domestic Needlework, 1660–1860*. New York: Macmillan Co., 1961.

Hunter, George Leland. *Decorative Textiles*. Grand Rapids, Mich.: Dean-Hicks Co., 1918.

Hunton, W. Gordon. *English Decorative Textiles*. London: John Tiranti and Co., 1930.

Ickis, Marguerite. *The Standard Book of Quilt-Making and Collecting*. New York: Dover Publishers, 1949.

Irwin, John, and Katharine Brett. *Origins of Chintz*. London: Her Majesty's Stationery Office, 1970.

James, John. *History of the Worsted Manufacture in England*. London: Longmans, Brown, Green, Roberts, Stanfield, and Bradford, 1857.

Johnson, Madam. *Every Young Woman's Companion in Useful and Universal Knowledge*. 3rd ed. London, 1765.

Jones, Emily G. *A Manual of Plain Needlework and Cutting-Out*. London: Longmans, Green and Co., 1887.

Jones, Stella. *Hawaiian Quilts*. Honolulu: Honolulu Academy of Arts, 1930.

Joy, E. T. "English Furniture Exports to America, 1697–1830." *Antiques*, January 1964, pp. 92ff.

Katzenberg, Dena S. *The Great American Cover-Up: Counterpanes of the Eighteenth and Nineteenth Centuries*. Baltimore: Baltimore Museum of Art, 1971.

Kauffman, Henry J. *Pennsylvania Dutch American Folk Art*. Dover, 1946.

Kendall, Elaine. "Beyond Mother's Knee." *American Heritage: The Magazine of History* 24 (June 1973): 16ff.

Kendrick, A. F. *English Needlework*. London: A. and C. Black, 1933.

King, Elizabeth. *Quilting*. Leisure League of America, 1934.

Koke, Richard J. "American Quilts: An Exhibition." *New-York Historical Society Quarterly* 32 (1948): 114–17.

Lane, Rose Wilder. *Woman's Day Book of American Needlework*. New York: Simon and Schuster, 1963.

Laury, Jean Ray. *Quilts and Coverlets*. New York: Van Nostrand-Reinhold, 1970.

Leene, J. E., ed. *Textile Conservation*. Washington, D.C.: Smithsonian Institution Press, 1972.

Lichten, Frances. *Folk Art of Rural Pennsylvania*. New York: Charles Scribner's Sons, 1946.

Lipman, Jean. *American Folk Decoration*. Oxford University Press, 1951.

Little, Frances. *Early American Textiles*. New York: Century Co., 1931.

Little, Nina Fletcher. *Floor Coverings in New England Before 1850*. Sturbridge, Mass.: Old Sturbridge Village Booklet Series, 1967.

———. *American Decorative Wall Painting, 1700–1850*. New York: E. P. Dutton and Co., 1972.

Lord, Priscilla Sawyer, and Daniel J. Foley. *The Folk Arts and Crafts of New England*. Philadelphia: Chilton Books, 1965.

MacIver, Percival. *The Chintz Book*. New York: Frederick A. Stokes Co., 1923.

McClellan, Elizabeth. *History of American Costume*. Tudor Publishing Co., 1969. Originally published as *Historic Dress in America*, George W. Jacobs and Co., 1904.

McClelland, Nancy. *Historic Wall-Papers*. Philadelphia and London: J. B. Lippincott Co., 1924.

McClinton, Katharine Morrison. *Antiques Past and Present*. New York: Clarkson N. Potter, 1971.

McKim, Ruby. *101 Patchwork Patterns*. New York: Dover, 1962.

Mailey, Jean. "Printed Textiles in America." *Antiques*, May 1956, pp. 422ff.

Mann, Kathleen. *Appliqué Design and Method*. London: A. and C. Black, 1937.

Marston, Doris E. *Patchwork Today*. Charles T. Branford Co., 1968.

Marting, Elizabeth. "Of American Quilts and Quilters." *American Collector*, March 1948, pp. 6–8.

Mayer, Christa Charlotte. *Masterpieces of Western Textiles*. Chicago: Art Institute of Chicago, 1969.

Memoirs of an American Lady. Boston: Wells, Wait and Co., 1809.

Montgomery, Florence M. *Printed Textiles, English and American Cottons and Linens 1700–1850*. A Winterthur Book. New York: Viking Press, 1970.

Montague, Peregrine. *The Family Pocket-Book: Or Fountain of True and Useful Knowledge*. London, eighteenth century.

Morris, Barbara. *Victorian Embroidery*. New York: Thomas Nelson and Sons, Victorian Collector Series, 1962.

———. *English Embroidery*. London: Victoria and Albert Museum, 1951.

Murray, Anne Wood. "The Attitude of the Eagle." *Antiques* 52 (July 1947): 28–30.

Nason, Elias. "A New England Village Quilting Party in the Olden Times." *Granite Monthly* 8 (1885).

Needle-work and Cutting Out. Dublin: Commissioners of National Education in Ireland, 1846.

Nevinson, John L. *Catalogue of English Domestic Embroidery.* London: Victoria and Albert Museum, 1938 (1950).

Nye, Russel Blaine. *1776–1830: The Cultural Life of the New Nation.* New York: Harper and Row Publishers, 1963.

"An Ohio Quilt (c. 1835); Quilt with Appliqué and Embroidery." *Antiques,* January 1930, pp. 26–28.

Ormsbee, Thomas Hamilton. *Collecting Antiques in America.* New York: Robert McBride, 1936.

Paddleford, Clementine. *Patchwork Quilts: A Collection of Forty-one Old Time Blocks.* New York: Farm and Fireside, n.d.

"A Patriotic Quilt." *Antiques,* June 1939, p. 304ff.

Peto, Florence. "Age of Heirloom Quilts." *Antiques* 42 (July 1942): 32–35.

———. *American Quilts and Coverlets.* New York: Chanticleer Press, 1949.

———. "Birds—Quilted, Patched and Woven." *Antiques* 36 (November 1939): 226–29.

———. "British Empire in Patchwork." *Antiques* 40 (September 1941): 145.

———. "Hand-made Elegance." *Antiques* 53 (March 1948): 214–16.

———. *Historic Quilts.* New York: American Historical Co., 1939.

———. "New York Quilts." *New York State Antiques,* July 1949, pp. 328–39.

———. "Quilts and Coverlets from New York and Long Island." *Antiques* 33 (May 1938): 265–67.

———. "A Textile Discovery." *Antiques* 64 (August 1953): 120–21.

———. "Three Generations of Quilts." *Antiques* 45 (July 1944): 306–7.

Pettit, Florence H. *America's Printed and Painted Fabrics: 1600–1900.* New York: Hastings House Publishers, 1970.

Polley, Robert L., ed. *America's Folk Art.* New York: G. P. Putnam's Sons and Country Beautiful Foundation, 1968.

Preston, Paula Sampson. *Printed Cottons at Old Sturbridge Village.* Sturbridge, Mass.: Sturbridge Village Publication, 1969.

Prime, Alfred Coxe. *The Arts and Crafts in Philadelphia, Maryland, and South Carolina 1721–1785.* Topsfield, Mass.: Walpole Society, 1929.

———. *The Arts and Crafts in Philadelphia, Maryland and South Carolina 1786–1800, Series Two, Gleanings from Newspapers.* Topsfield, Mass.: Walpole Society, 1932.

Pullan, Mrs. *The Lady's Manual of Fancy-Work.* New York: Dick and Fitzgerald, 1859.

Ramsey, J.G.M. *The Annals of Tennessee.* Charleston, South Carolina, 1853.

The Real Pen-Work Self-Instructor in Penmanship. Pittsfield, Mass.: Knowles and Maxim, 1881.

Reinert, Guy F. *Pennsylvania German Coverlets.* Kutztown: Mrs. C. N. Keyser, 1947.

Richards, Caroline Cowles. *Village Life in America.* New York: Henry Holt and Co., 1913.

Rinhart, Floyd and Marion. *America's Affluent Age.* South Brunswick and New York: A. S. Barnes and Co., 1971.

Robacker, Earl F. *Touch of the Dutchland.* New York: A. S. Barnes and Co., 1965.

Robertson, Elizabeth Wells. *American Quilts.* New York: Studio Publications, 1948.

Roth, Rodris. *Floor Coverings in 18th-Century America.* Washington, D.C.: Smithsonian Institution Press, 1967.

Safford, Carleton L., and Robert Bishop. *America's Quilts and Coverlets.* New York: E. P. Dutton and Co., 1972.

Schetky, Ethel Jane M., ed. "Dye Plants and Dyeing." *Plants and Gardens* 20, no. 3, 1972.

Schiffer, Margaret B. *Historical Needlework of Pennsylvania.* New York: Charles Scribner's Sons, 1968.

Sexton, Carlie. *Yesterday's Quilts in Homes of Today.* Des Moines: Meredith Publishing Co., 1930.

———. *Early American Quilts.* Southhampton, N.Y.: Crackerbarrel Press, 1924.

Shaffer, Sandra C. "Sewing Tools in the Collection of Colonial Williamsburg." *Antiques* 104 (August 1973): 233–40.

Sieber, Roy. *African Textiles and Decorative Arts.* New York: Museum of Modern Art, 1972.

Slayton, Mariette Paine. *Early American Decorating Techniques.* New York: Macmillan Co., 1972.

"Stars and Feathers." *Antiques,* January 1940, p. 15ff.

Stearns, Martha Genung. *Homespun and Blue.* New York: Charles Scribner's Sons, 1963.

Stevens, Napua. *The Hawaiian Quilt.* Honolulu: Service Printers, 1971.

Stoudt, John Joseph. *Early Pennsylvania Arts and Crafts.* A. S. Barnes and Co., 1964.

Stowe, Harriet Beecher. *The Minister's Wooing.* Boston: James R. Osgood and Co., 1875.

Swain, Margaret H. *Historical Needlework: A Study of the Influences in Scotland and Northern England.* New York: Charles Scribner's Sons, 1970.

———. *The Needlework of Mary Queen of Scots.* New York: Van Nostrand-Reinhold Co., 1973.

Swygert, Mrs. Luther. *Heirlooms from Old Looms.* Chicago: R. R. Donnelley, 1955.

Symonds, Mary (Mrs. Guy Antrobus). *Needlework in Religion.* London: Sir Isaac Pitman and Sons, n.d.

Symonds, Mary (Mrs. Guy Antrobus), and Louisa Precce. *Needlework through the Ages.* London: Hodder and Stoughton, 1928.

The Teacher's Assistant in Needlework. 3rd ed. London: J. Hatchard and Son, 1820.

Tomkins, Calvin. *The Bride & The Bachelors: Five Masters of the Avant Garde.* New York: Viking Press, 1968.

University of Kansas Museum of Art. *150 Years of American Quilts.* Lawrence, Kans., 1973.

Urmstone, John. "Self-Reliance on the Frontier." *The Annals of America; Discovery of a New World.* Vol. 1: 1493–1754. Chicago: Encyclopaedia Britannica, 1968.

Victoria and Albert Museum. *English Chintz.* London: Her Majesty's Stationery Office, 1955.

———. *Notes on Quilting*. London: His Majesty's Stationery Office, 1949.

———. *Notes on Applied Work and Patchwork*. London: His Majesty's Stationery Office, 1949.

Walton, Perry. *The Story of Textiles*. New York: Tudor Publishing Co., 1925.

Waring, Janet. *Early American Stencils*. New York: Dover Publications, 1968 (1937).

Warwick, E., H. C. Pitz, and A. Wyckoff. *Early American Dress*. New York: Benjamin Blom, 1965.

Webster, Marie D. *Quilts: Their Story and How to Make Them*. Tudor Publishing Co., 1948. Doubleday, Page, and Co., 1915.

"What Is American Folk Art? A Symposium." *Antiques* 575 (May 1950): 355–62.

Whiffen, Marcus. *American Architecture since 1780*. Cambridge: M.I.T. Press, 1969.

White, Margaret E. *Handwoven Coverlets in the Newark Museum*. Newark: Newark Museum Association, 1947.

———. *Quilts and Counterpanes in the Newark Museum*. Newark: Newark Museum Association, 1948.

———. "Wrought with the Needle." *Museum* (Newark) 10 (Spring 1958).

Whiting, Gertrude. *Old Time Tools and Toys of Needlework*. New York: Dover Publications, 1971.

Whittemore, Margaret. "A Doctor Syntax Quilt." *Antiques*, March 1949, pp. 182–83.

Winchester, Alice. *The Antiques Book*. New York: Bonanza Books, 1950.

———. "Stenciled Coverlets." *Antiques*, September 1945, pp. 145ff.

Wingate, Isabel B. *Textile Fabrics and Their Selection*. 5th ed. Englewood Cliffs, N.J.: Prentice-Hall, 1964.

Winthrop, John. *Journal, American Literature: The 17th and 18th Centuries*. Carl Bode, Leon Howard, and Louis B. Wright, eds. New York: Washington Square Press, 1966.

Wooster, Ann-Sargent. *Quiltmaking: The Modern Approach to a Traditional Craft*. New York: Drake Publishers, 1972.

Index

Picture Credits

Abby Aldrich Rockefeller Folk Art Center: plate 189. America Hurrah: plates 48, 57, 126, 181, 283, 304, 306. American Museum in Britain: plate 314. Mr. and Mrs. George Anderson: plate 277. *Antiques* (Helga photo): plates 149, 150. Antiques on Peaceable Street: plate 177. The Art Institute of Chicago: plates 29, 70, 124, 213, 281, 309. Authors' collection: plates 10, 90, 101, 106, 107, 117, 128, 130, 145, 147, 170, 208, 233, 234, 247, 248, 250, 256, 259. Mr. and Mrs. Leonard Balish: plates 120, 152. Baltimore Museum of Art: plates 4, 162, 263, 312. Linda Bartlett: plate 39. Marion Bennett: plate 214. Pauline Pretzfelder Blumenfeld: plate 78. Mary Borkowski: plate 123. Mrs. Frank Brazel: plates 253, 257, 265. Brooklyn Museum: plates 36, 104, 224, 235, 236. Charleston Museum: plate 291. Chester County Historical Society (David Townsend House): plates 113, 155. Cincinnati Art Museum: plates 24, 91, 279, 310. Colonial Williamsburg Collection: plates 100, 131, 183, 185, 186. Connecticut Historical Society: plate 44. Miss Louise Judson Cooke: plate 121. President Coolidge Homestead: plate 16. David Cornwell, photographer: plate 204. Darien Historical Society: plate 169. DAR Museum: 64, 65, 151, 219, 220. Jack Delano: plate 134. Denver Art Museum: plates 270, 274, 308. M.H. DeYoung Memorial Museum: plate 76. Dwight D. Eisenhower Birthplace Museum: plate 15. Fall River Historical Society Collection: plate 62. Louise Emerson Francke: plates 49 (© 1991 John Bigelow Taylor), 215, 216, 217, 271. Bill Gallick and Tony Ellis: plates 180, 282, 298, 299, 300, 301. Mrs. G. Gordon Gatchell: plate 52. Mrs. William B. Gillette: plate 258. Phyllis Haders: plate 199. Henry Ford Museum and Greenfield Village: plates 22, 72, 172, 182, 311. Mrs. George Hill, III: plate 283. Historic Deerfield, Inc.: plates 83, 95 (photo by Amanda Merullo), 187. Historical Society of York County, Pennsylvania (Herr Collection): plate 26. Jonathan and Gail Holstein: plates 43 (photo by Scott Bowron), 176, 197. Honolulu Academy of Arts: plates 205, 206. Illinois State Museum: plate 164. Mrs. Gemmell Jainschigg: plate 293. Mrs. Morton C. Katzenberg: plate 81. Mrs. Robert Keegan: plate 80. Mr. and Mrs. James O. Keene: plate 225. Jolie Kelter and Michael Malcé: plate 297. Kentucky Historical Society: plates 209, 210. Kate and Joel Kopp: plate 315. Barbara Ladd: plate 137. Russel Lee: plate 118. Log Cabin Village Museum: plate 280. Lycoming County Historical Society: plates 231, 232, 254. Mrs. R. MacFarlane: plate 35. Collection of Paul Madden: plate 31. Mr. and Mrs. Alastair B. Martin: plate 148. Maryland Historical Society: plates 41, 66, 75, 226, 227, 228, 272, 313. Massillon Museum: plate 38. Boleslaw and Marie-Louise d'Otrange Mastai, *The Stars and Stripes*—(from the Mastai Collection of American Flags): plate 56 (photo by Barbara Hansen). Mattatuck Museum: plates 132, 267. Nancy McClelland, *Historic Wallpapers*: plate 109. Mrs. John B. McIlhenny: plate 138. Memorial Hall (Deerfield): plates 115, 116. © 1992 by The Metropolitan Museum of Art: plates 173 (photo by John Bigelow Taylor), 178, 198, 289. Mr. and Mrs. Ben Mildwoff: plates 45, 79. Mississippi Department of Archives and History: plate 92. Moravian Museum of Bethlehem: plate 168. Museum of the City of New York: plate 11. Museum of Fine Arts (Boston): plates 119, 154, 171, 241, 296. National Gallery: plate 249. Nebraska State Historical Society: plates 19, 20. The Newark Museum: plates 50 (photo by Armen), 73, 125. The New-York Historical Society: plates 30, 53, 98, 143, 261, 262, 290, 294. New York State Historical Association: plates 99, 179, 188. Mrs. Robert Wright Northrop: plates 59, 67. The Ohio Historical Society: plates 77, 316. Old Sturbridge Village: plates 63, 85, 96 (photo by Thomas Neill), 103, 127, 133, 194, 201. Bill Pearson (photos by Roy Hale): plates 122, 286. Pennsylvania Historical and Museum Commission: plate 51. Philadelphia Museum of Art (A. J. Wyatt, staff photographer): plates 28, 33, 71, 175. Pioneer Museum and Haggin Galleries: plate 307. Mr. and Mrs. Michael Plisko: plate 302. Queen Anne's County Historical Society: plate 129. Quilt Gallery, Inc. (Rhea Goodman): plates 141, 196, 239, 242, 284, 303, 305. Royal Ontario Museum: plates 60, 61, 102, 105, 252. The St. Louis Art Museum: plate 25. Governor and Mrs. Leverett Saltonstall: plate 3. The San Antonio Museum Association: plates 166, 278. Schenectady Museum Collection (photos by Robert T. Staron, curator): plates 69, 264. George Schoellkopf, Inc.: plates 195, 200, 207, 230, 237, 251, 266, 269, 288. Shelburne Museum, photos by John M. Miller: plates 37, 40, 108, 244, 292; photos by Ken Burris: plates 9, 82, 136, 191, 192, 260. John and Jacqueline Sideli: plate 276. The Smithsonian Institution: page 16; plates 5, 17, 27, 84, 86, 87, 88, 93, 94, 110, 111, 112, 139, 146, 156, 157, 158, 165, 211, 212, 268, 295. Fannie Lou Spelce Associates (courtesy of The Kennedy Gallery): plate 12. Spencer Museum of Art, The University of Kansas, photos by Jim Enyeart: plates 21, 46, 240, 243, 255, 275; photo by Jon Blumb: plate 47. Staempfli Gallery (estate of Adeline Harris Sears): plate 142. Mary Strickler's Quilt Gallery (photo by Roy Hale): plate 114. Frances Stenge Traynor: plates 13, 14. Valentine Museum: plates 6, 7, 8, 89, 167. Victoria and Albert Museum, London: plates 1, 2, 174. Vigo County Historical Society, Inc.: plates 229, 245, 246. Wadsworth Atheneum: plates 153, 190 (© 1992 Wadsworth Atheneum), 238. Dr. and Mrs. W. Clough Wallace and Roberta Wallace (photo by Henry Elrod): plates 159, 160, 161. Mr. and Mrs. John S. Walton: plate 144. Noah Webster Foundation (Joseph Szaszfai, photographer): frontispiece. The White House: plate 140. The Henry Francis du Pont Winterthur Museum: plates 18, 23, 42, 54, 55, 58, 68, 74, 97, 135, 163, 184, 193, 202, 203. Collection of Tom Woodard and Blanche Greenstein: plates 32, 273, 285, 287. Woodlawn Plantation: plate 218.